HOME MISSIONS
ON THE AMERICAN
Frontier

HOME MISSIONS
ON THE AMERICAN
Frontier

With Particular Reference to the American
Home Missionary Society

BY

COLIN BRUMMITT GOODYKOONTZ

PROFESSOR OF HISTORY
UNIVERSITY OF COLORADO

The CAXTON PRINTERS, Ltd.
Caldwell, Idaho
1939

Printed and bound in the United States of America by
The CAXTON PRINTERS, Ltd.
Caldwell, Idaho
53664

TO THE MEMORY OF
MY MOTHER

PREFACE

HIS BOOK, WHICH is the outgrowth of a doctoral dissertation prepared at Harvard University under the direction of the late Professor Frederick Jackson Turner, deals with only one phase of the home missionary movement in the United States, namely, the work of Protestants from the East in the new settlements on the Western frontier. Local missionary activities in Eastern states and cities, Indian missions, missions among the Negroes, and the work of the Roman Catholic Church have either been omitted or treated incidentally to the main topic. For the sake of clarity emphasis has been put on the work of the Congregationalists and Presbyterians, especially their joint activities through the agency of the American Home Missionary Society. As a union society for more than a third of a century (1826-61), it had a significance beyond that of any of the strictly denominational home missionary organizations. Moreover, its work is especially interesting because it was the chief means through which the missionary spirit of New England was made effective in the West. The papers of the American Home Missionary Society, one of the major collections of manuscript source material for American religious and frontier history, have been used extensively in this study. Less attention has been paid to the work of other missionary societies; but in order to show the general character of the movement, and for purposes of comparison, brief accounts have been given of the home missionary activities of three other Protestant groups, the Baptists, the Methodists, and the Protestant Episcopalians. Home missionary activities of other religious bodies have been omitted, except for casual references, not because they are unimportant—for that is not true—but because it seemed that their inclusion would have greatly increased the amount of detail without a corresponding contribution to the significance of the movement as a whole.

This book does not purport to be an Encyclopedia of Home Missions. Of the tens of thousands of devoted men

and women who gave their lives in missionary service in the West, the names of only a few hundred appear here. Obviously some have been cited because of their prominence in the movement. The names of certain other persons have been mentioned in order to illustrate various phases of the work; perhaps in some cases others might just as well have been chosen. In life thousands of earnest Christian ministers gladly "buried" themselves in obscure villages on the frontier for the sake of a cause; in this book it has seemed necessary to omit many names of persons and places in order that the outlines of a great religious and social movement might not be obscured.

The viewpoint is secular throughout. An effort has been made to study the home missionary movement in its relation to contemporary political and economic conditions. The work of home missionaries in the introduction of moral principles and religious and educational institutions into the new settlements has been studied as one would examine any other social development.

To a considerable extent in the descriptions of the problems and activities of the individual missionaries, they have been allowed to tell their own stories in their own words. In these quotations the original spelling, capitalization, punctuation, and abbreviations have been retained; however, raised letters have been lowered for convenience in printing, and obvious typographical errors in printed accounts have been corrected.

The period covered in some detail in this study is roughly the nineteenth century. As a background, the preliminary work of the eighteenth century has been sketched and a summary statement has been made of religious conditions in the United States at the close of the War for Independence. The revival in religion which came at the end of the eighteenth century gave a new impulse to missionary activities, and new agencies were then devised to deal with the problem presented by the rapid settlement of the West. To follow the frontiersmen with religious institutions was the great object of the home missionary movement. In 1890 the Superintendent of the Census made the oft-quoted statement that the unsettled area of the United States had been so broken into by isolated bodies of settlement that there could hardly be said to be a frontier line any longer. Although frontier conditions still obtained in many parts of

the West, this statement called attention to a great change that was taking place in American life. The passing of the frontier, on the one hand, and the massing of large groups of aliens in our great cities, on the other, have so changed the nature of the home missionary problem that the last decade of the nineteenth century has seemed to be the natural point at which to end this study of Home Missions on the American Frontier.

I appreciate the many courtesies shown me by the authorities and attendants at the following libraries, societies, and institutions: Congregational Home Missionary Society (New York), Hammond Library of the Chicago Theological Seminary, Connecticut Missionary Society (Hartford), Congregational House (Boston), New England Baptist Library (Boston), Presbyterian Historical Society (Philadelphia), Wisconsin Historical Society, Missouri Historical Society (St. Louis), Kansas Historical Society, Nebraska Historical Society, Iowa Historical Society, State Historical Society of Colorado, Library of Congress, British Museum, Lambeth Palace (London), Harvard University, Andover Theological Seminary, Yale University, Crozer Theological Seminary, University of Chicago, University of Wisconsin, Washington University (St. Louis), University of Colorado, Colorado College, John Crerar Library (Chicago), Newberry Library (Chicago), Boston Public Library, New York Public Library, Chicago Public Library, and the Denver Public Library. To mention by name all the men and women in these institutions who have been helpful is impossible. However, it is only fair considering the nature of my work that I should express more definitely my gratitude to those persons who have given me unlimited access to the papers of the American Home Missionary Society; I am especially indebted to Dr. Matthew Spinka and Miss Evah Ostrander, of the Hammond Library of the Chicago Theological Seminary, to Dr. Ernest M. Halliday, General Secretary of the Church Extension Division, Board of Home Missions of the Congregational and Christian Churches, and to the Reverend William S. Beard, formerly Assistant Secretary of the Congregational Home Missionary Society. I am grateful also to the late Professor James Field Willard, of the University of Colorado, for encouragement and permission to use his collection of Americana, to Miss Martha Morrison, of Denver, Colorado, for

access to family letters and diaries, and to Mrs. Dorothy Printup Hulbert Wing, of Colorado Springs, for permission to quote from the manuscript of the unpublished eighth volume of Hulbert, *Overland to the Pacific*.

Among the friends and scholars who have given counsel regarding the form and content of this book and assistance in its preparation, mention should be made first of Professor Frederick Jackson Turner. My indebtedness to him for stimulating suggestions and helpful criticisms on that part of this study which came under his eye is incalculable. The manuscript has been read in whole or in part by my colleagues Professor Carl C. Eckhardt and Dr. Lucius F. Reed, of the University of Colorado, and by Dr. Louie Miner, of Brooklyn College of the City of New York. Professor Earl Swisher, of the University of Colorado, and Dr. Lynn Perrigo, of the University of Kansas City, have verified certain references for me. The members of my immediate family, my wife, my daughter, and my father, have given assistance beyond measure. To all those named and unnamed, who have helped me, I am deeply grateful.

C. B. G.

TABLE OF CONTENTS

HOME MISSIONS
ON THE AMERICAN
Frontier

ABBREVIATIONS USED IN FOOTNOTES

A.B.H.M.S.—American Baptist Home Mission Society.

A.H.M.S.—American Home Missionary Society.

B.N.P.E.—Board of National Popular Education.

C.H.M.S.—Congregational Home Missionary Society.

C.T.S.—Chicago Theological Seminary.

M.S.M.E.Ch.—Missionary Society of the Methodist Episcopal Church.

S.P.C.T.E.W.—Society for the Promotion of Collegiate and Theological Education at the West.

S.P.G.—Society for the Propagation of the Gospel.

CHAPTER I

MOTIVES FOR HOME MISSIONS

The East has always feared the result of an unregulated advance of the frontier, and has tried to check and guide it.—*Frederick Jackson Turner*.

THE THEME of this book is the organized effort of Protestants in the older parts of the United States—and particularly those who supported the American Home Missionary Society—to carry religious and educational institutions to the inhabitants of the frontier regions. What motives produced this home missionary movement? Why have the residents in one part of this nominally Christian republic thought it necessary to send missionaries to other parts? Why have the people of the East, and especially of New England, regarded it as their duty to attempt to convert or enlighten the West? Inasmuch as the supporters of home missions believed that their own systems and principles were superior to those of their beneficiaries, an answer to these questions involves a consideration both of the state of mind that prevailed in the East and of the conditions that existed, or were supposed to exist, in the West.

New England, which in proportion to its size and population has probably furnished more men, money, and zeal for home missions than any other part of our country, was regarded by its own people in the early part of the nineteenth century as being especially blessed. Its population was still remarkably homogeneous racially. Religion occupied a large place in the lives of its inhabitants. The churches were mainly Puritan in origin, Calvinistic in theology, and congregational in organization. The ministers were dignified and well educated. Sunday was generally a day of quiet and rest. Most of the sober and substantial members of the community attended church services with reasonable regularity. Life and property were safe. Outwardly the New England towns appeared to be inhabited by honest, thrifty,

god-fearing Christians. Beneath the surface, however, there were many signs that the "old Adam" in human nature had not been entirely eradicated. Certainly the preachers spoke out against greed, envy, jealousy, strife, and violations of the seventh commandment. But even so, New Englanders regarded themselves as God's chosen people in the New World—"winnowed grain"—and the exponents of the purest form of Protestantism. People who sincerely believed this about themselves and who felt some responsibility for others naturally wished to spread their principles. To do so was both a privilege and a duty.

In the Middle States, the stronghold of Presbyterianism, the population was less homogeneous than that of New England; but intermarriage for several generations had changed most of the English, Scotch-Irish, Dutch, and Germans into Americans. Although there were many denominations—Presbyterians rubbed elbows with Episcopalians, and they with Quakers and Baptists, and all looked askance at enthusiastic Methodists—Calvinism was the dominant form of theology. In addition to the Presbyterians, the Dutch Reformed, the German Reformed, and the Associate Reformed were of this persuasion; even among Baptists and Episcopalians there were traces of the influence of the great theologian of Geneva. In New York and Pennsylvania, as in Massachusetts and Connecticut, outward attention to religious observance was generally regarded as evidence of stability and respectability.

The people of the East, then, believed that their religious institutions were good enough and sufficiently well established to warrant them in attempting to carry them into the West. There may be inherent in such an attitude of mind a sense of superiority on the part of the benefactors, but it need not be to them a source of spiritual pride; they may be so aware of their own shortcomings, so conscious of their responsibility for the welfare of others, and so touched by the needs of those less fortunate than themselves, that compassion and brotherly love completely efface self-complacency. Ideally, it is always so; practically, it has sometimes appeared to the Western objects of Eastern missionary enthusiasm that their pious patrons spent too much time thanking God that they were not as other men. Since missions are carried on by imperfect men in an imperfect world, we need not be surprised to find that among

the motives of the supporters of the movement there have been secular and selfish, as well as altruistic and religious, elements. But if at times the home missionary movement has appeared narrowly sectarian and partisan, it has been in the main an honest expression of disinterested Christian benevolence.

THE FRONTIER

A basic fact in home missions in the United States has been the frontier. It was the settlement of the West, one of the most stupendous achievements in our history, which called the home missionary movement into existence.

English colonization in America in the sixteenth, seventeenth, and eighteenth centuries, as compared with Spanish and French, had been strangely lacking in expansive force. The Spaniards had overrun most of South and Central America, Mexico, and the southern part of the present United States before the English had planted a single permanent colony in the New World. The early English settlers hugged the Atlantic coast, while the French, who began their settlements in Canada about the same time that Virginia was founded, were lured far into the interior. How insignificant seemed the narrow and broken line of English settlements between Maine and Georgia as compared with the vast expanse of French Canada and Louisiana, and yet what an element of strength lay in its compactness!

At the outbreak of the American War for Independence, after 170 years of English colonization, the frontier line, except for a few scattered settlements west of the Appalachians, had not been pushed more than one eighth of the way across the continent. Within the next 120 years practically all the land comprised within the other seven eighths was occupied, superficially at least. It was as though the barrier of mountains, forests, and red men, which had held back the tide of humanity, had burst in the days of the Revolution, releasing a flood that swept across the Great Valley and over the Rockies to the Pacific with torrential force. Considering the magnitude of the distance, the number and diversity of the people involved, and the rapidity of the movement, the occupation of the trans-Allegheny West in the nineteenth century was one of the greatest colonizing achievements in history.

To keep pace with the pioneers was the task of the Church; and since the days when Christianity set out to con-

vert the Roman Empire it has seldom faced a more prodigious undertaking. Practically the whole of the territory of the United States has been at some time missionary ground. Before the American Revolution the original thirteen colonies, or parts of them, attracted the attention of pious and benevolent persons in England, Holland, and Germany; while in the colonies themselves there were some who were touched by the religious destitution of the Old West, the land lying between the Alleghenies and the "fall line" on the rivers flowing into the Atlantic. Even during the Revolution the frontier of settlement was shifting into the Great Valley of the Mississippi. By the opening of the nineteenth century this vast Western area, now more than doubled in size by the purchase of Louisiana in 1803, was becoming not only a theater for commercial rivalries, political contests, and sectional struggles, but also a moral and spiritual battleground on which the Christian churches fought their common enemy—and one another. Men who were concerned about the religious development of the country reflected on the problem presented by the rapid settlement of the West. One who signed himself "Minoris" wrote, as he surveyed the field in 1801, "The American Church is placed in a new and interesting situation; and there is a new and more solemn obligation than was ever found on Christians before, arising from the removal of our children into the wilderness."[1] As the century wore on the situation became more, rather than less, serious from the point of view of persons interested in home missions. Later stages of territorial advance opened to settlement with startling rapidity areas larger than old and powerful European states: Texas, for example, is larger than Germany, New Mexico than Italy, Arizona than the British Isles. It is little wonder that Daniel Webster, who was Secretary of State (1850) soon after those territorial acquisitions, attempted to put the haughty Austrian chargé d'affaires, Hülsemann, in his place by informing him that in comparison with the extent of the United States the possessions of the House of Hapsburg were "but as a patch on the earth's surface"; but to men concerned over the spiritual welfare of the rapidly expanding republic, it was a sobering thought.

---

[1] *Connecticut Evangelical Magazine*, I (1801), 324.

The problem of dealing with this extensive missionary field was complicated by the heterogeneity of its population. The frontier has been called a melting pot in which were thrown together people of different races and languages, of different habits and creeds, and from different sections and countries. Said a man thoroughly familiar with the West:

> The shrewd Yankee, the luxurious Southerner, the positive Englishman, the metaphysical Scotchman, the jovial Irishman, the excitable Frenchman, the passionate Spaniard, the voluptuous Italian, the debased African—and who not?—are flung together into this mighty crucible. The antagonistic elements are in contact but refuse to unite, and, as yet, no chemical agent has been found sufficiently potent to reduce them to splendid unity.[2]

One may take exception to certain of these trite and superficial characterizations of the representatives of various races and nations and yet recognize the truth of the contention that the normal Western community throughout the nineteenth century was not homogeneous. To be sure, the white population of the Old Southwest was mainly of Southern stock; and in the Old Northwest there were a few transplanted New England villages. But in that broad middle zone where the streams of settlement from New England, the Middle States, and the South met such homogeneous settlements were exceptional. Missionaries, particularly those of New England origin, frequently commented on this phase of Western life. One of them described the inhabitants of western New York, at a time when that part of the Empire State was still new, as "a strange compound—a chaotic mass," in their habits, manners, and religious opinions "a rope of sand."[3]

The difficulty of fusing these discordant elements into a unity was greatly increased by the isolation, the individualism, and the migratory habits of many of the first settlers. Some of them were improvident ne'er-do-wells who drifted about until through inertia they found precarious lodgment

---

[2] J. F. Tuttle, "The West and Western Eloquence," in *Biblical Repository*, 3rd Ser., No. 4 (1845), 644.

[3] Jesse Colton, Royalton, N. Y., April 18, 1826, to Exec. Com. of United Domestic Missionary Society, American Home Missionary Society papers in Chicago Theological Seminary (hereafter abbreviated as A.H.M.S. papers, C.T.S.). Unless otherwise noted, A.H.M.S. papers referred to in this book are reports from missionaries to the officers of the Society; hence only the name of the writer and the place and date of writing will be given.

in some pine barren or swamp in which they were not apt to be molested and from which they were not likely to be forced out by ambitious, energetic farmers. But ambition often caused the energetic to move on in search of better opportunities. Speculation in land, the search for the best soils, and an extensive system of agriculture induced pioneers to take up large tracts of land; but such action was not immediately conducive to community life. Nor did the land policy of the Federal Government compel compact settlement of the West, since squatting on the public domain was usually permitted or even encouraged. Apart from the danger from Indians, a force that operated only occasionally and in limited areas, there was almost nothing but self-interest to compel the people to live in compact communities. Some did so from preference; but the man who thought it was time to move on when neighbors came so near that he could see the smoke from their fires was a familiar figure in early Western society. The squatters especially, having little to tie them down, were prone to move about. Morris Birkbeck, an English traveler, reported that he stopped one night with a man in Illinois who was living in the third cabin he had built within twelve months, and who needed only a slender motive to send him off to another before the coming of winter.[4] It was no doubt such restless persons that Timothy Flint, missionary in Missouri, had in mind when he said of the Westerners that "they might almost as well, like the Tartars, dwell in tents." "Everything," he continued, "shifts under your eye. The present occupants sell, pack up, depart. Strangers replace them. Before they have gained the confidence of their neighbors, they hear of a better place, pack up, and follow their precursors."[5]

To the home missionary the migratory character of so many pioneers was important because on the one hand it added greatly to the physical labor necessary to find and minister to the spiritual wants of these isolated men and women, while on the other the need for such ministrations

---

[4] M. Birkbeck, *Notes on a Journey in America* (London, 1818), 122.

[5] T. Flint, *Recollections* (Boston, 1826), 76; after a long trip through the Southwest, G. F. Pierce wrote, in his *Incidents of Western Travel* (Nashville, 1857), 137: "I was very much struck by the *unsettledness* of the people. One great change seems to have unhinged them for life."

was increased by the brutalizing tendencies of this solitary life in the wilderness. On this unhappy phase of Western life an economist wrote about the middle of the nineteenth century:

... Widely separated from each other, amply supplied with food by the bounty of nature, but destitute of the manufactured articles on which depend the comforts and even the decencies of life, out of the reach of the law, and beyond the sphere of education, they [the pioneers] rapidly approximate the condition of the savages whom they have just dispossessed. They become "squatters," "bushmen," "backwoodsmen," whose only enjoyments are hunting and intoxication, whose only schoolroom is the forest, and whose sense of justice is manifested only by the processes of Lynch law. They are doomed to the solitary, violent, brutal existence, which destroys all true civilization, all sympathy with other men, though it increases strength of body, adroitness, courage, and the spirit of adventure. The want of local attachments, and an insatiable thirst for wandering and adventure, are, I fear, the most striking traits in the character of the whole population of our Mississippi valley. Their homes even in that fair region are but homes of yesterday; they had only pitched their camps on the banks of the Ohio and the Wabash, while on their way to the Sacramento and the Columbia. The truant disposition which carried them over the Alleghanies, hurries them onward to the Rocky Mountains. I do not go as far as an eminent thinker of our own day, who has expressed in eloquent language his fears lest these constant migrations should lead our countrymen back to barbarism; but it is certain that the "pioneers of civilization," as they have been fondly called, leave laws, education, and the arts, all the essential elements of civilization, behind them. They may be the means of partially civilizing others, but they are in great danger of brutalizing themselves.[6]

Such generalizations mean more if illustrated by specific examples. Here is one from the pen of John M. Peck, pioneer Baptist missionary in Missouri and Illinois. On one of his tours through the former state he came upon a migratory squatter family which he described as follows:

... The single log cabin, of the most primitive structure, was situated at some distance within the corn field. In and around it were the patriarchal head and his wife, two married daughters and their husbands, with three or four little children and a son and daughter grown up to manhood and womanhood. The old man said he could read but "mighty poorly." The old woman wanted a *hyme* book, but could not read one. The rest of this romantic household had no use for books or "any such trash." ... The "traveling missionary" was received with all the hospitality the old people had the ability or knew how to exercise. The younger class were shy and kept out of

---

[6] F. Bowen, *Principles of Political Economy* (Boston, 1856), 95.

the cabin and could not be persuaded to come and hear the missionary
read the Scriptures and offer a prayer. There was evidence of backwardness, or some other propensity, attending all the domestic arrangements. It was nine o'clock when I reached the squatter's cabin,
and yet no preparations had been made for breakfast. The beds,
such as they were, remained in the same condition as when the
lodgers first crawled from their nests in the morning. The young
women appeared listless. Their heads, faces, hands, clothing, all
indicated slothfulness and habitual neglect. Soon the old woman made
some preparations for breakfast ... the culinary operations were
performed out of doors. ...

Not a table, chair, or any article of furniture could be seen. These
deficiencies were common on the frontiers, for emigrations from the
"settlements" were often made on pack-horses and no domestic con-
veniences could be transported, except the most indispensable cooking-
utensils, bedding, and a change or two of clothing. But the head of
the family must be shiftless indeed, and void of all backwood's skill
and enterprise, who could not make a table for family use. ...

Our landlady having nothing in the shape of a table, substituted a
box. On this she spread a cloth that might have answered any other
purpose than a tablecloth. ... The rancid bacon when boiled could
have been detected by a foetid atmosphere across the yard, had there
been one. The snap-beans ... were not half-boiled. The sour butter-
milk ... was "no go." ...[7]

To make the story complete, it should be added that a few
days later Mr. Peck came upon this identical family on
their way to a new frontier. A newcomer had bought their
"crap" and claim for an old wagon and a yoke of steers,
and off they started for a new settlement of squatters and
bear hunters on the Big Black.

On the frontiers the amenities of civilized life were
often ignored either from necessity or indifference. Cabins
were small, families were large, inns were remote, and the
people in the main hospitable. Sleeping arrangements,
consequently, sometimes seemed to the people from the
East to be unconventional almost to the point of indecency.
An Episcopal missionary writing from Wisconsin in 1842
said:

You can have but little conception of the *sangfroid* wherewith you
will be showed to a bed to sleep in, that is in the same room where all
the rest of the family sleep. When I first came out, I felt awfully
bad at such vile barbarities; but I am getting somewhat wild myself;
and, following the example of my good Bishop, can carry on a conversation with the family after having gone to bed. Thus we live up

---

[7] R. Babcock, *Memoir of John Mason Peck* (Philadelphia [1864]),
101-03.

to the principle of carrying out our Churchmanship under every circumstance. When the Bishop last visited us, we once slept eight in a
room, and the tattling old woman kept the Bishop awake a long time.

What is civilizing this land is neither education nor Christianity,
but the introduction of *saw-mills!*[8]

In the course of time the rudely furnished one-room
cabins of the first settlers were replaced by larger dwellings
in which the members of the family and their guests had
more privacy; ultimately squatters took root and evolved
into permanent settlers or moved on to a new frontier,
yielding their places to men of higher material standards.
With such a natural evolution in the mode of life and standards of value, the problem of the missionary changed but
did not disappear. The basis of Western life was essentially
materialistic; people went West for land, for homes, for
wealth. With a few exceptions, it can be stated that the
West was occupied by men who were in search of neither
political liberty nor religious freedom; they had those in
the East. The dominant motive was economic; and it was
probably stronger in the industrious, thrifty, ambitious
settlers than in their shiftless, migratory predecessors or
contemporaries. To some religious leaders in the East materialism seemed to be the greatest danger to the spiritual
life in the West. "There is much hasting to be rich," said
one of the missionaries. Alfred Brunson, a Methodist circuit
rider, made the observation when he visited the lead-mining
district in southwestern Wisconsin in 1835 that "the spirit
of money making seemed to absorb the whole community,"
with the result that religion occupied little or no place in
the thoughts of the people.[9]

Furthermore, the task of the missionary from the East
was made more difficult by reason of the fact that it was
often the class that was discontented with its economic or
social status in the older communities, or that was restive
under the strict moral and religious system of Puritan New
England, that had gone West. Such men were apt to look

---

[8] C. Breck, *Life of the Reverend James Lloyd Breck* (New York,
1883), 28; the bishop who was kept awake was probably Jackson
Kemper. For examples of church trials growing out of alleged im-
proper conduct under such circumstances, see W. W. Sweet. *Religion
on the American Frontier ... Presbyterians* (New York and London,
1936), 250-55, 558-62.

[9] A. Brunson, "A Methodist Circuit Rider's Horseback Tour," in
Wisconsin Historical Collections, XV (Madison, 1900), 287.

upon the missionary as the symbol of unpleasant ideas and institutions. Timothy Dwight, distinguished president of Yale College, knew these dissatisfied men on the borders of New England; but the frontier spirit was much the same wherever it manifested itself. Concerning these restless, self-confident malcontents, Dwight wrote:

...A considerable part of those, who *begin* the cultivation of the wilderness, may be denominated *foresters* or *Pioneers*. The business of these persons is no other than to cut down trees, build log-houses, lay open forested grounds to cultivation, and prepare the way for those who come after them. These men cannot live in regular society. They are too idle; too talkative; too passionate; too prodigal; and shiftless; to acquire either property or character. They are impatient of the restraints of law, religion, and morality; grumble about the taxes, by which Rulers, Ministers, and School-masters are supported; and complain incessantly, as well as bitterly, of the extortions of mechanics, farmers, merchants, and physicians; to whom they are always indebted. At the same time, they are usually possessed in their own view, of uncommon wisdom; understand medical science, politics, and religion, better than those who have studied them through life; and, although they manage their own concerns worse than any other men, feel perfectly satisfied, that they could manage those of the nation far better than the agents, to whom they are committed by the public. After displaying their own talents, and worth; after censuring the weakness, and wickedness, of their superiors; after exposing the injustice of the community in neglecting to invest persons of such merit with public offices; in many an eloquent harangue, uttered by many a kitchen fire, in every blacksmith's shop, and in every corner of the streets; and finding all their efforts vain; they become at length discouraged: and under the pressure of poverty, the fear of a gaol, and the consciousness of public contempt, leave their native places, and betake themselves to the wilderness.... [10]

There can be no doubt as to President Dwight's answer to the old question of whether the ablest and most progressive individuals or the shiftless and incompetent made up the bulk of the westward-moving mass. In the departure of the disgruntled he found one crumb of comfort. "In mercy," he said, "to the sober, industrious, and well-disposed, inhabitants, Providence has opened in the vast Western wilderness a retreat, sufficiently alluring to draw them away from the land of their nativity. We have many troubles even now; but we should have many more if this body of foresters had remained at home."[11]

[10] T. Dwight, *Travels; in New-England and New-York* (New Haven, 1821-22), II, 459.
[11] *Ibid.*, 462.

President Dwight's antipathy towards frontiersmen was matched in many instances by their dislike for him and what he represented. The *Vermont Gazette* early in the nineteenth century, in commenting on the coming of missionaries from Connecticut, remarked: "The wolves in sheeps' clothing thrust forth by his holiness, Pope Dwight . . . get few hearts and less thanks in Vermont."[12] Such interchanges of un-complimentary remarks reveal the clash of interests between the frontier and coastal regions. This divergence developed almost as soon as there was a frontier, certainly by the time of Bacon's Rebellion (1676); it has persisted down to recent times with farmers from the prairie states com-plaining about Wall Street domination of Washington, and a New England senator branding Western progressives as "Sons of the Wild Jack-asses." Before the Civil War an espe-cially pronounced phase of sectional hostility was the dislike for Yankees which prevailed throughout the South and West. The typical Yankee was supposed to be a sanctimonious hypocrite who cheated in horse trades and made wooden nutmegs. This feeling made it difficult for a missionary from New England to work in many parts of the West, but the fact that he was disliked usually strengthened his conviction that his labors were needed among a people whose customs and ideas were not in harmony with those of the "Land of Settled Habits."

FRONTIER MORALS

It is especially important to keep this mutual sectional distrust and misunderstanding in mind when dealing with the moral condition of the frontier. Much of our informa-tion comes from Easterners and foreigners who visited the West. The reports of the missionaries contain long accounts of "moral wastes," "spiritual destitutions," and "seas of iniquity" on the frontiers. A bill of particulars usually in-cludes such offenses as Sabbath-breaking, profanity, gam-bling, drunkenness, fighting, murders, thefts, and general lawlessness. References to sexual irregularities are relatively few in the letters of the missionaries, an indication perhaps of the reticence of an age less frank than our own rather than a tribute to the purity of the frontier communities. How much truth is there in such charges of moral delin-

---

[12] Quoted by R. J. Purcell, *Connecticut in Transition, 1775-1818* (Washington, 1918), 324, Note 45.

quency? There can be no question about the honesty and sincerity of the missionaries who made the reports; whether they were accurate and unbiased is another matter. In the case of men making missionary tours allowance must be made for the inaccuracies so often found in the tales of travelers. In the case of settled ministers no such allowance need be made, but it must be remembered that these men were looking at Western life through the blue glasses of Puritanism. In the West they found habits, as of Sunday observance, that differed from those to which they were accustomed, and then, ignorant of or indifferent to the close connection between habits and morals, they were prone to call the possessors of strange habits immoral.

There is abundant evidence from other and secular sources, however, that among many Western people and in many parts of the frontier moral standards were deplorably low. Probably no Western preacher was more outspoken in his criticism of Eastern missionaries—"hot-house preachers" he called them—than Peter Cartwright, famous Methodist circuit rider in the Ohio Valley, but his testimony regarding the lawlessness in the frontier community in which his father lived in Kentucky is explicit. Logan County, when Cartwright's father moved to it about 1793, was called "Rogues' Harbor" because so many murderers, horse thieves, highway robbers, and counterfeiters had taken refuge there.[13] Lay travelers through the West were often shocked by vulgarity, profanity, intoxication, and brutality in fighting and in sports.[14] A passenger on a steamboat on the Ohio River about 1832 described his fellow travelers as disgusting and detestable in manners and morals. "The conversation in the cabin," he wrote, "was interlarded with the vilest blasphemy, not uttered in a state of mental excitement, but with a coolness and deliberation truly fiend-like."[15] If it be granted that these statements are accurate—and they might

[13] P. Cartwright, *Autobiography* (Cincinnati, [1856]), 24.

[14] F. A. Michaux, "Travels to the West of the Alleghany Mountains," in R. G. Thwaites, *Early Western Travels* (Cleveland, 1904), III, 144.

[15] [T. Hamilton], *Men and Manners in America* (Philadelphia, 1833), 296; E. Davies, *American Scenes* (London, 1849), 88, characterized the mass of men on a Mississippi River boat as rude and filthy beyond description; C. A. Murray, *Travels in North America* (London, 1839), 220, said, "...the swearing of some of the lower orders in the West...would shock ears accustomed to the language of Billingsgate or a London gin-shop, so full is it of blasphemy: and

be continued indefinitely—what do they prove about the West? There were doubtless shocking instances of drunkenness and profanity in the East too. The significance of such statements is to be found in the fact that they help make up the composite picture which men in the East were forming about the West. Whether the picture was fair or not made little difference. The attitude of the East towards the West was determined not by what actually existed there but by what the East thought existed.

The West has often been regarded as the part of the country where crimes of violence were common and where society protected itself by such extralegal devices as Vigilantes and Regulators. Countless examples, taken from river towns and cow towns, from mining camps and lumber camps, could be given of assaults, of murders, and of robberies. Again, what does it all prove? There were many such crimes in Eastern cities. However, at home and abroad, the West, especially to the generation following the Civil War, was the picturesque abode of two-gun men, of stagecoach bandits, and of sheriffs who shot to kill. There was lawlessness in the West, but it was a passing phase of life. Peculiar circumstances sometimes forced the pioneers to act in advance of legal processes. They sometimes found themselves so far ahead of organized government that it was of little use to them. Unfortunately, their practice of taking law into their own hands, however justifiable it may have been under the circumstances, "bred a lawlessness in certain matters which their children inherited for generations."[16]

The sins of the pioneers were in the main the sins of the flesh. The frontier was of the earth, earthy. It stood in need of refining influences.

But there is the other side of the picture. To generalize about Western morals solely on the basis of gloomy missionary reports and unfriendly travelers' notes would be to give as distorted a view as would be obtained now by representing contemporary life only as it has been caught by the reporters for the tabloid newspapers. The fundamental virtues on which society rests, loyalty, fidelity, honesty, love, and sacrifice, were so common in the West—as elsewhere—

---

uttered in a deliberate and determinate tone, such as to induce the belief that the speaker really wishes the fulfilment of the curses which he imprecates."

16 T. Roosevelt, *Winning of the West* (New York, 1889), IV, 256.

that they were taken for granted. Moreover, certain desirable social traits, such as hospitality, neighborliness, and generosity, were probably more fully developed there than in the older communities. Timothy Flint, who knew intimately the life of the West as well as that of the East, admitted that there were bad men—"gamblers, and gougers, and outlaws"—on the frontier, but he contended that there were fewer of them than might be expected "from the nature of things." Furthermore, he continued:

The backwoodsman of the west, as I have seen him, is generally an amiable and virtuous man. His general motive for coming here is to be a freeholder, to have plenty of rich land, and to be able to settle his children about him. . . . You find, in truth, that he has vices and barbarisms, peculiar to his situation. His manners are rough. . . . He carries a knife, or a dirk in his bosom, and when in the woods has a rifle on his back, and a pack of dogs at his heels. . . . Enter his door, and tell him you are benighted, and wish the shelter of his cabin for the night. The welcome is indeed seemingly ungracious: "I reckon you can stay," or "I suppose we must let you stay." But this apparent ungraciousness is the harbinger of every kindness that he can bestow, and every comfort that his cabin can afford.[17]

In the West, as elsewhere, the good and the bad, the strong and the weak, lived side by side. On the frontier extremes met. As Theodore Roosevelt put it:

. . . The two extremes of society, the strongest, best, and most adventurous, and the weakest, most shiftless, and vicious, are those which seem naturally to drift to the border. . . . All qualities, good and bad, are intensified and accentuated in the life on the wilderness. The man who in civilization is merely sullen and bad-tempered becomes a murderous, treacherous ruffian when transplanted into the wilds; while on the other hand his cheery, quiet neighbor develops into a hero, ready uncomplainingly to lay down his life for his friend.[18]

In standards of living, intellectual abilities, and personal ambitions, as in morals, sharp contrasts were found among frontiersmen. On the one hand there were the lazy, shiftless squatters, steeped in ignorance and superstition, who, although they might gladly share their dirt and bugs with a stranger, were not the most desirable elements in a community. On the other hand, there were many enterprising and ambitious men and women who had gone West to grow up with the country. De Tocqueville, French observer and

---

[17] T. Flint, *Recollections*, 176-77.
[18] T. Roosevelt, *Winning of the West*, I, 130-31.

commentator, was so impressed by the enlightened character of the backwoodsman that his description of him appears a bit idyllic:

> ...Everything about him is primitive and wild, but he is himself the result of the labor and experience of eighteen centuries. He wears the dress and speaks the language of the cities; he is acquainted with the past, curious about the future, and ready for argument upon the present; he is, in short, a highly civilized being, who consents for a time to inhabit the backwoods, and who penetrates into the wilds of the New World with the Bible, an axe and some newspapers. It is difficult to imagine the incredible rapidity with which thought circulates in the midst of these deserts. I do not think that so much intellectual activity exists in the most enlightened and populous districts of France.[19]

RELIGION ON THE FRONTIER

The religious situation on the frontier was complex. Whether viewed longitudinally in time or transversely in space, the frontier was so vast that on it one might expect to find somewhere, some time, all shades of belief from atheism to mysticism, all varieties of religious practice from crude camp meetings to elaborate ritual. This was the inevitable result of the diversity in origin of the people and their individualism. To men reared in New England at a time when there was normally but one church in a town or village, the multiplicity of sects in a small Western community was a source of dismay.[20] One missionary writing from Ohio in 1839 said plaintively: "The chh of which I have charge is a little flock, much scattered & thickly interspersed with almost every description of character & sentiment: Baptists, Methodists, Camelites, Chrystians, Episcopalians, & Universalists of two kinds: No-hellers & hell redemptionists."[21] The situation in the little community of Willow Springs, Wisconsin, was typical of what existed throughout the whole of the West. A missionary reported

---

[19] Alexis de Tocqueville, *Democracy in America* (Cambridge, 1863), I, 406.

[20] Julian Sturtevant, one of the members of the Yale Illinois Band, states in his *Autobiography* (New York, [1896]), 23, that when he was a boy in Connecticut the local church was not regarded as the representative of a denomination, but simply as a branch of the Church of Christ. "If in my childhood," he says, "I had heard our place of worship mentioned as Congregational I would have needed to ask an explanation of the unusual term."

[21] J. Crawford, Berlin, Ohio, May 1, 1839, in A.H.M.S. papers, C.T.S.

in 1848 that there were representatives of fourteen denominations in that town, and that they had come from seventeen different states and foreign countries.[22] In each community the members of those religious groups that were strongest in numbers or faith united in congregations, so that it was not unusual to find as many as five or six struggling churches in one small town. By and large the people of the West, particularly those who lived on the farms and in the little country towns, were not irreligious.

But they were in danger, in the opinion of many in the East, of worshiping false gods. More alarming than the number was the nature of some of the religious beliefs that found adherents in the West. Venable, historian of literary culture in the Ohio Valley, said:

Propounders of original views, dissenters and reformers of all shades of belief and unbelief, came to the valley. They considered the new country a *tabula rasa,* upon which every man who had a positive idea was free to write a theory.... [23]

In his list of strange cults that developed or flourished on the frontier an orthodox Easterner would probably have included, among others, Mormonism, which was founded in western New York "by a migrating New England family";[24] Millerism, with its proof by fifteen different calculations that the world would come to an end in 1843;[25] the system of Jemima Wilkinson, the "Universal Friend," who taught that the Divine Spirit had entered into her body;[26] the Leatherwood God, who deceived the credulous in eastern Ohio;[27] and the Pilgrims who, chanting with a peculiar twang the phrase "Praise God! Praise God!" as they marched along, came to the lower Mississippi Valley to establish a more perfect society upon earth.[28]

Presbyterians and Congregationalists, with whose activities in the West we are chiefly concerned in this study,

---

[22] *Home Missionary,* XXI (1848), 106.

[23] W. H. Venable, *Beginnings of Literary Culture in the Ohio Valley* (Cincinnati, 1891), 222.

[24] F. J. Turner, *Rise of the New West* (New York, 1906), 23.

[25] W. Miller, *Evidence from Scripture and History of the Second Coming of Christ about the Year 1843* (Boston, 1841).

[26] O. Turner, *History of the Pioneer Settlement of Phelps and Gorham's Purchase* (Rochester, 1851), 153-62.

[27] R. H. Taneyhill, *The Leatherwood God* (Cincinnati, 1870).

[28] T. Flint, *Recollections,* 275 ff.

looked with disfavor also on the principles and practices of some of the well-recognized Protestant denominations which were obviously more successful in winning converts among the mass of people than they were. They criticized Methodists because of their emotionalism and exuberance in religious exercises; they found fault with Baptists because so many of them in the West were opposed to Sunday schools, missionary and other benevolent societies; they disparaged both Methodists and Baptists on account of the alleged ignorance and illiteracy of some of their preachers. But Baptists and Methodists joined voices with Presbyterians and Congregationalists in disapprobation of an aggressive new religious movement which developed and became strong in the Middle West in the nineteenth century, that of the Christians or Disciples of Christ. Called "Campbellites" (after the Scotch-Irish Thomas Campbell and his son Alexander) by their religious neighbors, they were accused of holding out false hopes to those who accepted their way of salvation and of filling up their churches with persons who lacked those experiences which gave assurance that they were the elect of God. Such errors, said the Protestants of the East, must be combated by the preaching of the "sound gospel."

Thus in denominational rivalries among Protestants is to be found one of the compelling motives for home missions, but an even stronger reason was found at times in the fear of the spread of Roman Catholicism in the West. The rising tide of immigration after 1830, the large number of Irish and German Catholics who made their way to the West, the expenditures of the Catholic missionary societies in the United States, the zeal of the priests, the number and size of the Catholic schools and churches in the new states and territories, and the educational activities of the Jesuits all helped stir up the latent fear of Rome that had lain dormant in this country since the Revolutionary War. Some anti-Catholic zealots in the days of Native American enthusiasm and Know-Nothing secrecy resorted to violence, as though the merits of Protestantism could best be shown in the light of burning convents, but men of sounder judgment adhered to the American principle of full religious toleration; the latter recognized the right of Catholics to do their utmost to conserve the faith of their own people, and even to try to win converts. Throughout most of the Protestant churches

the antidote for Romanism was simple and peaceful: to match church for church and school for school.[29]

Another feature of Western religious life which was viewed with disapproval in the East was its emotional character as exhibited in revivals and camp meetings. Among a people forced to live in more or less isolation these were important social as well as religious gatherings. Nervous tension produced by the dangers and uncertainties of frontier life provided the psychological background for the wild excitement of some of these old-time religious exercises. Shouting and singing, jerking and falling into trances, the people of the West let their emotions run riot.[30] After the tremendous excitement of the Great Revival in the West (1797-1805) died down, religious practices on the frontier were more restrained; however, the custom of having a "big meeting" every year or so continued, especially among the more popular religious groups. It was generally believed in the East that these later revivals, although free from the more objectionable features of the earlier camp meetings, still overemphasized the emotional aspects of religion and often did more harm than good. The following unfriendly, but not especially unfair, description of Western religious practices which appeared in the *Home Missionary,* the organ of the American Home Missionary Society, in 1851 under the heading, "Getting Religion in the Southwest," is reproduced here because it represents the picture of a normal Western revival as visualized by an average conservative in religion in the East:

The mass of the people are made to believe that the Presbyterians[31] think themselves above them, and hence they treat us much after the same manner as they do most of the modern improvements in agriculture and mechanics. They go to hear the "larned" preacher, and to see the new fashioned plow, and the deep furrows which it makes; and then they return home, and partly from sloth, and partly from envy, cling the tighter to the old rickety plow, and to the see-saw, hum and spit preacher, feeling that improvements are for others. They seem glad enough to hear Presbyterian preaching, provided it costs them nothing; but when it comes to "jinin" the church, why, to be sure, that

---

[29] A more detailed discussion of Catholic activities in the West as a motive for Protestant home missions will be found in Chapter VII.

[30] F. M. Davenport, *Primitive Traits in Religious Revivals* (New York, 1905).

[31] Before the Civil War, Congregationalists in the West were often classed with the Presbyterians.

must take place at a "big meeting," where there is a great deal of
shouting and "hallelujah singing a going on." And then to see the
way they "get religion" as they call it! After a passionate appeal,
(which is evidently intended to reach the weaker part of the congregation first) about departed friends, and a vindication of shouting,
the mourners are called for. And then the singing and shouting
commences, and the mourners are brought in, and required to kneel
down. In this, often painful position, they are sometimes kept for
hours at a time, until wearied out, they sink down and stretch themselves upon the floor. This is considered a favorable symptom, and
the news circulates throughout the country, that "they have got
Mr. —— and Mrs. —— and Miss—— down." After awhile, through
suffocation and exhaustion, a profuse sweat breaks out upon them, and
they are made to feel as they "never felt before." This they conclude
is the "witness of the Spirit," and then as it is expected they relieve
themselves from their procumbent situation, by springing upon their
feet, and hopping about, and clapping their hands, and screaming out
with loud percussive emphasis, "Glory, glory, glory hallelujah, I've
got it" &c., and then all say that such a one "has got religion," and then
there is a great deal of religious laughing and shaking of hands
&c &c.... [32]

And then the ignorant and illiterate preachers of the
West! Their mistakes in grammar, their ludicrous explana-
tions of obscure texts in the Bible,[33] and their lack of dignity
in the pulpit were pointed to as proof of unsatisfactory religious conditions on the frontier. These criticisms were
directed mainly at the Baptists and Methodists, whose
preachers in the early days were often men who had not
enjoyed the benefits of a formal education. But they, in
turn, conscious of their own achievements, had a good deal
of contempt for missionary ministers from the East—the
products of "a theological factory, where they dress up little
pedantic things they call preachers."[34] John M. Peck, a
Baptist missionary of New England origin, was probably
fair in his evaluation of his fellow ministers in the West.
In his *Guide for Emigrants* he estimated that there were
about 240 preachers in Illinois in 1831, of whom "one third
may be rated as doing positive injury to religion, one third
as of minor service, and the rest as possessing various
qualifications, of a higher grade for usefulness in the
ministry."[35] The illiterate preachers, he said, were usually

[32] *Home Missionary*, XXIV (1851), 49.

[33] H. W. Pierson, *In the Brush* (New York, 1881), 246-48, gives
illustrations.

[34] P. Cartwright, *Autobiography*, 486.

[35] J. M. Peck, *Guide for Emigrants* (Boston, 1831), 261.

"proud, conceited, and influenced by a spirit far removed from the meek, docile, benevolent, and charitable spirit of the gospel."

Equally discouraging, in the minds of many, was the obvious interest of some Western preachers in secular pursuits, especially farming and speculation in land. Soon after John M. Peck reached Missouri as a Baptist missionary, he unburdened himself to a friend in regard to the land hunger of the preachers of his own denomination in the West. "The longer I live," he wrote, "the more I am impressed with the folly of the Baptists in ordaining so many to the sacred, high & responsible work of the ministry who will not first solemnly pledge themselves to make the gospel the *first* and *great business* of *their lives*."[36] Several months later, when he was debating in his mind the instructions he had received to abandon his field in Missouri, he wrote: "To leave a region nearly destitute of a gospel ministry is distressing and I see not the least prospect that this region is to receive any supply from emigration. The truth is the good land is all held by old claims and the ministers who emigrate to this state seem to be chiefly bent after *good land*."[37] If Peck made such comments about the Western preachers in his own denomination, one need not be surprised to find in the letters of Presbyterian and Congregational missionaries frequent disparaging references to the secular activities of native Western religious leaders, especially the Baptists. In such a situation the Easterners saw further evidence of the need for their good influence on frontier society.

EASTERN INTEREST IN THE WEST

Even the most unsympathetic New England critic of Western religious life recognized that there were many God-fearing men and women who had gone to the new settlements and had remained true to their early training.[38]

---

[36] J. M. Peck, St. Charles, Mo., March 8, 1820, to Isaac McCoy, McCoy MSS., II, No. 25, in Kansas State Historical Society.

[37] J. M. Peck, St. Louis Co., Sept. 4, 1820, to Isaac McCoy, McCoy MSS., II, No. 67, in Kansas State Historical Society.

[38] Albert Barnes in his *Plea in Behalf of Western Colleges* (Philadelphia, 1846), 16-18, insisted that the West because of the religious inheritance of its settlers would not be irreligious; the question, he said, was not whether there should be any religion in the West, but whether it should be true or false.

Again and again these pious pioneers appealed to their friends in the East for help in maintaining ministers and erecting churches. They longed for the forms of worship to which they had been accustomed in the old home; they were concerned about the moral and spiritual welfare of their children. But they needed assistance. The West has usually been a debtor section, and the frontiersmen have been poor. However well intentioned they may have been, it was in most cases quite impossible for the first generation of pioneers to perform the rough labor necessary to clear the ground, drain the swamps, build houses, make roads, raise crops, fight Indians occasionally, and still have sufficient time or money left with which to provide adequate religious and educational facilities. Even New England with a homogeneous population vitally interested in religion had not been able to do this; it had received some help from the old country, not the least of which was a goodly supply of ministers trained in the English universities.

Furthermore, when the people of New England became fully conscious as to their responsibility towards the West early in the nineteenth century, they knew that they themselves had inherited private and public improvements, and religious and educational institutions from the generations that had preceded them. "Freely ye have received, freely give." They knew also that they were accumulating a surplus of capital for investment—in the West, perhaps. Even the financial stake that the East had in the West was occasionally urged as a reason for contributing to home missions. In 1864 a Boston preacher in discussing the reasons for which the people of Massachusetts supported missions said:

And when men have made money, they are fond of good investments. And in the West we have made them. The iron horse flies over the prairies because fifty millions of New England capital aid in furnishing the track, and this mostly from Massachusetts. Fifty millions more are invested in land, manufactures, and loans; while twenty-five millions more are employed in mining operations.

Now, sir, the men who are shrewd enough to make the money are shrewd enough to see that they had better create a good moral atmosphere in the communities where they have made investments. They know that bonds and stocks and mortgages are all the more valuable for being within the sound of the *church*-going bell. Well do they know that the greater the intelligence and the higher the moral principles of the people, the more sure they can be that all their obligations will be fulfilled. Well do they know that an enlightened, living,

powerful conscience is a better guardian of silver and gold than any system of vengeance to the evil doer that the sagacity of man has ever invented. And also, well do they know that such intelligence, such Christian principles, and such power of conscience are created by and only by the blessed Gospel. Wherever it goes in its power, it creates a moral atmosphere which men cannot breathe without being faithful to all their obligations.[39]

In fairness to the cause and to the man whose statement has just been quoted, it should be added that he expressed regret that any one should support missions for purely mercenary reasons, and that he gave it as his opinion that the great body of contributors in New England did have higher motives. One of these he found in family ties between the East and the West. Massachusetts alone in 1864, he said, had nineteen thousand of her sons and daughters in Illinois; sixteen thousand in Ohio; twelve thousand in Wisconsin; nine thousand in Michigan; five thousand in Iowa.[40] Not through prayers alone, but also through gifts to missions, did Christian parents in the East indicate their solicitude for the younger generation in the West.

From time to time discouraged missionaries, as their thoughts turned back to the pillars of the church they had known in the East, expressed the desire that colonies of pious laymen, preferably of their own denomination, would move into the West to form centers of Christian influence. They pointed out that in so doing such emigrants would not only benefit themselves economically but would help in the spread of the Kingdom by giving their support to religious institutions in the new settlements. Eastern religious leaders on the whole did not give much encouragement to the idea. Many of them felt that only the less stable and more adventurous were likely to go to the frontiers, and that such persons were not the sort who might be expected either to support religion actively or to set a good example. Secretary David Greene, of the American Board of Commissioners for Foreign Missions, in reply to such a suggestion from Dr. Marcus Whitman, of Oregon, set forth this point of view very clearly when he wrote:

---

[39] H. B. Hooker, in *Home Missionary*, XXXVII (1864), 87.

[40] The exact figures for the free population of these states according to the Census for 1860 were: Illinois, 19,053; Ohio, 16,313; Wisconsin, 12,115; Michigan, 9,873; Iowa, 6,214.

What influence we can exert directly, to induce moral and intelligent men to go as settlers to the Oregon country, I do not know. I doubt very much if we ought to attempt anything of the kind. If we should, we probably should have little success. It is the unsettled, restless, adventurous, and generally not the thrifty or well-principled class of persons who would be disposed to undertake such a journey. Men who have a fair standing and fair prospects in the old states will not be much disposed to venture on the uncertainties, both to themselves & their families, which are to be encountered in such a new country, with the scanty social, educational, or religious advantages there to be enjoyed.... Besides, we have seen so much of the falling away of apparently good men, when deprived of their usual incentives to good conduct growing out of Christian instruction and the restraints of public sentiment & exposed to temptation, that we should be slow to advise or in any manner induce men to enter on such an enterprise whose character we had not seen [?] to be very thoroughly tried....[41]

If professing Christians themselves could not be trusted to keep their faith as they moved to the West, that region stood all the more in need of missionary influence.

As the pious men and women of the East looked out over the West they saw a vast area, thinly populated by shifting groups of people whose origins and interests were so diverse that it seemed hopeless to expect them to unite in the establishment of "sound and proper" religious institutions. From the nature of the case the primary concern of the frontiersmen was the satisfaction of material wants, and their manners and morals ofttimes took on the color of the barbarism which surrounded them. In religion there was diversity in place of the unity which New England had had but was losing at the very time that its lack in the West was the cause of so much concern. Diversity brought variation from certain ideals cherished by Calvinists, and to many of these persons the degree of divergence from orthodox Calvinism was assumed to be the measure of the extent of error and delusion. Could a man who believed that he was his brother's keeper look on idly? The New Englander felt his responsibility for others. He was familiar with a system in which the state lent its aid to morals and religion by laws intended to compel church attendance, the observance of Sunday, and the payment of money for the support of ministers. Calvinistic theology required introspection, otherwise a wrong answer might be given to the all-important question "Am I one of the elect of God?" It was an easy

---

[41] Greene to Whitman, April 14, 1845. Quoted by permission from the manuscript of Hulbert, *Overland to the Pacific*, VIII.

step for a conscience which had been sharpened by reflection on this problem, and then satisfied by an affirmative answer, to pass on to the affairs of its neighbor. The New England Conscience looked out as well as in.

It is also important to remember that ever since Christianity became the state religion in the Roman Empire there had been in Western civilization some form of union between church and state. This practice was brought to America. It was as difficult for our colonial forefathers to conceive of an enduring state without the support of religion as it is for us to imagine the long existence of a democracy without an educated citizenry. Before the Revolutionary War the state supported religion for the same reason that it supports education now. As one of the results of the War for Independence the United States launched upon the experiment of divorcing church and state. Men who opposed the change, and some of those who approved it, were convinced that the state would not endure without religion to teach men obedience, reverence, and honesty.[42] But what would happen to religion, and ultimately to the state, under the voluntary system of church support? Never since the days of the Roman Empire had such a plan been tried among Christians in so vast an area or among people of such diverse interests. Would it work? It might, but many people in the East were convinced that they themselves must take up part of the burden the state had laid down.

If correct religious ideas are essential to the life of the republic, then is the republic in danger when any part of it falls into infidelity or is carried away by error. The situation appeared the more serious by reason of the fact that the nineteenth century was not far advanced before it was realized in the East that the West was bound to grow so rapidly that it would soon hold the balance of power politically in the nation. With each reapportionment of seats in the House of Representatives the size of the Western delegation grew. The West would soon control the country. But what influences were to control the West? The men of the East who tried to answer this question through the home missionary movement did it in the firm belief that their

---

[42] Cf. E. N. Kirk, *The Church Essential to the Republic. A Sermon* ... (New York, 1848) ; S. F. Jarvis, *A Sermon, Preached before the Auxiliary Education Society of the Young Men of Boston* (Boston, 1822).

action was in the highest degree patriotic. When they gave
their assent to such a proposition as this, "Resolved, that
the influence which the Protestant Missionary exerts for
the proper organization, regulation and general welfare of
society at the West, entitles him to the confidence and support, not only of the Christian, but also of the patriot," they
were not mouthing empty words; they meant it.

The home missionary movement was the resultant of
many forces: Christian idealism, denominational rivalries,
humanitarianism, nationalism, and enlightened self-interest
all had their effect in producing and directing a movement
designed to mold the West according to orthodox Protestant standards.[43]

---

[43] New Englanders thought of the movement as an attempt to re-
organize society in the Western states "after the New England model."
[E. Judson], "The Evangelization of the West," in *The New Englander*, IV (1846), 29-39.

CHAPTER II

A MISSIONARY FRONTIER OF EUROPE

Wee are credibly informed, that in many of our Plantacons, Colonies and Factories beyond the Seas, belonging to our Kingdome of England, the Provision for Ministers is very mean; And many of Our said Plantacons, Colonies and Factories are wholly destitute, and unprovided of a Mainteynance for Ministers, and the Publick Worshipp of God; and for Lack and Support and Mainteynance for such, many of our Loveing Subjects doe want the administration of God's Word and Sacraments, and seem to be abandoned to Atheism and Infidelity.— *Preamble of Charter of the Society for the Propagation of the Gospel.*

ALTHOUGH the eighteenth was not a century of great missionary activity in the English colonies, there were during its course certain important developments which prepared the way for organized home missions among American Protestants. First of all, Christian institutions, where not already in existence, were established from Maine to Georgia, either by the colonists themselves or with the help of friendly persons in the Old World; in addition, revival characteristics were imposed on American Protestantism by the Great Awakening, and some efforts were made by those who lived in the older communities to carry the gospel to the new settlements; and finally, the principle of a free church in a free state was established, thus securing to all religious groups an equal opportunity to expand in the West.

The settlers in the English colonies had naturally brought with them the religious institutions and beliefs they had known in the old country. The Church of England had been introduced into Virginia with the founding of Jamestown; in New England, Congregationalism had evolved among the Puritans; Maryland was traditionally the colony of the Roman Catholics; in the Middle Colonies, as varied in religion as they were heterogeneous in race, Anglicans, Quakers, Scotch-Irish Presbyterians, and members of the many Dutch and German sects lived side by side. Religion had been one of the great forces which had led to the migra-

tion to America. And yet some pious Englishmen were convinced by the opening of the eighteenth century that "The very Indian darkness was not more gloomy and horrid, than that in which some of the English Inhabitants of the Colonies lived."[1] This comment was based partly on the feeling that it was bad, very bad, not to conform to the Church of England—and the majority of the colonists who made any profession of religion were nonconformists. But even if it be granted that the dissenters were as deserving of the name Christian as the Episcopalians, the religious outlook in the colonies was not bright. More people had come to America for economic gain and social advancement than for religious freedom. Even among those with whom religion had been the primary consideration it had been hard to maintain the pristine purity of the faith in the wilderness. Everywhere, even in New England, by the opening of the eighteenth century there were signs of indifference in religion, formalism in worship, and laxness in moral standards. The colonies, although nominally Christian, were a proper field for missionary endeavor—and all the more so since, according to good Richard Hakluyt (Discourse on Western Planting, 1584), one of the reasons for English colonization was to "inlarge the glory of the gospell, and from England plant sincere religion."

THE CHURCH OF ENGLAND

The first form of religion to be introduced into the English colonies was that of the State Church of England, but it was not until the beginning of the eighteenth century that it began organized missionary activity in America. One reason it began then, after a century of apparent indifference, was to be found in the political situation. England had recently expelled a Catholic king, James II (1688), and was engaged in war with France, a Catholic state. The colonies were involved in the struggle. The French in Canada, Catholics all, and the Indians on the borders of English America, most of whom were believed to be under Jesuit influence, were regarded as a threat to the safety of the English empire. In the eyes of Anglicans, America with its variety of dissenting sects was at loose ends religiously;

---

[1] D. Humphreys, Historical Account of the Incorporated Society for the Propagation of the Gospel (London, 1730), 20-21.

hence it seemed desirable that the State Church should take a hand in an effort to bolster up Protestantism as interpreted officially in the mother country.

A second reason may be found in the moderate growth of a spirit of reform within the Anglican Church. The restoration of the Stuarts in 1660 had been followed by a reaction from Puritan asceticism which had plunged England into the muck of sensualism. The moral condition of that country seems never to have been quite so bad as it was in the last half of the seventeenth century. Licentiousness, drunkenness, profanity, and gambling were common vices; robbery and murder, frequent crimes. A reaction came, as it always has, against such conditions. About the turn of the century various religious and moral societies were founded in England in an effort to combat irreligion and immorality.[2] Some of them were concerned primarily with the detection and punishment of vice and crime, but one of them, the Society for Promoting Christian Knowledge,[3] which was organized in 1698, had the more constructive program of preventing immorality and the spread of atheism by educating the people in Christian principles. That the scope of this Society embraced the colonies as well as England was due probably to the fact that its chief founder, Dr. Thomas Bray, was greatly interested in the religious situation in America by virtue of his office as Commissary in Maryland for the Bishop of London. Inasmuch as Dr. Bray was especially concerned about the scarcity of good books in the colonies, the new Society took as one of its chief objects "the fixing of Parochial Libraries throughout the Plantations." It was soon realized that, useful as was the dissemination of Christian literature, a more vigorous agency was needed if the Church of England were to make any progress in the English colonies. Accordingly the Society for the Propagation of the Gospel in Foreign Parts was organized in London in 1701; among the founders were the Archbishop of Canterbury and the bishops of London, Bangor, Chichester, and Gloucester.

---

[2] J. Woodward, *An Account of the Rise and Progress of the Religious Societies* (3rd ed., London, 1701); G. V. Portus, *Caritas Anglicana* (London [1912]), 8 ff.

[3] W. O. B. Allen and Edmund McClure, *Two Hundred Years: the History of the Society for Promoting Christian Knowledge* (London, 1898).

THE S. P. G.

The first missionary sent to the American colonies by this Society, whose long name is usually abbreviated to S. P. G., was George Keith, a native of Scotland, who had been successively a Presbyterian, a Quaker, and an Anglican; he had already lived for twelve years in America, and while there had been a leader among the Friends.[4] His return to the colonies in 1702 in the rôle of missionary for the English State Church naturally annoyed his erstwhile Quaker associates. They were his chief opponents, he said, in his missionary journeys (1702-04) "betwixt Piscataway-River in New-England, and Coretuck in North Carolina."[5] He and his companion, John Talbot, apparently without invitation, attempted to speak in the Quaker meetings, and then complained indignantly at the rude treatment they received. But in spite of heated disputations with the Quakers—some of whom, according to Talbot, "ought to be taken up, & put in Bedlam, rather than be sufferd. to goe abt. railing & raving agst. the Laws & Orders of Christ & his Church"[6]—Keith reported that he found the people in the colonies generally well affected towards the doctrines he preached among them and willing to join "decently in the Liturgy, and Publick Prayers, and Administration of the Holy Sacraments, after the Usage of the Church of *England*."[7] He made special mention of the fact that he was treated civilly at "Cambridge Colledge in N. England," and expressed the belief that "were it not for the poysonous doctrines that have been infused into the scholars and youths there and deep prejudices agt. the Church of England by Mr. Increase Mather, formerly President of the Colledge there, and Mr. Samuel Willard, now President there, the Scholars and students there would soon be brought over to the Church."[8]

Following Keith's reconnaissance of the field, the Society began to send out resident missionaries whose task it was to

---

[4] Society for the Propagation of the Gospel (abbreviated hereafter to S.P.G.), *Classified Digest of the Records of the Society for the Propagation of the Gospel* (London, 1893), 9-10.

[5] G. Keith, *Journal of Travels from New-Hampshire to Caratuck.* ... (London, 1706), 82.

[6] J. Talbot, Philadelphia, Sept. 1, 1703, to Secy., S.P.G., S.P.G. papers, Series A, Vol. I, in Library of Congress Transcripts, Great Britain, Vol. 376.

[7] G. Keith, *Journal of Travels*, 82.

[8] S.P.G., *Classified Digest of Records*, 42.

organize congregations and to perform the regular ministerial offices. At the outset the S. P. G. confined its activities mainly to the middle and southern colonies. By the
middle of the eighteenth century New England was receiving considerable attention from the Society, too much,
indeed, to suit the dominant religious group there. The
Puritans protested. The Reverend Mr. G. Muirson, who
tried to organize an Anglican church in Stratford, Connecticut, was warned by the local officials that he was acting
illegally in attempting to introduce a "New Way of Worship." The ministers and magistrates, he reported,

... left no means untryed both foul and fair, to prevent the settling of
the Church among them. ... The people were ... threatened with
Imprisonment and a forfeiture of £5 for coming to hearing me. ...
They spare not openly to speak reproachfully and with great contempt
of our Church; they say that the sign of the Cross is the Mark of the
Beast and the sign of the Devil and that those who receive it are
given to the Devil.[9]

The number of S. P. G. missionaries in New England
increased from three in 1718 to thirty in 1761. In the latter
year the Society had sixteen representatives in New York,
ten in New Jersey, nine in Pennsylvania, five in each of the
two Carolinas, and one in Georgia.[10] It appeared to the
Puritans that the great English missionary society was dis-
tributing its agents in inverse ratio to the needs of the
people. Surely other parts of America needed missionaries
more than pious New England! In 1734 the associated
ministers of the County of Hampshire, Massachusetts, with
Jonathan Edwards acting as scribe, sent a letter of protest
to the Bishop of London. They expressed the opinion that
the sending of Episcopal missionaries either to their com-
monwealth or to the neighboring colony of Connecticut did
not answer the "good & noble professed design" of the royal
charter of the Society and was injurious to the interests of
the Kingdom of Christ. "We think," they wrote, "we may
justly claim the name of a Christian Country, or people already." Furthermore, "the Missionaries that come among us
shew a very uncharitable & unchristian spirit, particularly
by insinuating that our Ministry is no Ministry, not having

---

[9] S.P.G., *Classified Digest of Records*, 43.

[10] It was not necessary to send S.P.G. missionaries to Maryland or
Virginia, since the Anglican clergy in those colonies were supported
from public funds.

had Episcopal Ordination." This state of affairs, they added, tended to breed disorder and confusion in their churches "by cherishing a small number of *disaffected persons* in several places, to the ill example of a whole town."[11] Other Puritan ministers fired broadsides of sermons and pamphlets at the S. P. G. They accused it of having become a society for the propagation of episcopacy rather than the gospel;[12] they reproached it for neglect of the Indians and suggested that this negligence had permitted French and Catholic influences to grow dangerously on their borders;[13] they professed fear of a design to establish a bishop in America, an official whose very presence in the country would threaten both political and religious liberty.[14]

As might be expected, the Venerable Society, as the S. P. G. was known affectionately to its friends, had vigorous defenders on both sides of the Atlantic. Its champions pointed out that the great objects of the Society were to combat Romanism and infidelity; these ends, they insisted, could best be reached by establishing an orthodox or Church

---

[11] W. S. Perry, *Historical Collections Relating to the American Colonial Church* (Hartford, 1870-78), III, 299-301.

[12] George Whitefield, an ardent Anglican revivalist who traveled extensively in the colonies, criticized the S.P.G. for the disproportionate attention it gave New England. In a letter to the Bishop of Oxford, July 28, 1741, he wrote: "I could not but further observe in looking over the list of Missionaries, that there are no less than twenty employed in preaching & teaching school in the Province of New-England, (where certainly the Gospel is preached wh. greater purity than at home) & but two settled Missionaries in all North Carolina.... Does this not look too much like making a Party of Religion?" Lambeth Palace MSS., No. 1123, I, 29.

[13] This idea is developed in a letter from Jonathan Edwards, Stockbridge, Feb. 24, 1752, to Joseph Paice, London; copy in Lambeth Palace MSS., No. 1123, I, 60. Cf. N. Hobart, *Serious Address to the Members of the Episcopal Separation in New-England* (Boston, 1748); John Beach, S.P.G. missionary, came to the defense of the Society in his *Calm and Dispassionate Vindication* (Boston, 1749); Hobart replied in a *Second Address* (Boston, 1751).

In a letter of Sept. 27, 1758, to Samuel Johnson, first president of King's College (Columbia), the Archbishop of Canterbury admitted that the S.P.G. ought to change its policy so as to put more of its missionaries on the frontiers. "For Missionaries there might counteract the Artifices of the French Papists; and do considerable services, religious and political at once, amongst the neighboring Indians; both which points the Society hath been heavily charged, on occasion of the present war, with having neglected." Lambeth Palace MSS., No. 1123, II, 121.

[14] For general discussion of this question, see A. L. Cross, *Anglican Episcopate and the American Colonies* (New York, 1902).

of England ministry in the colonies. The lamentations of
the New England divines on the wretched moral state of the
country were quoted to prove that there was need for missionary work. With respect to the Indians, the Puritans
were asked what they had done for these heathen who were
at their own door. And so the controversy went on with
each side accusing the other of mistakes and bad faith.[15]
It is significant in part as an illustration of the resentment
usually shown by members of self-satisfied communities
when outsiders enter in an effort to convert them to some
supposedly higher religious or social system. In the middle
of the eighteenth century the Puritans asked why Episcopal
missionaries were being sent to New England, the most
godly part of America. Fifty years later the men of Vermont
wanted to know why Puritan missionaries were being sent
from Connecticut to the Green Mountain State; it was not
a heathen land. In the middle of the nineteenth century
some of the people of Iowa expressed resentment over the
arrival of a band of Congregational and Presbyterian missionaries from New England; they thought they could get
along very well without them. The Mormons in their turn
protested against the sending of missionaries to Utah—and
so it went across the continent, with the sponsors of the
missionaries very sure in each instance that their actions
were justifiable.

The work of the Venerable Society was educational as
well as religious. Schools were sometimes maintained in
connection with the mission churches, part of the stipend
of the schoolmaster coming from England.[16] The function of
the school was to inculcate the doctrines of the Church of

---

[15] Of the many pamphlets and tracts issued in this battle of words
only a few titles are given below: East Apthorp's *Considerations on
the Institution and Conduct of the Society for the Propagation of the
Gospel* (Boston, 1763), was a defense of the S.P.G. by its missionary
in Cambridge, Mass.; Jonathan Mayhew, of Boston, replied in *Observations on the Charter and Conduct of the Society for the Propagation of the Gospel* (Boston, 1763); in answer to this Samuel Johnson, of Stratford, Conn., published anonymously his *Candid Examination of Dr. Mayhew's Observations* (Boston, 1763); in a counter-
reply entitled *A Defence of the Observations* (Boston, 1763), Dr.
Mayhew compared the methods of his unknown foe to those of the
Indians. The controversy continued, with pamphlet answering pamphlet, until the eve of the Revolution.

[16] S.P.G. Minutes, May 21, 1762, and July 16, 1762, in Lambeth
Palace MSS., No. 1124, II, 49, 57.

England as well as to give secular instruction.[17] The practice of Master Ellis at Burlington, New Jersey, was perhaps typical of the methods used in these schools. He wrote in one of his reports:

...In ye first place after morning prayer each Class reads a Chapter or Two in ye old or New Testament; the remaining part of the Morning they are Employed in Cyphering writing & reading, except ye small children in spelling & reading. Att 11 of ye Clock they all (except the Quakers) goe to Church commonly every day, in ye afternoon they onely read & write untill 4 of ye Clock, the other hour being sett apart for Spelling & Evening prayer, on Tuesdays, Thursdays & Saturdays in every week I Catechize those Children yt are of the Church, and others when suffer'd, and every Sunday they (as many as are able) are Catechized in ye church; children of Christian Parents are abt. 24 in Number; Quakers six.[18]

In the eighteenth century school teaching was not a highly specialized craft, and it is significant that one would-be pedagogue thought that the following qualifications adequately fitted him for admission to the ranks of S. P. G. teachers:

...Although I am no great Linguist, (having only had some small Education in the Latin Tongue, which by reason of my being took early from School and my time otherways employed, I have almost forgot, yet such effect it has had that) I can spell true English, and know how to divide the Sillables of Words, which so far as I can gather, will be as much as can at present be made use of, to a People, who, (as I may say) knows not their A B C. As for my life and Conversation, I hope upon enquiry you'l find it such that (setting aside youthful follies, which there are scarce any, or none, but what are subject to) I may be admitted into the Number of those, who are to be sent over.[19]

The distribution of prayer books and tracts was another educational means used extensively by the Society for the Propagation of the Gospel.[20] Ordinarily each missionary

---

[17] For summary of instructions by S.P.G. to schoolmasters, see C. H. Brewer, *History of Religious Education in the Episcopal Church to 1835* (New Haven, 1924), 28.

[18] R. Ellis, Burlington, Oct. 8, 1715, S.P.G. papers, Series A, Vol. XI, 262, in Lib. of Cong. Transcripts, Great Britain, Vol. 381.

[19] T. Fishwicke, London, June 14, 1711, S.P.G. papers, Series A, Vol. VI, 84, Lib. of Cong. Transcripts, Great Britain, Vol. 378.

[20] In S.P.G. Minutes, Lambeth Palace MSS., there are frequent references to gifts of books to missionaries or parishes in America; *e.g.*, No. 1124, I, 2, 3, 4, 5, 6; II, 2, 5, 7.

when he went out was furnished with books to the value of £10, provided no such library had already been sent to the place to which he was appointed; in addition he was given £5 worth of tracts to distribute.[21] Gifts were made also to some colonial colleges. King's College, out of which grew Columbia University, received a grant of £500 in 1759.[22] At the suggestion of the Reverend East Apthorp, missionary in Cambridge, the Society voted a gift of books to the value of £100 to Harvard College after its library had been destroyed by fire in 1764.[23]

Between 1702 and 1783 the S. P. G. maintained in whole or part 309 ordained missionaries in the Thirteen Colonies.[24] Some were good, some were bad. George Whitefield's accusation in 1740 that most of them were "corrupt in their principles, and immoral in their practices,"[25] was an exaggerated statement, but there is no doubt that some of them were dissolute. Commissary William Vesey, of New York, made complaint regarding one of them that he had "in Debauchery Really out done the Most Profane and profligate Wretch that Ever Came into these Parts."[26] Concerning one of the roistering parsons of the Carolinas, it was said that he did more to retard the spread of Christianity and the growth of the Church of England there than all other causes combined; it was this profane cleric who called North Carolina a "hell of a hole" and who declared that he would rather be vicar to the bear garden than bishop of that province.[27] However, the missionaries were not all profane and immoral; many of them were a credit to their church and their calling. On the roll of the S. P. G. appear such names as those of Dr. Timothy Cutler, sometime rector of Yale College; Dr. Samuel Johnson, first president of King's College; James MacSparran, on whom Oxford University

---

[21] D. Humphreys, *Historical Account*, 72-73.

[22] S.P.G. Minutes, March 16, 1759, Lambeth Palace MSS., No. 1124, I, 36.

[23] S.P.G. Minutes, July 20, 1764. and Jan. 25, 1765, Lambeth Palace MSS., No. 1124, II, 256; III, 15.

[24] S.P.G., *Classified Digest of Records*, 847.

[25] G. Whitefield, Nov. 30, 1740, to Secy. S.P.G., copy in Lambeth Palace MSS., No. 1123, I, 27.

[26] W. Vesey, New York, July 26, 1732, S.P.G. papers, Series A, Vol. XXIV, 219, Lib. of Cong. Transcripts, Great Britain, Vol. 387.

[27] S. B. Weeks, *Church and State in North Carolina* (Baltimore, 1893), 19.

conferred the degree of Doctor of Sacred Theology;[28] and John Wesley, founder of Methodism.[29]

The Society for the Propagation of the Gospel was the chief agency through which was distributed in the North American colonies the bounty of the Church of England, and to it, in the words of the Preface to the *Book of Common Prayer*, "the Protestant Episcopal Church in these States is indebted, under God, for her first foundation and a long continuance of nursing care and protection."

GERMAN "CHURCH PEOPLE" AND "SECTARIANS"

During the seventeenth century, save for the Dutch in New York and the Swedes on the Delaware, the English colonies had been almost entirely English in population. In the eighteenth century, especially with the coming in of thousands of Germans and Scotch-Irish, they began to lose their Anglican character; the colonists were becoming Americans. New racial groups added to the number and variety of sects found between Maine and Georgia, and nowhere was variety more in evidence than among the Germans.

War, famine, pestilence, and religious persecution impelled many thousands of Germans to leave their native land for America between 1685 and 1750. Although the religious controversy that had helped bring on the Thirty Years' War had been ended by the adoption of the principle of *cujus regio, ejus religio* in the Peace of Westphalia (1648), this was not an entirely satisfactory arrangement in that it recognized only the three major religious groups, Roman Catholic, Lutheran, and Reformed; furthermore, it left the way open for persecution or trouble whenever a prince changed his religion. Then came the wars of the League of Augsburg (1688-97) and of the Spanish Succession (1701-14) in which were ravished the farms of Rhenish peasants who had not the slightest interest in the dynastic quarrels and commercial rivalries that had produced these conflicts. In the midst of the turmoil agents of William Penn appeared in Germany seeking settlers for that Quaker statesman's new colony in America. Penn's terms were liberal. The

---

[28] D. Goodwin, ed., *Letter Book ... By the Revd. James MacSparran* (Boston, 1899), xxxv.

[29] S.P.G., *Classified Digest of Records*, 27-28.

prospects of religious freedom, political liberty, and cheap land were sufficient inducements to cause the Germans to move to Pennsylvania in such numbers that presently the English authorities began to ponder the problem of assimilation.[30] Not all of the Teutons settled in Penn's Woods; some of them made their way south and west into the back country of Virginia and the Carolinas, while a few took up land in the Mohawk Valley in New York.

The eighteenth-century German immigrants were on the whole devoutly religious. Not only had many of them left the Fatherland because of religious persecution, but often one of their most cherished possessions was the Family Bible. In their religious affiliations they were divided into two classes, the "church people" and the "sectarians." The members of the two state churches in the various German principalities—Lutherans and Reformed—were known as the church people; the adherents of the many small and often persecuted groups, such as Dunkers, Mennonites, Schwenkfelders, Sabbatarians, Inspired, and New Born, were called sectarians. In between the church people and the sectarians, sometimes classified with one and sometimes with the other, stood the Moravians. The church people were the more numerous of the two groups in America. In 1740 it was estimated that there were in Pennsylvania fifteen or sixteen thousand members of the Reformed Church and about the same number of Lutherans. The adherents of the "sects" probably did not exceed ten thousand in number. In general the latter were characterized by their simplicity of life, their refusal to bear arms, and their mysticism.[31]

In spite of all this religiosity, religious conditions among the Germans in America in the first half of the eighteenth century were often unsatisfactory. This was due partly to the drop in intellectual and moral standards which almost invariably occurs among a people whose energies are devoted mainly to an effort to wrest a living from untamed nature. It was partly the result of a dearth of properly trained religious leaders. So eager were the Germans for pastors that they sometimes elected the first educated man who appeared in the guise of a preacher without waiting for recommendations or certificates. This encouraged

[30] Max Farrand, "Immigration in the Light of History," *New Republic*, IX (1916), 116-18.

[31] W. J. Hinke, *Life and Letters of the Rev. John Philip Boehm* (Philadelphia, 1916), 83-84.

charlatans, for in an hour even "shoemakers, tailors or linen-weavers" might be metamorphosed into clergymen.[32] To say that the Germans in America were in danger of lapsing into heathenism is an exaggeration; that they were becoming indifferent towards religion is true.

THE GERMAN REFORMED

Missionary work among the members of the German Reformed Church in this country began as an outgrowth of the efforts of John Philip Boehm, a German schoolteacher, who came to Pennsylvania in 1720. Although untrained for such work and unordained, he yielded to the request of his own church people that he act as pastor. About 1727 a regularly ordained Reformed minister, George Michael Weiss, arrived; he at once protested against Boehm's irregular actions. The latter, at the suggestion of his friends, appealed to and received ordination from the Reformed Dutch Church in New York.[33] This unusual request for ordination and the appeal from Weiss to the Palatinate Consistory, which was forwarded to the Synod of South Holland, aroused the interest of the Dutch in the spiritual welfare of the Germans in the New World. In 1730 Weiss and Jacob Reiff visited Europe and collected over two thousand florins in Holland for the work in the English colonies; unfortunately the proceeds were invested in merchandise which was held for customs in England, with the result that the religiously destitute Germans in America received no immediate benefit from Dutch generosity. However, as one result of the connections thus established with the Netherlands, Michael Schlatter, a native of St. Gall, Switzerland, was sent by the Classis of Amsterdam in 1746 to visit the members of the German Reformed Church in America, to organize them in congregations, and to unite them more closely with one another and with those of their faith in Europe. After extensive missionary journeys—more than eight thousand miles on horseback in Pennsylvania, Maryland, and Virginia between 1747 and 1751—Schlatter recrossed the Atlantic to arouse further interest in the work

---

[32] W. J. Hinke, ed., "Diary of the Rev. Michael Schlatter," *Jour. Pres. Hist. Soc.*, III (1905-06), 119.

[33] W. J. Hinke, *Life and Letters of the Rev. John Philip Boehm* 20 ff; J. H. Dubbs, *Reformed Church in Pennsylvania* (Lancaster, 1902), 80-83.

he had undertaken.[34] He collected money and books in Germany, Switzerland, and the Netherlands, and induced six young men to join him in the American mission. The States of Holland and West Friesland promised two thousand florins annually for five years; this gift was three times renewed.[35]

THE CHARITY SCHOOLS

Among those in the Netherlands whose interest had been aroused in the Germans in America was David Thomson, pastor of the English Reformed Church in Amsterdam. Through him certain persons in Britain had their attention called to the religious and moral conditions that prevailed among the Germans in their overseas possessions. As one result of Thomson's visit to England and Scotland in 1752 the Assembly of the Church of Scotland (Presbyterian) ordered that a collection be taken up at the doors of all their churches; this produced "upwards of twelve hundred pounds sterling."[36] A more important consequence was the formation in 1753 in England of the Society for the Propagation of Christian Knowledge among the Germans in Pennsylvania. Among the officers of the Society was the Earl of Shaftesbury, who served as president; among the contributors was the King of England, who gave a thousand pounds.

Behind this outburst of charity among Englishmen, some of whom probably had no particular interest in the religious welfare of "Pennsylvania Dutch," were secular as well as religious motives. The number of Germans in Penn's colony had grown to such an extent that English leaders there and in the mother country had become concerned about the problem of anglicization. There were political ramifications also. Some feared that if the pacifist Quaker politicians got control of the German voters, especially in the sects opposed to war, they would continue to dominate the provincial as-

---

[34] For Schlatter's Journal see W. J. Hinke, "The Diary of the Rev. Michael Schlatter," *Jour. Pres. Hist. Soc.*, III (1905-06), 105-21, 158-76; H. Harbaugh, *Life of Rev. Michael Schlatter* (Philadelphia, 1857), 215 ff.

[35] J. H. Dubbs, *Reformed Church in Pennsylvania*, 145-62; on the "Holland Stipend" see also *Minutes and Letters of the Coetus of the Reformed Congregations in Pennsylvania, 1747-1792* (Philadelphia, 1903), 131, 149, 183, 200.

[36] S. E. Weber, *Charity School Movement in Colonial Pennsylvania* (Philadelphia, [1905]), 25.

sembly and, by their failure to make adequate provision for defense, expose the colony to the inroads of the French and the Indians. A pamphlet of 1755, published anonymously but attributed to William Smith, Provost of the College of Philadelphia, contained the charge that the Friends had persuaded the Germans that

there was a Design to enslave them; to force their young men to be Soldiers, make them serve as Pioneers, and go down to work upon our Fortifications;—that a military Law was to be made, insupportable Taxes to be laid upon them, and in a Word, that all the Miseries they suffered in *Germany*, with heavy Aggravations, would be their Lot, unless they joined to keep in the Quakers. . . .

In consequence of this, the *Germans*, who had hitherto continued peaceful, without meddling in Elections, came down in Shoals, and carried all before them. . . .

More serious, in view of the fact that the hostilities out of which were to grow the Seven Years' War had already started in the backwoods of Pennsylvania, was the statement that

The French have turned their Hopes upon this great body of Germans. They know the Germans are ignorant—they are sending Jesuitical Emissaries among them. They will offer the Germans easy settlements on their lands. The French are preparing to put their Grand Scheme into Execution.

Fortunately for such evils there was a remedy:

Now there is no Way of preventing these dreadful Misfortunes with which we are threatened, but to open the Eyes of the *Germans* to their true Interests, and soften their stubborn Genius . . . by means of *Instruction*. Faithful Protestant Ministers and Schoolmasters, should be sent and supported among them, to warn them against the Horrors of *Popish* Slavery; to teach them sound Principles of Government, and instruct their Children in the *English* Tongue, and the Value of those Privileges to which they are born among us. . . . [37]

It was to provide just this sort of education and propaganda that the Society for the Propagation of Christian Knowledge among the Germans in Pennsylvania had been organized. The work of the Society, for which the sum of about £20,000 was collected in England, was to be done

[37] [William Smith], *Brief State of the Province of Pennsylvania* (London, 1755), 27-43. Smith, in two letters to the Bishop of Oxford, Oct. 17, 1754, Nov. 1, 1756, urged that Protestant missionaries be sent to the frontiers of Pennsylvania in order that they might counteract the intrigues of the French. Lambeth Palace MSS., No. 1123, I, 83; II, 105.

mainly through schools. The plan of organization called for a superintendent, an advisory committee of prominent men, and a local committee for each school. As superintendent the Society chose Mr. Michael Schlatter, whose work among the Germans has already been noted. Among those appointed to the provincial advisory committee were Benjamin Franklin, Governor James Hamilton, Justice William Allen, Secretary Richard Peters, Provost Smith, and Conrad Weiser, the latter a well-known Indian agent. Schlatter, who began his work as superintendent in 1755, soon had schools established at Reading, York, Easton, Lancaster, Skippack, and Hanover.

In general this Charity School movement met with the approval of the "church people" among the Germans and the disapproval of the "sects." The latter had not forgotten the religious persecutions in Germany and were suspicious of any movement in which the organized churches took the lead. They raised the cry that German nationality and language were in danger and thus succeeded in alienating from the movement some of the German Reformed and Lutherans who had been friendly at first. The leader in the opposition to the schools was the Dunker Christopher Saur, of Germantown, the chief German printer in the province. He insisted that the object of the English in supporting the schools was political rather than religious, because, as he pointed out, some of the trustees were notoriously irreligious. In a letter to Conrad Weiser he said:

> Touching Hamilton, Peters, Allen, Turner, Shippen and Franklin, I know very well that they care little about religion, much less about improving the Germans; no farther than the stupid Germans could be used as militia-men to protect their property. For such persons know not what faith is, or what it is to confide in God. Their wealth is their God; and they are mortified that they cannot compel the people to protect their Gods. . . . [38]

Probably because of the opposition that had developed among the Germans, Schlatter resigned the superintendency in 1756. The work prospered for a few years; the report of the Society for 1759 shows that it was then maintaining eight schools with more than four hundred boys enrolled.[39] Beginning with the year 1760, however, the donations from

---

[38] H. Harbaugh, *Life of Rev. Michael Schlatter*, 293 (Note).

[39] S. E. Weber, *Charity School Movement*, 47.

the Society in London became so irregular and scanty that the schools had to be closed except as the Germans were able or cared to continue them for themselves. Thus ended an early effort to assimilate the foreign-born.

THE LUTHERANS

The Lutherans in Pennsylvania were about as numerous as the members of the Reformed Church and as destitute of competent ministers in the early part of the eighteenth century. The first pastor of note among them was John Caspar Stoever, who arrived in America in 1728. For thirty-five years he acted as missionary and pastor, traveling from settlement to settlement, preaching to the people, marrying them, baptizing their children, and offering them the consolations of religion.[40] In 1733 three Lutheran congregations in Philadelphia and vicinity joined in sending a deputation to England, Holland, and Germany to raise money for the purpose of maintaining churches and schools in Pennsylvania. Dr. Ziegenhagen, court chaplain in London to Britain's German king George II, endorsed the appeal because he remembered the touching calls he had received from the spiritually destitute in America. Assistance came also through the University of Halle, a pietistic center in Germany. A Lutheran missionary society was organized there, and in 1742 Henry M. Muhlenburg was sent to America; additional pastors and catechists were sent later. Muhlenburg, because he was the great organizer of his denomination in the English colonies, is known as the Father of the Lutheran Church in America.

On the eve of the Revolutionary War the Lutheran congregations in North Carolina appealed to Europe for help. In 1772 men from Rowan and Mecklenburg counties were sent to Hanover to ask for preachers and teachers. Perhaps it was because the King of England was also the Elector of Hanover that they approached this particular German principality. They obtained the services of a pastor and a schoolmaster. The promise of pecuniary assistance and a further supply of preachers and teachers was made but not fulfilled because of the outbreak of the American Revolution.[41]

---

[40] T. E. Schmauk, *History of the Lutheran Church in Pennsylvania* (Philadelphia, 1903), I, 247-69.

[41] G. D. Bernheim, *History of the German Settlements and of the Lutheran Church in North and South Carolina* (Philadelphia, 1872), 256-57.

THE MORAVIANS

The most zealous of the German missionaries in the colonial period were the Moravians. The Unitas Fratrum, or Moravian Church, which was founded by the followers of John Huss in 1457, had been crushed but not exterminated by the Thirty Years' War. A remnant who had secretly cherished their faith in Bohemia and Moravia took refuge in 1722 on the estates of Count Zinzendorf at Herrnhut in Saxony, as did also the representatives of other persecuted sects. To deal with the doctrinal controversies that arose from the mingling of these various religious enthusiasts, Zinzendorf proposed a plan that would permit individuals to hold their peculiar beliefs while all constituted one household of brethren in respect to those articles of faith and discipline that were commonly accepted.[42] Although Zinzendorf's notion of a church within a church—"the Congregation of God in the Spirit"—was agreed to by the Moravians at Herrnhut, they never completely abondoned the hope of rebuilding the church of their fathers; one result of thus keeping alive two policies, the one sectarian, the other nonsectarian, was at times an inconsistency of action. Count Zinzendorf and his Moravian associates agreed heartily on the necessity for missionary activity and the desirability of working in America. Their attention had been drawn to the spiritual needs of the Germans in the English colonies; furthermore, it seemed the part of wisdom to provide a refuge in the New World to which they might escape in case they were again molested in the Old. A threefold plan of missionary endeavor was evolved: they proposed to preach, to teach, and to work. Work was an essential part of the missionary program; the results of their toil were to be used to support the preachers and teachers.

The first attempt of the Moravians to organize a community in America was made in Georgia in 1735. It was never a flourishing settlement, and the environment was not congenial; when their Georgia neighbors insisted that they bear their share of the fighting in border warfare with the Spanish in Florida, in spite of the fact that they had been promised exemption from military service by the trustees of the colony, they decided to look for a place where they

---

[42] W. N. Schwarze, "Early Moravian Settlements in America," *Papers Amer. Soc. Ch. Hist.*, 2nd Ser., VII, 73.

might enjoy greater freedom of conscience and action.[43] Pennsylvania was selected on account of its reputation for religious freedom; and there the Moravians founded Bethlehem in 1741 and Nazareth in 1742. For twenty years the inhabitants of these two communities maintained a co-operative union or "Economy," a voluntary arrangement in which all the members worked for a common cause. They were divided into two groups: the members of the Pilgrim Congregation were those who were called to go out as preachers and teachers; the Home Congregation produced the necessary food and other supplies for the support of themselves and the missionaries.[44] The results were astonishing. By 1747, in addition to several farms, thirty-two different industries were in operation at Bethlehem. In 1753 it was reported that over one hundred distinct commodities could be produced in their shops and on their farms. At no time during the period of the "Economy" did the population of Bethlehem exceed six hundred, while the number of itinerant preachers and teachers sometimes reached fifty. With their work among the Indians, for which they are justly famous, we are not concerned here; their labors among the whites were confined mainly to the Germans in Pennsylvania and the southern colonies.

The diaries of the Moravian missionaries tell interesting stories of the simple faith and devotion of these men of God who sought out the scattered families of Germans in the back country. The hardships of travel on the frontiers they accepted without complaint. Such entries as the following in the diary of Brothers John Brandmueller and Leonhard Schnell, who made a journey into Virginia in the autumn of 1749, are typical:

November 15.... Travelling was difficult to-day, for we had to cross rather high mountains, and moreover it rained. Night overtook us before we reached a house and had passed through the water. At last we could no longer see the way and had to stay where we were. Fortunately, we found a little hut, in which no one was at home. Here we stayed, thanking God for the shelter. We made fire, and after

---

[43] Bishop John Ettwein, Bethlehem, March 15, 1793, to Benjamin Trumbull, MS. in Widener Library, Harvard University.

[44] J. T. Hamilton, *History of the ... Moravian Church*, in *Moravian Historical Society Transactions*, VI (Bethlehem, 1900), 138. For general discussion of Moravian missionary activities, see H. E. Stocker, *Home Mission History of the Moravian Church in the United States and Canada* (N.p., 1924).

drying our clothes we slept as well as we could. As we had nothing to eat, we had to fast, thanking the Lord that he had protected us this day.... [45]

In spite of their disinterested motives the Moravians met with considerable opposition from their own countrymen as well as from the English and Scotch-Irish. Some of the Lutheran and Reformed ministers objected when the Moravians preached to members of their flocks and accused them of trying to make proselytes, although that was not their purpose. Because of their insistence upon personal piety and their practice of itinerating, they were often associated in men's minds with the enthusiasts responsible for the excitement of the Great Awakening. In his proclamation of April 3, 1747, Governor Gooch of Virginia authorized all magistrates to discourage and prohibit so far as they could legally "all Itinerant Preachers, whether they be New Lights, Moravians or Methodists," from teaching, preaching, or holding any meeting in the colony.[46]

After Bethlehem and Nazareth, the principal Moravian settlement in the colonies was at Wachovia in North Carolina. Probably one reason for planting this new community was the desire to establish an additional base from which missionary work might be undertaken. In the autumn of 1753 a small party under the leadership of Brother Bernhard Adam Grube made the five-hundred-mile journey from Bethlehem to Wachovia to lay the foundations of the new colony.[47] There were many problems and difficulties on the way. One they met, so the record tells us, by simply "going four miles beyond Carl Isles [to make camp] so as not to be too near the Irish Presbyterians."[48] To get their heavily loaded wagon through the rough back country of Virginia and North Carolina was a task that called for both skill and patience. "It was uphill and down," and the brethren had to push the wagon or hold it back by ropes. At the approach to the James River the road was so steep that they had to fasten a small tree to the back of the wagon, "and

---

[45] W. J. Hinke and C. E. Kemper, "Moravian Diaries of Travels through Virginia," *Virginia Magazine of History*, XI (1903), 122-23.

[46] *Virginia Magazine of History*, XI (1904), 228.

[47] J. H. Clewell, *History of Wachovia* (New York, 1902), 3-15.

[48] N. D. Mereness, *Travels in the American Colonies* (New York, 1916), 332.

the Brethren held back by the tree with all their might," but even then the wagon went down so fast that most of them lost their footing. When they reached their destination they gave thanks to God in song and prayer. Brother Gottlob began the singing with this stanza:

> We hold arrival Lovefeast here,
>   In Carolina land,
> A Company of Brethren true,
>   A little Pilgrim Band,
> Called by the Lord to be of those
>   Who through the whole world go
> To bear Him witness everywhere
> And nought but Jesus know.[49]

Wachovia, like Bethlehem and Nazareth, became a center of missionary activities, but on a smaller scale. The home missionary work of the Moravians was disrupted by the Revolutionary War and never again became so important in proportion to their numbers as it had been in the middle of the eighteenth century. Indeed, for a time they practically abandoned missionary work within the United States and turned their attention mainly to the foreign field; it was not until about 1850 that a Moravian Home Missionary Society was organized.

THE PRESBYTERIANS

One of the indirect results of the beginning of missionary work in the colonies by the Church of England was the stimulation of American and British Presbyterians to greater activities in the New World. Soon after the arrival of George Keith as a representative of the Society for the Propagation of the Gospel, Francis Makemie, a leader among American Presbyterians, went to England in an effort to interest Presbyterians there in the propagation of their principles in the colonies.

Makemie, who has been called the "Father of American Presbyterianism," had come to America about 1683 in response to an appeal for a minister which had been sent to the Presbytery of Laggan in Ireland by a group of Presbyterians living on the eastern shore of Maryland. Little is known about his activities for several years, except that he com-

---

[49] A. L. Fries, *Records of the Moravians in North Carolina* (Pubs. of North Carolina Hist. Comm.), I, 79.

bined preaching with trade and farming and had interests sufficiently wide to give Governor Cornbury of New York, at whose instigation he was arrested in 1707 on the charge that he had violated the laws of that province regarding public preaching, an opportunity to describe him to the authorities in England as a "Jack-at-all-trades; . . . a preacher, a doctor of physic, a merchant, an attorney, a counsellor at law, and which is worst of all, a disturber of governments."[50]

In 1704 Makemie went to London and sought to interest British dissenters in the religious situation in the colonies in general and the needs of Presbyterians in particular. He was promised support for two missionaries for two years. With his two recruits, John Hampton and George McNish, Irish and Scotch respectively, he returned to America in 1705. In the following year they and a few Puritan ministers from New England who were living in the Middle Colonies formed the Presbytery of Philadelphia.[51] For many years the new presbytery looked across the Atlantic for moral and financial support. In 1709, for example, American Presbyterians called the attention of sympathetic dissenting ministers in London to their own weaknesses and to the advantages enjoyed by the S. P. G. missionaries on account of "the settled fund of their Church which not only liberally supports them here, but encourages so many insolencies both against our persons and interest, which sorrowfully looking on we cannot but lament and crave your remedy."[52] In 1718 the Synod of Philadelphia pointed out, in an appeal to the Presbytery of Dublin, that

. . . the paucity and poverty of these people render them utterly incapable to support the ministry among them, could they obtain it; and there lies, therefore, upon them a deplorable necessity of still continuing in the same circumstances of darkness that they are now in, which may render both themselves and posterity miserable Pagans, unless some methods can be found out for their speedy assistance in the maintaining of such ministers as we would direct them to. . . . [53]

---

[50] L. P. Bowen, "Makemie and Rehoboth," in *Jour. Pres. Hist. Soc.*, VI (1911-12), 159.

[51] C. A. Briggs, *American Presbyterianism* (New York, 1885), 138-40.

[52] *Records of the Presbyterian Church in the United States of America*, W. M. Engles, ed. (Philadelphia, [1841]), 16.

[53] *Ibid.*, 53.

A letter addressed to the Principal of the College of Glasgow in 1716 urged Scottish benefactions to the American churches partly for the reason that

there are a great many young men merchts who come from your parts, soberly ... educated & brought up att home, who, when they arive here, are meer rakes, stap or stand att no sin or vice almost that falls in their way, swearing whoring Sabbath breaking drunkennesse are as common vices, with a great many of them, as if they tho't there was no evil in the commission of any of these; ... [54]

From time to time British Presbyterians responded to these and other appeals with men and money. In 1706 two ministers were sent to South Carolina with help from the Presbyterian Fund which had been established in London. In 1711 Scottish Presbyterians contributed nearly £600 for the cause in America; two years later they sent a preacher to Pennsylvania. In 1719 the Synod of Philadelphia empowered a committee "to receive the collection of the Synod of Glasgow and Air, if it arrives safe in goods, and put them into the hands of some substantial persons, to be sold for the best advantage for money ... and receive the neat produce for the use of the fund."[55] These contributions, supplemented by gifts in America, enabled the Presbyterian Church to begin its long and effective career as a missionary agency in the new settlements.

CONGREGATIONALISTS AND BAPTISTS

The founders of New England Congregationalism were indebted to the mother country for a goodly cultural heritage, which included, in addition to books and institutions, the education received in the English universities by the first generation of ministers. But because of the unity of purpose in the Bible Commonwealths and their compactness of settlement, there was little necessity for their spirtual kinsmen in England to engage in missionary work among them; and, as was pointed out above, when the Anglican Society for the Propagation of the Gospel sent its representatives into their midst, they resented it.

Although in the colonial period the American Baptists

---

[54] C. A. Briggs, *American Presbyterianism*, App. xx.

[55] *Records of the Presbyterian Church in U.S.A.*, 56-57; C. A. Briggs, *American Presbyterianism*, 174 ff.

were neither so numerous nor so compact as the Congregationalists, and hence stood more in need of outside assistance, they seem to have received comparatively little direct help from their co-religionists in England. Perhaps this was the necessary consequence of Baptist individualism and the lack of any authoritative directing body among them; however, there are occasional references to the sending of both men and money to the colonies by the English Baptists. Among the Particular Baptists there was an unofficial body known as the Society of Ministers of the Particular Baptist Persuasion, which corresponded with colonial Baptists and gave them counsel and some financial assistance.[56] The General Baptists of London in 1714 sent two ministers to Virginia in response to an appeal from that colony. Occasionally personal gifts were made by English Baptists for religious and educational work in America. One of the chief donors was Thomas Hollis, who met Dr. Increase Mather during a visit of the latter to England, and who, in appreciation of the courtesy shown by the Mathers to the Baptists in Boston, made gifts to Harvard College and provided for the education in that center of Puritanism of a number of Baptist ministerial candidates. After the Baptists founded a college of their own in America (Rhode Island College, later Brown University), they sent an emissary to England to solicit funds for its support.

The settlers in the English North American colonies had brought with them not only their beds and books, their clothes and customs, their languages and laws, but also their religious beliefs and practices. In various ways they had received missionary assistance from the Old World. Christian institutions, under different names and in divers forms, had been introduced from Maine to Georgia. The new American nation was to start with a Christian endowment, but that necessarily implied that the people along the coast should assume some responsibility for the religious welfare of the frontiersmen.

---

[56] A. H. Newman, *Century of Baptist Achievement* (Philadelphia, 1901), 12.

CHAPTER III

THE COLONIAL PERIOD

If the state of society and manners, from the commencement of the settlements in this [western] country, ... owing to the sanguinary character of the Indian mode of warfare ... was in a state of retrogression, ... If ignorance is more easily induced than science, If society more speedily deteriorates than improves: If it be much easier for the civilized man to become wild, than for the wild man to become civilized, what means have arrested the progress of the early inhabitants of the western region towards barbarism?—*Joseph Doddridge.*

THE OLD WEST

BY THE MIDDLE OF THE seventeenth century, fifty years or so after the founding of Jamestown, the English had secured little more than a good foothold in America. Their settlements in Virginia and Maryland, in Massachusetts, Rhode Island, and Connecticut were all near the sea. Between the Chesapeake Bay colonies and New England stood the Dutch at the mouth of the Hudson, the most important point on the whole North American coast. Within the next hundred years there were two important changes in the settled area of the English North American colonies: first, the gaps along the shore line were filled in by the conquest of New Netherland and by the founding of Pennsylvania, the Carolinas, and Georgia; secondly, the westward movement of population carried the frontier line out to the Alleghenies.

The West of the first half of the eighteenth century is known as the Old West.[1] In New England it included the southwestern corner of Maine, the Berkshires in western Massachusetts, and the fingers of settlement which had thrust themselves up the Merrimac and Connecticut valleys into southern New Hampshire and Vermont. In New York

---

[1] F. J. Turner, "The Old West," in *Proceedings of the State Historical Society of Wisconsin for 1908.*

the frontier was to be found in the upper Hudson and lower Mohawk valleys. In Pennsylvania a band of new settlements lay athwart the middle reaches of the Delaware, the Schuylkill, and the Susquehanna rivers, while some adventurous frontiersmen had begun to penetrate the Kittatiny Mountains. In Virginia the Old West was the piedmont, the land between the fall line and the Blue Ridge, but there were already pioneers in the Shenandoah Valley. So new was North Carolina—William Byrd's "Lubberland"—that practically all parts of that province partook of frontier characteristics. In South Carolina and Georgia the edge of settlement had barely reached the fall line by 1760. Here and there the Old West, which stretched in a thin ragged line from Maine to Georgia, extended out as far as the Appalachian barrier.

This advance of settlers into the interior was of great significance in the religious as well as the political, economic, and social development of early America. In this, our first, West the people—at least some of them—were busy making homes out of the wilderness. Most of them were poor in worldly goods. By reason of their exposed position they had to bear the brunt of the Indian fighting. The feeling among the backwoodsmen that they had more than their share of this was one of many factors that helped bring about divergence between the coast and the frontier. Even as early as the latter part of the seventeenth century there were signs of cleavage between the two sections. There were disputes over representation in the colonial assemblies, the administration of justice, and the collection of taxes, as well as methods of Indian warfare and defense. The back country, although a region of rude plenty, was a place of hard labor in which the monotony of life was broken by rough sports and such practical diversions as hunting, trapping, and fishing. There was little time or means for the niceties of life. The coast towns, on the other hand, thanks to the accumulation of a little capital and the emergence of a small class that had some leisure time, were developing a polite society; the townsmen were becoming urbane.

The back country diverged also from the coast in racial stocks. The seaboard settlements were mainly English; the frontier, as a result of the entrance of several non-English groups, notably the Scotch-Irish and the Germans, and their intermingling, was becoming American. As the number of

the non-English increased the West tended more and more to be a region of dissent from the established churches of the coastal communities, while the poverty of the people and their preoccupation with other matters often made it difficult or impossible for them to provide themselves with ministers of the gospel. In this Old West, near as it was to the coast, an opportunity was offered for missionary endeavor.

RELIGION IN THE COLONIES

To outward appearance the religious life of the English colonies did not seem flourishing in the early years of the eighteenth century. The State Church of England was neither active nor effective in the provinces in which it was established by law. In some instances the lives of the clergy were a disgrace to their holy calling. In Maryland and Virginia, where they were supported by public taxation and inadequately supervised, so many of the Anglican clergy were guilty of licentiousness and drunkenness that the roistering parson came to be generally, although unfairly, regarded as typical of his class. The situation was so bad, however, that a governor of Virginia early in the eighteenth century complained to the authorities about the "most unworthy and scandalous carriage of some Ministers of the Church who by their corrupt Conversation and vicious practice do demolish more in one year, then even a Wise Master Builder could re-edify in a much longer space of time."[2]

Among the Puritan clergy in New England a higher moral standard was maintained, but even in their churches there were many signs of spiritual decay. The people as a whole were more tolerant than their fathers had been, but it was a tolerance born of apathy; for it is clear that "the New England of 1700 was meaner, narrower, in every way less inspired with the sense of a mission to accomplish and an ideal to uphold, than the New England of 1650."[3] It was with a sense of sadness that the good old days had gone that Dr. Increase Mather wrote in 1702 a book entitled *The Glory Departing from New England.* By 1714, according to the Assembly of Connecticut, "the Glory" had already de-

---

2 W. S. Perry, *Historical Collections,* I, 332.

3 W. Walker, *Creeds and Platforms of Congregationalism* (New York, 1893), 466.

parted from that colony, and the "reverend elders" were enjoined to make strict inquiry into the state of religion in the several parishes.[4] We may grant with a present-day historian that the people of New England probably touched their lowest point intellectually and spiritually in the opening years of the eighteenth century,[5] and yet realize that much that disturbed the professional religious leaders of that time was only the by-product of a period of social and intellectual change. Life in New England was being secularized. The people were turning from the state of mind that had made possible the witchcraft excitement at Salem. New interests in commerce and science were arising to claim a larger share of attention. There was less thought about the "Divell" and his works.

THE GREAT AWAKENING

Just as the English colonies had felt the effects of the religious and moral depression of the post-restoration period, so they shared in the religious revival that marked the middle years of the eighteenth century. This quickening of the spiritual life was not confined to one country or creed. In Germany, where it was called Pietism, sects that emphasized the mystical union of the believer with God sprang up and flourished; private devotional societies were organized within the existing churches; emotionalism in religion and reformation of conduct were stressed.[6] In England Methodism was born within the state church, but before the end of the century it had burst the bounds of this communion and had started to spread over the earth in its own name and way. So significant was the work of John Wesley and his followers that the great religious movement of the eighteenth century has sometimes been called the Methodist Revival; in America it is usually referred to as the Great Awakening.

The origins of this religious storm which swept over the English North American colonies were both internal and external. They were internal in so far as they were the

---

[4] *Public Records of the Colony of Connecticut* (Hartford, 1850-90), V, 436.

[5] J. T. Adams, *Revolutionary New England* (Boston, 1923), 35.

[6] C. H. Maxson, *Great Awakening in the Middle Colonies* (Chicago, 1920), 3-4.

result of the zeal and fervor of such earnest preachers as Jonathan Edwards in New England and of the Tennents in the Middle Colonies; they were external in so far as German Pietism influenced the Dutch and German settlers in New York and Pennsylvania, and above all in the effects of the visits of the great English revivalist, George Whitefield.

The youthful Edwards, minister at Northampton, Massachusetts, had for some time grieved over the seeming indifference of his people to spiritual concerns. "Extraordinary Dullness in Religion" had produced unseemly conduct. According to Edwards the youth of the town, before the revival started, were

very much addicted to Night-walking, and frequenting the Tavern, and lewd Practices, wherein some, by their Example exceedingly corrupted others. It was their Manner very frequently to get together, in Conventions of both Sexes, for Mirth and Jollity, which they called Frolicks; and they would often spend the greater part of the Night in them, without regard to any Order in the Families they belonged to; and indeed Family-Government did too much fail in the Town.[7]

Edwards attributed this decline in religion and morals to the inroads of Arminianism, a pernicious error, he said, which taught men to rely on good works for salvation. To combat this notion he began in 1734 a series of sermons on salvation by faith, in which he restated the Calvinistic teachings of the awfulness of sin, the sovereignty of God, the helplessness of man, predestination, and election. It was a hard doctrine that he preached, and the result, whether it be attributed to the working of the Holy Spirit or to the effects of fear and superstition playing on the imagination of an untrained and uncritical people, was the starting of a religious revival whose influence extended far beyond the confines of Northampton. Sweet music in the ears of Edwards was this "Noise amongst the Dry Bones." Men conversed almost entirely on religious subjects. "There was scarcely a single Person in the Town, either old or young," said Edwards, "that was left unconcerned about the great things of the eternal World. Those that were wont to be vainest and loosest, and those that had been disposed to think, and speak slightly of vital and experimental Religion, were now generally subject to great awakenings."

---

[7] J. Edwards, *Faithful Narrative of the Surprising Work of God* (3rd ed., Boston, 1738), 4.

Within a year "the Town seemed to be full of the Persence [sic] of God: It was never so full of *Love*, nor so full of *Joy;* and yet so full of Distress, as it was then."[8]

A second root of the Great Awakening can be traced back to Neshaminy, in Pennsylvania, the home of William Tennent. This Presbyterian preacher and teacher, Irish by birth, had come to the colonies in 1718. The cabin he built in which to educate his four sons and such other young men as came to him for instruction was called in derision the Log College, but it is now held in veneration as the germ out of which developed Princeton University. Tennent and those of his way of thinking were ardent evangelists. They believed in conversion as a definite experience and insisted that it was possible for mortal men to distinguish between the converted and the unconverted. A conservative group among the Presbyterians not only questioned this but looked with disfavor on the methods of the revivalists.

German Pietism made its contribution to the Great Awakening through the godly lives and preaching of various religious leaders among the Germans in Pennsylvania and the Dutch in New York. The Mennonites and the Dunkers, two of the chief pietistic sects in Pennsylvania, were not numerous, but on account of their earnestness had an influence out of proportion to their numbers. The leader of the evangelistic movement among the Dutch was Theodorus J. Frelinghuysen, who had come under pietistic influences in Germany. After his arrival in New York in 1720, he preached the necessity for conversion and the futility of reliance upon formalism in religion.

Thus in New England and in the Middle Colonies, among Congregationalists, Presbyterians, Dutch Reformed, and various German sects, there were local and occasional stirrings of the revival spirit. But the movement had not been general throughout the colonies nor had it attracted wide attention. With the coming of George Whitefield in 1739 the Awakening entered upon a new stage. He linked the American movement with English Methodism and transformed a series of local, sporadic revivals into an intercolonial, nonsectarian religious disturbance which shook colonial society to its foundations.

Whitefield had fallen under the influence of John and

---

[8] J. Edwards, *Faithful Narrative of the Surprising Work of God*, 9.

Charles Wesley while at Pembroke College, Oxford. He began to preach in 1736 and soon became the most effective revivalist in England. Like some of his successors, he was often violent in his methods, censorious in his judgments, and denunciatory in his language. Reports of his open-air preaching in England and of his first visit to the English colonies in 1738 in the interest of the orphanage he had started in Georgia had been printed in the colonial newspapers. When he returned to America in 1739 and began his first great tour through the colonies, people flocked to see and hear him. In Boston, said a disgruntled New England divine, "he was received as though he had been an *Angel of God: yea a God come down in the Likeness of Man.*"[9] According to Whitefield's own statement he preached to one audience of six thousand persons in one of the Boston meetinghouses; in another the aisles and doors were so blocked by the throng that he had to enter by a window; on a third occasion the crowd was so great that five were killed and others dangerously wounded. As in England, Whitefield frequently preached in the open. One of his audiences on Boston Common he estimated at fifteen thousand; another, on the occasion of his farewell sermon there, at thirty thousand.[10]

Under the preaching of the eighteenth-century revivalists, the auditors were moved to shouts and groans and tears. In describing a meeting in May, 1740, at which he preached "to near 12,000 hearers," Whitefield wrote:

> I had not spoke long, but I perceived Numbers melting. As I proceeded, the Power increased, till at last, both in the Morning and Afternoon, Thousands cried out, so that they almost drowned my Voice. Never before did I see a more glorious Sight! Oh what strong Cryings and Tears were shed and poured forth after the dear Lord Jesus.—Some fainted; and when they had got a little Strength, they would hear and faint again.... [11]

[9] Charles Chauncy, *Letter ... Concerning the State of Religion in New-England* (Edinburgh, 1742), 6.

[10] G. Whitefield, *Continuation of the Reverend Mr. Whitefield's Journal.... The Seventh Journal* (London, 1741), 26-41. In support of Whitefield's estimates of the size of his outdoor audiences, Benjamin Franklin's computation that he might have been heard by more than 30,000 is significant. Franklin, *Autobiography* (Boston, 1840), I, 139-40. William Seward, Whitefield's "Companion in Travel," in his *Journal of a Voyage* (London, 1740), 11, 13, refers to the "multitudes" who came to hear Whitefield.

[11] G. Whitefield, *Continuation of the Reverend Mr. Whitefield's Journal*, 43.

It is said that those who heard Jonathan Edwards preach his famous sermon on "Sinners in the Hands of an Angry God"—the one in which he represented the Almighty as holding sinful man over the pit of hell much as one might hold a spider or some other loathsome insect over the fire—were so convulsed in agony that the preacher had to bid them be more quiet in order that he might continue his discourse.

The excitement and physical manifestations which attended the Great Awakening brought reproach upon the revival movement. Conservatives in religion protested. Although Whitefield was a minister of the Church of England, the Anglican clergy in America were almost unanimous in their denunciation of the revivalists and their methods. Many comments similar to the following may be found in the reports of the missionaries of the Society for the Propagation of the Gospel:

... It is impossible to relate the convulsions into which the whole country is thrown by a set of Enthusiasts yt strole about harangueing the admiring Vulgar in *extempore* nonsense, nor is it confined to these only, for Men, Women, Children, Servants & Nigros are now become (as they phrase it) Exhorters. Their behavior is indeed as shocking, as uncommon, their groans, cries, screams, & agonies must affect the Spectators were they never so obdurate & draw tears even from ye most resolute, whilst the ridiculous & frantic gestures of others cannot but excite both laughter & contempt, some leaping, some laughing, some singing, some clapping one another upon the back, &c.... [12]

Among the dominant religious group in New England, the Congregationalists, there was also much opposition to the revival, and this despite the fact that the most distinguished Puritan preacher of the time, Jonathan Edwards, had helped bring it about and had taken up his pen in its defense. Admitting that the movement was attended by some undesirable features, Edwards contended that the good results far outweighed the bad.[13] The Reverend Charles Chauncy, of Boston, was foremost among those who held the opposite view. He could not see that the people were much if any better after the revival than before; he objected to busybodies going about the country and stirring up trouble in other men's churches; and he complained about

---

[12] W. S. Perry, *Historical Collections*, III, 353.

[13] J. Edwards, *Some Thoughts Concerning the Present Revival of Religion in New-England* (Boston, 1742), 39-55.

the censoriousness of the revival preachers and illustrated
his point by quoting a choice collection of opprobrious
terms hurled by Mr. Tennent at the ministers who opposed
the movement: "Hirelings; Caterpillars;...plaistered
Hypocrites; Varlets; the Seed of the Serpent;...dry
Nurses; dead dogs that cannot bark;...Daubers with un-
tempered Mortar; moral Negroes; Salt without Savour,
that stink in the Nostrils of God and Man;...Swarms of
Locusts;...blind Leaders of the Blind."[14] Did men who
used such expressions about their fellow ministers have the
spirit of the meek and lowly Nazarene? Chauncy thought
not.

So hostile was the established church in Connecticut to
the revival that some of those interested in keeping alive
the evangelistic spirit of the Great Awakening withdrew
and set up their own churches under the name of the Strict
Congregationalists or Separates.[15] The controversy in Connecticut between the advocates and opponents of revival-
istic methods resulted also in the passage of a reactionary
law for the purpose of preventing the growth of dissenting
congregations and the preaching of sermons by itinerant
evangelists. Any resident minister who presumed to preach
in the parish of another without his consent was to be
denied the right to share in the advantages of state support
for religion; while any "foreign" minister who attempted to
preach in any town without the permission of the settled
pastor and the major part of the local church was to be
treated as a vagrant and sent from constable to constable out
of the bounds of the province.[16] By virtue of this "transportation law" the Reverend Mr. Finley, later president of
Princeton, was once expelled from the colony graced by
Yale.[17]

Among Presbyterians the revival brought to a head a
dispute over regeneration which had been brewing for some
time between the conservative Old Side party and the re-

---

[14] C. Chauncy, *Seasonable Thoughts on the State of Religion in
New England* (Boston, 1743), 249-50; Chauncy also wrote *A Letter
To the Reverend Mr. George Whitefield, Publickly Calling upon him
to Vindicate his Conduct or Confess his Faults* (Boston, 1744).

[15] S. L. Blake, *Separates or Strict Congregationalists of New England* (Boston, [1902]).

[16] *Public Records of the Colony of Connecticut*, VIII, 455-57.

[17] B. Trumbull, *Complete History of Connecticut* (New Haven,
1818), II, 177.

vivalistic New Side group. The latter, who favored the admission to the ministry and the privileges of the Lord's Table of none but the regenerate, that is, those who could present clear evidence of their conversion, were protested out of the Synod of Philadelphia in 1741. They withdrew and set up their own Synod of New York. When the breach was healed by the union of the two synods in 1758, it was on a platform of evangelistic principles.[18]

As one weighs the consequences of the Great Awakening[19] the scales seem to tip on the side of the good and constructive influences. Divided churches, quarreling Christians, harsh language, and censorious judgments were unfortunate but temporary results of the storm. More hurtful were the fanaticism, the excessive emotionalism, and the baneful delusions encouraged by the appeals to fear and terror on the part of the revival leaders.[20] On the other hand must be set the general quickening of the spiritual life and reformation—perhaps only temporary—of manners and morals. According to Jonathan Edwards the revival caused throughout New England "a great Increase of a Spirit of Seriousness, and sober Consideration of the things of the eternal World." The young people, he noted, had been brought to forsake their bad habits: "Frolicking, vain Company-keeping, Night-walking, their Mirth and Jollity their impure Language, and lewd Songs." Amongst old and young there was a great alteration "as to Drinking, Tavern-haunting, profane speaking, and Extravagance in Apparel."[21] Whitefield likewise stressed the check imposed by the revival on worldly vanities. As a result of his preaching in South Carolina the jewelers and dancing masters of Charleston, he said, complained that their crafts were in danger. "A vast Alteration," he added, "is discernible in the Lady's Dress: And some, whilst I have been speaking, have been so convinced of the Sin of wearing Jewels, that I have seen them, with Blushes, put up their Hands and cover their Jewels with their Mobs."[22]

---

[18] *Records of the Presbyterian Church in U.S.A.*, 157-60, 286-88.

[19] J. Tracy, *Great Awakening* (Boston, 1842), 388 ff., summarizes the beneficial results of the Great Awakening.

[20] Cf. F. M. Davenport, *Primitive Traits in Religious Revivals*, 100.

[21] J. Edwards, *Some Thoughts Concerning the Present Revival of Religion in New-England*, 51-53.

[22] G. Whitefield, *Continuation of the Reverend Mr. Whitefield's Journal*, 8-9.

A consideration of the question of the degree of sinfulness involved in "Mirth and Jollity" and the wearing of jewels may be omitted here, but the rather sudden reaction from the exalted enthusiasm of the revival cannot be dismissed so lightly. Taking the colonies as a whole, it seems that there soon came a return to a state of religious indifference and moral laxness quite as discouraging as that which had preceded the Awakening.[23] Certainly the lamentations of the preachers are just as lugubrious after as before the falling of the "refreshing showers" on the hard hearts of the colonists. As the years go by the successive Fast Day resolutions of the Presbyterian Synod, for example, deplore the "abounding of profanity, luxury, infidelity, error and ignorance," the "prevailing of vice and immorality in the land," and the "lamentable decay of vital piety."[24]

But even though the immediate results of the Great Awakening were disappointing, it still remains the outstanding event in the religious history of the English colonies. Out of this period of controversy and excitement came ideas and principles of far-reaching consequence for the churches of America. The revival was largely responsible for the establishment among Evangelicals of the principle that only the regenerate, or those who had had the experience of conversion, should be regarded as church members: this was the platform upon which the New Side Presbyterians had taken their stand; Congregationalists began to abandon the Half-Way Covenant,[25] an arrangement under which limited membership had been allowed moral, baptized persons who made no claim to conversion; the Baptists, who profited greatly by the revival, and the Methodists, who were soon to sweep over the land in evangelistic fervor, both emphasized the necessity for conversion. The Great Awakening imposed revival characteristics on American Protestantism, and therein lies its chief significance for the home missionary movement. If only the regenerate may be church members, then converts must be made; if converts are to be made, the gospel must be preached to the people;

---

23 C. Hodge, *Constitutional History of the Presbyterian Church* (Philadelphia, [1851]), II, 54.

24 *Records of the Presbyterian Church in U.S.A.*, 229, 276, 290, 398, 426, 481.

25 P. E. Lauer, *Church and State in New England* (Baltimore, 1892), 58 ff.; W. Walker, *Creeds and Platforms of Congregationalism*, 245 ff.

if the gospel is to be preached, special arrangements and extraordinary efforts are needed on the frontiers. Furthermore, if only the "twice-born" are to be church members, then the proposal to separate church and state becomes reasonable from the standpoint of the theologian as well as from that of the statesman. Thus was the way prepared for the disestablishment of the churches in the United States. The Great Awakening encouraged the movement towards democracy in religion, because it helped break up the parish system in which there was one church and one minister for an entire community. Granted the evils of unnecessary duplication of effort in maintaining churches and the multiplication of wrangling sects, there is something to be said for an arrangement under which the individual may follow the spiritual leader of his own choice and attend the religious exercise which seems best to meet his own needs. The Great Awakening is important also because it gave an impetus to, although it did not originate, missions in the colonies. We now turn to a consideration of these, especially the efforts of two denominations, the Presbyterians and Congregationalists, which were later to join forces in the formation of the American Home Missionary Society.

THE PRESBYTERIANS

Early in the eighteenth century the Presbyterians, even while they were looking to the British Isles for help, began to take an interest in missions to the frontiers. One of the first resolutions adopted by the Presbytery of Philadelphia (1707) was that all of its ministers should supply "desolate places where a minister is wanting, and opportunity of doing good offers."[26] Within a few years the mandate was made more specific, as in 1714 when, in consideration of "the desolate condition of the people in Kent County," Mr. James Anderson was appointed to "supply them with preaching, &c. one Sabbath in the month till the next Presbytery."[27] In 1717, the presbytery having meantime been enlarged into a synod, a fund for pious uses was created to help weak churches and to aid in missionary undertakings.[28] The rapidity with which the back country was filling up with

---

[26] *Records of the Presbyterian Church in U.S.A.*, 10.
[27] *Ibid.*, 35-36.
[28] *Ibid.*, 49, 77, 103, 111, 121, 147.

Scotch-Irish immigrants during the first half of the eighteenth century not only gave the Presbyterian Church an unrivaled opportunity for establishing itself upon the frontiers but also called out its missionary powers.

Between 1700 and 1730 some twenty thousand Scotch-Irish, dissatisfied with the treatment they had received in Ulster, sought new economic opportunities and greater religious freedom in America. The lands along the coast being more or less taken up by earlier settlers, they pushed into the interior; soon their cabins were to be found in the back country all the way from New England to the Carolinas. Those who settled in Pennsylvania were a great source of annoyance to the provincial authorities. They squatted on unoccupied lands, refused to pay the quitrents, and, when challenged, made answer that it was against "the laws of God and nature, that so much land should be idle while so many Christians wanted it to labor on, and raise their bread." James Logan, agent for the Penns, said that five families of these land-hungry republicans from Ireland gave him more trouble than fifty of any other people. Stubborn in insisting on their rights, pious and acquisitive, —"they kept the Sabbath and everything else they could get their hands on," according to one writer,—the Ulster Presbyterians made good frontiersmen; but they also stood in need of prayer.

As pointed out above, the Presbyterians in America split into two factions over the question of regeneration. In 1741 the "New Side" New Brunswick Presbytery was excluded from the Synod of Philadelphia; four years later it joined with the presbyteries of New Castle and New York to form the Synod of New York. The New Side party, composed mainly of men from England, Wales, and New England, was strong to the north of Philadelphia. The Old Side party, which continued in control of the Synod of Philadelphia, found its strength geographically in the territory south of that town and racially among the Scotch-Irish. This division reveals the composite nature of American Presbyterianism; essentially the same line of cleavage was to appear again in 1837 when the Old School and New School churches were formed.

Both Old Side and New Side Presbyterians were active in missionary work during their brief schism. Practically every year between 1748 and 1756 such entries as these ap-

pear in the records of the Old Side Synod: "In pursuance to a supplication from Virginia, . . . Ordered, That Mr. Richard Zanchy supply eight Sabbaths in the back parts of Virginia this fall; and that Mr. Steel supply eight weeks in the spring, and return before next Synod;"[29] or, "Mr McCannan ordered to supply congregations of North and South Mountain, Timber Grove, North River, and Cook's Creek, and at John Hinson's until the middle of October next;"[30] or, Mr. John Allison ordered to supply back parts of Virginia and North Carolina and "to treat ministers from the Synod of New York in a brotherly manner."[31] The New Side Synod at New York was equally solicitous about the religious needs of the frontiersmen. In 1745, for example, it recommended that Mr. Robinson go to Virginia to preach, and that he reside there several months.[32] Again, in 1754, this Synod appointed four men to spend three months each in visiting the destitute settlements in Virginia and North Carolina; in the following year one of the three, who was instructed to go to the same general region, was told to supply vacancies at Rocky River and Sugar Creek, at the Hawfields, and on the Enno, Ilico, and Dan rivers.[33]

In 1758 the Old Side-New Side schism was healed by the formation of the united Synod of New York and Philadelphia. Interest in the frontiers continued, and the cessation of hostilities at the close of the French and Indian War opened the way again to the West. In 1762 the Synod appointed Messrs. Beatty and Brainerd "to preach to the distressed frontier inhabitants," and asked them to report "what new congregations are a forming, and what is necessary to be done to promote the spread of the gospel among them."[34] This mission was not carried out because of the unexpected outbreak of Pontiac's War. In 1766, the frontiers being again quiet, the Synod renewed the appointment of Mr. Beatty and gave him Mr. Duffield as his associate. In

---

[29] *Records of the Presbyterian Church in U.S.A.*, 193-94.

[30] *Ibid.*, 206.

[31] *Ibid.*, 220.

[32] *Ibid.*, 234; for the missionary labors of William Robinson, see A. Alexander, *Biographical Sketches of the Founder and Principal Alumni of the Log College* (Philadelphia, [1851]), 216-30, and S. Davies, *State of Religion among the Protestant Dissenters in Virginia* (Boston, 1751), 12.

[33] *Records of the Presbyterian Church in U.S.A.*, 262-65.

[34] *Ibid.*, 326.

the autumn of that year these two men visited Fort Pitt and
went as far west as the Muskingum River. On their return
from this journey, which for its time was unusually extensive, they reported that the people of the frontier were
anxious to have churches formed among them and that,
although they were in needy circumstances as a result of
their losses during the late war, they would do their utmost
to support the gospel.[35] This missionary tour gave a fresh
impetus to the efforts of the Synod in behalf of the West.
In 1766 it was ordered that collections be made in all congregations for a fund "for the propagation of the gospel in
such parts as cannot otherwise enjoy it," and four men were
appointed to visit needy settlements in Virginia, the Carolinas, and Georgia.[36] The Synod in 1768 received a long list
of applications for assistance on the frontiers. There were
appeals from the Long Cane settlement in South Carolina;
from Mecklenburg County, Cathey's settlement, and Fourth
Creek in North Carolina; from Upper Haw River, Deep
River, and Timber Ridge in Virginia.[37] Such place names are
significant, because they indicate that it was the back country of the Carolinas, Virginia, and Pennsylvania—the
stronghold of the Scotch-Irish—which was the missionary
field of the Presbyterian Church in the eighteenth century.
Earnest efforts were made to answer these calls for help.
At the meeting of the Synod in 1768 one minister was instructed to set off as soon as possible for the western frontier
of Pennsylvania, where he was to preach for at least twelve
Sabbaths under the direction of the Donnegall Presbytery;
as compensation he was to receive twenty shillings for every
Sabbath on which he preached "on the other side of
Kittatinning Mountain."[38]

It was thus that the Presbyterian Church sought to
conserve its strength among its natural constituency, the
Scotch-Irish. These men from Ulster were aggressive, hard-
headed individuals. They had been tried by fire in the old
country and had come to America looking for religious and
political freedom as well as better economic conditions.
They knew their rights as men and they held to them

[35] C. Beatty, *Journal of a Two Months Tour* (London, 1768), 15;
J. Smith, *Old Redstone* (Philadelphia, 1854), 115-16.
[36] *Records of the Presbyterian Church in U.S.A.*, 361.
[37] *Ibid.*, 386-87.
[38] *Ibid.*, 389.

tenaciously. From such a sturdy stock came and to them went a group of picturesque frontier preachers, men who combined the rigid classical training required of Presbyterian ministerial candidates with a knowledge of the West gained at first hand. They followed the pioneers into western Pennsylvania on the eve of the Revolution; and they lived among them, in spite of Indian dangers, during that conflict, laying deep foundations for Presbyterianism. One of them, John McMillan, was the first settled Protestant pastor west of the Alleghenies.

As might be expected among a people who insisted on a properly trained ministry, education received much attention among the Presbyterians. William Tennent's Log College at Neshaminy, Pennsylvania, a school of the prophets during the revival period, ceased to exist when its founder died in 1746, but its ideals were carried on by the College of New Jersey (Princeton) which was chartered soon after by the New Side party. In 1753 Gilbert Tennent and Samuel Davies were sent to Britain to solicit funds for the new school, with the result that from Presbyterians and Congregationalists in England, Scotland, and Ireland a sum amounting to more than four thousand pounds was obtained.[39]

In missionary spirit and in work done on the frontiers the Presbyterians were surpassed by no group among Protestants in the eighteenth century.

THE CONGREGATIONALISTS

Although the New England Independents were the most numerous and probably the most influential religious group in the colonies, they were one of the least active in the field of home missions. This inactivity was partly the result of a political and social arrangement which lessened the need for missions to the frontier settlements, but it was also an indication of that spiritual deadness against which Jonathan Edwards and other religious leaders had spoken out. In Massachusetts, Connecticut, and New Hampshire, where Congregationalism stood somewhat in the position of a state church, the colonial governments took care that the great majority of communities in their respective jurisdictions were supplied with an "orthodox gospel ministry."

---

[39] C. A. Briggs, *American Presbyterianism*, 308-09.

When new towns were laid out it was customary to make provision for the support of a minister and the erection of a meetinghouse. Ordinarily permission to go to the new town could not be obtained by the prospective settlers, nor would land grants be made to them, until the provincial authorities had been assured with respect to the new community that there would be "security against ennemyes, and more comfort for Xtian comunion and enjoyment of Gods worship, & education of children in schooles, & civility, wth [sic] other good ends."[40] But even with the best intentions frontier settlers found themselves hard pressed at times to build their churches and support their ministers. In such exigencies they naturally turned to the appropriate colonial assembly for relief. Between 1693 and 1711 at least fifty applications for help were made to the Great and General Court of Massachusetts by feeble or "destitute" parishes. The petition of the inhabitants of Brookfield (1698) was typical:

It is an intolerable burden to continue as we have done, without the preaching of the Word. . . . We are but twelve families, and are not of estate sufficient to give suitable encouragement to a minister. . . . If this Honorable Court would please to pity us, and grant us some help for a few years for the maintenance of a godly, able minister, besides the advantage that it may be to those few families that are here, it would be a means to draw many other inhabitants to us, whereby we shall be able to uphold the worship of God, and not be burdensome to others.[41]

The appropriations for such needy communities in the Bay Colony amounted to about one thousand pounds between 1693 and 1711. For the year 1717 alone the colonial records show that at least five such grants were made, ranging in amount from £10 to Tisbury and £20 to Falmouth (Portland, Maine), to £150 for a meetinghouse on "Cape Codd."[42]

Similar appeals were made to the Assembly in Connecticut. The relief offered there occasionally took the form of a grant of money[43] or the authorization of a special collec-

---

[40] Law of 1679, in *Records of the Governor and Company of Massachusetts Bay in New England*, V, 214.

[41] J. S. Clark, *Historical Sketch of the Congregational Churches in Massachusetts* (Boston, 1858), 114 (Note).

[42] *Journals of the House of Representatives of Massachusetts, 1715-1717* (Mass. Hist. Soc., 1919), 184, 206, 211, 214, 247.

[43] *Public Records of the Colony of Connecticut*, VII, 510, 550.

tion in the various parishes of the colony.[44] More often the Assembly remitted the taxes of a needy town for a term of years on condition that the money "be improved" for the local minister or church.[45] Frequently a special tax was authorized either on all the land in the "destitute" town or only on the unimproved lands.[46] The petitions to the colonial legislatures sometimes revealed the clash of interests that had developed even in the early part of the eighteenth century between the settlers and the nonresident proprietors of the New England towns. It had become common for men in the older communities who had accumulated a surplus for investment to take shares in proposed towns without any intention of settling in them. The actual settlers in a new town might or might not be proprietors, but, whether they were or not, they usually felt that their burdens of defense, of clearing the land, of building roads and bridges, of providing a school, of erecting a meetinghouse, and of supporting a minister, in addition to making a living for their families, were heavy. It was to their interest to shift a part of the load over to the shoulders of the nonresident proprietors. This attitude and the reasons for desiring a special tax for the support of the ministry are shown in the following petition from the inhabitants of Epping to the New Hampshire Assembly in 1747. After a recital of hardships and difficulties the petition "humbly sheweth":

That there is Scarce one Fifth Part of the Land in the Parish Improved the owners of many Large tracts Living out of the Parish who are not obliged by any Law in Force to bear any Part of the Publick Charges So that the Improvers and Settlers alone have Hitherto been obliged to bear not only the Burend of Taxes but to Clear and Repair the High Ways and to Maintain Several very Chargable Bridges and all this under the Troubles and Hardships of the War.—That the value of the Non Resident Lands is much Increased by the Settlements which we are making amongst them in almost all Parts of the Parish.—And that the Building of a Meeting House and Settlement of a Minister being Designed for the Good of the Whole Parish it is Likely that many of those owners of Lands Here who are not at Present Inhabitants may be Equal Sharers with us in the Benefits Accruing therefrom.[47]

---

[44] *Ibid.*, VII, 137.

[45] *Ibid.*, V, 310, 336; VI, 214; VII, 24; VIII, 71, 149.

[46] *Ibid.*, V, 284, 381; VI, 465; VII, 258, 434, 548-49; VIII, 153, 181, 241, 477, 542; IX, 375.

[47] New Hampshire, *Town Papers*, I. W. Hammond, ed. (Concord, 1882), XI, 618.

Although the response by the colonial governments to such appeals can hardly be called "missions," it does help explain the apparent lack of interest in home missions among pre-Revolutionary Congregationalists. The unchurched frontiersman, although not entirely absent, did not present so serious a problem in New England as in other parts of the colonies.

It is not so easy to find an entirely satisfactory explanation for the apparent indifference of the godly New Englanders to the spiritual condition of their less fortunate neighbors in the middle and southern colonies. Spiritual lethargy, provincialism, and the comparative isolation of New England were probably all more or less responsible. To be sure, the Puritans were not entirely indifferent to the welfare of others. Governor John Winthrop tells of the arrival in Massachusetts Bay in 1642 of a gentleman who brought letters "from many well disposed people of the upper new farms in Virginia ... bewailing their sad condition for want of the means of salvation, and earnestly entreating a supply of faithful ministers, whom, upon experience of their gifts and godliness, they might call to office."[48] Three ministers were sent to Virginia in response to this appeal; but they returned the next summer because "the rulers of the country did in a sense drive them out, by making an order that all who did not conform to the discipline of the English Church should depart by a certain day."[49] Another appeal to New England from the southern colonies came in 1695 when some pious persons in South Carolina requested that measures be taken "to encourage the settlement of churches, and the promotion of religion in the southern plantations." In response to this call the Reverend Joseph Lord of Dorchester, Massachusetts, with eight companions went to South Carolina "to settell the gospell ther."[50] Before this band of Christian emigrants set out they were organized into a church. The farewell sermon preached to speed their departure was full of the missionary spirit, and those who were departing were

---

48 John Winthrop, *History of New England, 1630-1649* (New York, 1908), II, 73.

49 W. Hubbard, *General History of New England* (Cambridge, 1815), 411.

50 *Records of the First Church at Dorchester in New England* (Boston, 1891), 109.

referred to as "New England's offering to the Lord Jesus Christ for the services of his Kingdom."[51] They established a New England community at Dorchester on the Ashley River.[52] Economic motives doubtless played their full part in this migration from New England; hence it is hardly to be regarded as a part of the home missionary movement. Probably other examples of New England benevolence might be found, but all put together do not make an impressive showing. The missionary spirit was not strong among the Congregationalists throughout most of the eighteenth century. With the Great Awakening a new spirit began to stir among the dry bones in New England. A new school of religious thinkers began the formulation of the "New England Theology," a modified form of Calvinism. In this the duty of Christian benevolence was stressed, and thus was laid the basis in theory for the reform and missionary activities in which Congregationalists distinguished themselves in the nineteenth century.[53] Signs of the new day are evident as early as June, 1774, when the General Association of Connecticut, in session at Mansfield, made the following pronouncement:

> This Association, taking into consideration the state of the settlements now forming in the wilderness, to the westward and northwestward of us, who are mostly destitute of a preached gospel; many of whom are of our brethren, emigrants from this colony; think it advisable that an attempt should be made to send missionaries among them: ... [54]

It was intended that two pastors should visit the new settlements in Vermont and New York in the spring of 1775, and a sum of money was raised for this purpose by collections in the various churches of the colony; but the guns at Lexington and Concord diverted attention from spiritual to physical conflicts.

---

[51] J. H. Means, "The First Home Missionaries of New England," *Congregational Quarterly*, Whole No. 38, X (1868), 167-71.

[52] There is an account of the Dorchester colony in Committee of Dorchester Antiquarian and Historical Society, *History of the Town of Dorchester, Massachusetts* (Boston, 1859), 261-64.

[53] G. L. Walker, *Some Aspects of the Religious Life of New England* (New York, 1897), 127-54.

[54] *Connecticut Evangelical Magazine and Religious Intelligencer*, VI (1813), 339.

THE BAPTISTS

Prior to the Great Awakening the Baptists in the English colonies were few in number and without great influence. On the whole they stood aloof from the revival, and yet no religious group profited more from it. The Great Awakening had stressed the necessity of personal salvation and the new birth, and both were principles in accord with the Baptist teaching that only repentant believers who had been baptized of their own volition should constitute a church. The Baptists emphasized individual responsibility and allowed full play to emotionalism in religion. The spread of the Baptists in the colonial period was not the result of organized missionary activity; it was rather the result of the evangelical zeal of individual preachers and laymen. In so far as there were any organized missionary efforts they were to be found in the local or regional associations of which the oldest, the Philadelphia Association, was formed in 1707. One of the earliest records of such action by Baptists is found in the Minutes of this Association, which voted in 1755 "that one ministering brother from the Jerseys and one from Pennsylvania, [should] visit North Carolina: the several churches to contribute to bear their expenses."[55] This Association in 1766 began the creation of a missionary fund for the assistance of destitute churches and the support of itinerant evangelists. In 1771 it appointed Morgan Edwards evangelist-at-large, and in the following year thanked him "for his services in traveling and visiting the churches southward."[56]

Of the early itinerant Baptist preachers in the South one of the most famous was John Gano, who had been sent into Virginia and the Carolinas by the Philadelphia Association about 1755. The French and Indian War had just begun; in some places the suspicious backwoodsmen misjudged Gano's motive in coming among them. In the Tar River district of North Carolina the report had gone out that Gano was a French spy—he was of French descent—so he rode to muster and preached to the men, telling them that he was loyal to King George but that the King of Kings

---

[55] A. D. Gillette, ed., *Minutes of the Philadelphia Baptist Association* (Philadelphia, 1851), 72.

[56] A. L. Vail, *Morning Hour of American Baptist Missions* (Philadelphia, [1907]), 73.

ought to be served first. In another place he was taken for the pressmaster, there being at the time a demand for men and horses for Braddock's army. Gano admitted that he was a "pressmaster" and that he even took married men, but he assured the alarmed rustic that the Master he wished him to serve was good, that the wages were high, and that it would be to his advantage to enlist.[57]

Another noteworthy pioneer missionary in the South was Thomas Etheridge of North Carolina; his life was sometimes in danger in his tours as, for example, when a mob in Princess Anne County, Virginia, threatened to pull him down from the trunk of a tree he was using as a pulpit.[58] Because of their refusal to comply with the Virginia laws regarding the registration of dissenting preachers, the Baptists were frequently in trouble there in the decade preceding the outbreak of the Revolution. Among the recalcitrants were John Waller and two companions, men who, according to the charge made against them in Spottsylvania County in 1768, could not "meet a man upon the road, but they must ram a text of scripture down his throat."[59]

In New England the number of Baptist churches increased rapidly after the Great Awakening, the increase being due in part to accessions to their ranks from former members of the Strict Congregational or Separate churches. Some of the men most active in the spread of Baptist principles were brought up among the Separates. Isaac Backus, remembered for his history of the Baptists in New England, was one of these. Another noteworthy figure in early New England Baptist annals was Hezekiah Smith, or Chaplain Smith as he was often called on account of his services during the Revolutionary War, who endured persecution as a result of his successful efforts to establish a Baptist church in Haverhill, Massachusetts. He made frequent excursions into neighboring towns and was largely instrumental in the founding of several new Baptist churches.[60] The Warren Association in Rhode Island, formed in 1767,

---

[57] D. Benedict, *General History of the Baptist Denomination in America* (Boston, 1813), II, 311-13.

[58] V. I. Masters, *Baptist Missions in the South* ([Atlanta], 1915), 100.

[59] R. B. Semple, *History of the Rise and Progress of the Baptists in Virginia* (Richmond, 1810), 15.

[60] Isaac Backus, *Abridgment of the Church History of New England* (Boston, 1804), 199-200.

was one of the most active missionary centers among the Baptists, and from it itinerant preachers were sent to the frontiers of New England.

The missionary tours of evangelists not only resulted in conversions and the formation of new churches, but they also promoted acquaintance and fellowship throughout the Baptist brotherhood. The Baptists in their hostility to ecclesiastical absolutism had gone to the other extreme of local independence. Their polity was congregational, but unlike the Congregationalists they were widely scattered through the colonies and thus missed the unifying influence of contiguity. There were important doctrinal differences among them, some being Calvinists, while others were Arminians. Through the interchange of visits they tended to approach doctrinal uniformity.

Between the Great Awakening and the outbreak of the Revolution the Baptists grew rapidly in numbers in America. Their membership was well scattered throughout the colonies, but their churches were small and not closely bound together. Their ministry on the whole was poorly trained, but made up in enthusiasm what it lacked in formal education. The Baptists insisted on a personal experience in religion and appealed to those who desired a more vital form of piety than was offered by the more conservative state churches. They were aggressive and, as yet, missionary in spirit; later an exaggerated form of Calvinism was to kill all interest in missions among some of them. Their church organization was democratic, their preaching popular in character.

THE METHODISTS

Although during the Great Revival some of the enthusiasts had been referred to disparagingly as "Methodists," it was apparently not until 1766 that John Wesley's followers appeared in the English colonies.[61] Richard Boardman and Joseph Pilmoor, the first missionaries sent to

---

[61] J. M. Buckley, *History of Methodism in the United States (Amer. Ch. Hist. Ser.,* V, New York, 1896), 110, makes the statement that in the first Methodist church built in America (New York, 1768) it was necessary to have a fireplace and chimney in order to evade the law which prohibited the erection of churches not under control of the Church of England. Since church buildings at that time were unheated, a building with a fireplace was obviously not a "church."

America by the Methodist Conference,[62] arrived in 1769, bringing with them a gift of £50 for needy brethren in the New World.[63] New York and Philadelphia were the chief early centers of American Methodism, but societies were soon organized in other towns in the Middle Colonies. Missionary tours were made into New England on the north and into Virginia and North Carolina on the south. The first Methodist preachers were zealous, but the work remained unorganized until after the coming in 1771 of Francis Asbury, the real founder of Methodism in America; Asbury's prodigious missionary labors, however, belong properly to a later period and will receive attention in the next chapter. The appearance in the colonies of "strolling Methodists" seemed to the clergy of the Church of England to confound still further the confusion already created by "religious fanaticks," but the slight ruffling of the religious seas by these early breezes was as nothing compared to the storms that were soon to come.

---

[62] J. Atkinson, *History of the Origin of the Wesleyan Movement in America* (Jersey City, 1896), 112.

[63] J. M. Buckley, *History of Methodism*, 120-21.

CHAPTER IV

AN INTERLUDE, 1776-98

Congress shall make no law respecting an establishment of religion, or prohibiting the free exercise thereof.—*The Constitution of the United States.*

T HE QUARTER of a century following the outbreak of the American Revolution was an interlude between colonial and national missionary activities. It was a period of readjustment rather than of stagnation. Henceforth, since little or no help could be expected from the Old World, the Protestant churches of America would be under the necessity of solving for themselves the problem of carrying the gospel to the frontiers. In the closing years of the eighteenth century they began to sense the magnitude of the problem, with the result that this period ends and a new one begins with the introduction of more elaborate missionary machinery than had been thought necessary in the colonial era. Although it was a time in which infidelity and deism flourished perhaps as never before or since in America, at least two religious groups, the Baptists and Methodists, made phenomenal gains in numbers. The chief constructive development of general interest in the religious history of the country was the weakening almost to the point of collapse of the age-old principle of the union of church and state, and the substitution therefor of the voluntary system of church support. Significant also was the organization of independent national churches, a concomitant in the ecclesiastical realm of the stirrings of nationalism in the political sphere.

DARK DAYS

The various religious bodies represented in America went through a trying time during the eight years of the War for Independence. Churches were desecrated or destroyed, congregations scattered, ministers driven away, colleges closed, nascent missionary operations suspended.

As usual, the effects of war were demoralizing: the value of human life was cheapened; speculation was encouraged; private and public credit were lowered.

The blow fell first and most heavily on the Church of England. Its connection with the English government naturally brought it under suspicion. Many of the Episcopal clergy, and especially the S. P. G. missionaries, were natives of England; moreover, at the time of admission to holy orders they had taken oaths of loyalty to the Crown. It is not surprising that many of these men viewed the quarrel from the English standpoint and remained faithful to the mother country. Some of the most outspoken loyalists were Anglican clergymen; Samuel Seabury and Jonathan Boucher, for example, both used pen and tongue vigorously in support of the English cause.[1] But the statement sometimes loosely made that all the clergy of the Church of England in America were Tories is not accurate.[2] In Philadelphia, for example, the patriot cause received strong support from certain Anglican ministers. John Adams, while attending the First Continental Congress, wrote to his wife from the City of Brotherly Love that he had never heard anyone pray for the American cause with such fervor, such ardor, such earnestness and pathos, and in language so elegant and sublime, as did Mr. Duché, an Episcopal clergyman.[3]

In general it may be said that most of the clergy of the Church of England in New York and New England were on the Tory side, while in Pennsylvania, Maryland, and Virginia they were more friendly to the American cause. This alignment was due, in part at least, to the fact that in the middle and southern colonies the Anglican ministers depended more on their parishioners for support and less on the bounty of the English missionary society than was true in the northern colonies.[4]

Many complaints were sent to England by clergymen who were persecuted because of their loyalist attitude. One of them wrote from Lancaster, Pennsylvania, in 1776:

[1] E. E. Beardsley, *Life and Correspondence of the Right Reverend Samuel Seabury* (Boston, 1881), 28 ff.; C. F. Pascoe, *Two Hundred Years of the S.P.G.*, 75.

[2] W. S. Perry, *Alleged "Toryism" of the Clergy of the United States* (n.p., n.d.), *passim.*

[3] John Adams, *Works* (Boston, 1850), II, 369 (Note).

[4] W. S. Perry, *History of the American Episcopal Church* (Boston, 1885), I, 447-48.

... I have been obliged to shut my Churches to avoid the fury of the populace who would not suffer the Liturgy to be used unless the Collects & Prayers for the King & Royal Family were omitted, which neither my conscience nor the Declaration I made & subscribed when ordained would allow me to comply with; and altho' I used every prudent step to give no offence even to those who usurped authority & Rule & exercised the severest Tyranny over us, yet my life and property have been threatened upon the mere *suspicion* of being unfriendly to what is called the American cause. Indeed every clergyman of the *Church of England* who dared to act upon proper principles was marked out for infamy and insult, in consequence of which the *Missionaries* in particular have suffered greatly. Some of them have been dragged from their horses, assaulted with stones & dirt, ducked in water; obliged to flie for their lives, driven from their habitations & families, laid under arrests & imprisoned![5]

A mob in Norwalk, Connecticut, expressed its disapproval of one Anglican priest by defacing his picture and nailing it to a signpost with the head down.[6] Upon a Dedham, Massachusetts, man of the cloth the local patriot party imposed the unusual, if not cruel, punishment of shutting him up in a room "for 3/4 of an hour, to view the Picture of Oliver Cromwell."[7] At another place in the Bay Colony the Episcopal church edifice was defiled and the minister was outlawed because of his refusal to sign the "Association."[8] When the War of Independence had run about half of its course, Thomas Barton wrote to the Secretary of the S. P. G. as follows:

The clergy of America, the missionaries in particular, have suffered beyond example, and indeed beyond the records of any history in this day of trial. Most of them have lost their all, many of them are now in a state of melancholy pilgrimage and poverty; and some of them have lately (from grief and despondency, it is said) paid the last debt of nature.... We may exclaim, *Quis furor, O cives!* What have we done to deserve this treatment from our former friends and fellow-citizens? We have not intermeddled with any matters inconsistent with our callings and functions. We have studied to be quiet and to give no offence to the present rulers. We have obeyed the laws and government now in being as far as our consciences and prior obligations would permit. We know no crime that can be alleged against us, except an honest avowal of our principles can be deemed such, and for these have we suffered a persecution as cruel as the bed of Procrustes.[9]

---

[5] W. S. Perry, *Historical Collections*, II, 490.

[6] C. F. Pascoe, *Two Hundred Years of the S.P.G.*, 50.

[7] *Ibid.*, 49.

[8] *Ibid.*, 49.

[9] Quoted by E. E. Beardsley, *Life and Correspondence of the Right Reverend Samuel Seabury*, 57.

At the outbreak of the Revolution there were seventy-seven Church of England missionaries in the rebellious colonies. A few of them were dropped from the roll because they joined the American party;[10] many of them returned to England or shifted their field of labor to the Maritime Provinces; some of them remained at their posts and eked out a precarious existence among people who suspected them of disaffection and treated them accordingly. At the close of the war the S. P. G. officially abandoned work within the limits of the United States, since by winning independence the Thirteen Colonies passed beyond the field in which it had been authorized to work by its charter.[11]

THE FRENCH CRAZE

Not only were religious institutions left in a weak condition after the war, but before the post-Revolutionary period of political, economic, and social readjustment was over a new flood of secular ideas and emotions swept over the land. The War for Independence left the American people feeling mildly grateful to the country of Lafayette for its help in disrupting the British Empire, but there was no great outburst of enthusiasm for *la belle France* until the French Revolution startled the world. A Revolution in France? Chains of bondage and shackles of tyranny being struck from the downtrodden masses of an Old World monarchy? Who would have dreamed that the glorious American Revolution could have made its influence felt so quickly and so mightily? Their Revolution was our triumph. In contemplating the epoch-making events in France in 1789 the Boston *Gazette* predicted the beginning of the Golden Age, and pointed out that the "seraphic contagion was caught from Britain, it crossed the Atlantic to North America, from whence the flame has been communicated to France."[12] With the coming of Citizen Genêt in 1793 the excitement reached its height. "What hugging and tugging!

---

[10] W. S. Perry, *Historical Collections*, III, 609.

[11] The 309 missionaries whom the S.P.G. had maintained in the colonies between 1702 and 1785 had been distributed as follows: New England, 83; New York, 58; New Jersey, 44; Pennsylvania and Delaware, 47; Maryland, 5; Virginia, 2; North Carolina, 33; South Carolina, 54; Georgia, 13. S.P.G., *Classified Digest of the Records*, 80.

[12] C. D. Hazen, *Contemporary American Opinion of the French Revolution* (Baltimore, 1897), 142.

what addressing and caressing! What mountebanking and chanting, with liberty caps and other wretched trumpery of sansculotte foolery," exclaimed one unfriendly observer in retrospect.[13] Men addressed one another by the new French equalitarian title of "Citizen"; they wore the tri-color and sang revolutionary songs; they formed democratic clubs to cherish and spread the principles of liberty, equality, and fraternity. Under such circumstances it is not sur-prising that "French infidelity," which had already won converts in America, swept over the land. It became the fashion for young men of education to scoff at religion as superstition. According to President Timothy Dwight of Yale:

... From France, Germany, and Great-Britain, the dregs of Infidelity were vomited upon us at once. From the Systeme de la Nature and the Philosophical Dictionary, down to the Political Justice of Godwin, and the Age of Reason, the whole mass of polution was emptied on this country. The two last publications, particularly, flowed in upon us as a deluge. An enormous edition of the Age of Reason was published in France, and sent over to America, to be sold for a few pence the copy; and where it could not be sold it was given away. You may perhaps be astonished, that such men as these, the mere outcasts of creation, could do harm at all. In my apprehension they were exactly fitted for a sphere of mischief.... Satan needs his scullions and scavengers, as well as his nobles and heroes.... They were conven-iently lost to principle, and to shame; and uttered villainy, obscenity, and blasphemy, not merely with a brazen front, but with the sober, intrepid serenity of apparent conviction....[14]

Skepticism was prevalent in the colleges. Lyman Beecher said that Yale College, about the time when he entered in 1793,

was in a most ungodly state. The college church was almost extinct. Most of the students were skeptical, and rowdies were plenty. Wine and liquors were kept in many rooms; intemperance, profanity, gambling, and licentiousness were common....

That was the day of the infidelity of the Tom Paine school. Boys that dressed flax in the barn, as I used to, read Tom Paine and believed him ... most of the class before me were infidels and called each other Voltaire, Rousseau, D'Alembert, etc., etc.[15]

There was danger that the infection might spread among the sons of John Harvard; so to combat the influence of

---

[13] *Ibid.*, 185.
[14] Timothy Dwight, *Travels*, IV, 380.
[15] Lyman Beecher, *Autobiography* (New York, 1864), I, 43.

Paine's *Age of Reason* and similar books, the authorities of Harvard College in 1796 provided their students with copies of Watson's *Apology for the Bible* at the expense of the corporation.[16]

When New England, the "land of settled habits," lost its head over French thought and principles, what must have been the situation in the more excitable South and West? Infidelity flourished in the backwoods; religion fell into neglect for a time. From one end of the country to the other, men interested in the old ways and the old religious principles were disheartened by what they saw and heard. Dark indeed was the picture painted in 1798 by the Presbyterian General Assembly in its pastoral letter:

... When formidable innovations and convulsions in Europe threaten destruction to morals and religion; when scenes of devastation and bloodshed, unexampled in the history of modern nations, have convulsed the world; and when our country is threatened with similar calamities, insensibility in us would be stupidity; silence would be criminal.... We perceive, with pain and fearful apprehension, a general dereliction of religious principle and practice among our fellow-citizens, ... a visible and prevailing impiety and contempt for the laws and institutions of religion, and an abounding infidelity which, in many instances, tends to Atheism itself.... Formality and deadness, not to say hypocrisy; a contempt for vital goodness, and the spirit of fervent piety; a desertion of the ordinances, or a cold and unprofitable attendance upon them, visibly pervade every part of the church.... The profligacy and corruption of the public morals have advanced with a progress proportioned to our declension in religion.— Profaneness, pride, luxury, injustice, intemperance, lewdness, and every species of debauchery and loose indulgence greatly abound.... [17]

However, lest this be taken too seriously, it should be remembered that much that these good Presbyterian preachers regarded as irreligious, or even immoral, was probably nothing more than an expression of new conceptions and of changing customs in a period of social and political upheaval. American life was still basically sound and wholesome.[18]

SEPARATION OF CHURCH AND STATE

Even though there was a decline in interest in religion in the closing years of the eighteenth century, it was also a

---

[16] V. Stauffer, *New England and the Bavarian Illuminati* (New York, 1918), 76 (Note).

[17] *Acts and Proceedings of the General Assembly of the Presbyterian Church* (Philadelphia, 1798), 11-14.

[18] Cf. V. Stauffer, *New England and the Bavarian Illuminati*, 25-32.

time of some significant achievements in the ecclesiastical realm. The War of Independence tended to promote democracy in religion as well as in politics. It stimulated the movement for the separation of church and state, and thus helped produce one of the marked characteristics of American Christianity, "a free church in a free state, or a self-supporting and self-governing Christianity in independent but friendly relation to the civil government."[19] Before the Revolution no one of the original Thirteen Colonies, with the possible exception of Rhode Island,[20] had entirely discarded the principle dominant in Christendom since the time of Constantine, that there should be some form of union between church and state. The degree of union maintained in the colonies varied from the collection of taxes for the support of an established church, as in Massachusetts, Connecticut, Maryland, and Virginia, to the imposition in Pennsylvania of an oath of office that could not be taken by a conscientious Roman Catholic or Unitarian. The old system of insistence on religious uniformity and the persecution of dissenters from the state religion had already been abandoned, even in those colonies where it had been applied most vigorously. In Connecticut, where Congregationalism was established by law and all were taxed for the support of religion, Episcopalians after 1727 and Quakers and Baptists after 1729 could have their share of the taxes diverted to their respective ministers.[21] Similar regulations were in effect in Massachusetts and New Hampshire. It was an unsatisfactory arrangement in that only dissenters who worshiped regularly in organized congregations derived any benefit from the diversion plan; and to be put in a position of legal inferiority to Congregationalists was resented by people of other churches. Congregationalism, however, was so firmly entrenched in New England that the Revolution produced little immediate change in the situation. The Massachusetts Constitution of 1780 guaranteed liberty of conscience in religion, but made it the duty of every town or parish to make provision for the public

---

19 P. Schaff, *Church and State in the United States* (New York, 1888), 9.

20 Rhode Island had on her statute books a discriminative suffrage law which apparently was not enforced; see I. B. Richman, *Rhode Island* (Boston, 1905), 180-84.

21 *Public Records of the Colony of Connecticut*, VII, 107, 237; P. E. Lauer, *Church and State in New England*, 85-87.

teaching of piety, religion, and morality. For this purpose public taxes were to be levied; but, as before the Revolution, non-Congregationalists might direct the transfer of their share of the tax money to their own ministers. Massachusetts retained this law until 1833; a similar rule prevailed in Connecticut until 1818, and in New Hampshire until 1819.[22]

In Maryland, Virginia, the Carolinas, Georgia, and in four counties in New York[23] the Church of England had stood in a favored position before the law. Unlike the Congregational establishment, which might be regarded as a native institution, the Episcopal Church appeared foreign during and immediately following the Revolution; moreover, to some patriots it seemed to be the handmaid of a hated and tyrannical government. In this difference probably is to be found the explanation of the failure of the Episcopal establishments to survive the shock of the War for Independence, whereas Congregationalism retained its special position in New England for a generation longer.

The contest over the disestablishment of the Church of England attracted more attention in Virginia than elsewhere; this was due in part to the violence and duration of the struggle there as well as to the prominence of the leaders of the opposing camps—Jefferson and Madison for the liberals, and Patrick Henry for the conservatives. In the seventeenth century Virginia had insisted upon religious uniformity quite as much as Massachusetts; in the eighteenth century religious dissenters were tolerated in the Old Dominion if they complied with the terms of the English Act of Toleration, which had been repassed in Virginia in 1699, registered their meetinghouses, and behaved peaceably towards the government. This arrangement appears to have satisfied the Presbyterians, but not the Baptists. The former complied with the law, while the latter, who found toleration intolerable, violated it wilfully. The active struggle for

---

[22] P. E. Lauer, *Church and State in New England*, 98-106; Allan Nevins, *American States during and after the Revolution* (New York, 1924), 421-26; W. A. Robinson, *Jeffersonian Democracy in New England* (New Haven, 1916), 144.

[23] The law of 1693 which provided for an established church in four counties in New York contained no specific mention of the Church of England, but the colonial officials acted on the assumption that it had been established by this law; see S. H. Cobb, *Rise of Religious Liberty in America* (New York, 1902), 338-39.

disestablishment began when the first Virginia legislature met in 1776. The first step was the passage of a law exempting dissenters from paying taxes for the support of the state church and suspending for a year the payment of tithes by the Episcopalians. Never again were taxes collected in Virginia for the support of an established church, for obviously no one could be compelled to pay church rates against his will when he could escape by declaring himself a dissenter. Then followed a controversy over a proposal to levy a general tax for the support of religion and morality. The conservatives under the leadership of Patrick Henry— the same Patrick Henry who once stirred America with his "Give me Liberty or give me Death"—sponsored this plan; they were alarmed at the dislike of restraint manifested by the people generally, at their attempts to evade their obligations, at their leveling tendencies, and at the spread of infidelity. They feared that the structure of society would crumble without the cement of religion and morals. They asked for state aid for religion for about the same reasons that we now grant it so freely for education. After long discussion in the legislature and among the people, the proposal to levy a tax for the support of religion was defeated; the supporters of the complete separation of church and state then seized the opportunity to revive Thomas Jefferson's bill for religious freedom which had been introduced into the assembly six years earlier. Now it became a law (1786), and henceforth in Virginia no man was to be compelled to frequent or support any religious worship, place, or ministry whatsoever, nor was he to be "enforced, restrained, molested or burdened in his body or goods" on account of his religious opinions or beliefs. Jefferson rightly regarded this law as a landmark in the history of man's struggle for freedom, and requested that it be included along with the writing of the Declaration of Independence and the founding of the University of Virginia as the achievements of his life worthy of mention on his tombstone.[24]

---

[24] On the stone over Jefferson's grave at Monticello are cut these words: "Here was buried Thomas Jefferson, Author of the Declaration of American Independence, of the Statute of Virginia for Religious Freedom, and Father of the University of Virginia."
Much has been written on the struggle over disestablishment in Virginia, e.g., H. J. Eckenrode, *Separation of Church and State in Virginia* (Richmond, 1910); H. R. McIlwaine, *Struggle of Protestant*

By the close of the eighteenth century taxation for the support of a privileged church had been abolished in all the states except Massachusetts, Connecticut, and New Hampshire. Absolute separation of church and state had not yet been achieved, however, except in Virginia and Rhode Island; the other states still retained vestiges of the older arrangements, such as the limitation of office holding to Protestants, or to those who declared their belief in the divine inspiration of the Bible and in a state of future rewards and punishments.[25] Not until Jacksonian Democracy began to make its influence felt in the East were such restrictions generally removed from the statute books of the original states. Although the first amendment to the Federal Constitution, by which Congress is prohibited from passing any law "respecting the establishment of religion or prohibiting the free exercise thereof," is not a limitation on the powers of the states,[26] the principles of complete separation of church and state have been uniformly adopted in the American commonwealths.[27] Thus at a time when the various denominations were preparing to extend their influence into the West through home missions they were assured a free field and equality of treatment so far as state interference was concerned. Furthermore, the abolition of taxation for religion meant dependence on voluntary church support. It was fortunate that it was so; it is not likely that any state church would or could have assumed the burden of following the pioneers with Christian institutions when they began to swarm over the whole of the Mississippi Valley. It was a matter of record that the Congregational and Episcopal establishments in America had not been strongly missionary in spirit. The problem of Christianizing the trans-Allegheny West called for a system better calculated to develop a feeling of responsibility throughout the churches than one in which it was the business of the state.

Dissenters for Religious Toleration in Virginia (Baltimore, 1894); E. F. Humphrey, *Nationalism and Religion in America* (Boston, 1924), 366-404; S. H. Cobb, *Rise of Religious Liberty in America*, 490-99.

[25] S. H. Cobb, *Rise of Religious Liberty in America*, 507.

[26] *Eilenbecker* v. *District Court of Plymouth County* (1890), 134 U.S., 31; *Ohio ex rel. Lloyd* v. *Dollison* (1904), 194 U.S., 445.

[27] S. H. Cobb, *Rise of Religious Liberty in America*, 520, gives a convenient summary of the basic principles of religious freedom upon which the several states are in agreement.

THE WEST OF THE PERIOD

The region of new settlements in the last quarter of the eighteenth century stretched in a great arc from Maine, through western Pennsylvania and Kentucky, to Georgia. In 1775 the pioneer farmers had not penetrated or pushed beyond the Allegheny barrier except here and there in Pennsylvania, Virginia, and North Carolina. At the outbreak of the Revolution the settled area in New England included Massachusetts, Connecticut, Rhode Island, and southern New Hampshire. In Maine a narrow ribbon of settlement hugged the shore as far as the Penobscot, while in Vermont there was only a thin line of towns on the west bank of the Connecticut River, an indication that the home of the Green Mountain Boys was still in the frontier stage of development. In New York the area of settlement included the Hudson and Mohawk valleys and the upper waters of the Delaware and Susquehanna in the southeast corner of the colony. In Pennsylvania the frontiersmen were as far west as Fort Pitt, but the northwestern and the north central sections of this province were unoccupied. In Virginia and North Carolina the settlements reached out roughly to the Blue Ridge with certain remote frontier communities established in the Shenandoah Valley and in the Watauga country. Practically all of South Carolina had been occupied, but in Georgia the land taken up for plantations and farms comprised only a narrow strip extending from the Atlantic Ocean to the foothills along the west bank of the Savannah River.

Even during the Revolutionary War, in spite of unusual Indian hazards, adventurous pioneers pushed into the Indian country; some began their clearings on the Ohio below Pittsburgh; others settled in the blue grass region of Kentucky, or in the vicinity of Nashville on the Cumberland. The period of financial and economic confusion which followed the Revolution saw a great movement of people towards the frontiers. Hard times in the East have, under certain conditions, set the discontented on the move in search of better opportunities in the West. The return of prosperity about the time that the Constitution of 1787 was being drafted, and the outbreak of war in Europe in connection with the French Revolution, retarded the movement somewhat; the increased demands for foodstuffs and other supplies in war-busy Europe meant improved economic conditions in the

seaboard towns and on the Eastern farms.[28] But even so, the last quarter of the eighteenth century was a time of noteworthy advance against the wilderness. By the end of the period here under consideration the settled area in Maine had been extended along the coast "way down East" to the St. Croix River. Northern New Hampshire and practically all of Vermont had been brought within the frontier line. In New York pioneers to the north of the Mohawk and east of Lake Champlain were pushing into the edges of the Adirondacks, while others were penetrating the old Iroquois country in the lovely Finger Lake region. In Pennsylvania the newly settled parts included the upper Susquehanna Valley to the New York line, the lower valley of the Juniata, and the extreme southwestern corner of the state. In Virginia much of the mountainous area had been occupied, especially the Blue Ridge section, the upper part of the Shenandoah Valley, and the Kanawha and its tributaries. Practically all the western part of North Carolina had been taken up. Although Kentucky and Tennessee had been in the Union since 1792 and 1796 respectively, neither was fully settled in 1800; in both, conditions were still primitive. Small but thriving settlements along the north bank of the Ohio above the mouth of the Miami presaged the speedy admission of a new member (Ohio) to the family of states.

Obviously much of the frontier region of this period lay in or near the Appalachian mountain system. Although these mountains were not high, they were an important barrier to westward-moving settlers because they were heavily wooded and there were often several parallel ranges of hills through which the way must be laboriously picked. Some of the pioneers who pushed into the hill districts of Virginia, the Carolinas, Tennessee, and Kentucky in these years became stranded in coves or other remote spots. As the decades passed the main currents of American life swept by them without affecting them very much. There they lived, handing down to their children the customs and modes of thought of the pioneers of the latter part of the eighteenth century. In racial stock they remained as they began, almost entirely British, if not English. The early part of the eighteenth century had seen a great migration of non-English peoples, especially Germans and Scotch-Irish to America. During

---

[28] Cf. J. B. McMaster, *History of the People of the United States* (New York, 1883-1910), IV, 381-82.

the Revolution the movement was sharply retarded, thus affording some opportunity for amalgamation and assimilation. Hence the pioneers who settled the Appalachian highlands might properly be called "Americans." Nor were they and their descendants much affected by the great inundation of the foreign-born which poured into the country in the nineteenth century, with the result that these mountain whites have remained remarkably homogeneous in racial strains.

Life was simple and primitive in the eighteenth-century backwoods. In general the people lived in one-room log cabins set in tiny clearings in the vast forest which stretched in almost unbroken grandeur from the eastern foothills of the Alleghenies to the Mississippi. Household utensils and furniture were of the simplest sort;[29] the clothing was made of homespun and leather. A shotgun or rifle was indispensable not only for defense but also for livelihood, since the family larder was so dependent on the hunters' skill; and skilled they were, not only in hunting but in woodcraft. Of book learning they had little, and their ignorance was sometimes the mother of superstition. Joseph Doddridge, in describing society among the first settlers in western Virginia and Pennsylvania, wrote:

> The wilderness was a region of superstition. The adventurous hunter sought for ominous presages of his future good, or bad luck, in everything about him. Much of his success depended on the state of the weather; snow and rain were favorable, because in the former he could track his game, and the latter prevented them from hearing the rustling of the leaves beneath his feet. The appearance of the sky, morning and evening, gave him the signs of the times, with regard to the weather. So far he was a philosopher.... The croaking of a raven, the howling of a dog, and the screech of an owl, were as prophetic of future misfortunes among the first adventurers into this country, as they were amongst the ancient pagans; but above all their dreams were regarded as ominous of good or ill success....
>
> Let not the reader be surprised at the superstition which existed among the first adventurers into the western wilderness. Superstition is universally associated with ignorance, in all those who occupy perilous situations in life....
>
> The passion of fear excited by danger, the parent of superstition, operated powerfully on the first adventurers into this country. Exiled from society, and the comforts of life, their situation was perilous in

---

[29] J. W. Monette, *History of the Discovery and Settlement of the Valley of the Mississippi* (New York, 1846), I, 359.

the extreme. The bite of a serpent, a broken limb, a wound of any kind, or a fit of sickness in the wilderness, without those accommodations, which wounds and sickness require, was a dreadful calamity.... [30]

In some parts of this West the settlers had come in ahead of state authority or before conflicting claims to jurisdiction had been resolved. There were lawless and reckless men among them; there was often a period of little law and order during which public opinion or unofficial bands of regulators operated as the chief check on evildoers. "The punishment for idleness, lying, dishonesty, and ill fame generally, was that of 'Hating the offender out,' as they expressed it, ... a public expression, in various ways, of a general sentiment of indignation against such as transgressed the moral maxims of the community to which they belonged."[31] They were rude and rough in manners, but given to hospitality; they were warm in their friendships, revengeful in their quarrels, quick in their emotional responses.

And they held the frontiers, protecting the more urbane and cultured people of the East, during a period of sanguinary Indian fighting. These were the days of Daniel Boone and Simon Kenton in Kentucky; of John Sevier and James Robertson in Tennessee; of St. Clair's defeat in the woods north of Cincinnati and Anthony Wayne's victory at Fallen Timbers. These people were worthy of some consideration at the hands of the East—and they were sorely in need of civilizing and refining influences.

CONDITIONS OF MISSIONARY LABOR

Missionaries who worked among a people so situated were continually exposed to dangers and hardships. The normal mode of travel was on horseback over uncertain trails, across unbridged streams, and through a sparsely settled country where inns were almost unknown. Anyone who spent most of his time traveling thus needed a strong body to endure the inclemencies of weather and the miserable living conditions to which he was subjected; fortunately the outdoor life compensated in part for these difficulties. From the *Journals* of Francis Asbury, one of the founders

---

[30] J. Doddridge, *Notes on the Settlement and Indian Wars ...*, (Wellsburg, Va., 1824), 22-24.

[31] J. Doddridge, *op. cit.*, 168-69.

16 5 8

of the Methodist Episcopal Church in America, we get glimpses of the experiences of an itinerant missionary during this period. In Bishop Asbury's vast field of operations, which included the back country of all the seaboard states as well as the more thickly settled communities, he was often discommoded for lack of decent shelter at night, occasionally made ill by exposure, and sometimes brought close to death through Indian attack. Once, in describing his experiences in the mountainous region of North Carolina, he wrote: "We were spoken to on our way by most awful thunder and lightning, accompanied by heavy rain. We crept for shelter into a little dirty house where the filth might have been taken from the floor by a spade: we felt the want of a fire but could get little wood to make it, and what we gathered was wet."[32] Four pages farther on in the *Journal* we come to this entry (December, 1788):

> We had to cross the Alleghany mountains again [in Virginia], at a bad passage. Our course lay over mountains and through valleys, and the mud and the mire was such as might scarcely be expected in December.... I lay along the floor on a few deer skins with the flees.
> ... O, how glad should I be of a plain, clean plank to lie on, as preferable to most of the beds; and where the beds are in a bad state, the floors are worse. The gnats are almost as troublesome here, as the moschetoes in the lowlands of the sea-board. This country will require much work to make it tolerable. The people are, many of them, of the boldest cast of adventurers, and with some the decencies of civilized society are scarcely regarded.[33]

Four years later he made this note while in Kentucky:

> After crossing the Laurel River, which we were compelled to swim, we came to Rock Castle station where we found such a set of sinners as made it next to hell itself....
> Wednesday 5 [April]. This morning we again swam the river, and also the west fork thereof.... I was steeped in the water up to the waist,... How much I have suffered in this journey is only known to God and myself. What added much to its disagreeableness, is the extreme filthiness of the houses.[34]

NATIONAL CHURCHES AND MISSIONARY BEGINNINGS

In this postwar transition period there was one further development of significance in connection with the subsequent efforts to Christianize the West, namely, the organiza-

---

[32] F. Asbury, *Journal* (New York, 1821), II, 31.

[33] *Ibid.*, II, 35-36.

[34] *Ibid.*, II, 126.

tion of independent, national churches. In the case of the Episcopalians and Methodists this involved the severing of ties that had bound them to England; among the Presbyterians, with minor exceptions, it meant simply the logical development of a form of church organization that was already in existence. These changes resulted in the creation of religious bodies that were better organized and consequently better able to handle a problem of such magnitude as the home missionary undertaking was soon found to be. And yet, paradoxically, the denomination that was to be one of the most active in missions in the new period, the Congregational, did not form a national organization, nor did the Baptists, who, while not so active in missions as some of their religious neighbors, did, nevertheless, increase rapidly in numbers.

THE EPISCOPALIANS

As explained above, the Protestant Episcopal Church was weak in the United States at the close of the War for Independence. In the words of one of her own historical writers:

> It would be difficult to imagine a more desperate situation than that of the Episcopal Church at the close of the Revolution. Her members were a seemingly hopeless little band compared with the Puritan hosts about her. She was regarded,—to use the quaint phrase of the late Bishop Williams of Connecticut,—as "a piece of heavy baggage which the British had left behind when they evacuated New York and Boston." No religious organization, with the possible exception of the Church of Rome, could have been more unwelcome to the rank and file of the people, or more severely condemned by the popular judgment of the period. She was the offspring of a State Church, and therefore to be suspected, however much she might protest her separation from politics. The very features which constitute her abiding value and influence were unwelcome, if not abhorred. A bishop smacked of courts and crowns, of stately carriages and aristocratic pomp. No other kind could be imagined by the sturdy Puritans. Her liturgical worship was counted as deadly formalism, and all the order, beauty and glory of the Christian Year,—of Feast and Fast and Sacrament, were but so many Rags of Popery; from all which, together with the Bishop of Rome, the stout Protestants of the day prayed that they might be delivered.[35]

---

[35] H. L. Burleson, *Conquest of the Continent* (New York, [1911]), 36-37.

However, the Episcopalians quickly rallied their forces and closed their ranks. One of the first steps in reorganization was the election of bishops. Samuel Seabury, the first to be chosen, received ordination at the hands of Scottish bishops in Aberdeen; the next two, William White and Samuel Provoost, were consecrated in England, the mother Church having by that time withdrawn opposition, since it had become apparent that the American daughter was disposed to follow English doctrine and discipline.[36] By 1787 there were three Episcopal bishops in the United States, and others followed in rapid succession until the whole of the territory of the original states had been organized into dioceses. But the Episcopal Church was not an active missionary force. Its members, who came to a considerable extent from the socially prominent and wealthy groups, were not ordinarily of the discontented classes usually found on the frontiers. Being conservative and opposed to emotionalism, Episcopalianism did not offer the type of religion which was most popular in the West; nor did it make much effort to reach the West at this time. It was not, however, completely indifferent to the problem of home missions; in 1792 a General Convention approved a plan by which an annual missionary sermon was to be preached by each of its ministers and an offering was to be made for missions. The next General Convention relegated the conduct of missions to the diocesan conventions, and there it remained in a quiescent state for a full generation.[37]

THE METHODISTS

The Methodists also organized a new national church soon after the Revolution. John Wesley's Methodism had started within the Church of England. It had not been a church at all. It had begun as a group of societies for the promotion of holiness—an early "Christian Endeavor" movement. Its places of assembly had been called meeting-houses or chapels rather than churches. Its preachers had usually been laymen; its members had been mainly communicants of the Church of England and dependent on the Anglican clergy for the administration of the ordinances.[38]

---

[36] E. F. Humphrey, *Nationalism and Religion in America*, 220-28.

[37] W. S. Perry, *Missions and Missionary Bishops* (privately printed, 1877), 4.

[38] E. F. Humphrey, *Nationalism and Religion in America*, 167-68.

In this situation is to be found at least a partial explanation of the disfavor with which the early Methodist missionaries were viewed in America during the War for Independence. They were Englishmen, lately arrived from the mother country and naturally sympathetic towards the English position in the controversy. The first Methodist sermon was preached in America in 1766, the year after the Stamp Act had been passed; the first missionaries sent to the colonies by the Methodist Conference arrived in 1769, the year preceding the Boston Massacre; Francis Asbury, the real founder of Methodism in America, did not come until 1771—only four years before the early-morning skirmish on Lexington Green.

The first Methodist preachers in America were zealous and made extensive missionary tours as far as New England on the north and North Carolina on the south, but the work remained unorganized until Asbury took charge. Asbury was a successful preacher, but not a great orator; his skill lay in his "capacity for developing, leading, and governing the Methodist itinerant forces of America."[39] From the outset he stressed the importance of itinerancy and complained—unfairly, it seems—that his predecessors in the American mission had not been sufficiently active. In his *Journal* the following entry appears for November 22, 1771: "At present I am dissatisfied. I judge we are to be shut up in the cities this winter. My brethren seem unwilling to leave the cities, but I think I shall show them the way."[40] He did. The Methodist Church has never had an itinerant who surpassed Asbury in boundless energy or in the extent of his perigrinations.

The Revolutionary War was a trying period for John Wesley's American followers. Not only were they, as members of the Church of England, under suspicion of holding to Tory principles, but Wesley's defense of England's conduct in his borrowed *Calm Address to the American Colonies* (1775)[41] made the position of his disciples in the colonies still more uncomfortable. By 1775 all the English Metho-

---

[39] J. Atkinson, *History of the Origin of the Wesleyan Movement in America*, 290.

[40] F. Asbury, *Journal*, I, 6.

[41] Wesley's *Calm Address* was an abridgment of Dr. Samuel Johnson's *Taxation No Tyranny*. E. F. Humphrey, *Nationalism and Religion*, 124.

dist preachers save one were ready to leave the land of the rebels and return home. That one was Francis Asbury. In his *Journal* for August 7, 1775, occurs this significant entry:

I received a letter from Mr. T. R. [Thomas Rankin] in which he informed me that himself, Mr. R. [Rodda] and Mr. D. [Dempster] had consulted and deliberately concluded it would be best to return to England. But I can by no means agree to leave such a field for gathering souls to Christ, as we have in America. It would be an eternal dishonour to the Methodists, that we should all leave three thousand souls, who desire to commit themselves to our care; neither is it the part of a good shepherd to leave his flock in time of danger; therefore, I am determined, by the grace of God, not to leave them, let the consequence be what it may.[42]

Asbury's decision had important results; if he too had left the infant Methodist societies at that critical time, they probably would have broken up, and the development of Methodism in the United States would have been delayed for a decade or more. Nay, more, if the attempt had been made to introduce Methodism into the United States after the Revolutionary War, it would have come under a distinct handicap of its English origin; as it turned out, Methodism was well Americanized by the end of the Revolution. It had also gained tremendously in strength. Asbury and the native preachers working under his direction continued their labors during the War with astonishing results. In 1775 Methodism had been an insignificant movement within the Church of England; ten years later it had grown into a distinct denomination. In 1775 there were about three thousand members in the American Methodist societies and nineteen preachers; in 1784 there were fifteen thousand members and eighty-four itinerant preachers.[43] What other religious body had multiplied fivefold during the turbulent years of the Revolution?

John Wesley realized that the winning of independence had so altered relations between the United States and England that he could no longer expect to keep American Methodism under his personal direction; nor would it do to turn his American followers adrift. Accordingly, with the help of some presbyters of the Church of England, he

[42] F. Asbury, *Journal*, I, 118-19.
[43] *Minutes of the Methodist Conferences, Annually Held in America from 1773 to 1794* (Philadelphia, 1795), 14, 70.

ordained Thomas Coke as superintendent or bishop for the United States, and sent him over the ocean with instructions to ordain Francis Asbury as his co-superintendent. Asbury knew enough about the temper of America to wait until he had been elected to the episcopacy by his fellow preachers before he accepted the new office.[44] It is not likely that Wesley had intended that the American Methodists should review or ratify his plan, but they did. At a conference held in Baltimore in December, 1784, they voted to organize themselves into a Methodist Episcopal Church, with bishops, elders, and deacons. Coke and Asbury were elected the first bishops.[45] Although American Methodists venerated John Wesley, they were too independent to take orders from him. A constitution was adopted, and thus what had been a weak and apparently unimportant religious society a few years earlier had been transformed into a fully organized church.

Methodism continued to expand after the War was over. According to Jesse Lee, an early Methodist historian,

The revolutionary war being now closed, and a general peace established, we could go into all parts of the country without fear; and we soon began to enlarge our borders, and to preach in many places where we had not been before. . . .
One thing in particular, that opened the way for the spreading of the gospel by our preachers was this: during the war, . . . many of the members of our societies had, through fear, necessity or choice, moved into the back settlements, and into new parts of the country: and as soon as the national peace was settled, and the way was open, they solicited us to come among them; . . . [46]

To trace in detail the spread of Methodism in the West during these years is impossible here; some idea of its progress may be gained, though, by noting that in 1786 two regular itinerants appointed by the Baltimore Conference of that year appeared in Kentucky; and that the first Methodist sermon was preached in Ohio in 1787, while the first itinerants sent to that territory by Bishop Asbury arrived about 1796.

The foremost itinerant among the Methodists was Bishop Asbury himself. Year after year he rode from one end of his vast American diocese to the other. North in the sum-

---

[44] F. Asbury, *Journal*, I, 376.

[45] F. Asbury, *Journal*, I, 377-78.

[46] Jesse Lee, *Short History of the Methodists, in the United States of America* (Baltimore, 1810), 84.

mer, south in the winter, west in the spring or autumn he went, visiting the Conferences, marshaling his spiritual army, and inspiring the people as he passed by their clearings or through their straggling villages. As an illustration of his journeys year after year, consider his itinerary for 1792: January found him in North Carolina; in February he visited South Carolina and Georgia; in March he traveled through the two Carolinas and Virginia into Tennessee; he was in Kentucky in April, back in Virginia in May, and in Pennsylvania, Maryland, and Virginia again in June; in July he was in New Jersey, New York, Connecticut, and Massachusetts; then he made his way to the South through the late summer, autumn, and early winter, the entry in his *Journal* for December 25 being made in South Carolina. Towards the end of his career he wrote:

... In the year 1774 I first visited Virginia and North Carolina: in the year 1780 I repeated my visit; and since that time, yearly. In the year 1785 I first visited South Carolina and Georgia; and to these states have since paid (except one year) an annual visit, until now, (1814). I suppose I have crossed the Alleghany mountains sixty times.[47]

With such an example before them, is it any wonder that the early Methodists in the United States, preachers and laymen alike, were distinguished for their missionary zeal and fervor? Methodism was aggressive, dynamic, evangelistic. It appealed to the emotions. It did not spend its time on finespun theological distinctions. Its assault on Calvinistic predestination and foreordination suited the spirit of the democratic West. "Whosoever will may drink freely of the water of life," was a favorite text. Methodism was a religious system adapted to the needs of the common people, and they heard its message gladly.

THE BAPTISTS

The Baptists were like the Methodists in their wide popular appeal but unlike them in that they had no Old World ecclesiastical ties to sever at the close of the War for Independence. In the colonial period Baptist churches had been bound together loosely in regional or district associations; after the Revolution their insistence on local congregational

---

[47] F. Asbury, *Journal*, III, 361.

independence made them look with disfavor on any attempt to create a national church-governing body. In the closing years of the eighteenth century, then, one must look among Baptists to the various regional associations for direction of missionary work. As before the Revolution, one of the most active of these associations was that of Philadelphia. There are many references in its records between 1778 and 1798 to the granting of supplies to destitute churches or to the sending of the gospel to the new communities in western Pennsylvania.[48] The Warren, Rhode Island, Association was also active in missions, sending men especially to the frontiers of New England.[49] One of its representatives, Isaac Backus, made a missionary tour into Virginia and North Carolina in 1789, in response to an appeal for help from Southern Baptists.[50] This was a time of revival among Baptists in Virginia; they were increasing both in numbers and influence. As Semple says in his contemporary account:

> From this revival great changes took place among the Baptists, some for the better, and others for the worse. Their preachers were become much more correct in their manner of preaching: A great many odd tones, disgusting whoops and awkward jestures were disused: In their matter also, they had more of sound sense and strong reasoning. Their zeal was less mixed with enthusiasm, and their piety became more rational. They were much more numerous, and of course, in the eyes of the world, more respectable. Besides, they were joined by persons of much greater weight, in civil society: Their congregations became more numerous, than those of any other Christian sect; and, in short, they might be considered, from this period, as taking the lead in matters of religion, in many places of the State.[51]

At the opening of the American War for Independence the number of Baptists in the colonies was estimated at ten thousand; by 1800 their numbers had grown to about one hundred thousand. One of the reasons for this remarkable increase in numbers in a period ordinarily thought of as one in which irreligion and scepticism flourished was the interest in missions on the part of the early Baptist preachers; other contributing causes were the granting of full

---

[48] *Minutes of the Philadelphia Baptist Association*, 159, 174, 181, 201, 218, 248, 271.

[49] D. Benedict, *General History of the Baptist Denomination in America*, I, 325.

[50] *Ibid.*, II, 272.

[51] R. S. Semple, *History of Rise and Progress of Baptists in Virginia*, 38.

religious freedom in the various states, and the harmony
between the democratic spirit of the people and the congregational polity of the Baptist churches. For several reasons
Baptists might be expected to play an important part in
the religious development of the West. Their membership
was well scattered through the states, and by personal in-
clination as well as by geographical location would share
largely in the westward movement. Their ministry was aggressive and evangelistic, although generally inferior in its
formal training to that of the Episcopalians, Presbyterians,
and Congregationalists. In the struggle for national independence the Baptists had stood enthusiastically on the
American side; in the contest for religious freedom no
group had been more active in working for, and none de-
serves more credit for bringing about, the separation of
church and state.

THE PRESBYTERIANS

The Presbyterians, generally speaking, had no official
ties binding them to any European ecclesiastical body.[52]
Readjustment for them in the post-Revolutionary period
was simple, and involved mainly the extension of their
representative system of church government by the erection of a General Assembly above the synods. The first
General Assembly met in 1789, the year in which was in-
augurated the new Federal Government—an appropriate
date for the completion of a church organization which
from local session to national assembly corresponds so
closely to the framework of our political system. The Synod
of New York and Philadelphia, which had been so active
in missionary work in the colonial period, had not abandoned entirely its benevolent activities during the Revolution; on the return of peace, and especially after the formation of the General Assembly, the problem of the new
settlements was taken up with renewed interest. The first
General Assembly requested each of the synods to recommend two members well qualified to be employed in missions
to the frontier inhabitants; and in order to provide means
for defraying the expenses of such missions it was strictly

---

[52] The Scots' Presbyterian Church of Philadelphia was subordinate
to the Associate Synod of Edinburgh, Scotland. Louie Miner, *Our
Rude Forefathers* (Cedar Rapids, Iowa, 1937), 70.

enjoined on the several presbyteries that collections be taken in all of their congregations.[53] As before the Revolution, the method used was the sending of pastors and licentiates on short tours to the frontiers. In 1794 the Assembly drafted a letter to the inhabitants visited by the missionaries explaining their concern for the spiritual state of the frontier, and containing suggestions of ways in which the people in the "destitute" communities might improve conditions even without the help of ministers. They were warned not to neglect the catechetical instruction of their children, because ignorance of spiritual concerns is "the fruitful parent of immorality and licentiousness." The evils of the profanation of the Lord's Day were pointed out, and the suggestion was made that in the absence of preaching they meet for social prayer and praise. "By this method," so the letter ran, "your social attachments will be strengthened; your religious affections cherished; your habits of worship improved."[54] Although the General Assembly took the lead in missions, it was not the only agency of benevolence within the Presbyterian Church; some of the synods conducted their missionary operations independently of the Assembly. Of these perhaps the most active was the Synod of Virginia; it appropriately made Kentucky its special field, sending there eight young preachers between 1791 and 1800.[55] Into Tennessee too went the zealous Presbyterian missionaries. One of the best known of these was Samuel Doak, son of Princeton, who, in the words of Theodore Roosevelt, followed the blazed trails across the Alleghenies about 1777 to the Holston settlements, "driving before him an old 'flea-bitten grey' horse, loaded with a sackful of books." He founded Salem church near Jonesboro, and built a log high school "which soon became Washington College, the first institution of the kind west of the Alleghanies."[56]

Among the Presbyterians this period of missionary activity differed in no essential respect from the one that had

[53] *Acts and Proceedings of the General Assembly of the Presbyterian Church* (Philadelphia, 1789), 8.

[54] *Acts and Proceedings of the General Assembly of the Presbyterian Church* (Philadelphia, 1794), 11-14.

[55] R. Davidson, *History of the Presbyterian Church in the State of Kentucky* (New York, 1847), 104-05.

[56] T. Roosevelt, *Winning of the West*, II, 223.

preceded it. If little was accomplished, it was largely because of circumstances over which they had no control. They had, however, developed an ecclesiastical organization which could be used effectively in the future. Presbyterian polity has shown itself to be well adapted to the needs of an expanding church. It has combined representative self-government with sufficient rigidity to provide for concerted action and close supervision over morals and doctrine. In organization, in the character of its leaders, in experience on the frontiers, and in the geographical location of its numerous Scotch-Irish constituency, the Presbyterian Church was well prepared to undertake vigorously missionary work in the wider field that opened at the dawn of the nineteenth century.

THE CONGREGATIONALISTS

In the Revolutionary period the Congregationalists of New England were the most numerous and probably the most powerful religious group in the United States. Their membership stood high morally and intellectually; their ministry was able and well trained; their influence was thrown actively on the American side. Their church organization was democratic, and had thus far served their needs. They saw no reason to change, and hence retained their principle of local or congregational autonomy at a time when the tendency in most other denominations was towards the setting up of some national agency of control or supervision. There was among them no central body similar, for example, to the Presbyterian General Assembly. Perhaps if they had had such an organization they might have made more progress in the West; if so, a high price was paid for local independence. However, in Connecticut there was a consociation of churches which resembled somewhat the Presbyterian organization; and, indeed, Congregational churches in this colony in the eighteenth century were sometimes referred to as Presbyterian.

Among Congregationalists, Connecticut was the chief center of missionary interest and activities in this period. This was probably due, first of all, to the influential state association of churches just noted. In Connecticut too there was greater loyalty to the old faith than in Massachusetts, which was soon to witness the Unitarian defection from

orthodox Congregationalism. Moreover, there was being developed in Connecticut, and especially at Yale, the main outlines of the "New England Theology" or the "New Divinity." In this theological system, which represented an attempt to reinterpret Calvinism after the Great Awakening, one of the cardinal points was that the essence of sin is selfishness and an essential quality of holiness is benevolence.[57] In such a proposition is to be found the theoretical background for the scores of reform and benevolent societies—Bible, Missionary, Tract, and Moral—which sprang up in New England in the early part of the nineteenth century.

Since it is to Connecticut that we must look for Congregational missionary activity in the closing years of the eighteenth century, let us turn back to that meeting of the General Association at Mansfield in June, 1774, at which it was decided that missionaries should be sent to the new settlements then forming "in the wilderness to the westward and northwestward." As was pointed out in the preceding chapter,[58] plans were made to send out two pastors in the spring of 1775. But when the Association met in June of that year—the month in which the Battle of Bunker Hill was fought—it made record of the fact that "the perplexed & melancholy State of public Affairs has been a Discouragement to this Design, & a Reason why the Collections have not been brought in, as was expected." But the project was not forgotten, and in 1780, even before the War had ended, the Association asked two pastors to go as missionaries to Vermont.[59] In 1788 the General Association recommended to the individual associations that they send out members of their respective bodies on short tours, while in 1792 they presented a petition to the General Assembly of the state asking that contributions might be made for the support of the missions. In October, 1792, the Connecticut legislature authorized "Contributions in the several Religious Societies and Congregations on this state, on the first Sabbath in the month of May, annually, for the term of three years."[60] In addition to the way in which this ac-

---

[57] G. L. Walker, *Some Aspects of the Religious Life of New England*, 127-54.

[58] See above, page 82.

[59] E. P. Parker, *Historical Discourse* (Hartford, 1898), 8.

[60] Missionary Society of Connecticut, *Twenty-Third Annual Narrative of Missions ... 1821* (Hartford, 1822), 3-4.

tion illustrates the close connection between church and state at the time, it is also of interest in that the first of these state-sponsored collections (May, 1793) produced twelve hundred dollars. Besides preaching to the people and performing other ministerial functions, the missionaries were instructed to obtain "as accurate a state of the countries through which they pass as may be," and "information with respect to the sentiments and feelings of the inhabitants of the New-settlements respecting our sending missionaries among them."[61] A typical commission was that of the Reverend Mr. Eells, who "was appointed to go two months, ... on Mohawk river and to proceed westward as far as Fort Stanwix, visiting all settlements north and south of said river, to such a distance as he shall judge proper, and as can be accomplished with convenience during the term allotted him."[62] Sometimes the missionary on his return illustrated the report of his tour with rough sketch maps of the regions visited; there are still preserved in the archives of the Connecticut Missionary Society at Hartford interesting maps of central and western New York made about 1793 by Aaron Kinne, one of the early missionaries to that country.[63] Mr. Kinne's report on the people in the Genesee settlements was complimentary. "The principal parts of the inhabitants," he said, "are directly or indirectly from New England, and retain the spirit and manners of their native States, are very distinguishable from the settlers from other States by their mien, address, and taste in domestic life, are exemplary in their reverence for the Sabbath, zeal for religious worship and the decent manner in which they attend." But "Alas! the poor people of Tioga! intemperate, contentious, with[out] law, without order, without ministers, without Sabbaths, & without God in the world."[64]

The plan of the missions used by the Connecticut group

---

[61] "Minutes of the Doings of the Committee of the General Association of the State of Connecticut, relative to the Missionaries to be sent into the New Settlements: begun June 20th, 1793," Yale Library MSS., entry for July 16, 1793.

[62] *Ibid.*

[63] Missionary Society of Connecticut, MS. Letters, 1793. Filed with the reports are also letters of thanks which were received occasionally from the people visited.

[64] Aaron Kinne, "Journal of a Missionary Tour.... Sept. 1793 to Jan. 1794," Conn. Miss. Soc., MS. Letters and Journals, 1793-99.

at this time was the sending of pastors on short tours to the near-by frontiers; Vermont and central New York were the regions most frequently visited. But the method was haphazard and the work limited in scope. In order that a larger number of people might become interested in missions and in the expectation that the work would be more efficiently managed, there was formed in 1798 the first important voluntary missionary society in America, the Missionary Society of Connecticut—and with its organization a new period in the history of home missions begins.

CHAPTER V

MISSIONS FROM MAINE TO MISSISSIPPI, 1798-1820

Such a wave of feeling [Romanticism], we may be sure, could not fail to transmit itself across the Atlantic, and to be manifested in some form in the America of 1800, still colonially dependent upon the European mind. We do indeed trace a slight romantic movement in American literature, a faint heightening of American patriotism, slowly mustering courage for the War of 1812. But if we would seek the most powerful and pervasive manifestation of the movement, the best analogy which the poverty of American culture permitted, we can find it nowhere else than in the wonderful religious revivals which in those years swept through America and especially through the forest camp-meetings of the non-literary West.—*J. Franklin Jameson.*

$\mathcal{G}$T IS AN OLD SAYING that the blackest hour of the night is just before dawn. The nadir of the post-Revolutionary period of religious indifference and moral laxness was touched in the closing years of the eighteenth century. But even at the very time that the Presbyterian clergy, convened in their General Assembly of 1798, were bemoaning the prevalence of "profaneness, pride, luxury, injustice, intemperance, lewdness, and every species of debauchery and loose indulgence," a remarkable religious revival was starting in the West, a new spirit was stirring among the Christians of New England, and scores of moral, Bible, and missionary societies were on the point of organization in the East.

In the history of home missions the distinctive characteristic of the opening years of the nineteenth century is the formation of a large number of local and state voluntary missionary societies. It is difficult to fix exact dates for either the beginning or the end of this movement, because there is no set of dates that applies exactly to all of the denominations concerned. The year 1798, however, has been chosen to mark the beginning of this chapter because it was then that the first important state organiza-

tion, the Missionary Society of Connecticut, was established. For the next two decades the supervision of home missionary work was mainly in charge of this and similar organizations. In the years following the War of 1812 there was a general movement to substitute national for local societies; consequently, the year 1820 has been arbitrarily set as the close of this period.

The formation of these state or local societies marked a great advance in the method of conducting home missions. Hitherto the work had been more or less haphazard. When the representatives of some denomination had met in their ecclesiastical convention—General Assembly, Synod, Classis, Association, or Conference—men had been appointed to go on missionary tours. At the next regular meeting, usually a year later, reports were received and new appointments were made. In the interval between these annual meetings the work was inadequately supervised. By the opening of the nineteenth century the problem of carrying religious institutions to the frontier had become so great that it seemed wise to devise a more efficient means of conducting missionary activities.

THE WEST

The new frontier line was to be found in the Great Valley of the Mississippi. By 1800 it was evident that a flood of human beings was soon to pour over the Allegheny barrier. Moreover, a young and virile nation on the march might be expected to demand territorial expansion to natural boundaries. In the first two decades of the nineteenth century the original area of the United States was doubled by the purchase of Louisiana in 1803 and Florida in 1819. In these twenty years the population of the country nearly doubled (5,300,000 in 1800; 9,600,000 in 1820), but even more significant for the home missionary movement was the increase in numbers in the western parts of some of the original states, such as Georgia, Virginia, Pennsylvania, and New York, and the rapid filling up of the new western states. Between 1800 and 1820 seven states—Ohio, Louisiana, Indiana, Mississippi, Illinois, Alabama, and Maine—entered the Union, and arrangements had been completed for the admission of still another, Missouri. All of these, including Maine, were frontier states. The West was grow-

ing at an amazing rate. The population of Ohio grew from
45,000 in 1800 to 580,000 in 1820; Indiana, from 5,600 to
nearly 150,000; Kentucky, from 220,000 to 564,000; Tennessee, from 105,000 to 420,000; Mississippi, from 8,800 to
75,000. The movement into the West was especially rapid
after the close of the War of 1812. The victories of William
Henry Harrison and Andrew Jackson over the Indians before and during the war with England opened to settlement
fertile lands north of the Ohio River and in the rich cotton
belt of Alabama and Mississippi. Furthermore, the economic revolution that was taking place in New England,—
the shifting of capital from commerce and shipping to manufacturing and internal improvement projects, and the relative decline of agriculture,—necessitated readjustments
which compelled or encouraged people to seek easier living
conditions in the West.[1] Over the new National Road and
down the Ohio River the flood poured into the Old Northwest; through passes in the lower part of the Appalachian
mountain system, or around the southern end of that barrier, planters made their way from well-worn fields in seaboard states to virgin soils in Alabama, Mississippi, and
Louisiana. Thus by 1820 practically all of New York, Ohio,
Kentucky, and Tennessee had been opened to settlement;
the southern half of Indiana, the lower third of Illinois, the
central and western parts of Alabama, and southern Mississippi had been brought within the frontier line; west of
the Mississippi, in the Louisiana Purchase territory, there
were settlements along the rivers in the state of Louisiana
and in Arkansas and Missouri. Within one generation the
settled area of the United States had about doubled. To be
sure, these new states and territories were only sparsely
populated, but it was precisely this scattered character of
western settlement which made the problem of introducing
religious institutions so difficult. Western New York and
Pennsylvania, the Ohio Valley, the new Southwest of Alabama and Mississippi, and isolated settlements near the
Mississippi River, especially in Missouri, comprise the chief
fields of missionary operations in the period here under
consideration.

In this West the population, like that of the remainder
of the United States at the time, was remarkably homo-

---

[1] F. J. Turner, *Rise of the New West*, 12-15.

geneous. There were, to be sure, a few thousand French in the Illinois country, in Louisiana, and in Missouri, and also a few Spaniards on the borders of the rapidly disintegrating Spanish empire in North America; migrating planters were taking their Negro slaves into the Southwest; but even so, never before nor after in the eighteenth and nineteenth centuries was the West so distinctly Anglo-American. There had been sufficient time for the amalgamation of the great mass of the non-English groups that had come into the colonies in the eighteenth century; on the other hand, for four or five decades after the Revolution the migration of the foreign-born into the United States was comparatively insignificant and presented no important problem of assimilation. Consequently, the Westerners of the early part of the nineteenth century were overwhelmingly "Americans" with an English, or a Scotch-Irish, or a German racial background.

As was usual on the agricultural frontiers these people were in the main young men and women, married, and with large families coming on. They were optimistic. They knew the lands on which they had settled were rich and productive, and they looked forward to the time when these lands would give them economic comfort or even affluence. Their speculative instincts were encouraged by the Harrison Land Law of 1800, which required the down payment of only one fourth of the purchase price of public lands and allowed credit on the balance due for a four-year term.

But this was also a West of hard labor. Except for the prairies of Illinois, most of the land as far west as the Mississippi River was heavily forested when the whites entered. There were countless trees to be cut down, made into logs for cabins, or split into rails for fences, or perhaps just rolled into piles and burned. There were almost endless swamps to be drained, not only in order that corn and wheat might be grown, but also that the country might be rid of the ague, a malady which caused its unhappy victims alternately to burn with fever and shake with chills. The tools available in the conquest of the West were still of the simplest sort, the ax, the spade, the shovel, and the hoe. The two most important beasts of burden were the horse and the ox. Except for the explosive force of gunpowder and for a few steamboats chugging noisily on the western waters after 1811, almost all the power used in

the occupation of the West up to 1820 was produced by men and domestic animals.

As on previous frontiers, the men of the West were in close contact with the Indians and exposed to attack. Wayne's victory at Fallen Timbers (1794) had quieted the Indians north of the Ohio for a time, but under the able leadership of Tecumseh they soon began to make plans to stem the advancing tide of whites. It was in vain; the battle of Tippecanoe (1811) cleared the way for a new advance of land-hungry frontiersmen into the Northwest. In the Southwest the Creeks, who had also gone on the warpath, brought down on their heads the wrath of Andrew Jackson and his Tennessee militia at Horseshoe Bend (1814).

Nor were Indians the only danger to life on the frontier. There were few physicians, competent or incompetent, who could be called to care for a woman in the pains of labor, to set a broken arm, to amputate a crushed leg, or to bring relief to the victim of a snakebite. Each family was thrown largely on its own resources. If there were neighbors, they would probably be friendly and helpful, but often they were too far removed to be of assistance in an emergency.

All in all, the West of the early years of the nineteenth century was a region of aggressive, individualistic, materialistic, and yet emotional Americans who had outrun the cultural institutions of social control, and who were necessarily tremendously absorbed in their tasks of erecting cabins, laying out towns, digging ditches, building roads, and fighting Indians. With respect to religion and morals these people, in the eyes of eastern Christians, were "destitute."

REVIVALS IN RELIGION

The effort in the United States to deal with the religious problem presented by the West was closely related to a revival of interest in religion and missionary projects which seems to have been general among European as well as American Christians at this time. A reaction had set in against the skepticism and infidelity so evident in the eighteenth century. One who signed himself "Eusebius," writing in the *Massachusetts Missionary Magazine* in 1804, called attention to the fact that the Protestants of Great Britain had begun to engage in world-wide evangelization: the

Missionary Society of London had agents in the Islands of the Pacific and in South Africa; the Edinburgh Missionary Society had established a mission in Russian Tartary; the Baptist Association had reported that its work in India was prospering; the Moravians had at least 166 missionaries at work in places as widely separated as Greenland and Labrador in the North, central Africa in the South, and Ceylon in the Far East.[2] Among European Roman Catholics a new period of missionary activity was beginning, one in which an appeal was made to the people rather than to states for financial support for missions. To stimulate and conserve this popular interest in missions among Catholics such benevolent organizations as the Society for the Propagation of the Faith, the Association of the Holy Childhood, the Society of St. Francis Xavier in Aix-la-Chapelle, the Ludwigmissionsverein in Bavaria, and the Leopoldine Stiftung in Austria were formed in the first third of the nineteenth century.[3]

The reforming spirit was also in the air, especially in New England. Bible societies, tract societies, and moral societies were being formed to correlate the benevolent efforts of those who felt some responsibility for the welfare of their fellows who lacked the Bible and other good books, or who were indifferent to the claims of religion, or were careless in their observance of the moral code. By 1814 there were at least fifty Bible societies in the United States;[4] some of these organizations, such as the Philadelphia Bible Society, which helped bear the expenses of a tour into the interior in 1814-15 by Messrs. Samuel J. Mills and Daniel Smith,[5] were active in the distribution of Bibles and the formation of branch societies throughout the West. Many societies were also formed to distribute religious tracts and books. The spirit in which this work was undertaken is well illustrated by the constitution of the Massachusetts Society for Promoting Christian Knowledge. It declared that "No atheistical, deistical, skeptical, heretical,

---

2 *Massachusetts Missionary Magazine*, II (1804), 159-61.

3 E. J. Hickey, *Society for the Propagation of the Faith (Cath. Univ. of Amer. Studies in Amer. Ch. Hist.*, III, 1922), 5-6; [Joseph Freri], *Society for the Propagation of the Faith and Catholic Missions, 1822-1900* (Baltimore, 1902), 3-4.

4 *Conn. Evan. Mag. and Rel. Intel.*, VII (1814), 474.

5 See below, page 141.

nor immoral book or tract, nor any book or tract that is tinc-
tured by any such principle or sentiment, shall ever be
purchased, printed, published, or distributed by this society."[6] And then there were the numerous societies for
the Promotion of Good Morals, or, as they were sometimes
more pessimistically called, societies for the Suppression of
Vice and Immorality. The policy announced by the Wolcot
branch of the Connecticut Society for the Promotion of
Good Morals was typical: its members resolved "to hold, in
due contempt, all persons who spend their time in idleness,
gambling, profane swearing, and excessive drinking; to
notice carefully violations of the Sabbath and neglecters of
public worship; and to feel themselves pledged individually
to bear testimony by example, exhortation, admonition, and
reproof, against all immoral conduct within their personal
knowledge."[7] The New England Conscience was still
vigorous.

In Connecticut, where these moral, tract, and Bible societies were especially active, the charge was made that
they were more political than religious in their nature and
that their object was the propagation of Federalism instead
of Christianity. But how was a Federalist to distinguish
between his politics and his religion when one seemed to
supplement the other and both appeared to him to be the
last word of excellence in their respective spheres? The
officers and directors of the various Bible, moral, and missionary societies in New England were for the most part
members of the old families, men who were eminently respectable, conservative, well-to-do, and, of course, Feder-
alists in politics. In their minds good morals and pure religion were just as much identified with Federalism as were
infidelity and atheism with Jeffersonian Republicanism. It
was not an academic question with these men; they were
earnestly trying to preserve cherished institutions and
ideals. They had seen infidelity invade Yale College, which
had been founded as a bulwark for orthodoxy. They knew
that in their communities there was an increasingly large
number of men who were opposed to what little was left
of the Congregational establishment and who were insisting
on the complete separation of church and state. They knew
also that many of these men were the followers of Thomas

---

6 *Mass. Miss. Mag.*, V (1808), 390.

7 *Conn. Evan. Mag. and Rel. Intel.*, VII (1814), 305.

Jefferson, champion of the French Revolution and of free thought. They had seen the spread of such "subversive" ideas as democracy and rationalism, and had even witnessed the elevation of the high priest of these principles to the presidency of the United States. Granted their conceptions and prejudices, it is no wonder that they turned to moral and religious societies as a means of defending and spreading those institutions and principles upon which they believed society rested and without which the nation might perish.[8]

The spiritual impulse for these many moral, Bible, and tract societies, as well as for the missionary societies that are to be considered in detail later, came from a series of religious revivals which broke out in various parts of the country in the closing years of the eighteenth century. A revival usually begins among professing Christians who become aware of their own spiritual deadness and sins; and from them it spreads to "the world." The revival movement in New England, which started in 1797 and lasted for five years, has been called the Second Great Awakening.[9] Beyond the Alleghenies the religious disturbance which began about the same time is known as the Great Revival in the West.[10] Among members of the rival denominations there had been, in the words of a participant in the movement, "envy and strife, railing and backbiting." The people as a whole had acted "more like devils than Christians." But a few men who were under conviction of sin, who fasted and prayed and searched the Scriptures diligently, and who found a comfortable hope of salvation, "were constrained to cry out, with tears and trembling, and testify a full and free salvation in Christ for all that would come."[11] Thus did a great religious awakening begin.

The revival in the West commenced in Logan County, Kentucky, in 1797 under the preaching of James McGready,

---

[8] See W. A. Robinson, *Jeffersonian Democracy in New England*, 128-50, for the connection between Republicanism and opposition to the Congregational Church.

[9] There is a good factual account of missionary activities during this period in O. W. Elsbree, *Rise of the Missionary Spirit in America, 1790-1815* (Williamsport, Pa., 1928).

[10] The best study of this religious movement is Catherine C. Cleveland's *Great Revival in the West, 1795-1805* (Chicago, [1916]).

[11] Richard M'Nemar, *Kentucky Revival* (New York, 1846), 8-20, *passim*.

a Presbyterian minister. From there it spread over the remainder of Kentucky, into Tennessee, North and South Carolina, western Virginia, and across the Ohio River into Ohio and western Pennsylvania. The Great Revival in the West resembled in many respects the Great Awakening of the eighteenth century. The state of society in the West in 1800 was similar to that found in the back parts of the seaboard colonies a half century earlier. In each case the people involved were exposed to the dangers of frontier life and were subject to emotional excesses. Both revival movements were accompanied by various physical phenomena, but those which attended the second were much more violent than those which had brought discredit upon the first. In both, there were groans from those who feared that they were lost and shouts of joy from those who believed that they had been saved; in both, enthusiasts saw visions and went into trances. But never before or since in this country has religious enthusiasm carried such large numbers of people into such excesses as were common in the West between 1797 and 1803. One reason the excitement of the Great Revival surpassed that of the Great Awakening was the introduction of camp meetings about this time. People came such distances and in such numbers to some of the western revival exercises that the only way in which they could be cared for was to allow them to camp on the grounds. On one "sacramental occasion" twenty thousand persons are reported to have assembled at Cane Ridge, Kentucky.[12] All sorts and conditions of men came together in these vast gatherings. Earnest Christians who yearned for spiritual food and the fellowship of the saints rubbed elbows with politicians seeking votes. Some were there because they had been convicted of sin and were looking for salvation; others had been drawn by curiosity and love of novelty and excitement. Doubtless many attended the camp meetings because they broke the monotony of existence and were a means of satisfying social longings.

Whatever the motives may have been which brought men, women, and children together on these occasions, they were all likely to fall under the spell of the excitement. These great assemblies, under the eerie light of the wood-

---

[12] R. Davidson, *History of the Presbyterian Church in the State of Kentucky*, 137; J. B. Finley, *Sketches of Western Methodism* (Cincinnati, 1857), 78-79.

land torch, of backwoodsmen who had lived for months or even years in comparative solitude subject to the dangers and uncertainties of frontier life, were like tinder which flared into wild flames of religious enthusiasm at the touch of "hell-fire and brimstone" preaching.[13] Under such conditions men who were little accustomed to the restraints of convention or law could not be expected to behave quietly. During the excitement of the revival the most common bodily manifestation of a conviction of sin was "falling." One observer declared that from two thirds to three fourths of those who had a genuine conviction of sin "fell."[14] They fell on all occasions—when alone, or at work, even in merry company, but most frequently at public worship when the psychological effect of the fall of one person was likely to bring others to the ground. Falling was attended by various degrees of bodily disturbance, from nervous agitation to deathlike weakness and inaction. The duration of the attack lasted anywhere from a few minutes to several days. All ages and classes—saints and sinners alike—were likely to fall. In the case of the "unrenewed sinners," according to a contemporary preacher, "the weight of sin, the wrath of God, the certainty of his vengeance, and the pains of hell, when brought feelingly to their view, come upon them with a load too great to be borne." Professing Christians also fell when a "view of the glories of the divine character, the wonders of sovereign grace, the riches of the Savior's love and the glorious work of man's redemption" opened to them with such a clearness that they could no more bear it "than Moses could a sight of God's glory."[15]

Two peculiar forms of emotional disturbance that appeared in parts of the West at the time of the Great Revival were the "jerks" and the "barks." In the one, the victim found himself unable to control the more or less violent jerking of his arms, legs, or head; in the other, he got down on all fours and growled, snapped, and barked like a dog.[16]

---

[13] Cf. F. M. Davenport, *Primitive Traits in Religious Revivals*, 77-84.

[14] Thomas Robbins, missionary to the Western Reserve, Ohio, writing in *Conn. Evan. Mag.*, IV (1804), 316.

[15] Thomas Robbins, Canfield, New Conn. (Western Reserve), Dec. 7, 1803, in Conn. Miss. Soc. MS. Letters and Journals, 1800-05. This letter was published with slight changes in *Conn. Evan. Mag.*, IV (1804), 316-18.

[16] R. Davidson, *History of the Presbyterian Church in the State of Kentucky*, 146-52.

According to the eccentric Lorenzo Dow, who preached in the Southwest during this time of excitement, those seized with the jerks sometimes caught hold of saplings and jumped up and down so often and so violently that the ground around looked as though it had been kicked up by "a horse stamping flies"![17] Perhaps it had been. Equally amazing is the statement that when the head of the victim was the seat of the jerks, his hair, if it were long, might be shaken with such quickness as to "crack and snap like the lash of a whip." Peter Cartwright, who was a young and energetic Methodist circuit rider at this time, says that he had seen more than five hundred persons jerking at one time in his own large congregations. "To see those proud young gentlemen and young ladies, dressed in their silks, jewelry, and prunella, from top to toe, take the *jerks*," he added, "would often excite my risibilities. The first jerk or so, you would see their fine bonnets, caps, and combs fly; and so sudden would be the jerking of the head that their long loose hair would crack almost as loud as a wagoner's whip."[18] But the jerks, according to Cartwright's own statement, sometimes had tragic consequences. He tells of a drunken rowdy who went to a camp meeting at "the Ridge" intending to help break it up. Instead, he took the jerks. He started to run, but jerked so powerfully he could not get away. He pulled out his bottle of whiskey and swore he would drink "the damned jerks to death." In the midst of his profane contortions "he fetched a very violent jerk, snapped his neck, fell, and soon expired, with his mouth full of cursing and bitterness."[19]

Such strange physical phenomena were excrescences on the revival, as were also the sexual irregularities that occasionally attended the free intermingling of men and women who were emotionally unbalanced. These disorders were not an essential part of the movement, which in some places was conducted with due propriety and solemnity. The latter seems to have been generally true in northern Ohio, judging by the descriptions of the revival meetings there written by Joseph Badger, representative of the Missionary Society of Connecticut, and other men from New

[17] L. Dow, *Perambulations of Cosmopolite* (Rochester, 1842), 134.

[18] P. Cartwright, *Autobiography*, 48-49.

[19] P. Cartwright, *Autobiography*, 50-51.

England. Concerning one of the meetings he attended on the Western Reserve in 1802, Badger wrote that at candle lighting the preachers repaired to the house of worship and found it so full that "it was difficult getting through the allies." The congregation had been singing hymns, and as the ministers entered the building "a person near one end of the house cryed out & became helpless. The publick exercises pretty soon began. Mr. Wick preached, there was great solemnity & many appeared under deep distress of soul; four other persons in the course of the evening cryed out, ... Their groans and cries indicated deep anguish of the soul; but most of the time for four hours they very nearly resembled persons who have just expired from full strength."[20] In describing a meeting at Salem he wrote:

Several fell in time of prayer; some were greatly agitated, cried out suddenly as they fell, and for a few moments struggled violently, but were immediately taken care of by those who sat near them; after struggling for a few moments, they lay for hours more resembling a dead corpse, than living creatures. Others fell without noise or struggle, and some as suddenly as if they were dead. Others discovered deep distress without noise or falling. At evening Mr. Wick preached; as the air was dry and still, candles were lighted and stuck up on trees and shed posts, sufficient to enlighten the whole congregation. The sermon, several prayers and singing of hymns lengthened out the exercises until about one o'clock when many retired and took a little sleep. I slept about three hours. Many of the distressed and others did not leave the place.[21]

The Great Revival had several important results. Camp meetings and "protracted meetings" became well established agencies in the spread of the gospel among the people of the West. With thousands of men and women a normal religious experience was regarded as one associated with the excitement of the "big meeting." The revival emphasized an emotional type of religion and gave a great impetus to the more popular denominations. In so far as the home missionary movement is concerned with the efforts of the various sects to increase their numbers in the West, this is of significance because it is one reason for the numerical preponderance obtained by the Baptists and Meth-

---

[20] Joseph Badger, Austinburg, New Conn., Nov. 19, 1802, in Conn. Miss. Soc. MS. Letters and Journals, 1800-05; parts of this letter were printed with some changes in Conn. Evan. Mag., III (1803), 319.

[21] Joseph Badger, Canfield, New Conn., July 19, 1803, in Conn. Evan. Mag., IV (1803), 113.

odists in the United States. At the same time the revival directed the minds of men toward religious subjects and temporarily, at least, made it easier for the missionaries of any denomination to work among them. It should be noted, however, that the representatives of the more conservative churches made many complaints about the difficulty of carrying on their work in the areas of the West that had been burned over by the fires of religious excitement. As to the effect on morals, opinions differed. According to one observer the character of Kentucky had been entirely changed by the Great Revival. Writing in 1802, this man said: "I found Kentucky to appearance the most moral place I had ever seen. A profane expression was hardly ever heard. A religious awe seemed to pervade the country; and some deistical characters had confessed that from whatever cause the revival might proceed, it made the people better."[22] This picture of Kentucky morals is very different from that painted by John F. Schermerhorn and Samuel J. Mills, representatives of the missionary societies of Massachusetts and Connecticut, at the time of their trip through the West ten years later; they found the morals of the people of Kentucky loose and reported that many of the inhabitants were extremely ignorant as well as very vicious, and that the most prevalent vices were profanity, gambling, horse-racing, fighting, drunkenness, and violation of the Sabbath.[23] No doubt there was a decline in moral standards and a subsidence in religious enthusiasm after the excitement of the revival had died down, but it is also probable that Kentucky was not so good in 1802, nor so bad in 1812, as the two reports would indicate.

NEW DENOMINATIONS

During the course of the revival relations between the principal denominations represented in the West appear to have been friendly. Their ministers sometimes preached from the same platform, and their members even united in the observance of the Lord's Supper. And yet out of this period of religious turmoil came schisms and the formation

---

[22] G. A. Baxter, Washington Academy, Jan. 1, 1802, in *Conn. Evan. Mag.*, II (1802), 355-56.

[23] J. F. Schermerhorn and S. J. Mills, *Correct View* (Hartford, 1814), 20.

of new churches. The Presbyterians suffered most from such factional contests, perhaps because they were most alert to detect and stamp out heresy.

The first of these major schisms resulted in the formation of the Cumberland Presbyterian Church. Many conservative western Presbyterians had opposed the revival because of its excesses; some churches in Kentucky and Tennessee had been locked against revivalists, and in some cases resort was had to violence.[24] However, as a result of the increased interest in religion the supply of preachers was inadequate to meet the needs of the people; hence the Cumberland Presbytery, which included counties in southern Kentucky and northern Tennessee, began about 1803 to accept as ministers pious men who could testify convincingly about their experimental religion but who had not received the academic and theological training ordinarily required by the Presbyterians.[25] A doctrinal controversy was also involved: the men licensed by the Cumberland Presbytery made reservations in adopting the Confession of Faith on the subjects of predestination and perseverance. The minority party in the presbytery, disturbed by such irregularities, appealed to the Synod of Kentucky, which appointed a commission, strongly antirevivalistic in sentiment, to investigate. This commission, in excess of its authority, according to the revivalists, suspended the majority of the presbytery. The action of the commission was approved by the Synod of Kentucky and ultimately by the General Assembly of the Presbyterian Church. The Cumberland Presbytery refused to recognize this action and in 1810 organized itself as a separate church. The Westminster Confession with the element of fatalism removed was adopted as the creed; a system of itinerant preachers was introduced.[26] For nearly a century the Cumberland Presbyterians maintained their separate identity, reunion with the parent body not being brought about until 1906.

---

[24] B. W. McDonnold, *History of the Cumberland Presbyterian Church* (Nashville, 1888), 40.

[25] W. W. Sweet, *Religion on the American Frontier . . . Presbyterians*, 287, 291.

[26] B. W. McDonnold, *History of the Cumberland Presbyterian Church*, 48-108; R. Davidson, *History of the Presbyterian Church in the State of Kentucky*, 223-63; F. R. Cossitt, *Life and Times of Rev. Finis Ewing* (Louisville, [1853]); W. W. Sweet, *Religion on the American Frontier . . . Presbyterians*, 91-94, 282-305.

About the time of the Cumberland disruption, the Synod of Kentucky had to deal with another controversy that likewise resulted in the formation of a new denomination. During the Great Revival certain Presbyterian ministers in Ohio and Kentucky taught doctrines contrary to the Calvinistic theory of predestination and election. One of these men of "unsound" faith, Richard McNemar by name, was brought to trial and condemned for preaching heresy; four other Presbyterian clergymen who had taught similar doctrines united with him in withdrawing from the Synod of Kentucky and in forming the Springfield Presbytery.[27] Up to this point they had regarded themselves as Presbyterians, but in 1804 they dissolved their newly created presbytery and promulgated a singular document entitled "The Last Will and Testament of the Springfield Presbytery"; in this they announced that henceforth they would take the Bible as their only rule of faith and practice and the name "Christian" in place of any sectarian or denominational designation.[28] The adherents of the new movement were called New Lights, or Stonites from one of the leaders, Barton W. Stone; but they called themselves simply "Christians." The movement was a protest in part against certain features of Calvinistic theology, but also against the sectarian spirit which divided Protestantism into hostile camps; it suggested as a way out of the difficulty that all man-made creeds and names be discarded, and that all Christians unite on the Bible.

So far as the home missionary movement is concerned these schisms are important because they indicate that in the West there was a desire for a simpler theology and a more emotional type of religion. Eastern Congregationalists and Presbyterians often found in the West an uncongenial atmosphere. To the extent that it was uncongenial they were strengthened in their conviction that the West sorely needed their doctrines; but slowly as time went by they were forced to make readjustments in their ideas and practices.

The story of denominational discord in this period would not be complete without some mention of the Unitarian defection among Congregationalists, but in this connection

---

[27] For their protest to the Synod of Kentucky, see W. W. Sweet, *Religion on the American Frontier . . . Presbyterians*, 318-19.

[28] B. W. Stone, *Autobiography*, in J. R. Rogers, *Cane Ridge Meeting-house* (Cincinnati, [1910]), 165-66.

nothing more need be said than to call attention to the fact that this schism was one of the forces which helped arouse the orthodox of New England, and especially of Massachusetts, to greater efforts on behalf of their faith. They hoped to compensate in the West for their losses in the East.

The score of years dealt with in this chapter comprise a turbulent period in American church history. The Great Revival had produced profound excitement throughout the West. Old churches were breaking up; new ones were being formed. Movements designed to combat sectarianism and to bring about the union of all Christians had been launched. It was in the midst of this religious excitement and confusion that the churches in the East took up the task of reorganizing their missionary methods in order to meet the new situation.

MISSIONARY SOCIETY OF CONNECTICUT

The first step toward the establishment of a more efficient missionary system among the Congregationalists was the formation of the Missionary Society of Connecticut. In 1797 the General Association of Connecticut had issued an address to the District Associations setting forth the need for an increased support for the missions to the new settlements.[29] At the meeting of the Association in 1798 a Missionary Society was formed whose purpose was to "Christianize the Heathen in North America, and to support and promote Christian Knowledge in the new settlements, within the United States."[30] In 1802, the funds having considerably increased, the trustees of the Society were vested with corporate powers by the General Assembly of Connecticut.[31] Moreover, the Society received official state endorsement; by resolution of the Assembly passed in 1801, and renewed at intervals of three years until 1820 at least, it was given authority to take up collections annually in the churches

---

[29] *An Address, of the General Association of Connecticut, to the District Associations on the Subject of a Missionary Society;...* (Norwich, 1797).

[30] *Constitution of the Missionary Society of Connecticut:...* (Hartford, 1800), 4.

[31] *An Act to Incorporate the Trustees of the Missionary Society of Connecticut:...* (Hartford, 1803); "On the Subject of Missions and a Statement of the Funds of the Missionary Society of Connecticut for the year 1804," Yale Univ. Lib. MSS.

of the state for the support of its work.[32] The people were urged to contribute because, as one minister put it, in no other way could they so eminently manifest their love and regard for their brethren in the new settlements.[33]

In its first year the Missionary Society of Connecticut sent out six missionaries to new settlements in Vermont, New York,[34] and Pennsylvania. Even on a frontier no farther removed than that of central New York, the missionaries reported that it was not uncommon to preach in communities where no sermon had been heard for a year. Much that they saw and heard among these New Yorkers was displeasing to the men from New England. One minister, Robert Porter, who went to the Black River communities in the vicinity of Utica shortly after the election of 1800, notes that when he reached "Boon's second settlement" the people had an Indian fiddler and were making preparations to celebrate Jefferson's election. "I thought them in no situation to hear preaching," he said, so he rode on to the next settlement.[35] In 1801 the number of missionaries had increased to fifteen, and the field of labor had been extended to include "New Connecticut" or the Western Reserve in northern Ohio, into which many people from Connecticut were already moving. In general the Society still retained the old plan of sending out pastors on missionary tours from four to eight weeks in length; but in the case of settlements so far removed as those of the Western Reserve, longer tours were necessary.

The first missionary sent to the Western Reserve by the Connecticut society was Joseph Badger, a veteran of the Revolutionary War and a graduate of Yale College. He began his work in New Connecticut in January 1801;[36] then fol-

---

[32] Conn. Miss. Soc., *Narrative on the Subject of Missions:... for the Year 1804* (Hartford, 1805), and following years.

[33] This paraphrase of a statement by Cyprian Strong, in *Sermon Preached at Hartford,... January 15th. A.D., 1800* (Hartford, 1800), is typical of the appeals that were made on the basis of benevolence.

[34] There is a good, brief account of Congregational and Presbyterian missionary activities in central and western New York in J. H. Hotchkin, *History of the Purchase and Settlement of Western New York* (New York, 1848), 176-99.

[35] Robert Porter, "Journal of a Missionary Tour among the Settlements on the Black River," in Conn. Miss. Soc. MS. Letters and Journals, 1800-05.

[36] Joseph Badger, Journal, 1800-01, in Conn. Miss. Soc. MS. Letters and Journals, 1800-05.

lowed a year of strenuous missionary endeavor at the end of which he said that he had visited and preached the gospel to all the families on the Reserve.[37] The number of families was small, but they were widely scattered; blazed trails had to be followed from one settlement to another. On the site of Cleveland, two families were living; at Euclid, one. There were two families at Painesville, and ten in Austinburg. Everywhere he encouraged the people with hopes of a brighter day, because, he said, the soil was good and industry would produce plenty. Christians who mourned the loss of their former religious privileges and who wondered why they had ever come to such a desolate country were assured by him that "they had been moved here by the hand of God to plant the church in this wilderness."[38] Before returning to New England, Badger formed at Austinburg the first church organized in the Western Reserve. When he reached home on New Year's Day, 1802, after an absence of more than thirteen months, he had completed in point of time and distance one of the longest home missionary journeys made in the United States up to its date. After Badger made his report to the Society at Hartford it was proposed that he return to the Western Reserve with his family. Missionaries resident in the frontier communities were thus introduced by the Missionary Society of Connecticut; in the years to come these settled pastors, each in charge of one or more churches, were to be the chief means employed by most of the denominations in their missionary operations in the West. Early in 1802 Badger moved his family, consisting of a wife and six children, with a small amount of furniture and clothing, on a wagon drawn by four horses, to Austinburg, Ohio, a distance of six hundred miles.[39] A cabin was built for the family. "It was a rough one, rough logs, without a chink; and only floored half-over with split stuff, and partly roofed with boards . . . with no chimney."[40] Badger remained in the employ of the Connecticut Mission-

---

37 *Memoir of Rev. Joseph Badger* (Hudson, Ohio, 1851), 25-35.

38 *Memoir of Rev. Joseph Badger*, 26.

39 For the hardships endured on this journey see Badger's letter from Austinburg, June 8, 1802, in Conn. Miss. Soc. MS. Letters and Journals, 1800-05.

40 *Memoir of Rev. Joseph Badger*, 39-40.

ary Society until 1806, during which period he was instrumental in founding several churches in northern Ohio.[41]

The Missionary Society of Connecticut very appropriately made "New Connecticut" in northern Ohio its special field. Not only was that region being settled principally by emigrants from Connecticut, but the Connecticut school system benefited from the proceeds of the sale of lands in the Western Reserve. "And in what more suitable way," asked the directors of the Society, "can we make compensation to the settlers than by furnishing them with the means of obtaining religious instruction?"[42] To list even the names of all the men sent to the Reserve by the Connecticut society is impossible here. It is a roll of honor. They were college-trained men, lovers of learning, with high moral standards. No man can measure the extent of their influence in northern Ohio in the formative period.[43]

The printed page was another agency on which the Missionary Society of Connecticut placed great emphasis— so much in fact that Joseph Badger sometimes complained about the number of books that were sent to him for distribution, although he did admit that the books were needed and were in great demand.[44] Among the books and pamphlets sent to the frontiers from New England such titles as the following occur frequently: *A Friendly Visit to the House of Mourning*, Beecher on *Divine Government*, Baxter's *Call to the Unconverted*, *Solemn Reasons for Infant Baptism*, Trumbull on *Family Prayer*, Beecher on *Waste Places*, *Summary of Christian Doctrine and Duties*, Baxter's *Saint's Rest, Guide to Heaven*, and the *Dairyman's Daugh-*

---

[41] Badger's closing years in the services of the Society were marred by misunderstandings: the officers complained because he spent too much of his time in Austinburg (Trustees of Conn. Miss. Soc., Hartford, Jan. 6, 1803, to J. Badger, Conn. Miss. Soc. MS. Letters and Journals, 1800-05); Badger felt that the Society had acted unfairly in reducing his allowance (*Memoir of Rev. Joseph Badger*, 110-11). Perhaps it was such controversies that Leonard Woolsey Bacon had in mind when he characterized the administration of the Connecticut Missionary Society in the early period as "incompetent, unjust, cruel and mean." *Home Missionary*, LXXI (1898), 92.

[42] Conn. Miss. Soc., *Narrative on the Subject of Missions:... Year 1801* (Hartford, 1802), 13.

[43] There are short biographical sketches of several of the early missionaries from New England to northern Ohio in W. S. Kennedy, *Plan of Union* (Hudson, Ohio, 1856), 55-81.

[44] *Memoir of Rev. Joseph Badger*, 111.

ter.[45] If these books were read, and there are many evidences that they were, it was because there was then a popular interest in theological minutiae and doctrinal disputation that is almost entirely lacking at the present time, and also because books of any nature were scarce on the frontier. In 1818 the Missionary Society of Connecticut reported that in the preceding year it had sent to the frontiers over five thousand volumes, making a total of nearly forty-two thousand books and tracts that it had distributed up to that time.[46] A somewhat different sort of appeal, one directed primarily to the scattered Christians in the frontier communities, was an "Address from the Trustees of the Missionary Society of Connecticut, to the Inhabitants of the New-Settlements, in the northern and western parts of the United States," warning them of the moral dangers to which they were exposed, and suggesting that until they could obtain the stated preaching of the gospel and the administration of the ordinances of the church, they should assemble for public worship every Lord's Day with their ablest and best men leading in prayers and reading sermons.[47]

The representatives of the Connecticut Missionary Society met with varied receptions on the frontiers. Usually they were well received; however, there were times and places when they were looked on with disfavor, partly because they were regarded as political emissaries. As stated above, the missionary and moral societies which flourished in Connecticut in the early part of the nineteenth century were directed by the conservative Federalist leaders of the state. In the list of officers and directors of the Missionary Society of Connecticut in this period may be found the names of such worthies as Jonathan Trumbull, Jedediah Huntington, and Theodore Dwight. They were of the "Standing Order," the political, economic, and social leaders of their communities. The connection between Federalism and Congregational missions in Connecticut was so close that Jeffersonian Republicans professed to believe that religion was only a

---

[45] For lists of books sent out by the Missionary Society of Connecticut, see its annual *Narratives of Missions*, e.g., for 1806, 18; for 1814, 26-27; for 1817, 23-24.

[46] Conn. Miss. Soc., *Nineteenth Annual Narrative of Missionary Service* (Hartford, 1818), 23-24.

[47] Original printed circular in Yale Univ. Lib.

cloak for political activity. To complaints against the dominant Federalist group were sometimes added economic
grievances. Men on the frontiers were often in debt to
well-to-do moneylenders of the coast towns or were paying
rent to absentee proprietors. To these men the missionary
might be an unpleasant reminder of agencies of control they
would like to shake off, or of obligations they would like to
forget. One of the Connecticut missionaries, Robert Porter,
—the man who disapproved of the celebration in New York
in honor of Jefferson's election,—came in contact in St.
Albans, Vermont, with some of these disgruntled men, who
asked him if the people of Connecticut thought that the
people of Vermont were too ignorant and too poor to pay
for their own preaching. After the missionary had explained the benevolent motives of the society which had sent
him out, his critics expressed the opinion that "the business
was quite overdone."[48] When the missionaries were not
well received they could always explain it on the ground
that evil-minded men naturally did not wish to have the
gospel preached among them.[49] Timothy Dwight, in his
well-known description of New England and New York,
paid his respects to the men on the frontiers of New England who complained about taxation for the support of religion, and who also objected to the various activities of the
Congregational establishment. He said:

> Of all religious sects, those which owe their existence to the
> reluctance, felt by every avaricious man, to support the public worship
> of God, are the worst in their character and the most hopeless of
> reformation.... To preserve his pelf, the man belies his conscience
> and insults his Maker. To appease the one, and soothe the other, and
> at the same time preserve some appearance of character among his
> neighbors, he endeavors to make up in the show of zeal what he so
> evidently lacks of common honesty. Hence he becomes enthusiastic,
> bigoted, censorious, impervious to conviction, a wanderer after every
> straggling exhorter, and every bewildered tenet; and thus veers from
> one folly and falsehood, to another, and another, throughout his life.[50]

In this exchange of left-handed compliments we find
another illustration of the divergence between the East and

---

[48] Robert Porter, "Journal of a Mission into the Northern and
Western Towns in the State of Vermont, 1800," in Conn. Miss. Soc.
MS. Letters and Journals, 1800-05.

[49] Conn. Miss. Soc., *Second Address from the Trustees* (Hartford,
1801), 13.

[50] T. Dwight, *Travels*, IV, 173-74.

the West, between the coast and the frontier. Among the people of the older communities there was a tendency to regard the frontier as a region of ignorant, opinionated, shiftless persons whose moral standards were low and whose religious condition was truly deplorable; among the frontiersmen there were many who resented the attitude of superiority assumed along the seaboard, and who felt that the East should mind its own business and keep its missionaries at home.

MASSACHUSETTS MISSIONARY SOCIETY

The Massachusetts Missionary Society, which was formed in Boston in May, 1799,[51] was similar to the Missionary Society of Connecticut in its objects and methods.[52] Its operations west of the Hudson were not so extensive as those of its sister society in Connecticut; it appropriately devoted a considerable part of its effort to work in the province of Maine, which, although a part of Massachusetts, was then as much frontier territory as western New York or Ohio. This society also sent men to the new settlements in New Hampshire, Vermont, and New York. One of its missionaries, Adoniram Judson, who went on "a mission to the interior parts of Vermont" in the summer of 1800,[53] was later a famous Baptist missionary pioneer in Burma. Another, Jacob Cram, left a report of his missionary tour through the new settlements of northern New Hampshire in 1808, which indicates that he had on the whole a cordial reception. He said:

> In thirty eight towns, I preached one hundred and sixty eight sermons, visited three hundred and twenty six families, visited one school, and attended one conference, and rod [sic] on my mission nine hundred ninety four miles.... The people in general have been very attentive to meeting, not only to go to meeting, but also to attend when they were there. But a very little disorder, has taken place on my whole Mission. Now and then among the Methodests an outbrakeing in the periodical *growns*, and *Amens*, and this *they* would call the hight of regularity, and, but now and then one would have

---

[51] *Mass. Miss. Mag.*, I (1803), 5.

[52] The Constitution of the Society, with the names of the original members, may be found in an address *To All, who are desirous of the Spread of the Gospel of our Lord Jesus Christ* (Boston, May 28, 1799).

[53] Mass. Miss. Soc., *An Historical Sketch of the Missions of the Massachusetts Missionary Society. From May 1800, to May 1801* ([Boston, 1801]), 9.

the ill manners, and bad breeding, to appear light and trifling when at meeting. But there were a general seriousness on the minds, and people did not only here attentively, but many appeared to feel sensibly the things that were delivered from time to time. . . . I have been perticularly requested to return to the society the greatful thanks, not only of the people in common but also of many of the first characters in the country, for my labors among them.[54]

In 1803 the Massachusetts society began the publication of the *Massachusetts Missionary Magazine*, the net proceeds from which were devoted to the support of missionary work. Unlike the *Connecticut Evangelical Magazine*, the organ of the Missionary Society of Connecticut, the Massachusetts publication contained very little information about home missionary activities; its pages were largely filled with doctrinal sermons, the explanation probably being found in the fact that it was the organ of orthodox Congregationalism in Massachusetts at a time when the Unitarian controversy was still acute.

OTHER NEW ENGLAND MISSIONARY SOCIETIES

Many other missionary societies, similar in objects and methods, but not so well known, were organized among the Congregationalists of New England during this same period. In 1798 there was formed the Congregational Missionary Society in the counties of Berkshire and Columbia for western Massachusetts and eastern New York. Its funds were never large, but in 1803, for illustration, it sent men to the new settlements of New York and Pennsylvania on missionary tours twelve to fifteen weeks in length.[55] One of its representatives, Joseph Avery, reported after a tour into western New York in 1805 that he had preached to a group of people in the vicinity of Batavia who had begun there "two years ago and never had a meeting of any kind on the Sabbath or any other day for religious worship."[56] The announced purpose of the New Hampshire Missionary Society, founded in September, 1801, was to spread abroad "the glad tidings of salvation among the Heathen, and

---

[54] Jacob Cram, *Journal of a Missionary Tour in 1808 Through the New Settlements of Northern New Hampshire and Vermont* (Rochester, 1909), 33.

[55] *Conn. Evan. Mag.*, IV (1804), 278-79.

[56] "Visit of Rev. Joseph Avery," in *Pub. of the Buffalo Hist. Soc.*, ed. by F. H. Severance, VI (Buffalo, 1903), 226.

others, in our frontier and infant settlements."[57]   In 1802 the Hampshire Missionary Society was organized in Massachusetts, taking its name from the county in which it was organized. In the first season four missionaries were sent out, two to Maine and two to New York.[58] One of these men, John Taylor, made some very uncomplimentary remarks about what he saw and heard in western New York. He complained that the Methodists were producing scenes such as are "transpiring in Kentucky," to wit, "Women here methodists, pray in their families instead of ye men— and with such strength of lungs as to be distinctly heard by their neighbors." Concerning a community in the Black River country, he wrote: "Here is a mixture of all the physical and moral evils that can well be conceived of. Here may be found filth of all kinds, such as dust, mud, fleas, bedbugs, gnats, rotten meat, and sour bread; and, as to moral evils, you may here find ignorance, self-will, self-sufficiency, ill manners, pride, boasting, fanaticism, and witchcraft."[59] Other local societies in New England included the Piscataqua Missionary Society, formed in eastern New Hampshire in 1803,[60] and the missionary societies of Vermont and Rhode Island. In addition to these state and county societies, there were also many purely local organizations designed to foster an interest in missions and to collect money for the larger societies. Among the women "Female Cent Associations," in which the members pledged themselves to contribute one cent each week for missionary purposes, were frequently formed.[61] The Boston Female Society for Missionary Purposes, formed in October, 1800, by Congregationalist and Baptist women was the first missionary organization of women in America.[62]

Within ten years the New England Congregationalists had formed many state and local missionary societies for the purpose of carrying the gospel to the frontiers, usually

---

[57] *Conn. Evan. Mag.*, V (1804), 37.

[58] *Conn. Evan. Mag.*, III (1802), 78.

[59] "Journal of Rev. John Taylor's Missionary Tour," in O'Callaghan, *Documentary History of the State of New York* (Albany, 1850), III, 1134, 1141-42.

[60] *Conn. Evan. Mag.*, IV (1804), 393-95.

[61] *Conn. Evan. Mag.*, V (1804), 148; *Mass. Miss. Mag.*, I (1803), 433.

[62] Williston Walker, *History of the Congregational Churches in the United States* (*Amer. Ch. Hist. Ser.*, III, New York, 1894), 313.

by means of short missionary tours. There was no clear line of demarcation between the spheres of influence of these various societies. In some parts of the West there was duplication of efforts, while many needy places were entirely neglected. The weakness of this system, or rather lack of system, led to the demand for unification of effort through national societies.

MISSIONARY SURVEYS OF THE WEST

One of the most notable services rendered by the Missionary Societies of Connecticut and Massachusetts was the survey of the religious and moral needs of the West by means of two extensive missionary tours in the Mississippi Valley. The first of these was made by Samuel J. Mills and John D. Schermerhorn in 1812-13.[63] Mills, the son of a Connecticut clergyman, had been a leader in the "Hay Stack Band" at Williams College, out of whose secluded devotions grew the American Board of Commissioners for Foreign Missions. Immediately after his graduation from Andover Theological Seminary in 1812, Mills and another Andover graduate, John F. Schermerhorn, of the Dutch Reformed Church, were sent on a tour to the mouth of the Mississippi River under the auspices of the two leading missionary societies of New England.[64] Their aim was to investigate the religious and moral condition of the West, the number of Bibles in the various communities, the number of clergymen in each county, profitable fields for missionary labor, the number of towns able and willing to support ministers, and the origin and characteristics of the people; they intended also to preach and to promote the establishment of Bible societies and other religious institutions. The route followed by the two young men took them down the Ohio to Indiana and then through Kentucky and Tennessee to the Mississippi River and thence to New Orleans.[65] About six months were

---

[63] Their report was published as J. F. Schermerhorn and S. J. Mills, *Correct View of that Part of the United States which lies West of the Alleghany Mountains* (Hartford, 1814); Mills' manuscript journal of the tour is in Conn. Miss. Soc. MS. Letters and Journals, 1812-15.

[64] Gardiner Spring, *Memoirs of the Rev. Samuel J. Mills* (New York, 1820), 59; Conn. Miss. Soc., *Missionary Address . . . 1812* (Hartford, 1813), 13.

[65] In a letter to Stephen Hempstead, St. Louis, Schermerhorn said that their plan had been to go by way of Vincennes through Illinois to

spent on the journey from the upper Ohio to the lower Mississippi. Their report contains much interesting information about the strength and characteristics of the various denominations in the West. As might be expected from men of their background, they characterized the Presbyterians— and they meant the New England Congregationalists too, since most of them became Presbyterians when they got out West—as "the most intelligent part of the community, lovers of order, and promoters of knowledge."[66] The Western Baptist preachers, they thought, were inadequately educated and too much given to efforts "to excite the passions, to terrify and raise into transports of joy, rather than to inform the mind, [and] convince the understanding."[67] As to Methodists, the customary tribute was paid to the efficiency of their organization and "their complete system of missions, which is by far the best for domestic missions ever yet adopted."[68]

Messrs. Mills and Schermerhorn also made suggestions for the conduct of home missions. They recommended that the appointment of missionaries be for a longer time than had been customary. On missionary tours of one, two, or even three months, they pointed out, a disproportionate amount of time was spent in going to and returning from the field of labor. Furthermore, the time was too short to accomplish much in a new place; the transient missionary might arouse interest, but when he left the door was opened "for preachers of different denominations to creep in, and propagate their peculiar sentiments." The suggestion was made that the field of missions be divided into circuits, and these into societies and places for preaching, so that a missionary by preaching three or four times a week could visit each society once a month. As stated above, these young men from New England were greatly impressed with the Methodist plan of itinerancy. They also urged that the great object in missionary activities should be the establishment of churches, otherwise there would be no means of conserving the moral and religious benefits derived from the mis-

---

St. Louis, but, having been advised by "Gentlemen of information" that that "rout" was not safe, they had passed through Kentucky and Tennessee. Schermerhorn to Hempstead, Ft. Massac, Jan. 24, 1813, Hempstead papers, Mo. Hist. Soc., St. Louis.

[66] Schermerhorn and Mills, *Correct View*, 37.

[67] *Ibid.*, 38-40, for discussion of Baptists.

[68] *Ibid.*, 40-41, on Methodists.

sionaries' labors. The evils of the existing decentralized method of conducting missions were pointed out, in that it resulted in duplication of effort in some places and the utter neglect of others; the remedy suggested was the co-ordination of the missionary activities of the Congrega-tionalists and Presbyterians.[69] They expressed the opinion also that one reason for the rapid growth of the Methodists and Baptists in the West was that their representatives ap-peared in the new communities while they were still in their infancy. The moral was obvious: "If we wish to introduce correct sentiments and Presbyterian churches,... we must send missionaries ... while the settlements are forming, for the people as a body when they immigrate to a place, are not fixed in their sentiments, but are eventually, what the preacher is, who is instrumental in calling their attention to the subject of religion."[70]

The Schermerhorn and Mills report had said much about the lack of Bibles and other religious books in the West. In order to meet this need another journey was undertaken by Mr. Mills, with Daniel Smith as his companion. Under the patronage of the Massachusetts Missionary Society, and with the aid of the Philadelphia Bible Society and the Phila-delphia Missionary Society, the two men set out from Phila-delphia in the summer of 1814, just about the time that the English General Ross was preparing to apply the torch to the capitol and the president's house in Washington. The missionaries went down the Ohio River, through Indiana and Illinois into Missouri, organizing Bible societies and dis-tributing copies of the Scriptures and religious tracts.[71] From St. Louis they returned through Illinois and Indiana to Kentucky, whence they went down the Ohio and Missis-sippi rivers to New Orleans. On their way down the river in January, 1815, they were gloomy about their prospects, having heard that the British had landed near New Orleans; they naturally supposed that everything would be in con-fusion and that it would be a poor time for their mission. But before their arrival General Jackson had repulsed the

---

[69] *Ibid.*, 43-44.

[70] *Ibid.*, 31.

[71] Mills and Smith forwarded to Stephen Hempstead for distribu-tion in and around St. Louis a box containing 259 French New Testa-ments and 50 English Bibles. S. J. Mills, Louisville, Jan. 2, 1815, to S. Hempstead, Hempstead papers, Mo. Hist. Soc.

enemy; the War of 1812 was over. The militia were glad to get copies of the Bible, and "many of the Tennessee detachment said they would carry them all the way home in their knapsacks, even though they should be obliged to leave a part of their baggage."[72] The French inhabitants of New Orleans were also happy to receive the New Testament in their native tongue and took a thousand copies within a week. The Roman Catholic bishop refused to have any part in the disposal of the Bibles, since they were not of the version authorized by his Church, but he made no objection to the distribution and said "that he should prefer to have the present version of the Testament in the possession of the people, rather than have them remain entirely ignorant of the Sacred Scriptures."[73]

The chief object of the Mills-Smith tour was to distribute Bibles and tracts, but some attention was paid to general religious conditions; and the report contained much information designed to encourage the work of the Congregational and Presbyterian missionary societies. One suggestion in the report is of particular significance, namely, that the Presbyterians and Congregationalists should pay especial attention to the towns and villages of the West, because their inhabitants were more destitute of religious privileges than the rural population. The Methodists and Baptists, it was admitted, had done a great work among the farmers and scattered backwoodsmen, but, in the judgment of these two observers, had found less encouragement in the towns, whose inhabitants, "having been long freed from the restraints of religion, have become much more vitiated in their morals, than those of the country."[74]

These two missionary tours had a great influence upon the missionary activities of the Presbyterians and Congregationalists. The religious needs of the West, as seen through the eyes of men trained in Calvinistic theology, had been vividly presented. Thousands of Bibles and religious tracts had been distributed, and the interest aroused by the tours had given an impetus to all the Eastern societies interested in the moral and religious condition of the West. Valuable

---

[72] Daniel Smith, New Orleans, Mar. 27, 1815, in Hempstead papers, Mo. Hist. Soc.

[73] S. J. Mills and D. Smith, *Report of a Missionary Tour* (Andover, 1815), 35.

[74] *Ibid.*, 21.

suggestions had been made for the co-ordination of the work of the various Presbyterian and Congregational organizations interested in home missions.

NEW ENGLAND MISSIONS IN MISSOURI

As one of the results of these reconnaissance tours the Missionary Society of Connecticut extended its operations west of the Mississippi by sending Timothy Flint and Salmon Giddings to Missouri. Timothy Flint, a Harvard graduate, was one of the most interesting and versatile of the long line of New England missionaries in the West. He spent the winter of 1815-16 preaching here and there in southern Ohio, Indiana, and Kentucky, using, among other places, the home of General William Henry Harrison at North Bend, Ohio, as a place of worship. Perhaps it was because he regarded the towns and villages along the Ohio River as "in a measure heathen" and inhabited by "wretched pagans" that he decided to shift his field of endeavor to Missouri.[75] He arrived in St. Louis, a straggling, run-down town of about two thousand inhabitants, in the spring of 1816. If Flint had expected to find there a more congenial environment for his missionary work than he had left behind in Ohio, he was soon disillusioned. St. Louis, as judged by New England standards, was a godless place in 1816. Whether it be true or not that men there had boasted that the Sabbath should never cross the Mississippi, its observance was almost unknown. A majority of the inhabitants of the town were probably adherents of the Roman Catholic Church and of course not interested in a new Protestant preacher. Before the year ended Flint had abandoned St. Louis, where, it seemed to him, "even the sentiment of a God was universally erased,"[76] and sought a new abode in St. Charles. Alas! conditions there were little, if any, better. Within six months Flint was describing the moral conditions about him as appalling. "There is no Sabbath—no moral restraints—& the profanity is, I believe, unparalleled. There is enough, God knows, in your [New England] towns & villages. But compared with yours, [this] country sends up a continual

---

[75] T. Flint, Cincinnati, Jan. 18, 1816, to Abel Flint, copy in Hempstead papers, Mo. Hist. Soc.

[76] T. Flint, St. Charles, Mo., Oct. 10, 1816, to Abel Flint, copy in Hempstead papers. Mo. Hist. Soc.

execration. ... I believe that Hindostan is not more strictly heathen, than this country. There is an overwhelming preponderance of bad example. The sinners are most of them the worst of all—Gospel sinners—who have relinquished, & lost all, that they once had, or knew, or heard in a more favored country."[77] It would appear from these strictures that Flint was "down on the West." Perhaps the West was down on Flint. That was true to a certain extent; he did meet with opposition and sharp criticism. His first handicap was his New England origin. Throughout the West and Southwest there was at this time a hatred and suspicion of Yankees based partly on jealousy and partly on recent memories of New England's unfriendly attitude toward the War of 1812. In describing his trip down the Ohio River, Flint said:

> Wherever we stopped at night and requested lodgings, we were constantly asked if we were Yankees; and when we answered that we were, we constantly saw a lengthening of visage ensue, but were generally complimented in the end with granting our request, and assurances that our appearance and my profession answered for us. We were then compelled to hear of impositions and petty tricks, and small thefts, and more than all, departure without paying off bills, which, they alleged, had been practiced upon them by Yankees.[78]

Another reason for Flint's difficulties in St. Louis was that he had laid himself open to criticism by bringing a stock of goods with him, thus arousing the enmity of the local merchants, and by engaging in land speculations.[79] There were also charges of a more serious nature, but they appear to have been the outgrowth of malice and without foundation. Flint's usefulness as a missionary in that region, however, had been impaired, and he resigned his commission from the Connecticut society in 1818.[80] The whole unfortunate affair is an illustration of the circumspection required of New England missionaries in the West, surrounded as they were by men who by reason of sectarian, partisan, or sectional prejudice were ready to seize upon

---

[77] T. Flint, St. Charles, Mo., Apr. 15, 1817, to Abel Flint, in Hempstead papers, Mo. Hist. Soc.

[78] T. Flint, *Recollections*, 32.

[79] The letters of Salmon Giddings, Jan. to May, 1818, contain a statement of the various charges that had been made against Flint. Conn. Miss. Soc. MS. Letters and Journals, 1816-19.

[80] J. E. Kirkpatrick, *Timothy Flint* (Cleveland, 1911), 291-96.

and magnify any mistake. Flint continued to live in the West for many years, and, as a result of his experiences there, wrote the books for which he is chiefly remembered. In Cincinnati he established in 1827 the *Western Monthly Review*, thus realizing one of the ambitions that had led him to go West. His *Recollections*, published in 1826, give an interesting picture of life and society in the Mississippi Valley as seen by an educated New Englander. His *Geography and History of the Western States* contains valuable information on the West as it was about 1828; his *Memoir of Daniel Boone* passed through fourteen editions between 1833 and 1868. Flint's other writings, too numerous to mention here, included magazine articles, poems, and novels, many of which were based directly on his own experiences in the West.

Salmon Giddings, who arrived in St. Louis in April, 1816,[81] after having made the twelve-hundred-mile journey from New England on horseback, was another representative of the Missionary Society of Connecticut who began work in Missouri about the same time that Flint went there. Giddings too met with opposition on the ground that he was a Yankee. If he had read—as he probably did—the local St. Louis newspaper issued about the time of his arrival he would have found there the following advice on how to treat New England missionaries:

The republican papers in the East inform us that the Osgoods and Parish's of New England, have in drill, a member [sic] of missionaries destined for the West. It is said that those intended *shepherds* are taught to propagate the doctrines of union of church and state, and to discountenance republicanism.

Certainly, ignorance in regard to religion, abominable wickedness and daring impiety may prevail in certain sections of the western country; yet we find that as the country become more populous, religion and orderly habits assume their empire. Are we to receive teachers from those who preached up non-resistance [to the] last war, who declared the war was impious and unnecessary, who declared that England done us no essential injury? No. I would advise my fellow citizens before they subscribe for the mantainance of a clergyman, to stipulate, that as soon as he made politicks a part of his sermon or presumed to censure any political or religious sect, to withdraw their support.[82]

---

[81] Timothy Hill, *Historical Outlines of the Presbyterian Church in Missouri* (Kansas City, Mo., 1871), 5.

[82] *Missouri Gazette*, St. Louis, April 6, 1816.

But Mr. Giddings, like many another missionary, apparently thought that the place where he was least wanted was exactly the place where he was most needed; so he stayed in Missouri[83] in spite of his lack of welcome there and served for several years as pastor of a Presbyterian church in St. Louis.[84]

THE PRESBYTERIANS

The missionary character of the Presbyterian Church in America had been clearly marked from the time of its organization early in the eighteenth century. The activities of the Synod of New York and Philadelphia have already been described,[85] and mention has been made of the formation of the General Assembly in 1789.[86] This body continued the missionary work of the synod out of which it had grown, but not until 1802 was there any significant change in the methods used. Up to that time missions had been taken up like any other business at the annual meetings of the Assembly. When the Assembly met a committee on missions was appointed to look over the reports of the missionaries, to investigate the needs of the field, and to make recommendations for future activities; when the Assembly adjourned the committee ceased to exist. By the opening of the nineteenth century the work had become so important that this method was no longer adequate; a more permanent body to direct the missionary work of the Church was needed. Hence there was formed in 1802 a Standing Committee of Missions, whose business it was "to collect, during the recess of the Assembly, all the information in their power relative to the concerns of missions and missionaries, to digest this information, and to report thereon at each meeting of the Assembly; to designate the places where, and specify the periods during which, the missionaries should be employed; to correspond with them if necessary, and with all other persons

---

[83] On one of his tours in Missouri, Giddings was entertained by Moses Austin, a Connecticut Yankee, who later became prominent in the history of Texas. Giddings described Austin as a friendly man who was anxious to have the gospel flourish in the West. S. Giddings, Kaskaskia, June 12, 1816, Conn. Miss. Soc. MS. Letters and Journals, 1816-19.

[84] J. C. Roy, "Salmon Giddings," in *The New Englander*, XXXIII (1874), 513-32.

[85] See above, page 76 f.

[86] See above, page 109.

on missionary business,[87] to nominate missionaries to the Assembly, and report the number which the funds will permit to be employed; to hear the reports of the missionaries."[88] Otherwise there was no change in the method of conducting missions: as before, pastors or licentiates were sent to the frontiers on tours varying from one to six months in length. The number of men sent out was not large; in 1802 the Assembly made eight appointments,[89] but by 1811 the number had grown to forty.[90] The amount of money available for the purpose was small, never exceeding $2,500 a year between 1802 and 1811.[91] The pay received by the missionaries was nominal. It is recorded that one missionary who traveled two thousand miles and preached over one hundred sermons received $45.32; that another served as a missionary for six weeks and received $3.755; while a third, who visited Mississippi Territory, served on his mission seven months and thirteen days and received $86.00.[92]

Books and tracts were distributed by the Presbyterian missionaries—even such secular works as a pamphlet on vaccination, two hundred and fifty copies of which were given in 1803 to the General Assembly by a group of Philadelphia citizens, the "friends of humanity," whose object was to hasten *"the total extermination of that loathsome*

---

[87] The instruction to the Committee to correspond with "all other persons on missionary business" was not interpreted in a narrow sectarian sense. A long and friendly letter from Ashbel Green, Chairman of the Committee, was printed in the *Massachusetts Baptist Missionary Magazine*, I (1804), 80-83.

[88] *Extracts from the Minutes of the General Assembly of the Presbyterian Church in the United States of America, A.D. 1802* (Philadelphia, 1802), 14.

[89] *Ibid.*, 14.

[90] *Extracts from the Minutes of the General Assembly of the Presbyterian Church in the United States of America: From A.D. 1803 to A. D. 1811* (Philadelphia, 1813), II, 323.

[91] The Treasurer's report in 1810 gives an interesting sidelight on banking conditions in the United States; he said he had experienced considerable embarrassment in consequence of members of remote presbyteries bringing all kinds of banknotes, some of which were not negotiable in Philadelphia. Of the money received at that session, he said that 20 dollars were counterfeit, 51 were doubtful, 55 were from unincorporated banks, and 16 were supposed to be good, but were from such distant banks that they were not negotiable. *Ibid.*, 277.

[92] E. H. Gillett, *History of the Presbyterian Church* (Philadelphia, [1864]), I, 461.

and fatal disease, the small-pox."[93] In 1805 it was recommended to the Committee of Missions that it publish a magazine "sacred to religion and morals," and devote the profits, if any, to the support of missions. Apparently there were no profits; publication was suspended in 1810.[94]

In addition to the men commissioned by the General Assembly, several missionaries were sent out annually by the various synods, especially by those of the Carolinas, Virginia, and Pittsburgh. Some of the first Presbyterian Churches in Kentucky were formed as a result of the missionary work of the Synod of Virginia. The Western Missionary Society of New Jersey, which was formed in 1800, conducted its missionary operations independently of the General Assembly.[95]

In 1816 the growing importance of home missions was recognized among the Presbyterians by the substitution of a Board of Missions for the Standing Committee.[96] To the new board was given full power to transact all missionary business, subject, of course, to review by the Assembly. It was believed by many Presbyterians that this method of conducting the missionary activities of the Church was more satisfactory than dependence upon voluntary societies not directly under ecclesiastical control. It was pointed out that the Board of Missions could act with all the vigor and unity of design that would be found in a society created especially to promote missions, while at the same time it would enjoy the benefit of the advice and counsel of the General Assembly.[97] On the other hand, there were some members of the Presbyterian Church who preferred to act through voluntary societies. The most important of these, after its organization in 1826, was the American Home Missionary Society. But it was the agency chiefly used by the Congregationalists. Thus was raised the question of the

---

[93] *Extracts from the Minutes of the General Assembly . . . 1803 to . . . 1811*, II, 17.

[94] E. L. Gillett, *History of the Presbyterian Church*, I, 442.

[95] Ashbel Green, *Historical Sketch or Compendious View of Domestic and Foreign Missions in the Presbyterian Church* (Philadelphia, 1838), 21-22.

[96] *Historical Sketch of the Board of Home Missions of the Presbyterian Church . . . 1802-1888*, in *Addresses Delivered at The Centennial Celebration of the General Assembly* (Philadelphia, 1888), 7.

[97] *Extracts from the Minutes of the General Assembly . . . 1816*, 307-08.

relationship between these two denominations on the mission field. In the period here under consideration the main
effort to bring about harmonious relations between Presbyterians and Congregationalists on the frontiers was
known as the Plan of Union.

THE PLAN OF UNION

In the closing years of the eighteenth and early years
of the nineteenth centuries the Presbyterian Church maintained close relations with other Calvinistic religious groups
in America. At the General Assembly in 1799 plans were
presented for intercourse with the Reformed Dutch Church
and the Associate Reformed Church, and delegates were
sent to and received from Congregational Associations in
New England. This friendly attitude made possible the
Plan of Union. Calvinistic Presbyterians and Congregationalists met on the frontier; missionaries of both persua-
sions were sometimes laboring in the same field; rival
churches holding doctrines that were practically the same,
and differing only in their form of church government,
were established in the same frontier community—and
often, too, in one in which it was hard to keep even one
church alive. Moreover, in spite of their differences Presbyterians and Congregationalists had enough in common to
create a bond of sympathy between them as opposed to their
other ecclesiastical rivals in the West. To promote harmony
and union between Presbyterians and Congregationalists
in the new settlements, a plan of co-operation was adopted
in 1801 by the General Assembly of the Presbyterian Church
and the General Association of Connecticut. It contem-
plated the establishment of three types of churches in the
new settlements: those that were entirely Presbyterian;
those that were purely Congregational; and those that combined the two systems of church organization. Stated briefly,
the terms of the Plan were as follows: missionaries were
enjoined to promote friendly relations between the Presbyterians and the Congregationalists; a Congregational or
Presbyterian church might settle a minister of the opposite
polity without surrendering its own method of church organization and discipline, but in case of a dispute between
such a minister and his own church, or any member of it,
the matter was to be referred either to the Presbytery or
the Association to which the minister belonged, or to a joint

council composed of both Congregationalists and Presbyterians; mixed churches, or those made up of both orders, were to be governed by a standing committee of members, Presbyterians having the right to appeal to the Presbytery, and Congregationalists to the body of male communicants of the church.[98]

To understand the spirit in which this agreement was made, it should be remembered that in the half century following the Great Awakening the conservative party in New England Congregationalism had been growing away from the liberal group and coming into closer relationship with the Presbyterians. Eastern New England tended to be liberal; western Massachusetts and Connecticut were conservative. Interest in doctrine supplanted interest in church polity. Because of essential doctrinal agreement the people of western New England came to regard the differences in polity between Presbyterianism and the Consociationism of Connecticut as immaterial; and, indeed, the Connecticut churches at this time were often referred to by their own pastors and members as Presbyterian.[99] Furthermore, it was assumed by many in New England that Congregationalism would not thrive in the West, since it was thought to be a form of church organization especially adapted to the compact type of town settlement which prevailed in New England. A stronger form of church government such as Presbyterianism provided was thought necessary for the more sparsely populated frontier communities. The later development of Congregationalism in the West has shown that such fears were groundless, but their prevalence in the early part of the nineteenth century was one of the influences which tended to increase Presbyterianism beyond the Hudson at the expense of Congregationalism. It should also be borne in mind that most of the New Englanders of this generation had been trained in towns or villages in which there was normally but one church, and that this was usually spoken of as the "Church of Christ" rather than the "Congregational Church." In such communities there had been no occasion to stress the differences between denominations; consequently, it was

[98] W. Walker, *Creeds and Platforms of Congregationalism*, 530-31; for documents on the working of the Plan, see W. W. Sweet, *Religion on the American Frontier ... Presbyterians*, 464-549.

[99] W. Walker, *History of the Congregational Churches*, 314-16.

comparatively easy for men so trained to affiliate in the West with other religious bodies holding similar beliefs.[100] Under such circumstances Congregationalism was likened to a river which took its origin in New England and flowed into a Presbyterian ocean in the West.

The Plan of Union had important consequences for both the participating denominations. Although the provisions of the Plan were identical with respect to both, it operated in favor of the Presbyterians. The center of their strength in the Middle States was nearer the scene of missionary labors; their denominational spirit was stronger than that of the Congregationalists; and their presbyteries, which were rapidly formed on the missionary field, provided centers of fellowship in which missionaries found a welcome. For the Congregationalists it meant the loss of many churches in the West—more than two thousand, according to one oft-quoted estimate.[101] This figure is probably much too large;[102] but as Congregational self-consciousness grew, the feeling that many Western congregations that had been founded by New Englanders had taken the Presbyterian name led to such pungent comments as that of the speaker at the Albany Conference of 1852 who said, "they have milked our Congregational cows, but have made nothing but Presbyterian butter and cheese."[103] The Congregational loss was the Presbyterian gain; but before a quarter of a century had passed conservative Presbyterians had come to regard it as a doubtful blessing, because it had introduced into their Western churches many preachers and laymen whose peculiar brand of Calvinism they came to distrust, and to whom they attributed, in some instances, the desire to subvert Presbyterianism. The result of this well-intentioned attempt at harmony was ultimately discord and strife, especially among the Presbyterians, where the presence in the Western churches of men trained as Congregationalists was a contributory cause of the division into "Old School" and "New School" in 1837. Nevertheless the Plan of Union rested on a sound idea—the desirability of decreasing the number of competing churches in the new settlements.

---

[100] L. W. Bacon, *History of American Christianity*, 138.

[101] W. Walker, *History of the Congregational Churches*, 318.

[102] R. H. Nichols, "The Plan of Union in New York," *Church History*, V (1936), 30.

[103] W. Walker, *Creeds and Platforms of Congregationalism*, 533.

THE BAPTISTS

Among the Baptists, as well as among the Presbyterians and Congregationalists, the early years of the nineteenth century were marked by efforts to co-ordinate and systematize missionary endeavors. In place of the sporadic missionary journeys of a Hezekiah Smith, a John Gano, or an Isaac Backus, local missionary societies were formed to send the gospel to the frontiers. The most important of these early Baptist organizations was the one formed in Massachusetts in 1802 "to furnish occasional preaching, and to promote knowledge of evangelistic truth in the new settlements within these United States; or further, if circumstances should render it proper."[104] The field of operations of this society was principally the frontier section of New England, eastern Maine, Vermont, and northern New Hampshire, but men were also sent to New York, Pennsylvania, and Canada. At the first meeting of the trustees two men were instructed to make a tour to Maine and the British Provinces, and one was appointed to the "Western Mission." It was voted at this meeting that each missionary be allowed traveling expenses (he finding his own horse) and five dollars a week as compensation for his labor, but that all money he might collect or receive as a gift should be accounted for to the trustees.[105]

In 1801 the Shaftsbury Association of Baptist Churches in Vermont and northeastern New York, having become interested in missions in the "Far West," voted to recommend to the churches that they consider maturely the raising of a fund for missionary purposes. Money was contributed as requested; when they met in 1802 a Board of Missions was created to take charge of the contributions, select missionaries, and decide where they should labor.[106] The amount of money at the disposal of the Board was small, less than two hundred dollars annually, but with it provision was made for the visit of two or three ministers each year to the new settlements in central and western New York and upper Canada. In 1803, for example, two

---

[104] The constitution is in *Massachusetts Baptist Missionary Magazine*, I (1803), 5-7.

[105] W. A. Eaton, *Historical Sketch of the Massachusetts Baptist Missionary Society and Convention* (Boston, [1903]), 13.

[106] S. Wright, *History of the Shaftsbury Baptist Association* (Troy, N. Y., 1858), 80-88.

men, Elders Warren and Covell, went into western New York as far as Buffalo village.[107] From 1802 to 1817 thirty-one missionary appointments were made, mainly to western New York and upper Canada; there is no record of any appointment after 1817, but money was collected thereafter —a few hundred dollars each year—and sent to the Baptist Board for Foreign Missions.[108] It is significant that among Baptists generally about this time home missions were being overshadowed by a growing interest in the newly developing foreign field.

As early as 1800 the question of the propriety of forming a missionary society was raised in the Philadelphia Baptist Association; in 1802 a committee was appointed to form a plan, and in 1803 the plan was approved and recommended to the churches.[109] The amount of money available was small, being only $121.28 in the first year (1804).[110] In 1810 seven missionaries were sent out on tours, four of them to western Pennsylvania and Ohio.[111] In 1804 the Maine Baptist Missionary Association was formed as an outgrowth of the Gospel Mission Plan adopted by the Bowdoinham Association in 1799.[112] The Baptists of New York, who had co-operated for several years in missionary work with Presbyterians, withdrew from the union organization in 1806 and formed a denominational society which devoted its attention chiefly to the needs of New York and Canada.[113] Still another local society among New York Baptists was that formed in Onandaga County in 1807 under the name of the Lake Baptist Missionary Society. Two years later its name was changed to the Hamilton Missionary Society. Auxiliary to it was a woman's organization which is remembered among Baptists for its gift to the parent society in 1812 of twenty yards of fulled cloth—a product of the

---

107 C. W. Brooks, *Century of Missions in the Empire State* (Philadelphia, 1909), 37; S. Wright, *History of the Shaftsbury Baptist Association*, 90.

108 S. Wright, *History of Shaftsbury Baptist Association*, 369-70.

109 *Minutes of the Philadelphia Baptist Association*, 350, 370, 381.

110 *Ibid.*, 395.

111 A. L. Vail, *Morning Hour of American Baptist Missions*, 113.

112 J. Millet, *History of the Baptists in Maine* (Portland, 1845), 425-26; H. S. Burrage, *History of the Baptists in Maine* (Portland, 1904), 108.

113 D. Benedict, *General History of the Baptist Denomination in America*, II, 441.

loving toil of its members.[114] Many other missionary societies were formed among Baptist women about this time, usually under the name of Female Cent or Female Mite Societies.[115] Perhaps the most noteworthy of these women's organizations was the Boston Female Society for Missionary Purposes, which was formed in 1800 by Baptist and Congregational women; as stated above, it was the first woman's missionary society in America.

From this brief sketch of the more important Baptist home missionary undertakings in the first decade of the nineteenth century it will be observed that there was a striking similarity between the developments in the Baptist and Congregational denominations. In both, it was a period in which many local societies were formed; in both, pastors were sent on short tours to the frontiers; in both, New England was the chief center of missionary enthusiasm.

The formation in 1814 of the General Baptist Convention was an important landmark in the missionary history of this denomination. A union of Baptists for missionary purposes was bound to come sooner or later, but it was hastened by the return to the United States in 1813 of Luther Rice, who came to ask the support of American Baptists for the missionary activities in India of Adoniram Judson and himself. These men, after having been sent out as foreign missionaries by the American Board of Commissioners for Foreign Missions, adopted Baptist principles and naturally turned to that denomination for assistance. When news of the step taken by Judson and Rice reached Boston, a "Baptist Society for Propagating the Gospel in India and other Foreign Parts" was formed. In February, 1814, Rice met the managers of this new society, and was appointed by them to travel in the middle and southern states in an effort to arouse the Baptists to their opportunities and responsibilities in the foreign field. In May, 1814, delegates from Baptist missionary societies and churches met in Philadelphia and organized the "General Missionary Convention of the Baptist Denomination

---

[114] H. L. Morehouse, "Historical Sketch of the American Baptist Home Mission Society for Fifty Years," in *Baptist Home Missions in North America* (New York, 1883), 293-94.

[115] A. L. Vail, *Morning Hour of American Baptist Missions*, 127-37, lists forty-three such societies which were formed between 1802 and 1814.

in the United States of America for Foreign Missions";
owing to the fact that it met every third year it was generally known as the Triennial Convention. This Philadelphia
meeting is of especial significance to American Baptists because it was their first general assemblage. Luther Rice's
interest was primarily in foreign missions, but he realized
that adequate support for these could come only from a
strong and vigorous denomination at home. Consequently
he urged the development of domestic missionary work
also; to him more than to any other man the Baptist denomination owes the organization of its home missionary
work.[116] At the second meeting of the Triennial Convention (1817), its constitution was so amended as to allow
domestic as well as foreign missionary work. An appropriation of a thousand dollars was made to defray the expenses
of John M. Peck, of Connecticut, and James E. Welch, of
Kentucky, on a mission to Missouri. In addition to regular
ministerial labors among the white settlers, they were instructed to establish schools and to pay particular attention
to the neighboring Indians, "the Fox, the Osage, the
Kanses."[117] Thus for the first time did the Baptist denomination as a whole assume responsibility for home missions.

It took Peck and his family 129 days to make the journey
from Connecticut to St. Louis in 1817 by way of Philadelphia and the Ohio River. Twenty-two of these days
were spent in going from Shawneetown, Illinois, to the
Mississippi River and up that stream to St. Louis. The
delay was due partly to wind and rain and partly to the
caution required in navigating the Mississippi, since this
was only the third time a steamer had made its way as far
north as St. Louis.[118] Peck did not confine his activities to
that city; he made many trips out into the surrounding
country both in Missouri and Illinois, preaching, organizing churches, and encouraging education. Peck had found
missionary ground. Concerning the schools he observed on
one trip out from St. Louis, he said that "at least three-
fourths of all the masters and schools were public nuisances,

116 J. B. Taylor, *Memoir of Rev. Luther Rice* (Baltimore, 1840), 296.

117 *American Baptist Magazine*, N. S., I (1817), 190.

118 A. K. de Blois and L. C. Barnes, *John Mason Peck* (New York,.
1917), 24-25.

and ought to have been indicted by the Grand Jury."[119] In describing conditions as he found them in the vicinity of St. Francois in 1818, he wrote:

> The people throughout these extreme frontier settlements were quite ignorant: few could read, and fewer had Bibles. They knew not the name of a single missionary on earth, and could not comprehend the reasons why money should be raised for the expenses, or why ministers should leave their own neighborhood to preach the gospel to the destitute. They manifested the same apathy in their worldly business. A small corn field and a truck patch was the height of their ambition. Venison, bear-meat and hog-meat dressed and cooked in the most slovenly and filthy manner, with corn-bread baked in the form of a pone, and when cold as hard as a brick-bat constituted their provisions. Coffee and tea were prohibited articles among their class; for had they possessed the articles, not one woman in ten knew how to cook them. Not a school had existed. A kind of half-savage life appeared to be their choice.[120]

In 1820, just at the time Peck was getting his work in Missouri well under way, the Baptist General Convention voted to close its Western mission among the whites and instructed him to move to an Indian mission at Fort Wayne. Mr. Peck refused to comply with the order on the ground that the work he had started at St. Louis was too important to be thus lightly cast aside, and because of his conviction that missions to the whites were essential in order to provide a proper foundation for Indian missions.[121] For several years he continued his work in Missouri supported only by the meager voluntary contributions of the people among whom he preached. In 1824 he received a commission from the Massachusetts Baptist Missionary Society, under whose direction he continued his work, with slight interruptions, until the formation of the American Baptist Home Mission Society in 1832.[122]

THE METHODISTS

Among the Methodists, in the opening years of the nineteenth century, there was nothing to correspond to the many local missionary societies which were then being formed

---

[119] R. Babcock, *Memoir of John Mason Peck*, 100.

[120] R. Babcock, *op. cit.*, 122.

[121] J. M. Peck, St. Charles, Mo., Aug. 1, 1819, to Isaac McCoy, McCoy MSS., I, No. 83, in Kansas State Historical Society.

[122] For a fuller treatment of Peck's work in the West, see below, page 201 ff.

among the Presbyterians, the Congregationalists, and the Baptists. This was not the result of any lack of interest in missions on the part of the followers of John Wesley; it was rather due to the fact that the Methodist Episcopal Church had not yet felt the need for a missionary organization separate from the Church itself. Every Conference was virtually a home missionary society; every itinerant, a missionary.[123]

The system of itinerant preaching used by the Methodists was well adapted to the needs of the frontier. Sparseness of settlement and the poverty of the people made it difficult if not impossible for the average backwoods community to support a minister, while, on the other hand, it was only by scattering their energies over a wide area that the relatively small number of preachers could reach the people with their message. The chief weakness in the occasional or sporadic missionary tour was that there was no satisfactory method of conserving the good accomplished by the itinerant. The Methodists saw to it that there was a Paul to reap where Apollos had planted and Cephas had watered—only with them the Apollos who planted usually came back in a month to water, and then in another month to reap. The Methodist itinerant was normally a circuit rider; when he preached in a community he ordinarily announced the exact day of his next visit, perhaps a month or six weeks later, and he was usually there just as he had promised. The Methodist traveling preachers won an enviable reputation throughout the West for dependability and punctuality. As Atkinson said:

> The early itinerants became familiar figures on the highways of the country. The grave, earnest countenance, the straight-breasted coat, the oil-skin covering of the hat, the leather saddle-bags, and the staid gait of the horse denoted the Methodist preacher, and usually they were "recognized by all that ever beheld or heard of one about as far as they were to be seen." Such was their faithfulness in filling

---

[123] Inasmuch as there are several good accounts of the methods and characteristics of Methodist circuit riders, the subject is treated here in summary fashion. See, among others, W. W. Sweet, *Rise of Methodism in the West* (Nashville, 1920), 11-70; W. B. Posey, *Development of Methodism in the Old Southwest* (Tuscaloosa, Ala., 1933); W. M. Gewehr, "Some Factors in the Expansion of Frontier Methodism, 1800-1811," *Journal of Religion*, VIII (1928), 98-120.

their appointments in the wide territory of their circuits that of a "bitterly cold winter it became almost a proverbial saying, 'There is nothing out today but crows and Methodist preachers.' "[124]

The circuit riders were usually young men. There was no rule of the Church to keep them from marrying, but their migratory habits and meager salaries acted as deterrents from matrimony. Bishop Asbury, who never married, encouraged celibacy among itinerants because he feared that as soon as they took wives they would wish to settle down or would be tempted to eke out their small incomes by secular employment. He noted with satisfaction that at the Virginia Conference of 1809 there were only three married preachers among the eighty-four present. In the light of the trouble produced among the Methodists when one of Asbury's successors in the episcopate, Bishop Andrews, married a slave owner, the comment the former made in his *Journal* at the time of this Virginia Conference is interesting:

The high taste of these southern folk will not permit their families to be degraded by an alliance with a Methodist traveling preacher; and thus, involuntary celibacy is imposed upon us; all the better— care and anxiety about worldly possessions do not stop us in our course, and we are saved from the pollution of negro slavery and oppression.[125]

Certainly circuit riders in general were not overburdened with worldly possessions. "The people are taught to believe," one of them said, "that the Methodist preachers are neither avaricious or extravagant, and they are taught truly. As a body there are no men in America, perhaps in the world, who live at so little expense, and are more economical in expending the donations of the generous benefactor."[126] Whether generous or not, the donations they received were usually small. Peter Cartwright, one of the best-known of the Western itinerants, reported that he received forty dollars for his work in the year 1806, but that many of the circuit riders did not receive half that amount; at another time he found himself, at the close of a period of hard work in a difficult Ohio circuit, five hundred miles

---

[124] J. Atkinson, *Centennial History of American Methodism* (New York, 1884), 164-65.

[125] F. Asbury, *Journal*, III, 257.

[126] J. Atkinson, *Centennial History of American Methodism*, 148.

from home, his horse gone blind, his saddle worn out, his clothes patched until it was difficult to detect the original cloth, and in his pocket seventy-five cents.[127] William Burke, a Kentucky circuit rider, in commenting on the state of his wardrobe, said: "My clothes were nearly all gone. I had patch upon patch, and patch by patch, and I received only money sufficient to buy a waistcoat, and not enough of that to pay for the making, during the two quarters I remained on the circuit."[128] William Moss, in his eleven years of itinerancy (1778-89) in Virginia and the Carolinas, received a total of $493, an average of less than $45 per year.[129] Whatever faults they may have had, such men were not hirelings.

Living as they did in the midst of rough frontier society, occasionally in peril from Indians[130] and wild beasts, and continually exposed to the inclemencies of the weather, the itinerants were necessarily exponents of a muscular Christianity. It was no time or place for physical weaklings. Peter Cartwright could handle a bully as well as he could preach damnation to sinners, or dispute with Baptists about immersion. While he was on the Scioto circuit in Ohio a crowd of lewd and base fellows, armed with dirks, clubs, knives, and horsewhips came to one of his camp meetings, swearing that they would break it up. When the dust of battle cleared away thirty of the rowdies found themselves in the custody of the preacher and his supporters.[131] Such stories of circuit-rider prowess, which probably lost nothing in the retelling, were common in the early days of the West; not infrequently after the villain had been soundly thrashed by the minister, he was converted. Perhaps the bullies had been misled by the sanctimonious demeanor of the Methodist ministers. Their appearance suggested sobriety and piety, and most of them, no doubt, were puritanical in their conduct. Not all, however, had attained to sainthood, if the references in the conference records to complaints about and investigations of immoral or unseemly

---

127 P. Cartwright, *Autobiography*, 96-102.

128 J. B. Finley, *Sketches of Western Methodism*, 41.

129 J. Atkinson, *Centennial History of American Methodism*, 148.

130 L. Garrett, *Recollections of the West* (Nashville, 1834), 96-97.

131 P. Cartwright, *Autobiography*, 90-92; there are many references to encounters with rowdies in this book, *e.g.*, 60-61, 131, 142, 223, 229, 236, 270, 321.

conduct on the part of some of the brethren are a basis for judgment.[132] But they were honest and frank with one another, and probably inquired into actions that among others would have passed without notice.

Frank as were these preachers in pointing out faults one to another, they were equally direct in telling the men of the world about their sins. They were democratic in their denunciations, convinced as they were that God is no respecter of persons. Once when Peter Cartwright was opening a church service General Andrew Jackson entered the building. Another preacher, awed by the presence of this great man, pulled Cartwright's coat and whispered, "General Jackson has come in; General Jackson has come in." In indignation Cartwright said so audibly that Jackson and the remainder of the congregation could hear him: "Who is General Jackson? If he don't get his soul converted, God will damn him as quick as he would a Guinea negro!" That was both good religion and good frontier doctrine, and next day the general told the preacher that he was a man after his own heart.[133]

Of formal instruction or "book learning" the Methodist itinerants usually had but little. They attended the hard school of experience and were apt pupils. They learned to preach by preaching. Their theology, which was on the whole simple and direct, they got by reading their Bibles, by conversation with their elders in the ministry, and from reflection, for which they had abundant opportunity on their lonely rides through the sparsely populated country. When lack of learning was urged as an objection to the admission of a young man to the itineracy, Bishop Asbury was wont to reply that "the saddle-bags were the best school for traveling preachers." It must not be thought from this that the Methodist circuit riders did not have access to books. Indeed, the distribution of books and pamphlets was one of their duties. The General Conference of 1796 announced that since the propagation of religious knowledge by means of the press is next in importance to preaching the gospel, pastors should give their deepest attention to the distribution of pious and useful books. Four years later

---

[132] W. W. Sweet, *Rise of Methodism in the West*, 86, 97, 111, 126, 130, 159, 179, 200, 203, for cases of investigation and discipline taken from the Journal of the Western Conference, 1800-11.

[133] P. Cartwright, *Autobiography*, 192-93.

the injunction was made more specific; the General Conference of 1800 announced that "it shall be the duty of every preacher, who has charge of a circuit, to see that his circuit be duly supplied with books, and to take charge of all books sent to . . . his circuit and account with the presiding elder for the same."[134] Messrs. Mills and Smith, in their journey through the West in 1814 for the Massachusetts Missionary Society, noted especially the activity of the Methodists in the distribution of books. Their comment was that the work of the Methodists in this respect "puts to blush all other charitable institutions in the United States."[135]

The gatherings of the Methodist preachers in their annual and general conferences were occasions of rejoicing and refreshing for weary warriors. After weeks or months of hardships, long hours of solitary journeys through the wilderness, and many conflicts with the Devil, the itinerants came together for fellowship and inspiration. They embraced one another and wept for joy when they met. They shed tears of sorrow when the time for parting came. Having received their assignments from the bishop or the presiding elder, they went back to the field of battle shouting their praises of the Lord God of Hosts.

It is doubtful if a missionary system better adapted to the needs of the frontier in the early part of the nineteenth century could have been found than that used by the Methodist Episcopal Church. The settlements were widely scattered; the people generally had not the means, and frequently not the desire, to call and settle ministers in their midst. The circuit rider did not wait for a call—he sought the people. Church buildings were rarely found, but that did not hinder the work of the itinerant; the cabin of a friendly settler would do at the outset. "Indeed, the Methodists were slow in securing houses of worship; they depended upon the cabins of settlers as preaching places long after the Baptists and Presbyterians had begun the erection of substantial buildings."[136] The Methodist circuit riders were the advance guard of American Christianity in

---

[134] Methodist Episcopal Church, *Journals of the General Conference* (New York, 1855), I, 17, 45.

[135] S. J. Mills and Daniel Smith, *Report of a Missionary Tour*, 49.

[136] W. W. Sweet, "The Coming of the Circuit Rider Across the Mountains," in *Miss. Val. Hist. Asso. Proceedings*, 1916-17, 280-81.

the occupation of the West. The Methodists have probably influenced the lives of more persons than any other Protestant body in America, and, what is equally important, their influence was exerted in the formative period in countless frontier communities.

The system of circuit riders did not, however, necessarily imply any particular concern for the West on the part of the East. But among a people so filled with missionary enthusiasm as the Methodists that was bound to manifest itself. It had definitely appeared by 1812; for in the General Conference of that year each annual conference was authorized to raise a fund for affording supplies for missionary purposes,[137] and Bishop Asbury himself took subscriptions for the purpose of securing money to finance the itinerants on some of the frontiers.[138]

THE EPISCOPALIANS

In the colonial period the Church of England had played an important part in missionary work in America through the Society for the Propagation of the Gospel. The Revolutionary War left the Protestant Episcopal Church in the United States weak and discredited on account of its supposed English tendencies. Accustomed to state support, it had to adjust itself suddenly to the voluntary system; cherishing an elaborate and beautiful ritual, it had to win tolerance from a Puritan opposition which professed to see therein signs of "Popery"; handicapped somewhat as the heir of colonial Anglicanism, it had to live down memories of moral laxness on the part of some of its clergy; inclined to formalism, it had to arouse an interest in religion among its people generally. All this took time. After the establishment of the American episcopate late in the eighteenth century, the Church slowly regained its prestige, but its strength continued to lie mainly in the older parts of the seaboard states. At a time when the other denominations were engaged in extending their borders in the West, the Episcopal Church did little missionary work in any organized manner. Joseph Doddridge, a pioneer Episcopal minister in Ohio, as early as 1818 called attention to the

---

137 Missionary Society, Methodist Episcopal Church, *Fortieth Annual Report* (1859), 51. (Abbreviated hereafter as M.S.M.E.Ch.).

138 M.S.M.E.Ch., *Forty-fifth Annual Report* (1864), 77.

indifference of his denomination to the West. "To the Presbyterians alone," he said, "we [of the West] are indebted for almost the whole of our literature. . . . Were it not for the herculean labors of the Methodist society, many of our remote settlements would have been at this day almost in a state of barbarism. . . . The Roman Catholic clergy, without making any ostentatious parade, are traversing every part of the country, carrying the ministry to almost every family of their people."[139]

But even while Dr. Doddridge was complaining about the lack of missionary zeal in the Episcopal Church, a new spirit was appearing. In place of a Bishop Provoost who resigned his episcopate in 1801 to busy himself with a translation of Tasso and the study of botany, such men as Bishop Hobart in New York, Bishop Moore in Virginia, and Bishop Griswold in New England assumed the leadership in the Church, with the result that evangelism and moral earnestness received more attention from the clergy themselves.[140] After 1814 diocesan reports to the General Convention tell of missionary work in the various dioceses; missionaries were employed in western New York; in Pennsylvania the Society for the Advancement of Christianity was formed in order to send missionaries beyond the Alleghenies. The first missionary employed by this Society was Jackson Kemper,[141] a man whose later activities in the West did much to regain for the Episcopal Church the position of influence it had temporarily lost.

The local society, sending out pastors on short missionary tours, was the normal agency through which home missionary work was carried on in the early part of the nineteenth century. But these local societies were often local only in name; many of them were national in their interests and activities. The Missionary Society of Connecticut, as was shown above, sent men as far west as Missouri. However, as each of these societies widened the scope of its interests, the danger of duplication of work increased. It

---

[139] Doddridge, "Memoir of the Rev. Dr. Joseph Doddridge," in J. Doddridge, *Notes on the Settlement and Indian Wars* . . . , (New ed., Albany, 1876), 20-21.

[140] H. B. Burleson, *Conquest of the Continent*, 40-47.

[141] See below, page 262 ff.

was becoming evident that co-ordination of effort was desirable, especially among religious groups that had as much in common as did the Presbyterians and the Congregationalists. It was for this purpose that the American Home Missionary Society, the origin of which will be described in the next chapter, was formed. Expanding needs and a growing sense of nationalism led naturally to the substitution of national for local agencies of control.

CHAPTER VI

FORMATION OF NATIONAL SOCIETIES, 1820-35

We are great, and rapidly—I was about to say fearfully—growing. This ... is our pride and danger—our weakness and our strength.— *John C. Calhoun.*

THE FIRST FOUR DECADES of the nineteenth century witnessed an amazing transformation in the size and power of the United States and in the spirit of its people. In 1800, despite the diplomatic achievements and the domestic triumphs of the Washington administration (1789-97), the new American Republic was still a puny youngster among the nations of the earth. Although its western boundary extended to the Mississippi River, its right to navigate the lower stretches of that stream depended on the whims of Spain. In respect to the Napoleonic wars in Europe it found itself between the upper and nether millstones; it was flouted by France and bullied by England. It had achieved political independence, but had not disentangled itself entirely from the European state system; and whether or not it could do so was a question to which the events antecedent to the War of 1812 gave temporarily a negative answer. But weak as was its political strength, the United States had more nearly attained to independence there by the beginning of the nineteenth century than in the realm of economics. It was still largely dependent on Europe for manufactured articles on the one hand and for markets for its raw products on the other. The Republic of the United States of America had not yet passed beyond the experimental stage; it had not yet won for itself absolutely the right to claim allegiance above that due from citizens to their several states. The sense of nationalism was weak.

NATIONALISM

By the end of the War of 1812 a new period in American history had started. The purchase of Louisiana (1803) and

the acquisition of Florida (1819) not only gave to Americans uninterrupted access to the Gulf of Mexico but also plenty of elbow room in the West. The War of 1812 had stimulated nationalism and aroused patriotic sentiments; furthermore, the obstructive policies of New England during the conflict had served, for the time being, to bring discredit upon narrow sectionalism. For a few years it seemed that the chief political leaders were more concerned about the welfare of the country as a whole than they were in sectional rivalries and advantages. This was the time when Henry Clay was developing his "American System," while John C. Calhoun, of South Carolina, in his desire to bind the country together, proposed the construction of roads and canals by the Federal Government. In the same period the Supreme Court under the leadership of John Marshall was handing down great nationalistic decisions in such famous cases as *McCullough* v. *Maryland, Gibbons* v. *Ogden,* and *Cohens* v. *Virginia.* Moreover, after the War of 1812, the end of which was synchronous with the conclusion of the long Napoleonic struggle in Europe, the people of the United States tended to lose interest in the Old World and its affairs; they turned their backs on Europe and faced the West. Their concern was now primarily in their own country; their engrossing problems included such purely domestic questions as internal improvements, the disposal of the public domain, banking and currency, and slavery. The War had stimulated the development of manufacturing in this country; and now the new infant industries, partially successful in their clamor for a high protective tariff, began not only to consume a larger share of the raw products of the land, but also to satisfy to a greater extent the American demand for manufactured goods.

Furthermore, the people of the new republic were buoyant, optimistic, proud. They felt that national honor had been vindicated by the War. The disasters and scandals of the conflict were conveniently forgotten; its victories were magnified until the Americans came to believe that they had soundly "licked the British" and forced them to respect their rights on the high seas. A spirit of spread-eagle patriotism swept over the land. Fourth-of-July orators called up memories of a glorious past, extolled the virtues of the present, and prophesied wonders for the future. And why not? After due allowance has been made for the

bumptious egotism of youth or the chauvinism of misdirected patriotism, the fact remains that any thoughtful man who looked at the boundless resources of the United States, the excellence of its government, and the character of its citizens, was justified in predicting a great and happy future for the American people. It was not by chance that the most famous pronouncement in the whole foreign policy of the United States, President Monroe's doctrine of America for Americans, should have been made in 1823 at a time when the tide of nationalism was running high.

THE NEW WEST

Of the many forces that helped produce this changed outlook, one of the most important was the growth of the West. As stated above, settlers poured into the Mississippi Valley in such numbers after the War of 1812 that Indiana, Mississippi, Illinois, Alabama, and Missouri were brought into the Union between 1816 and 1821. In all these new states there was still so much vacant land during the 1820's and 1830's that they were filled with busy, hustling frontier communities as the pioneers pushed in. Indiana's population of 147,000 in 1820 had grown to 685,000 in 1840; Illinois had 55,000 persons within its borders in 1820 and 476,000 twenty years later; in the same score of years the population of Missouri expanded from 66,000 to 383,000; that of Alabama from 127,000 to 500,000. During the same period settlers moved into the lower valley of the Arkansas and its tributaries in such numbers as to make a new state there in 1836; while Michigan, with settlements only in its southern end, was ready for statehood in the following year.

These were states; perhaps their orators referred to them as Sovereign States, but it can hardly be emphasized too strongly that they were frontier states. Even Ohio, which had been in the Union since 1803, still gave the impression of rawness and newness in 1830. A visitor from New York wrote:

... My anticipations were probably not singular, but they were erroneous, as to the proportion of agricultural cultivation already attained in the western states.—Knowing that the present population of Ohio, for instance, is estimated at about 1,000,000, I had expected to find the country more extensively cleared and occupied that it is, and as I passed through the northern and central part of the State, and beheld how few and small are the openings in the great wilderness

that remains yet to be subdued, and how everything in the appearance of farms, buildings, villages, roads, &c. bears the aspect of incipiency, I could hardly persuade myself that this was really the *great and powerful state of Ohio.* ... [1]

The West was raw and crude; it had been and still was remote from the East, but every year saw new ties drawn between it and the Atlantic seaboard. Better means of transportation were both a cause and an effect of the settlement of the West. Turnpikes, steamboats on the western rivers, the Erie Canal, and later the railroads made it easier for settlers to reach the new lands in the interior; as western communities developed they clamored for and sometimes obtained the internal improvements which they believed would—and often did—add to the population of their towns and counties and enhance the value of their lands. A nation was being born in a day.

The economic prosperity of the United States has been based to a great extent on the natural resources of the West: *there* were to be found raw materials in abundance for Eastern and even European factories; *there* were expanding markets for the products of the industrial section; *there* was a region whose wishes had to be taken into account in the formation of national policies. "The rise of the new west," said Professor Frederick J. Turner, "was the most significant fact in American history in the years immediately following the War of 1812."[2]

The influence of this New West in the councils of the nation was growing about as rapidly as the number of its inhabitants. Out of the West had come a new group of leaders. The youthful Henry Clay, of Kentucky, an ardent patriot, was made Speaker of the House of Representatives on the eve of the War of 1812; Andrew Jackson, of Tennessee, was another natural leader of Western democracy. Political power as measured by representation in Congress and in the Electoral College was passing to the West. With a few exceptions the Congressional delegations of the old Eastern states remained stationary or even decreased in size, but the representation of the new Western states increased with each new apportionment of seats. The electoral votes of New Hampshire, Rhode Island, New Jersey,

---

[1] A. Peters, in *Home Missionary*, II (1830), 156.

[2] F. J. Turner, *Rise of the New West*, 67.

Maryland, North Carolina, and South Carolina were no larger at the election of 1824 than they had been in the election of 1812; Connecticut, Vermont, Delaware, and Virginia had each lost one vote in this period of twelve years; Massachusetts dropped from twenty-two to fifteen voices, but this was due mainly to the division of the Old Bay State by the admission of Maine; in the same twelve years Pennsylvania and New York, both of which were states with an extensive Western back-country, gained respectively three and seven votes in the Electoral College. Turning to the West, we find everywhere signs of expansion. The eight votes of Ohio in 1812 had grown to sixteen by 1824; Kentucky and Louisiana had each increased its voting strength by two; Tennessee had gained three. The five Western states admitted to the Union in the six years following the close of the War of 1812 each cast from three to five votes in the election of 1824. It required no great foresight to see that the time would soon come when the West would hold the balance of power in the nation.

What was the nature of this West? After due allowance has been made for exceptions and variations, it can be said that in general the conditions of life under which the pioneers of the first quarter of the nineteenth century lived tended to make them individualistic, democratic, and nationalistic. They were individualists because only those survived or got ahead in the race who were able to adapt themselves to changed environment, or who were able to meet on their own initiative the crises of pioneer life. They were individualists because the simplicity of life and the comparative isolation of the family did not compel that continual regulation of personal conduct in actions affecting others, without which urban life under modern conditions would be intolerable. If a frontiersman chose to drive his horse on the left-hand side of the trail or to turn his cart around in the middle of a "block" when he got to town, nobody cared; if he wanted to shout and sing in the middle of the night, there were no near neighbors to object; if he tossed the refuse from his kitchen out the front door, it was his own business. Of course, there were occasions when the inhabitants of the new communities worked together for the common good, as in log-rollings, cattle roundups, or in defense against attack; but by and large the frontier put a premium on individualism in conduct. Whether or not it

encouraged individualism in thought is another matter; the preponderance of evidence indicates that it did not.

The frontier was democratic. Distinctions based on birth counted for little in the West of this period; a man was judged mainly on the basis of his own ability. Distinctions based on wealth were relatively unimportant since all stood on essentially the same level of economic equality. There were few in the West who could be called rich. All were faced with the same problem of getting food and shelter in the wilderness. The frontier may have had its aristocracy, but it was an aristocracy of ability and skill as shown in those personal characteristics that best fitted men for life in a new country.

The frontier was nationalistic. The wrench of leaving the old home had torn loose the roots of state or local pride; sufficient time had not elapsed to allow them to dig far down into the soil of the new abode. The foreign-born, many of whom made their way to the West, had come to "America," rather than to a particular "sovereign state" in the Union. Furthermore, the people of the frontiers in their inability to carry out ambitious projects for internal improvements without help, or in their eagerness for cheap lands, or in the desire for greater protection against the Indians, were continually calling on the Federal Government to act in their behalf; such action might directly or indirectly tend to increase the powers and responsibilities of the government in Washington. The frontier, to quote Professor Frederick J. Turner again, was the most nationalistic part of America. But, it should be added, along with this nationalistic attitude with respect to the powers of the central government there went also a good deal of suspicion regarding the East and especially New England.

The New West, individualistic, democratic, and nationalistic, gave promise soon of controlling the nation. But what forces, what influences, what ideas, what ideals should control the West? That was the question to which thoughtful men in the East began to turn their attention. One of them, a seminary student, put the question in this form:

... The hundreds and thousands of populous towns and cities which stretch along the shores and cover the hills and vallies of the Atlantic states will soon cease to characterize our nation and sway its councils. They will soon come to be but a small minority compared with the millions that shall roll in wealth and luxury beyond the Alleghany,

and even beyond the Mississippi. Already is the influence of the West beginning to be strongly felt in our halls of national legislation. A few years and of those who represent our nation in our council chambers, the majority will come over the Alleghany:—a few years more and that majority will cross the Mississippi on their way. And with what character shall they come?[3]

"And with what character shall they come?" The home missionary movement was conceived and carried out for the purpose of giving to that question an answer acceptable to a large and influential class in the East.

TENDENCIES IN RELIGION

The revival in religion, which was noted in the preceding chapter, was still in progress through the decade of the thirties. It was a time of keen interest in religious questions. Denominational rivalries were strong, and there were many acrimonious disputes between the advocates of this or that road to heaven. Camp meetings were still being held on the frontiers, while "protracted meetings" were occasions for especial emphasis on religion in communities which had passed beyond frontier conditions. One of the most famous revival preachers of the time was Charles G. Finney, who encouraged the saints and scared the sinners in New York state and Ohio by his methods and language. His emphasis in preaching, as was usual at the time, was upon personal salvation, upon the acceptance of Christ in order to escape hell and reach heaven. Finney had a Calvinistic background, but in his preaching the old Calvinistic doctrines of predestination and election had been so modified that the responsibility for the soul's welfare rested squarely on the individual himself. Each person must choose where he would spend eternity. Typical of Finney's methods was his attempt to force an immediate decision upon the members of one unresponsive congregation in western New York. They were suddenly offered the choice of accepting Christ publicly in accordance with the plan of sal-

---

[3] John Maltby, "Connexion between Domestic Missions and the Political Prospects of Our Country," an Address before the Society of Inquiry respecting Missions, Andover Theological Seminary, 1825, MS. copy in Congregational Home Missionary Society archives (abbreviated hereafter as C.H.M.S.), New York, box No. 2. I have not found this MS. in A.H.M.S. papers, C.T.S., although there is there a torn copy (1825) sent as a letter to M. Bruen of the United Domestic Missionary Society in New York.

vation advocated by the preacher or rejecting Him. All who would make their peace with God by accepting Christ were told to stand up. Surprised, bewildered, hesitant, all in the congregation sat still. Finney fixed his penetrating gaze upon them and pronounced the words of doom: you have made your choice; you have rejected Christ; your sins are on your own heads. Then he abruptly left the pulpit and the building, leaving behind a shocked and awe-struck group of people. Many were in great distress, and one young woman, so it is said, was dumb with terror for sixteen hours. But the results desired were obtained: converts were made, and a local revival of religion was brought about.

A renewed interest in religion in the opening years of the nineteenth century helped produce the home missionary movement, but methods such as those just described and the emotionalism which characterized so many frontier religious exercises brought continued support to the movement from Eastern conservatives. Among most of the New England Congregationalists and New York Presbyterians it was felt that missionaries should be sent to the West in an effort to introduce better religious practices and beliefs. They wanted a revival of interest in religion, but they preferred for it to come quietly. The lasting conversions, they thought, were those that came after enlightenment, long prayer, and much searching of the heart; those made under the stress of great emotional excitement were likely to be temporary.

NATIONAL SOCIETIES

In an effort to keep pace with the rapidly growing West and to curb excessive emotionalism there, Eastern Christians were led, in the decade following the close of the War of 1812, to an important readjustment in their method of conducting missionary and other benevolent undertakings. In politics and economics many men were thinking nationally; in religion some men had been thinking nationally for several years, but now, as never before, this point of view became general. Religious and benevolent institutions were reorganized on national lines. The American Education Society was founded in 1815 and the American Bible Society in 1816; the Sunday School Union was formed in 1824, the American Tract Society in 1825, the American

Society for Promoting Temperance in 1826, and the American Peace Society in 1828. The frequency with which these organizations made use of the word "American" in their titles is indicative of the spirit of the times.[4]

There was a corresponding movement among men interested in home missions. The local and state societies had proved inadequate to deal with the problem presented by the growth of the new settlements in the West. Co-ordination of effort was lacking; in some places there was needless duplication of work, while other communities were entirely neglected. No one of the local societies was large enough to attract general attention or to arouse widespread interest in the missionary cause. Among Congregationalists and Presbyterians the fusing of these local societies into a national organization is the most characteristic feature of this period of our home missionary history. A similar movement took place among the Baptists, who erected a general denominational society to do more efficiently the work hitherto entrusted to local associations and voluntary societies. During this period the Methodist Episcopal and the Protestant Episcopal churches likewise created denominational societies. The tendency to form these general denominational or union societies was so clearly apparent in the years immediately following the close of the War of 1812 that the date 1820 has been taken arbitrarily to mark the beginning of the movement. By the middle of the 1830's each one of the religious bodies with which we are concerned in this study had formed such organizations; hence the date 1835 has been set for the end of this chapter.

ORIGIN OF THE AMERICAN HOME MISSIONARY SOCIETY

The best example of the tendency toward nationalism in the missionary movement is to be found in the establishment of the American Home Missionary Society in 1826. This society is significant not only because it was the most important single home missionary agency among Protestants in the United States before the Civil War, but also because it represented an experiment in the co-operative conduct of missions by several religious groups.

The immediate forerunner of the American Home Mis-

---

[4] Cf. E. D. Adams, *Power of Ideals in American History* (New Haven, 1913), 102-03.

sionary Society was the United Domestic Missionary Society of New York. As the name of the latter indicates, it was formed by the union of several local societies. One was the Young Men's Missionary Society of New York, which had been organized about 1815. Its operations had not been conducted on an extensive scale, only nine men having been employed in 1821, the last year of its separate existence; they had been engaged chiefly in New York, Pennsylvania, and New Jersey. Another was the New York Evangelical Missionary Society, which was formed in 1816. In its final report it stated that it had in its employ ten men, nine of whom were in the state of New York; the tenth was in Missouri.[5] In May, 1822, delegates from these and other local missionary societies, all within the state of New York, met and formed the United Domestic Missionary Society.[6] The delegates were mainly from the Presbyterian Church, although the Dutch Reformed and the Associate Reformed churches were represented. The society which they created was not a denominational organization, although it was mainly under the control of Presbyterians. As a union society it was designed to eliminate some of the evils which resulted from the existence in the state of New York of several local societies, each with a small membership, limited resources, and a restricted field of operations. Two or more of these voluntary societies sometimes existed in the same district, solicited pecuniary aid from the same people, and wearied them by repeated appeals. There was unnecessary duplication of effort by the managers of these various organizations; the means of each was so limited that it was not able to accomplish much. It was thought that the formation of a union society would secure a more efficient and economical administration of the missionary business, attract attention by its size, and thus secure more adequate funds, and prevent useless duplication of effort on the missionary field.[7]

---

[5] A. Green, *Historical Sketch or Compendious View of Domestic and Foreign Missions*, 24-25; [G. Spring], *Brief View of the Facts which Gave Rise to the New York Evangelical Missionary Society of Young Men* (New York,1817).

[6] The text of the Act of Incorporation (Feb. 28, 1822) is in the Geneva, N. Y., *Gazette*, April 17, 1822.

[7] Printed circular letter issued by Genesee Missionary Society, Geneva, N. Y., Dec. 24, 1821, copy in C.H.M.S. (14th year, No. 55); not found in A.H.M.S. papers, C.T.S.

Hitherto the normal method of conducting missionary operations had been to send out a minister on a tour to the frontier. In any given community he would ordinarily preach, administer the ordinances of the church, visit and encourage the faithful, reprove the sinners, and then go on after a day or two to another settlement to repeat the process. The United Domestic Missionary Society of New York put the emphasis in its work on the establishment of churches and the support of pastors. To this end it assisted young or feeble churches in the new settlements by paying all or part of the salary of a minister. It did not employ itinerant missionaries. An innovation of this sort seemed to call for some explanation and defense, and in its first annual report the United Domestic Missionary Society set forth at length the reasons for its new policy. It was argued that the appearance in the new settlements of "travelling preachers, authorized and unauthorized, with which the country abounds," tended to keep alive the sectarian divisions, kept the people in ignorance of the proper religious principles, and failed to develop among them a sense of responsibility for the support of the ministry. In some parts of the state of New York, said the committee,

... it is less practicable now to settle ministers than it was many years ago, notwithstanding that the population has very much increased. The people, besides having adopted a variety of superficial and unharmonious notions on the subject, are a great deal less sensible of the necessity and importance of religion, and a great deal less willing to contribute any thing on account of it than they were on their first removal from the older parts of the country where they had in early life been used to the observances and instructions of the gospel. ... The committee ... would express their earnest hope that the practice of employing missionaries to travel from place to place preaching here and there a sermon, consuming a great portion of their time in journeying, and remaining at no one point long enough to accomplish any thing likely to be permanent, will be universally abandoned. In these occasional and transient labours the ablest missionary sent forth has no advantage over the uneducated and vociferous exhorters, who in their turn address the same hearers. Such competitors indeed by their numbers, and the methods they adopt, do actually succeed in obtaining each his partisans and followers, and creating divisions which no missionary, however gifted, can heal or counteract, except by a course of faithful, uninterrupted, and persevering labour. . . . [8]

---

[8] *First Report of the United Domestic Missionary Society* (New York, 1823), 9-14.

The new United Domestic Missionary Society was a success. By 1826 it had on its roll 127 missionaries, of whom one hundred were in the state of New York. The other twenty-seven were scattered from Vermont and lower Canada in the north and east to Florida in the south and Illinois, Indiana, and Missouri in the west. It was a non-sectarian voluntary society, but its management was mainly in the hands of, and its support was drawn from, Presbyterians. Close connections were maintained with the Congregationalists, and some of the men who went out from New England as missionaries went under the auspices of this Society. Indeed, it was in connection with the ordination in Boston in September, 1825, of three young prospective representatives of this Society, that the assembled friends of home missions took certain steps that led to the formation of the American Home Missionary Society.

In the story of the evolution of the American Home Missionary Society one other preliminary phase must be mentioned—that of the interest of a group of Andover divinity students in the creation of a national domestic missionary organization.[9] Andover Seminary had been established as a theological school for orthodox Congregationalism after it became evident by the election of Henry Ware to the Hollis Professorship of Divinity in Harvard College in 1805 that the Unitarians had secured control of English America's oldest and most famous seat of learning. The Andover students were interested in missions, both home and foreign, and had a Society of Inquiry for the study of mission fields and problems. As early as January, 1825, the idea was definitely advanced among a group of these young men that a national missionary society should be formed. The credit for first putting the idea into words apparently belongs to Nathaniel Bouton; it was elaborated in April of that year by John Maltby, a member of the Society of Inquiry, who read an essay he had written in which he set forth the advantages to be derived from a large general society for home missions. What was needed, he said, was a system "which shall have no sectional interests,—no local prejudices,—no party animosities,—no sectarian views; a system which shall bring the most remote parts of our

---

[9] N. Bouton, Concord, N. H., May 1, 1826, to A. Peters, A.H.M.S. papers, C.T.S.

nation into cordial cooperation, awaken mutual interest in the same grand and harmonious design, produce a new feeling of brotherhood, and thus bind us all together by a new cord of union." In the second place, a change in the method of conducting missions was needed in order that more money might be available. "We want a system," he continued, "which in its operation, shall have but one treasury, and that, as it were, the treasury of the nation." And finally, a change was needed that should secure the advantages of union in operation and permanency in effect. The object should not be mere itinerant missionary labor but the planting of men of learning and influence in every little community that was rising up throughout the land. In short, what was needed was a system which should gather the resources "of philanthropy, patriotism and Christian sympathy throughout our country, into one vast reservoir, from which a stream shall flow to Georgia, to Louisiana, to Missouri and to Maine, fertilizing every barren spot and causing our whole country to flourish like the garden of the Lord." Only a National Domestic Missionary Society could do all this.[10] Thus among New England Congregationalists as well as among New York Presbyterians there was a movement towards the formation of a large national home missionary society.

Six members of the senior class at Andover Seminary in 1825 had decided to go West as home missionaries; four of them, Augustus Pomeroy, Lucius Alden, John M. Ellis, and Hiram Chamberlain, intended to go out under the auspices of the United Domestic Missionary Society of New York. At the request of this Society three of these men were ordained at a council called for that purpose in the Old South Church, Boston, in September, 1825. Several of the men who came together on that occasion met and considered the advisability of forming a national domestic missionary society. A committee was appointed to make further inquiries and to arrange for a subsequent meeting, if desirable.[11] At this next meeting, which was held in

---

[10] John Maltby, "Connexion between Domestic Missions and the Political Prospects of our Country," MS. in C.H.M.S. (box No. 2); not found in A.H.M.S. papers, C.T.S., although there is there a torn 1825 copy of the original.

[11] E. Porter and J. Edwards, Andover, Mass., Dec. [14], 1825, to M. Bruen, in C.H.M.S. (box No. 2); not found in A.H.M.S. papers, C.T.S.

Boston in January, 1826, with twelve prominent New England religious leaders in attendance, it was unanimously resolved that it was expedient to attempt the formation of a new national society.[12] It was also agreed that in forming such a society a union of all denominations was not to be attempted, and that existing societies should not be impeded in their work or superseded, except in accordance with their own desires, but should rather be strengthened and stimulated. Inasmuch as there were several societies in existence whose interests or fields of labor might be affected by a new national society, careful attention was given to the best method of procedure. Because of the prominence of the United Domestic Missionary Society of New York, which already had under commission several young missionaries from the Congregational churches of New England, it was decided to ask it to issue the call for the convention to form the new organization. In accordance with this suggestion the Executive Committee of the New York society issued a circular (March 13, 1826) addressed to a number of Congregational, Presbyterian, Dutch Reformed, and Associate Reformed churches in different parts of the United States, inviting them to send representatives to New York in May, 1826, the time of the annual meeting of the American Bible Society, for the purpose of establishing a national domestic missionary society. Ministers and laymen to the number of 126, representing at least thirteen states and territories, and the four denominations named above, met at the time and place appointed (May 10, 1826) and formed the American Home Missionary Society. Then the United Domestic Society voted to merge with the new organization, which took over the work and continued the policies of its predecessor.[13] In view of the charge subsequently made that the creation of the American Home Missionary Society was a scheme of the New England Congregationalists to subvert Presbyterianism, it is noteworthy that more than half of the persons who took part in the

---

[12] B. B. Wisner, Boston, Jan. 12, 1826, to A. Peters, in C.H.M.S. (box No. 2) ; not found in A.H.M.S. papers, C.T.S.

[13] Nathaniel Bouton, "History of the Origin and Organization of the American Home Missionary Society," in *Home Missionary*, XXXIII (1860), 157-66.

1826 convention in New York City were Presbyterians, as were also the majority of the members of the first executive committee.[14]

OPERATION OF THE AMERICAN HOME MISSIONARY SOCIETY

The support for the American Home Missionary Society came mainly from Presbyterians and Congregationalists,[15] and it was the hope of the men in charge of the Society that it would be given supervision over all the home missionary activities of these two denominations. It did not aim to supplant their local or ecclesiastical organizations already in existence; but it did desire that they should become subordinate or auxiliary to the national society, turning over to it the money which they collected beyond their own local needs. This hope was realized in part. The principal New England societies, such as the Missionary Society of Connecticut and the Massachusetts Missionary Society, became auxiliaries; many of the local societies among the New York Presbyterians also affiliated with the new organization. The General Assembly of the Presbyterian Church, however, retained its own Board of Missions.

The expectation that the formation of a united missionary society would result in an increased interest in missions was justified by the results. In the last year of its separate existence the United Domestic Missionary Society had received about $12,000 and was helping support 127 missionaries. The receipts of the American Home Missionary Society were more than $18,000 in its first year, and it had on its roll 169 missionaries. Five years later (1831-32) the

---

[14] A. Peters, *Brief Answer to an Official Reply* (New York, 1831), 25; H. Woods, *History of the Presbyterian Controversy* (Louisville, 1843), 49.

[15] At the outset most of the financial support for the Society came apparently from Presbyterians. Of the $20,000 received in the second year (1827-28), $16,121.27 was credited to New York and only $1,641.34 to four New England states, A.H.M.S., *Second Report* (1828), 53-54. Although members of the Dutch Reformed and Associate Reformed churches had shared in the movement which led to the establishment of this union society, it appears that they soon withdrew. The Reformed Dutch Church had its own Standing Committee of Missions, which dated from 1806, and a Missionary Society which was formed in 1822. In 1831 a Board of Missions was created by the Synod to supervise all mission operations of the Church. E. T. Corwin, *Manual of the Reformed Church in America* (3rd ed., New York, 1879), 129-34.

annual receipts had increased to about $50,000 and the number of missionaries had grown to 509. In the tenth year (1835-36) the receipts were slightly more than $100,-000, while the number of representatives in the field had become 755.[16] Not all these missionaries, however, were in the West. Owing to the fact that several of the New England societies had become auxiliary to the national society,[17] their local missionaries counted in the total number; in 1835-36, for example, 319 of the 755 men listed were engaged in missionary work in the New England states, mainly in Vermont, New Hampshire, and Maine. But the number of missionaries in the West was increasing year by year. In the first annual report 33 were accredited to the West; in the tenth, 191. Of these 191 Western missionaries in 1836, 12 were in Tennessee, 9 in Kentucky, 80 in Ohio, 24 in Indiana, 32 in Illinois, 12 in Missouri, and 17 in Michigan.[18]

An examination of the geographical distribution of the men sent out by the American Home Missionary Society quickly reveals that, although this was a national society, comparatively few of its representatives were to be found in the South. Of the 755 men on the list in 1835-36, only 15 were in the slave states of the South and Southwest,[19] counting Kentucky, Tennessee, and Missouri as Western rather than Southern. The reasons for the comparative neglect of the South are obvious: most of the prospective missionaries came from New England and the Middle States; they had objections to settling in the South because of their dislike for slavery, the feeling that they would not be well received by the people, and fear of an enervating climate. Missionaries presumably go where need is greatest without much regard for personal comfort; however, when a Northerner had a choice between a needy field in, let us say, Arkansas and an equally needy field in Michigan, he would naturally choose the Northern post. Moreover, according to the officers of the Society, missionary operations in the slave states were generally more expensive and less suc-

---

16 A.H.M.S., *Tenth Report* (1836), 63.

17 On relations between A.H.M.S. and auxiliary societies see A.H. M.S., *Second Report* (1828), 69-75.

18 *Home Missionary*, LXIV (1891), 112-13.

19 They were distributed as follows: Del., 2; Md., 1; Va., 3; N. C., 1; Ga., 1; Ala., 1; Miss., 4; Ark., 2. *Idem.*

cessful than those in the free states of the West; the more compact settlement of the Northwest with many towns and villages gave better opportunity for the creation of religious societies that gave promise of attaining soon to self-sufficiency.[20]

It was the settled policy of the American Home Missionary Society, like that of the United Domestic Society before it, to assist in the development of churches in the West by subsidizing them to the extent necessary to enable them to engage a full-time or even a part-time pastor. In the Constitution of the Society (Art. II) it was declared that "the great object of this Society shall be to assist congregations that are unable to support the Gospel Ministry, and to send the Gospel to the destitute within the United States." In its first report the Society announced that it has "from the beginning been a prominent object with the Committee, to send out well qualified ministers to our frontier settlements, with instructions to gather new congregations, and labour as they may find opportunity, until with the choice and co-operation of the people, they may become permanently established in the pastoral office."[21] This policy was based on the firm conviction that the occasional missionary tour was ineffective; that whatever good had been accomplished by the itinerant was lost before some other missionary appeared in the same place. One man familiar with the West likened the old method of conducting missions through missionary tours to an attempt to burn a pile of green buckeye logs by setting fire to a bunch of shavings under them. When the missionary left the fire was burning brightly, but he was scarcely out of sight before the shavings had burned up and the logs were about as before, only a little blackened.[22] A local church with a minister in charge was needed to conserve whatever gains had been made. The Methodists met this problem by sending their itinerants on circuits; they appeared regularly to keep the fires burning. Although several of the representatives of the American Home Missionary Society in the West were convinced that the Methodist system was highly desirable and should be used,[23] the

---

[20] A. Peters, in *Home Missionary*, V (1833), 198-99.

[21] A.H.M.S., *First Report* (1827), 45-46.

[22] Calvin E. Stowe, in A.H.M.S., *Eighteenth Report* (1844), 106.

[23] John M. Ellis, Kaskaskia, Ill., Jan. 10, 1827, and May 23, 1827, A.H.M.S. papers, C.T.S.; Julius A. Reed, Fairfield, Iowa, Dec. 5, 1842,

Society continued to emphasize the establishment of churches and the maintenance of pastors over them. It should be remembered that Presbyterians and Congregationalists alike looked askance at religious declarations made hastily and under emotional stress. Fearing that such commitments would not be lasting, they generally disapproved "revivals" and preferred the less spectacular meth-' od of the settled pastor who presented his message quietly and logically Sunday after Sunday.[24]

In general the missionaries acting under the American Home Missionary Society fell into three classes: first, settled pastors, each in charge of one or more churches; second, men who went West with no definite location in mind; and third, agents. The majority of men on the roll of the Society belonged to the first class. Ordinarily the Society acted by giving financial assistance to a Western church to enable it to maintain a preacher. When one of these churches desired help it sent in a formal application stating the facts concerning its location, membership, financial condition, with the name and credentials of the man it wished to engage. Each congregation making application was expected to raise as much of the minister's salary as it could, normally three fourths, and the Society supplemented this by enough to give him a living wage. When the Society was founded it was estimated that in the average Western community a minister could live and support a family on $400 a year;[25] consequently, $100 was the annual grant most frequently made in the early years of the So-

---

ibid., wrote: "The truth is that a circuit rider brought up, perhaps he will boast, at the plough tail, exerts *more influence* than the most faithful of your missionaries in Iowa. The only way to meet the difficulties is to employ itinerants and reach every settlement." James Thomson, Wabash, Ind., April 4, 1844, suggested the use of itinerants to form nuclei and then settled pastors to serve the churches after they had been established. A.H.M.S. papers, C.T.S.

24 When A. H. M. S. representatives participated in revivals or camp meetings they carefully stressed the solemn nature of the proceedings in their reports; *e.g.*, P. S. Cleland, Greenwood, Ind., Sept. 26, 1842, A.H.M.S. papers, C.T.S.

25 James Hoge, writing from Ohio in 1827, stated that in county towns and "wealthy" villages a man could not live decently on less than $450 or $500 a year; in small villages $400 would be competent support; in retired places among poor people $300 or $350 a year would be sufficient. James Hoge, Columbus, Ohio, Feb. 15, 1827, in A.H.M.S. papers, C.T.S.

ciety's history.[26] In so far as possible the business was run on the principle of helping those that help themselves. Again and again local churches with or without good reasons failed to keep their pledges to their ministers. After a few years the number of defaulting churches had become so great that the Executive Committee adopted a rule that the Society would not renew its assistance to a church unless it presented a statement from its pastor to the effect that all pledges made to him in the preceding year had been met.[27] It was hoped that in a few years each of these churches would not only become self-supporting but would also send in gifts to enable the Society to carry on its work on newer frontiers.

To the more distant and newly settled states and territories, where fewer churches had been formed, a second class of missionaries was sometimes sent. These were the men who went out to the West without any definite location in mind. They were ordinarily provided with an outfit sufficient to pay their expenses to the field and a pledge of full support for twelve months, usually $400, including what they might receive from the people. These men were left somewhat to their own discretion in the selection of a location, subject to such general advice as they received from the officers and agents of the Society, with the general understanding that as soon as possible they should engage in permanent labor in some place where there was a prospect of gathering a congregation which would assume responsibility for all or a part of their support. If at the end of the first year further aid was needed, it would usually be granted only after application from the people. The missionary of the second class would then have become a member of the first group.

The American Home Missionary Society also had in the West a few representatives known as agents.[28] These

---

[26] In the Far West, including the Rocky Mountain region, the annual grants were often greater, since living expenses were so much higher than in the Middle West; for example, to Nathan Thompson, missionary in Boulder, Colo., the Society granted, in 1867, $1227 out of a total salary of $1500. A.H.M.S. Letter Bk., 1867-68, No. 272, in C.T.S.

[27] A.H.M.S., Minutes of the Executive Comm., 13th year (1838), entry 702, C.H.M.S.

[28] There were 12 of these agents in 1834, A.H.M.S., *Eighth Report* (1834), 70-71. Occasionally complaints were made that the agents

were usually ministers of maturity, experience, and executive ability who might or might not be in charge of a church. Their duties were manifold and important. They were expected to visit the Presbyterian and Congregational churches in their state or district as often as convenient for the purpose of raising money for and keeping up interest in missions; they were expected to visit destitute and needy parts of their country, to organize churches if possible and to help them secure pastors; they were also expected to give advice to new missionaries arriving in their districts and to keep the officers of the Society informed about the successes and failures of the various missionaries and about religious conditions in general. They were missionaries at large who held an important post between the officers of a society with headquarters in New York on the one hand and the local churches and missionaries on the other.[29] The duties of the agent corresponded in part to those of a missionary bishop in the Protestant Episcopal Church, but the former lacked the latter's prestige either among the people at large or among his colleagues.

The appointment and reappointment of the missionaries involved the question of the relationship between the American Home Missionary Society and the official church organizations to which the men belonged. This was a voluntary society under no ecclesiastical control, but its policy was one of close co-operation with the various Presbyterian presbyteries and Congregational associations. It recognized that they were the sole judges of the qualifications of their own

---

had too much influence; e.g., R. W. Patterson, Chicago, Ill., Oct. 24, 1845, A.H.M.S. Correspondence, 1845-46, No. 1689, C.T.S. Such criticisms were often related to the disputes between Congregationalists and Presbyterians.

[29] The A.H.M.S. Letter Books in C.T.S. contain many letters in answer to inquiries as to the conditions under which missionaries were sent out, e.g., A. Peters to J. Crawford, Sept. 1, 1826, Bk. A, 22-24; A. Peters to E. Child, Sept. 1, 1826, Bk. A, 19-22; A. Peters to E. Yale, June 9, 1827, Bk. A, 42-46; C. Hall to T. Cole, June 10, 1828, Bk. B, 594; C. Hall to W. Rankin, Nov. 7, 1828, Bk. B, 842; C. Hall to T. Thacher, Dec. 10, 1828, Bk. B, 884; C. Hall for A. Peters to T. Lippincott, Feb. 10, 1829, Bk. B, 1036; A. Peters to H. Hooker, [date illegible], Bk. C, 414; A. Peters to B. Laberee, Dec. 29, 1830, Bk. D, 419; C. Hall to W. Nichols, Apr. 24, 1833, Bk. F, 522; A. Peters to W. Henry, Sept. 29, 1834, Bk. H, 139. On general policy see also A.H.M.S., *First Report* (1827), 44-46; *Home Missionary*, IV (1831), 129-31.

members; hence the commission issued to the missionary required that his credentials be acceptable to the presbytery or association within whose bounds he was to labor. The various presbyteries and associations containing home mission churches were asked to appoint committees to receive applications for help from their own members, and to suggest to the Society the action proper in each case. The advice of such a committee was considered as of the highest authority in matters pertaining to the ecclesiastical standing of ministers and churches.[30] Missionary qualifications, such as age, experience, training, or fitness for a particular place, were a different matter. On these questions the Society sought information from the presbyteries and associations concerned, but reserved the right to make final decisions for itself.

The American Home Missionary Society discouraged its missionaries from engaging in secular pursuits. They were expected to keep themselves "unspotted from the world" and to spend their time in ministerial duties. One of the most common of the current adverse criticisms of the local Western preachers, especially the Baptists, was that so many of them spent their time during the week in farming or other worldly vocations. It was felt in the East that this lowered the dignity of the minister and seriously interfered with his efficiency. Representatives of the American Home Missionary Society were given to understand that it would be held against them if they engaged in farming or merchandising.[31]

---

[30] A. Peters, *Brief Answer to an Official Reply*, 37-38; *Home Missionary*, XXIV (1852), 219-20; A. Peters by C. Hall to S. Buck, May 8, 1830, A.H.M.S. Letter Bk. C, 454, in C.T.S.

[31] Occasionally spirited protests came back from missionaries who had been criticized for their secular activities. One wrote from Wisconsin in 1838: "How you could suppose I could devote my time exclusively to the work of the ministry & support my family on a little more than three hundred dollars a year I cannot conceive. It would have cost three hundred and fifty dollars to have hired and boarded a common laborer the first year of our residence here, & the case is but little altered now. House rent & everything I can think of except fuel is dearer here than in New York City. . . . I am told flour is now fifteen dollars per barrel in Chicago. The last salt was sold here in bulk at ten dollars per bl & retailed higher, now none is to be had. Pork in the hog, ten dolls. per hundred, butter 3/ per lb. Poor brown sugar 1/6 per lb. Molasses 6/ to 8/ per gall. Poor Coffee 20 cents per lb. If I get a bushel of corn or buckwheat I must carry it forty miles to mill or pay 3/ per bush for having it carried. . . . If I wish a days work of chopping wood or anything I must spend half a day in finding a man to do it & pay him one dollar cash in hand. If I hire a

They were discouraged from teaching, even though the officers of the Society were friendly to the cause of education and were well aware of the educational needs of the West. To one member of a group of young men at Yale who had an ambitious plan for combining teaching and preaching—a plan that resulted in the founding of Illinois College[32]—the Executive Committee said that while they wanted their missionaries to favor and promote the growth of literary institutions, they preferred that they should not themselves engage in teaching, but should give themselves entirely to their work of proclaiming the gospel.[33] It should also be noted in passing that one effect of this restriction on secular activities was to give the unfriendly critics of Presbyterian and Congregational missionaries in the West the chance to make the charge that they were hirelings—men who preached for money and were too burdensome for poor people to support.[34]

A commission was issued to each missionary;[35] it contained general instructions, stated specifically that his

mason I must pay him $3.50 per day and board. If I get a common coat made I must pay ten dollars. I can buy as good a coat in Troy N.Y. for $14 as I can get here for $30—but I wear my old coat. I am confident my family cannot be supported here without my own exertion for $800 a year.... Butter, cheese, sugar &c are used so sparingly with us that we scarcely know their relish. And even now with the rigid practice of economy that amounts almost to parsimony if when I sit down in my cold crowded cabin to write a sermon I sometimes have two duns in a day without being able to satisfy the demand. It is true I have not taken my bag on my shoulder & begged my bread & then spent my time in writing about it. I have preferred to take my plough & hoe & go into the field & trust God for a crop & he has blessed my efforts. I have not raised enough for our consumption but it will help us much...." C. Nichols, Racine, Wis., Dec. 22, 1838, in C.H.M.S. (13th year, No. 875); not found in A.H.M.S. papers, C.T.S.

Another missionary who felt the force of this rule complained that it was not applied uniformly. "But when it does not so suit [to waive it], a half-starved missionary ... cannot plant a hill of beans but he is becoming so extensive a farmer [that] it will be an entire perversion of funds to assist him." S. N. Grant, Macon, Neb., Feb. 27, 1877, in A.H.M.S. papers, C.T.S.

[32] See below, page 197.

[33] A. Peters by C. Hall to M. Governeur [Grosvenor], Jan. 8, 1829, A.H.M.S. Letter Bk. B, 1006, in C.T.S.

[34] There are many references to such charges in the missionary reports; e.g., John Brick, near Jacksonville, Ill., Feb. 6, 1827, A.H. M.S. papers, C.T.S.

[35] For form of commission in use in 1845, see A.H.M.S. Correspondence, 1845-46, No. 1734, A.H.M.S. papers, C.T.S.

credentials as a minister must be acceptable to the ecclesiastical organization within whose jurisdiction he labored, announced the terms on which the Society granted financial assistance, and made note of the amount of money he was entitled to receive from the Society in the course of the year. Payment was usually made quarterly and, theoretically, only after receipt of a written report of the missionary work performed during the preceding three months. These reports, which varied in length from a few lines to many closely written pages, are of widely different degrees of value to the student of history. Some were filled with conventional religious phraseology; others were of a statistical nature and recorded the number of additions to the church, the number of "scholars" in the Sunday school, the number of sermons preached and monthly "Concerts of Prayer" attended; still others, fortunately for the secular historian, contained interesting and illuminating comments on Western social, economic, and religious conditions.

In order to disseminate information and arouse interest in its work the American Home Missionary Society began in 1828 the publication of a monthly magazine called the *Home Missionary*.[36] In judging its value as a source of historical information it must be remembered that its primary object was to aid Presbyterian and Congregational missionary activities in the West. Obviously this magazine could not print all of the thousands of missionary reports that came in to the Society. Selection involves judgment in which even the wisest men may make mistakes. Some reports were encouraging, others discouraging. How to hold the proper balance between letters on the one hand that called attention to the great need for missionaries in the West and the trying conditions under which they lived and worked, and those on the other that emphasized the success that attended their efforts there, was a nice question. Furthermore, when a man wrote freely about religious or social conditions in the community in which he was stationed, his letter if published over his name might subject him to local hostility which would injure his usefulness or even make it so unpleasant for him that he would be forced to leave. Again and again missionaries who had made frank unfavorable comments

---

[36] Before 1828 the A.H.M.S. used the *New York Observer* as its medium of communication to the public.

about the people among whom they were working asked that their letters be not published.[37] To protect the missionary and to avoid unnecessary sectarian animosities the editors often either omitted the name of the writer and the place from which the letter had been sent, or they edited the report until it was innocuous. The Corresponding Secretary of the Society wrote to one missionary in Tennessee as follows: "We were very much affected with the statement which you give of the moral condition of the country. You will see in our August number of the Home Missionary that we have ventured to take some extracts from your letter, tho' we have been careful to cut out all that might cause trouble, if enemies should get hold of it."[38]

SOME EXPERIENCES OF MISSIONARIES IN THE WEST

As stated above, the work of the American Home Missionary Society in the West in its first decade (1826-35) was carried on mainly in western New York, Ohio, southern Michigan, Indiana, Illinois, Missouri, and Kentucky. This was "out West"; missionaries as well as everybody else there had to live under frontier conditions. It was a time and place of sharp denominational conflict; Presbyterians and Congregationalists often found themselves in a religious hubbub that was not to their liking. In all of the states and territories named above that touched on the Ohio and the Mississippi rivers the white population up to 1835 was mainly of southern or middle-state origin; men from New England had to meet sectional prejudices and dislikes. They described their experiences and told their tales of woe in their reports to the officers of the Society, and in so doing gave an intimate picture of certain phases of frontier life. Perhaps the best way to show those problems and difficulties is to let some of the men speak for themselves. The following letter from Ohio (1827) tells of some of the hardships of pioneer preaching:

---

[37] *E.g.*, "These hard sayings of mine must not be published," wrote J. Crawford, Jefferson Co., Ind., May 30, 1827; "These remarks about the Methodists I intend for your own eyes, not for the public," said H. Lyman, Portland, Ore., April, 1851; "I wish this letter to be kept private," was the request of G. H. Atkinson, Oregon City, Ore., Feb. 10, 1849. A.H.M.S. papers, C.T.S.

[38] A. Peters by C. Hall to N. Hood, Aug. 17, 1830, A.H.M.S. Letter Bk. D, 190, in C.T.S.

... Since I wrote you, I have preached in a house that had no windows & was under the necessity of getting the Hyms read by the light of a crack. I have preached in the entry of a schoolhouse, where one third of my audience were [on] the outside; & in a snowy day in February, to visit a sick man a [I] rode a three year old colt across a stream where the bottom could not be touched for 8 rods. These things, with riding in storms & sleeping where the wind and rain beat on my head are [too] hard for flesh & blood. ... The wants of the people, their urgent requests, & the prospect of doing them good, (which cannot be resisted) would move a heart of stone. ...[39]

From a missionary in southern Michigan came a story of sickness and suffering which moved the officers of the Society to make an extra allowance in spite of the low state of the treasury at the time. William Jones wrote in December, 1830:

I now write you as one lately risen from the borders of the grave. Soon after I last reported to you I was seized with the chill fever—from that it turned to the billous remitting fever—then the nervious fever & from that it changed to the typhoid nervious. ... [Describes his recovery, and his financial difficulties; has had to borrow money to buy food.] Add to this the expense of my present sickness besides various other indispensible expenditures. All this however could be met did I receive a moderate salary from the people among whom I labour—but believe me dear Sir all what I receive for a years labour will not on a fair calculation amount to more than $100 & not a dollar in money in all. Provisions and Mirchandize &c are the articles of subscription—& you must know that it will more than all be needed for my family consumption, being 4 in number.

The items are as follows—From Beardsleys Prarie 10 bushels of wheat—$5.00—From Elkhart $25. or $30.00 in wheat, corn, potatoes &c At this place the subscription amounts to $50.00—in Merchandize grain pork, labour & team work Add to this amount $10.00 which I may expect to receive from other places & you have all.

You may enquire the cause why the people subscribe no more. ... Most of the members of our church on my field of labour are the poor of this world—they are now scrubbing [?] & saving what they can to purchase their lands when they come for sale,—soon they will be able to bestow more—And as to mere worlings in this section—they are eager to become rich—riches seem to absorb the whole mind. ...

We have been obliged to live for the summer in an open house with another family.—the most part of the house has no doors or windows—they stood open night & day except it was merely planked with green planks which soon shrunk & left large crevices between & every beating storm found its way through the house. To the exposure of the night airs I may in a great measure I think attribute my illness

---

[39] Jacob Little, Belpre, Ohio, April 16, 1827, in A.H.M.S. papers, C.T.S.

—together with excessive fatigue. I have been under the necessity of traveling on foot 10 or 12 miles in performing my Missionary labours for I have not the means of buying a horse. . . .

We did expect with the assistance of the people to put up a small comfortable house for the winter—but aid from the people here I could not obtain—as every man had more than he could do for himself. . . . I had to abandon the object & put up a cabin 24 by 12—which is constructed of croches set into the ground—with a board & slab roof—& boarded all around. . . . [40]

Less serious, but still perplexing, were the problems of Charles Danforth, a missionary in Indiana and Ohio. He had located in Indiana, became discouraged, and had gone to New Connecticut, or the Western Reserve, in Ohio. Then, to let him tell his story in his own words,

. . . my mind became much exercised in relation to my future course. And as strange as it may seem, I soon came to the conclusion that it was my duty to return to Indiana. What brought me to this conclusion was—that my return would have a favourable bearing on the missionary cause— . . . After resolving to return to Indiana I had difficulties to contend with that were rather of a trying nature.—The parents and friends of my wife were exceedingly desirous that we should settle near them; & parting with her to go to Indiana seemed like parting with her no more to meet this side the grave. Other difficulties arose from my pecuniary circumstances—I borrowed money to bear my expenses from Indiana. My horse failed me at London & I was under the necessity of buying another for which I run in debt. I preached 4 Sabbaths in Austinburg, for which they raised for me sixteen dollars. —The only way that I could see by which we could go [back] to Indiana without becoming more deeply involved in debt, was to obtain a Dandy waggon & put my horse before it & consequently I [expended? (letter torn)] all my wife's dowry which amounted to $45.00 [to? (letter torn)] obtain a waggon & harness for my journey. We started from Austinburg the 4 day of May & reached London a distance of 225 miles in two weeks & a half—We found the road much of the way rough & in many places almost impassable for a slender dandy waggon. The skein broke twice which let off one of the wheels—this happened once when we were about two miles in the wilderness & after much exertion I got it mended & started on about dusk, but after going a little distance the end of a tree which lay partly across the road caught one of the wheels of my waggon, that I was under the necessity of leaving it there in the road until morning—found a house ahead about 2 miles & was thankful that nothing worse had happened—my horse likewise occasioned us considerable trouble being young and not much accustomed to labour— . . . [41]

[40] William Jones, White Pigeon, M. T., Dec. 13, 1830, in A.H.M.S. papers, C.T.S.

[41] Charles Danforth, Troy, Ohio, Aug. 24, 1830, in A.H.M.S. papers, C.T.S.

The troubles that disturbed Ellery Bascom at Lower Sandusky, Ohio, were of an entirely different nature. He wrote in 1834:

... This village [Lower Sandusky] ever since its first settlement has been famous for vice and Infidelity. It has been the famous resort for Counterfeiters, horse thieves, highway robbers &c &c in so much that it was unsafe for a stranger who had money about him to lodge here for a single night. And intem[perance] has made it a slaughter-house. Even when I came here vice & crime & sickness & Death had had such a transforming influence, that it seemed as if the great mass of the people had no hearts. The Moral faculties appeared to have been torn away from the human mind, as exhibited in this *Seat of Satan*, this *Canton* of his western Empire. But Glory to God the Scale is fast turning. Moral & religious influence begins to predominate. Even Infidels find it for their temporal interest to contribute to the support of the gospel.... [42]

From China, in southern Indiana, John W. Parsons wrote to state that he gave first place among his difficulties to

Ignorance & her squalid brood. A universal dearth of intellect. Total abstinence from literature is very generally practiced. Aside from br. Wilder & myself, there is not a literary man of any sort in the bounds. There is not a scholar in grammar or geography, or a *teacher capable* of *instructing* in *them*, to my knowledge. There are some neighborhoods in which there has *never been a school* of *any* kind. Parents and children are one dead level of ignorance. Others are supplied a few months in the year with the most antiquated & unreasonable forms of teaching reading, writing & *cyphering*. Master Ignoramus is a striking facsimile of them. They are never guilty of teaching any thing but "pure *school-master larnin*." Of course there is no kind of ambition for improvement; & it is no more disgrace for man woman or child to be unable to read, than to have a long nose. Our own church the other day elected a man to the eldership who is unable to read the bible. I dont know of ten families who take any kind of paper, political or religious, & the whole of their revenue to the Post office department is not as much as mine alone. Need I stop to remind you of the host of loathsome reptiles such a stagnant pool is fitted to breed! Croaking jealousy; bloated Bigotry; coiling suspicion; wormish blindness; crocodile malice!...[43]

From the same part of Indiana came a similar complaint, but one stated more sympathetically:

... The people are poor & far from market labouriously engaged in improving & cultivating their new land. Society here is in an unformed

[42] Ellery Bascom, Lower Sandusky, Ohio, July 1, 1834, in A.H.M.S. papers, C.T.S.

[43] John W. Parsons, China, Ind., Feb. 20, 1833, in A.H.M.S. papers, C.T.S.

state composed of persons from every part of the Union.... Religious sects are numerous & blind guides enough to swallow all the camels in Arabia—Some of these cant read—Some labour to preach down the Sabbath! & others to rob *Christ of his divinity!* and all harmoniously unite in decrying education—as requisite for a public teacher & in abusing the learned clergy who take wages for their services. When shall this reign of ignorance & error cease in the West?[44]

The lack of adequate facilities for holding public worship was often listed among the difficulties of work in the new communities. The following letter was written in Cleveland, Ohio, in 1830:

...We have long been in difficulty for want of a convenient meeting. Last spring the society was compelled by circumstances to do *something;* & after an unsuccessful effort to raise funds to build a house, they rented a spacious hall & fitted it up with good slips & a pulpit & rented the slips to support preaching. This was carried into execution during my absence. There were violent prejudices... against the plan of having select seats for families which drove many of our former congregation away from the meeting.... The Methodists who before had preached one half of the Sabbaths in town, but to a mere handful of hearers, now learning of our difficulties procured the Masonick hall, a spacious room & had preaching every sabbath & a preacher stationed in town. Multitudes had forsaken our meeting & gone to this. The Episcopalians have just finished their house & employed a preacher & numbers of the disaffected go there. And thus my congregation has been diminished nearly two-thirds.... [Resigns] You may therefore consider this place vacant & send here the first man you can find of solid & yet popular talents, who has iron nerves & can bear with fortitude & patience any amount of neglect or even abuse....[45]

Out of the bitterness of religious rivalry came this complaint from a town on the Ohio River in southern Indiana:

...In regard to *this* place [Evansville] it seems as if a cloud of seven-fold darkness rested upon it and the *curse* of the Allmighty to even *blacken* that darkness.... But against *Presbyterians* there is as *real* a *persecution* as ever existed under Nero or any other tyrant though not carried forward in the same manner; and in this the light of eternity will show that the influence of Methodists and some others is united with that of infidels and unbelievers. There is a deadly hatred towards *Presbyterians* because they are the firm advocates for the different benevolent institutions existing in our country....[46]

---

[44] James Crawford, Jefferson Co., Ind., Jan. 31, 1827, in A.H.M.S. papers, C.T.S.

[45] S. J. Bradstreet, Cleveland, Ohio, Jan. 1, 1830, in A.H.M.S. papers, C.T.S.

[46] Calvin Butler, Evansville, Ind., June 16, 1834, in A.H.M.S. papers, C.T.S.

Visiting on Sunday was common in many parts of the West; one earnest missionary described as follows the method he used to break up this "ungodly practice" among his own church members:

...When I came here [Spencer, Ind.] every thing was opposed to Presbyterians...with some of our Church members visiting was so common I had to rig an anxious seat before I could break down this ungodly practice. But the Lord blessed our course, and let me tell you the Devil stole away all my sermons after meeting for a long time but one day I saw him at the door I warned the congregation of the fact —then I gave the people one of the plainest talks ever mortals heard and tears and sobs were heard and seen all over the house. I made every man and woman and child to [go] to their own homes but before they left the house I made about ⅔ of the assembly make a solemn vow to have no visitor on the holy sabbath....[47]

A summary of difficulties, temporal and spiritual, was made by a missionary writing from a little town in central Illinois in 1833:

...The people are not dissipated & are generally industrious But 1. There are here strong sectional prejudices. We have a large neighborhood of Quakers, whose hand is against every man & every man's hand against them. The County Seat is not yet located—several different sections are laboring to secure it—& each manifests displeasure to every opposing section & to every thing transacted in its vicinity—2 The people here have come from different quarters of the United States—each have brought along with them their local prejudices—but few have come from the East & against that few there appears to be almost every thing said to destroy or lessen their influence, that can be. 3. There are prejudices existing between the different denominations of Christians, but all seem to be united in having something to say against Presbyterianism. Other denominations are sensible that our ministers are better educated than theirs; & that their clergy may be elevated to an equal standing with ours, it is very natural for them to whisper abroad "The Presbyterian minister is a very poor preacher for one who has spent 8 or 7 years learning to preach." And as preaching, in view of the people, consists in *Certain tones & an abundance of noise*, which the Presbyterian has not acquired; it is, perhaps, proclaimed through the community, that "He is no preacher at all."... 4 Another thing much in the way of doing here is, the people are generally poor & have been borrowing money at 25 or 50 percent to pay for their land & are now exceedingly harassed & perplexed in canceling the debt contracted. This embarrassed state of the community absorbs all the energies of the mind prevents the attention from being riveted to the subject of religion....5 An other thing which has much hindered the usefulness of your missionary in this country is there have been no laymen to take an active part in religious concerns.

---

[47] J. Hill, Spencer, Ind., Nov. 22, 1831, in A.H.M.S. papers, C.T.S.

There has been no resident among us to take charge of a Sabbath
School except myself & wife; & no member of our little church has
been willing to go round to the people with a subscription paper for
my support. If some of the pious laymen in the older states knew how
much good they might accomplish in this beautiful, rich & salubrious
section of our country, I think they would certainly locate themselves
in this vicinity. 6 There are not a few who have been pretty well
educated in the modern school of Infidelity. They manifest a greater
hatred to Presbyterianism than to any other denomination.... 7 An
other thing in the way of my usefulness is, I happen to go by the
name of "New-school man" & the three or four Presbyterians who
were here when I came & the Cumberland Presbyterians with their
two ministers are "old-school men." ...48

It would be a mistake to assume that all or even a
majority of the missionary reports were written in so pessi-
mistic a vein as those quoted above. It would be just as easy
to make a selection of letters in which the emphasis is placed
on achievements, churches organized, converts made, and
schools founded. And it must also be remembered that most
of the men who relieved their feelings by pouring out their
tales of woe to their superior officers in the East usually
stayed in the West, and some of them attained positions of
influence among the people of the West. Perhaps all that
was necessary was some slight readjustment in attitude
and manner on the part of the missionary himself. One of
the men from the East, Theron Baldwin, who had adjusted
himself to Western life warned the officers of the American
Home Missionary Society on this point:

> The Eastern preacher is not unfrequently the very "antipodes" of
> his audience—and sometimes looked upon as a mysterious, suspicious
> being from another hemisphere or another planet—Since my residence
> in the state I have travelled 2000 miles or more in different directions
> —and it is my settled conviction that for the Eastern preacher who
> expects to settle permanently in this state, it is all important that
> he at first travel a great deal and mingle with the people—acquaint
> himself with their manners and customs—their sentiments, preju-
> dices &c &c. He has as a general fact many points which must be
> *knocked off* before it is *possible* for him to come in close contact with
> this people—and if he is unable to do this, where is the prospect of
> his usefulness? ...49

48 C. M. Babbitt, Pekin, Ill., June 8, 1833, in A.H.M.S. papers, C.T.S.

49 T. Baldwin, Vandalia, Ill., Aug. 16, 1830, in A.H.M.S. papers,
C.T.S. A group of dissatisfied members of a mission church in Keo-
kuk, Iowa, made complaint in July, 1846, that their missionary pastor,
although "pious, orthodox, and devoted ... never unbends from the
stiffness (not to say formality) of almost magisterial dignity, to
manifest an interest in passing occurrences." *Ibid.*

THE ILLINOIS BAND

Of the early activities of the American Home Missionary Society, perhaps the one which attracted the most attention was the sending of the Yale Band to Illinois in 1829. It will be remembered that John M. Ellis of Andover Theological Seminary was one of the men ordained in the Old South Church, Boston, in September, 1825, and that he had gone West under the auspices of the United Domestic Missionary Society of New York. In his chosen field of labor, Illinois, he continued his work under the American Home Missionary Society after it was established.[50] Ellis was greatly interested in education; again and again in his missionary reports he called attention to the necessity of providing books for the people in the West.[51] As early as 1827 he began to look for a suitable site for a seminary or academy, which he proposed to establish in Illinois or Missouri. In 1828 he acquired for this purpose a quarter section of land near Jacksonville, Illinois; it was, he said, the most delightful spot he had ever seen.[52] Ellis' letter to the American Home Missionary Society, in which he made a brief statement regarding the proposed school, was printed in the *Home Missionary* for December, 1828,[53] and read by some students in the Yale Divinity School who were interested in domestic missions.[54] These young men had a Society of Inquiry concerning Missions and held monthly meetings for the purpose of providing and circulating among the students accurate information relative to fields of missionary labor. It had occurred to one of these men that it would be a good plan for a group of theological students who knew one another to form an association for the purpose of co-operating in the work of home missions and establishing a college in the West. One of the members of the group stated the plan and its merits as follows:

---

[50] J. E. Roy, "Fifty years of Home Missions in Illinois," in *The New Englander*, XXXV (1876), 567.

[51] *E.g.*, letters of Aug. 7 and 14, 1826, from Kaskaskia, Ill., in C.H.M.S. (Box 1, Bundle 1); not found in A.H.M.S. papers, C.T.S.

[52] John M. Ellis, Jacksonville, Ill., Sept. 25, 1828, in A.H.M.S. papers, C.T.S.

[53] *Home Missionary*, I (1828), 135-36.

[54] J. M. Sturtevant, *Historical Discourse* (New York, [1855],) 8-16.

A frontier state, or territory likely soon to become a state, was to be selected as a common field of labor. It was proposed to establish there an institution of learning, and by the united efforts of the association to foster its growth and efficiency, while the members strengthened each other's hands in the use of all evangelical instrumentalities. By this means they hoped to secure co-operation, which is often so difficult to obtain among the scattered population of the frontier, and to avoid that peculiar isolation which is among the greatest disadvantages of a home missionary on the borders of the wilderness.[55]

The letter from John M. Ellis appeared shortly after this happy suggestion had been made. The young men corresponded with Ellis, informed him of their plans, and suggested that they might be disposed to choose Illinois as their field of labor and assist in the establishment of his proposed seminary. The reply from Ellis as to his aims and ideals was satisfactory, and the organization of the Illinois Band was soon completed. Seven members of the Yale Theological School, Theron Baldwin, John F. Brooks, Mason Grosvenor, Elisha Jenney, William Kirby, Julian M. Sturtevant, and Asa Turner, signed a compact in February, 1829, in which they expressed their readiness "to go to the State of Illinois for the purpose of establishing a Seminary of learning such as shall best be adapted to the exigencies of that country—a part of us to engage in instruction in the Seminary—the others to occupy—as preachers important stations in the surrounding country—provided the undertaking be deemed practicable, and the location approved—and provided also the providence of God permit us to engage in it."[56]

The men who had entered into this agreement also pledged themselves to raise ten thousand dollars for the proposed college, and they in turn were to be given a share in its management. With the assistance of Mr. Ellis, who came East for that purpose, the money was secured.[57] Then they turned to the American Home Missionary Society for commissions and such financial support as might be necessary. The officers of the Society, apparently with some hesitation because of their feeling that they were allowed by

[55] J. M. Sturtevant, *Autobiography*, 135-36.

[56] J. M. Sturtevant, *Autobiography*, 138-39.

[57] Ellis later stated that he sacrificed the last fragment of his wife's patrimony, about $150, to make the trip East in behalf of the college. J. M. Ellis, Jacksonville, Ill., Nov. 2, 1830, in A.H.M.S. papers, C.T.S.

their constitution to send out none but preachers, agreed to give missionary commissions to the men in the Yale group as fast as they were individually prepared and ordained. But in order that there might be no misunderstanding it was stated and restated that the Executive Committee regarded preaching the gospel as the principal object of all missionaries, although they also expected of them "such a general cooperation in all that relates to the Civil & literary interests of the country where they labor as is becoming in Ministers in other situations."[58]

In the autumn of 1829 two members of the Band, Baldwin and Sturtevant, went to Jacksonville, "then a village of two years growth from the naked prairie," and on January 4, 1830, Illinois College was opened for the reception of students. Sturtevant took charge of the college, while Baldwin located as a missionary pastor at Vandalia, then the capital of the state. Other members of the Yale Band went to Illinois later, and, in addition to the original members whose names are given above, five others joined the association after 1829; their names were Romulus Barnes, William Carter, Flavel Bascom, Albert Hale, and Lucien Farnham. They were primarily ministers; but they were interested in and gave loyal support to the little college at Jacksonville, which became a center of Puritan influence in Illinois.[59]

THE PRESBYTERIAN BOARD OF MISSIONS

At the same time that certain Presbyterians were giving support to and helping administer the American Home Missionary Society, others adhered to the General Assembly's Board of Missions. As was pointed out in a previous chapter,[60] the Presbyterian Committee of Missions, which was formed in 1802, had been enlarged into a Board of Missions in 1816. The significance of the change is to be found in the fact that the Committee had been more or less temporary in its make-up, whereas the Board was a more permanent group, composed of men who spent much of their time in the supervision of missionary work. Adherents of the Board,

---

[58] A. Peters by C. Hall to M. Governeur [Grosvenor], Jan. 8, 1829, A.H.M.S. Letter Bk. B, 1006, C.T.S.

[59] C. P. Kofoid, "Puritan Influences in the Formative Years of Illinois History," in *Transactions of the Illinois State Historical Society*, 1905, 261-338.

[60] See above, page 148.

as opposed to the friends of voluntary societies, insisted that this plan combined unity of control and permanence of policy with the direct supervision of the Church through the General Assembly. As late as 1820 the operations of the Board were conducted on a small scale. In that year it had available in its missionary fund only $2,200; thirty-six missionary appointments were made for tours varying in length from one to nine months.[61] In the report of 1825 it was stated that 52 missionary appointments had been made that year; of these 8 were in New York, 14 in Pennsylvania, 5 in Ohio, 4 in Indiana, 3 in Illinois, 4 in Missouri, and 3 in Alabama.[62]

In 1827, the year after the creation of the American Home Missionary Society, the report of the Board of Missions contained a review of its previous history and an apology for or explanation of its unimpressive record as compared with that of its new and aggressive rival. The Board pointed out that its funds had been small, little more than $4,000 a year on the average for the preceding ten years, and that consequently it had not been able financially to make use of the plan, "recently adopted by the Home Missionary Society with flattering success," of settling pastors over weak churches. The Board did not disapprove the new plan; on the contrary, so the report goes, "we feel disposed to commend the endeavors made in this way to secure the permanent settlement of ministers in feeble and infant churches; and so far as our funds, and the relation the Board sustains to the Presbyterian Church at large will allow, we design to act more directly on it than heretofore."[63]

In 1828 the Board of Missions made a friendly gesture to the new society. The Secretary of the Board, Reverend E. S. Ely, addressed the Executive Committee of the American Home Missionary Society with a plea for co-operation. He said: "To prevent all interference in appointments, and to let you know the affairs of your brethren, we shall communicate to you, from time to time, our proceedings; and beg leave to assure you, that we shall not intentionally authorize any encroachment upon ground preoccupied by

---

[61] *Extracts from Minutes of the General Assembly of the Presbyterian Church*, IV, 341-43, 368.

[62] *Ibid.*, V, 279.

[63] *Ibid.*, VI, 155-57.

yourselves in the manner above described." As evidence that there was room for both agencies he pointed out that "at this moment [1828] there are 636 vacant churches connected with but 90 Presbyteries; which have no ministrations of the gospel but from itinerant preachers; and 502 more of our churches have only 226 pastors or stated supplies among them; so that 276 of the churches said to be supplied might with propriety be added to those which are denominated vacant."[64] In reply the Corresponding Secretary of the American Home Missionary Society, the Reverend Absalom Peters, wrote a lengthy defense of the method of conducting missions through a voluntary union society, and pointed out the evils of having in the same denomination two societies competing with one another for funds in the East and working at cross-purposes in the West.[65] His solution of the difficulty was not co-operation but consolidation. The two secretaries met as individuals and worked out a plan of union,[66] but it was rejected by the Board of Missions partly because it thought the proposed merger was inexpedient, and partly because it had no authority from the General Assembly to enter into any such arrangement;[67] there was also some opposition from some supporters of the American Home Missionary Society, and so the plan was dropped.[68]

---

[64] E. S. Ely, Philadelphia, July 4, 1828, to Executive Comm., A.H. M.S., in C.H.M.S. (unnumbered box, Bundle 16, No. 170); an extract from this letter was published in *Home Missionary*, I (1828), 60; I have not found the original letter in A.H.M.S. papers, C.T.S.

[65] A. Peters to Exec. Comm. of Board of Missions, N. Y. Aug. 13, 1828, copy in C.H.M.S. (unnumbered box, Bundle 16, No. 219); I have not found this letter in A.H.M.S. papers, C.T.S.

[66] The details of the plan are of little significance in the present study; it called for the annual appointment of fifty directors by the General Conference of Maine, the General Association of New Hampshire, the General Convention of Vermont, the General Association of Massachusetts, the General Association of Connecticut, the Evangelical Consociation of Rhode Island, the General Synod of the Reformed Dutch Church, the German Reformed Synod, and the General Assembly of the Presbyterian Church in the United States of America, in proportion to the number of ministers severally embraced in the above-named ecclesiastical bodies. Printed circular letter of the A.H.M.S., Feb. 5, 1829; also published in *Home Missionary*, I (1829), 206-11.

[67] Printed Circular of Board of Missions of the General Assembly, Philadelphia, Feb. 25, 1829, copy in C.H.M.S. (box No. 2); not found in A.H.M.S. papers, C.T.S.

[68] Exec. Com. of A.H.M.S. to the Christian Public, N. Y., March 10, 1829, in *The Philadelphian*, March 20, 1829.

The unfortunate result of this abortive attempt at union was that the two organizations were driven farther apart; rivalries soon passed the point of friendliness. The Board was the older of the two; its supporters insisted that missions should be conducted by the Church and not turned over to a voluntary society not under direct ecclesiastical control. The friends of the new organization contended that a large union society, which drew its support from two or more groups of Protestants whose practices and doctrines were so much alike, could handle home missions more effectively than the many small competing societies and boards. They pointed to the rapid growth of their society as evidence that the formation of a large union organization had aroused a new interest in missions and secured more financial support than all the little societies had ever been able to obtain. Furthermore, they insisted that the refusal of the Board to give way partly defeated the very objects for which the American Home Missionary Society had been created.[69] Letters were written and pamphlets were printed in an effort, on the one hand, to bring about consolidation, or, on the other, to drive the American Home Missionary Society out of the Presbyterian Church. But the voluntary society had a strong following in the Church, especially in New York; and in 1829 the General Assembly adopted a resolution to the effect that, although it would affectionately solicit the co-operation of the churches with its own Board of Missions, the "churches should be left entirely to their own unbiased and deliberate choice of the particular channel through which their charities shall flow forth to bless the perishing."[70] The controversy continued, however, and by 1837 had become so bitter as to help bring about schism in the Church.[71]

THE BAPTISTS

As was briefly described in the preceding chapter, the Baptists in 1814 organized their General Missionary Convention because their attention had been called in a striking manner to the foreign field. In 1817 they entered the home

---

[69] The controversial literature is voluminous; arguments on both sides may be found in A. Peters, *Brief Answer to an Official Reply.*

[70] *Extracts from the Minutes of the General Assembly of the Presbyterian Church,* VI, 374.

[71] See below, page 240 f.

field too and sent John M. Peck and James E. Welch to Missouri to work among both whites and Indians. Three years later the Convention voted to give up home missions. The reason given for this act of retrenchment was as strange as the act itself; it was that the Western settlements would soon be supplied with an abundance of preaching by the migration of ministers from the Eastern states.[72] Another reason was lack of funds for the support of missions among both the white population and the Indians. Still another factor in the decision to abandon home missions was the growing hostility to such work on the part of many Southern and Western Baptists. In the eighteenth century many Baptists had been zealous in missions. By the end of the second decade of the nineteenth century certain elements in the denomination had become strongly opposed to all forms of missionary activity. This antimission feeling was most noticeable in the West and the Southwest, where there were more of the uneducated ministers who resented the presence among them of the better-trained men from the East, and who, in common with large numbers of their self-satisfied neighbors, were unwilling to admit that their communities were in any way inferior to those of the East or that they stood in any particular need of missionary assistance. This feeling of resentment and jealousy is well illustrated by a story told in Peck's *Memoirs* of a man who rose in a Western Baptist Association to speak against missionaries. He said: "We don't care anything about them missionaries that's gone amongst them heathens way off yonder. But what do they want to come among us for? We don't want them here in Illinois." When the Moderator remarked that this is a free country and one did not have to hear the missionaries preach unless he wanted to do so, the man continued: "Well, if you must know, Brother Moderator, you know the big trees in the woods overshadow the little ones; and these missionaries will be all great, learned men, and the people will go to hear them preach, and we shall all be put down. That's the objection."[73] Furthermore, in the

---

[72] *Latter Day Luminary*, II (1820), 125; John M. Peck made the observation that Baptist ministers who moved to Missouri were apparently more interested in good land than in preaching. J. M. Peck, St. Louis Co., Sept. 4, 1820, to Isaac McCoy, McCoy MSS., II, No. 67, in Kansas Historical Society.

[73] R. Babcock, *Memoir of John Mason Peck*, 110-11.

West the Methodists were the chief rivals of the Baptists. Theological disputes with these Arminians forced many Baptists into an exaggerated form of Calvinism.[74] If the doctrines of election and predestination are carried to extremes, missions become not only unnecessary, but even impious. "What a manifestation of hatred to God, and puny rebellion against him," exclaimed one foe of missions, steeped in foreordination, "for puny worms to undertake to introduce as heirs of his last will and testament, such as he has not chosen, whose whole conduct prove them to be strange children, entirely of another spirit and principle."[75] Other Baptists who professed to believe in "gospel missions" objected to the formation of missionary societies on the ground that there was no authority for them in the Bible; they denounced the attempt to convert the world through the use of worldly means, gold and silver, rather than through the agency of the Holy Spirit. As one of the "Antis" put it, "No money, no converts"; hence obviously the whole missionary society scheme is a human contrivance devised by human wisdom and carried on by human skill.[76]

Whatever the reasons may have been, and probably a failure on the part of Eastern Baptists to realize the significance of the West was one of the most important, the Baptist General Convention in 1820 instructed John M. Peck, its principal home missionary, to cease his work among the white settlers and move to an Indian mission at Fort Wayne. Peck declined to comply with this order and continued his work in Missouri on his own responsibility. About 1824 he received a commission from the Massachusetts Baptist Missionary Society, in the service of which institution he remained with slight interruptions until the formation of the American Baptist Home Mission Society in 1832.[77]

John M. Peck is one of the outstanding figures in the

---

[74] The editor of the *Western Predestinarian*, Paris, Ill., wrote about 1842: "We consider the entire mission system predicated in rank Arminianism, and as such, a disgrace to the Baptist name." C. R. Henderson, "Early Home Mission Work in Indiana," *Baptist Home Mission Monthly*, V (1883), 76.

[75] Quoted by C. R. Henderson, "Early Home Mission Work in Indiana," *Baptist Home Mission Monthly*, V (1883), 76-77.

[76] G. Conklin, *Examination of a Pamphlet titled "Truth as it is"* (Alexandria, 1839), 15.

[77] W. H. Eaton, *Historical Sketch of the Massachusetts Baptist Missionary Society*, 34.

early religious history of the Middle West. He was a man of great animation and energy, one who made friends easily. It was greatly to his advantage that he lacked the stiffness and reserve which so often hampered the work of other New England missionaries in the West. His thorough familiarity with Western life and his skill in such homely tasks as building a campfire or making a bed out of boughs won him the respect of frontiersmen. Although broad-minded and tolerant in his relations with men of other creeds,[78] he labored earnestly to build up his own church in the West. In 1826 he submitted to the Massachusetts Baptist Missionary Society a plan for work. He proposed, first of all, to organize a system of circuits for Missouri, Illinois, and Indiana, because he believed that the system of itinerant missions was the cheapest and best method for the West; his second suggestion was that at St. Louis there should be stationed an able preacher who should devote a part of his time to teaching; and, finally, that a theological school for all these states be established in Illinois in order that Western men might be trained for the Baptist ministry.[79] About 1827, Peck having moved meantime to Illinois, the proposed school was started as the Rock Spring Theological and High School. Out of this ultimately grew Shurtleff College.[80] In 1829 the versatile Peck began the publication of a religious newspaper called *The Pioneer of the Valley of the Mississippi.*

Peck's notable work in the West attracted the attention of Eastern Baptists. He visited the East, after nine years' experience in the new states, and pointed out the needs of the country. While there he visited Dr. Jonathan Going, dynamic pastor of a Baptist Church in Worcester, Massachusetts, and one of the leading spirits in the Massachusetts

---

[78] The Presbyterian Salmon Giddings, St. Louis, July 23, 1818, in Conn. Miss. Soc. MS. Letters and Journals, 1816-19, paid a tribute to Peck's ability and Christian spirit; in one of his letters Peck referred to his friendly relations with Messrs. Giddings and Rice, both of whom were Presbyterian ministers. J. M. Peck, St. Louis, March 21, 1818, to Isaac McCoy. McCoy MSS. I, No. 37, in Kansas Historical Society. T. Lippincott wrote from Belleville, Ill., Feb. 10, 1840, that Mr. Peck had made his arrangements for preaching "with studied regard to mine, so that we each occupy half the time in different houses." A.H.M.S. papers, C.T.S.

[79] J. M. Peck, "Circular Address," in *American Baptist Magazine*, N. S., VI, 206; R. Babcock, *Memoir of John Mason Peck*, 220.

[80] See below, page 399.

Baptist Missionary Society. In 1831 Going made a journey through the Mississippi Valley to observe the religious conditions on the frontier. Peck accompanied him on a part of this tour; when they parted they had agreed that a general Baptist Home Missionary Society should be formed. On his return to New England, Going met with the Massachusetts Baptist Missionary Society in Boston and urged the formation of such a society. A resolution was adopted declaring that the Baptists of the United States ought to form a general society for home missionary work and that Dr. Going ought to relinquish his pastoral duties in order to direct the work of the new organization. A deputation was appointed to confer with the members of the New York Baptist Missionary Society, which also had missions in the West. As a result of this agitation the American Baptist Home Mission Society was organized in New York in April, 1832, with Jonathan Going as Corresponding Secretary.[81]

The Executive Committee of the new Society very properly began their work by making a survey of the field. "This survey," they said, "has disclosed a wide and fearful moral destitution, which calls loudly on all sections of the Christian community to immediately and liberally aid in efforts for its supply. To furnish a population of 13,000,000 with religious institutions there are only about 11,000 ministers of all denominations." They found much to lament in the condition of Baptists in the West. "Among these, and the cause of most other evils, is a lamentable want of the preaching of the gospel and of pastoral labor, arising, in a great measure, from a mistake in relation to the qualification of ministers, a deficiency in their support, and a misapprehension of the sacred nature of the pastoral office, and the importance of its responsible duties."[82]

The Western Baptists themselves were a field for missionary work with respect to missions, Sunday Schools, and all benevolent organizations.[83] Representatives of the

---

[81] *Proceedings of the Convention held in the City of New-York, on the 27th of April, 1832 for the Formation of the American Baptist Home Mission Society* (New York, 1832); H. L. Morehouse, "Historical Sketch of the American Baptist Home Mission Society for Fifty Years," in *Baptist Home Missions in North America*, 307-22.

[82] American Baptist Home Mission Society (cited hereafter as A.B.H.M.S.), *First Report* (1833), 6-7.

[83] On the rise of antimission Baptists see W. W. Sweet, *Religion on the American Frontier: The Baptists, 1783-1830* (New York, 1931), Chap. IV.

new Baptist society often found it difficult to obtain a hearing or support among their own people in the West. One reported from Illinois in 1833:

> The Baptists belonging to the Crooked Creek Association will not suffer me to preach in their houses. One of them invited me to do so, but when he found I was favorable to Sabbath Schools, he said his church would deal with him if he suffered a man of that character to preach in his house.[84]

Another missionary to Illinois about the same time was rejected because he expected the people to contribute something to his expenses. He wrote:

> Since my last report I have preached sixty-nine sermons, and baptized twenty-two persons, but the cause of missions is not flattering. Some there are who love in word and tongue, but not in deed and truth. They say, "We love to hear you preach. Come as often as you can." But when we say to them, "The laborer is worthy of his hire," they resent it and cry out "beggars," "missionary beggars," "money-hunters," and "deserters."[85]

Fifty missionaries were in the service of the Baptist Home Mission Society in its first year; they were located mainly in Ohio, Indiana, Illinois, Michigan, Missouri, and New York. In the second year eighty men were employed, and by the end of the fourth year the number had increased to more than one hundred; the annual receipts of the Society that year (1835-36) were about $17,000. During these early years missionary agents were also employed; they did not have charge of any one church, but traveled extensively, organized churches, sought out new fields of labor, and secured information for the Society. The methods used by this Baptist society were similar to those employed by the American Home Missionary Society, except that more use was made of local Western and Southern ministers. The Executive Committee of the American Baptist Home Mission Society gave their reasons for this policy in their first report:

> . . . They have not relied exclusively or chiefly [they said] on men from the North and East. They believed from the first that there were many on the ground, who, if aided and encouraged, would be highly useful in the work, and information has shown that the number of such is larger than they had supposed. These men resemble in principles, piety and qualifications, the founders and fathers of the

[84] A.B.H.M.S., *Thirty-ninth Report* (1871), 18.
[85] *Ibid.*, 17.

churches of the denomination in other sections of the country. Such
men will be, in several respects, more useful than strangers; they
know the people, are acquainted with their wants, their habits, and
their prejudices, and can readily accommodate themselves to these;—
they are also known to the public, and confidence is reposed in them.
Of these, hundreds will be found disposed to engage in the work of
fully preaching the gospel to those who are around them, as soon as
the funds of the Society will enable the Committee to loose them from
the embarrassment of their secular occupations for the support of
their families. . . . [86]

THE METHODISTS

In keeping with the spirit of the times the Methodists
organized a general missionary society in 1819. Although
the whole organization of the Methodist Episcopal Church
was essentially a missionary scheme, and despite Bishop
Asbury's collections for the support of itinerants in new
settlements, there were some who believed that the missionary work of the Church might be conducted more efficiently, especially among the Indians and the Negroes and
on the frontier circuits, if a society were formed for that
purpose. It was argued that the needs of the vast Western
and Southern fields had grown beyond the ability of the
various conferences to deal with them and that some plan
of systematic co-operation of all the conferences was desirable.[87] Hence the suggestion was made that a missionary
society be formed subject to the General Conference. There
was some opposition to the proposed organization, which
was to be both a Bible and a missionary society, on the
ground that Methodists ought to co-operate with the American Bible Society. The latter, however, came in for its
share of criticism then directed by certain Methodists towards all societies that assumed the name "American" or
set up a claim to be "National." Advocates of the new
society, notably Nathan Bangs, Freeborn Garrettson, and
Bishop Joshua Soule, persisted in their efforts, with the
result that the Missionary and Bible Society of the Methodist Episcopal Church in America was formed in New
York in April, 1819.[88] At the General Conference which met

---

[86] A.B.H.M.S., *First Report* (1833), 12-13.

[87] H. K. Carroll, *Missionary Growth of the Methodist Episcopal
Church* (Cincinnati, 1907), 10.

[88] Missionary and Bible Society of the Methodist Episcopal Church,
Constitution and First Annual Report (New York, 1820), 3.

in the following year the new society was given the official sanction of the Church, and, as had been hoped by the founders, nearly all the conferences became auxiliary societies.[89] The first missionary appointed by this society was Ebenezer Brown, who was sent to work among the French in Louisiana in 1820. Brown's work among the French did not meet with much success, but his efforts were of importance in connection with the spread of Methodism among the English-speaking population of New Orleans. In 1822 a missionary district was formed in the Tennessee Conference in what was known as the Jackson Purchase. Then followed in rapid succession the establishment of missions in the Highlands of New York, in the Hampshire section of Massachusetts, in the Piscataquis district in Maine, at St. Augustine, St. Johns, and Tallahassee, Florida, at St. Mary's in western Ohio, at St. Joseph's and Defiance in Michigan, at Logansport in Indiana, on Salt River and at Gasconage and West Prairie in Missouri, on the Fox River and at Galena in Wisconsin. The receipts of the Society in its first year (1820) were less than one thousand dollars, but they had grown to $13,000 by 1830 and $30,000 by 1835. At the end of the first ten years of its history the Society had thirty-seven mission stations and thirty missionaries.[90]

Meanwhile the circuit riders appeared so regularly and faithfully at their appointed times and places, that the Committee on Itinerancy in the General Conference of 1832 could report that "the general state of the itinerant connexion is not only very favorable, but its future prospects exceedingly flattering."[91]

THE EPISCOPALIANS

In the first two decades of the nineteenth century the Protestant Episcopal Church paid little attention to the West. Its membership was drawn mainly from the prosperous city dwellers in the North and the aristocratic planter population of the South. Comparatively few of

---

[89] J. M. Reid and J. T. Gracey, *Missions and Missionary Society of the Methodist Episcopal Church* (rev. ed., New York, 1896), I, 14-24; N. Bangs, *History of the Methodist Episcopal Church* (New York, 1857), III, 80-92.

[90] W. P. Strickland, *History of the Missions of the Methodist Episcopal Church* (Cincinnati, 1850), 52-61.

[91] Methodist Episcopal Church, *Journals of the General Conferences* (New York, 1855-56), I, 393.

these people went West; and even when men brought up in the Episcopal Church did go to the new settlements, they were usually so few in numbers compared with the adherents of the more popular creeds about them that they were unable to found churches in their new homes.

One indication of change in attitude towards the West was the formation in 1821 of the Domestic and Foreign Missionary Society of the Protestant Episcopal Church. Membership in the Society came as a result of the gift of money for the support of missions. The receipts were not large, amounting to less than $13,000 in the tenth year of the Society's history. Until 1829 the work of the Society was carried on entirely within the United States and mainly among the Indians. The principal mission was at Green Bay, Wisconsin, but others were maintained in Florida, Missouri, Mississippi, Tennessee, Kentucky, Michigan, and New York.[92]

Meanwhile Philander Chase had been making an interesting experiment in the establishment of the Episcopal Church and Episcopal institutions in a new Western state with almost no assistance from his co-religionists in the seaboard states. Chase, a New Englander and a graduate of Dartmouth College, had become an Episcopalian as a result of reading the Prayer Book. Immediately after his ordination as a deacon in 1798 he became an itinerant missionary in northern and western New York.[93] In 1805 he went to New Orleans, where he established an Episcopal Church. He returned to New England in 1811 and served as the rector of Christ Church in Hartford, Connecticut, until 1817. In March of that year he set out for Ohio to look over the ground with the view of locating there. The journey west from Buffalo over the ice of Lake Erie was not without its dangers. Chase and his traveling companion, who had hired a man to take them by sleigh to Cattaraugus Creek, about thirty-seven miles west of Buffalo, reached it just before nightfall. Ahead of them lay a dark,

---

[92] *Proceedings of the Board of Directors of the Domestic and Foreign Missionary Society of the Protestant Episcopal Church* (Philadelphia, 1831), 44; for the missions at Green Bay see Jackson Kemper, "Journal of an Episcopal Missionary's Tour to Green Bay, 1834," in *Wisconsin Historical Collections*, XIV (Madison, 1898), 394-449. The work of Jackson Kemper as a home missionary will be described in the next chapter.

[93] Philander Chase, *Reminiscences* (2nd ed., Boston, 1848), I, 23.

rolling stream which was pouring its early floodwaters out on the ice of the lake. The village where they had expected to spend the night was on the other side of the stream. A recent thaw had removed the ice on which they had expected to cross, and the creek, running with overflowing banks, was too deep to ford. The driver, contending that he had fulfilled his obligation when he brought them to Cattaraugus Creek, dumped their baggage on the beach and demanded his pay. Chase refused to pay the man until he took them on to some place where they could find shelter for the night; so they got in the sleigh again and drove out toward the center of the lake until they got beyond the ice that had been weakened by the warm, muddy water from the creek. Then they turned to the left and drove through the water flowing over the top of the ice. "It was terrific to the feelings, if not to the eye of reason," said Chase, "to hear the water pour over the runners of the sleigh as we crossed this muddy stream, in a dark night, so far out from the shore."[94]

Chase spent the summer of 1817 in Ohio, preaching, organizing parishes, and visiting different parts of the state in the interest of his Church. At Worthington he bought a tract of land and was appointed principal of the Worthington Academy. His importance among the members of the Episcopal Church in Ohio was quickly recognized, and at a meeting of the clergy and lay delegates held in June, 1818, he was elected Bishop of Ohio. It will be observed that in the formation of the diocese of Ohio the Episcopal Church in the Eastern states had assumed no responsibility and had given no help. In accordance with the theory of autonomy for the various dioceses, the clergy of a state were expected to organize a diocese and choose a bishop without any direction or interference from the outside when they became sufficiently numerous. This method of procedure was retained until 1835, at which time the Church as a whole assumed responsibility for the organization of churches on the frontier by the selection of a missionary bishop.[95] One of the weaknesses in the old arrangement was that if the clergy of a new state waited until they were sufficiently numerous and their churches sufficiently strong to provide

[94] P. Chase, *Reminiscences*, I, 120-24.

[95] The creation of missionary bishops will be discussed in the next chapter; see below, page 262.

adequate support for a bishop before they organized a new diocese, they were compelled to do without the services of a bishop at the very time they were most needed.

Under the newly elected Bishop of Ohio were five clergymen.[96] The Episcopal Church was so weak in Ohio at the time that funds were not available to provide adequate support for the bishop and his family. He was forced to engage in farming on a small scale to make a living. In 1820, on his return home from his episcopal visitations, Bishop Chase had to discharge his hired man for lack of money. Then the bishop himself had to thresh the grain, haul and cut wood, build the fires, and feed the stock. At times he felt that he had acted unwisely in accepting the episcopate in the absence of appropriations for the bishop's support, for he recalled the rule of the Church that "no ordained clergyman shall condescend to menial and servile employments."[97]

To found a college in the West where Western men might be trained for the ministry was one of Bishop Chase's chief desires. Considering the lack of interest in the West that had thus far been manifested by Episcopalians in the East, it is not surprising that Chase decided to look elsewhere first for assistance in his new venture. His proposal to go to England for help met with sharp opposition from some of his colleagues in the episcopacy, and one of them who went to that country about the same time Chase did in 1823 even issued a public warning there against him and his plans. In spite of this opposition, Bishop Chase was able to interest some influential Britishers in his proposed college, among them Lord Kenyon, Lord Gambier, and Lady Rosse. He secured about $30,000 in England for the new school, to which was given the name Kenyon College in honor of one of the chief benefactors; to commemorate another donor, the site chosen in Knox County, Ohio, was called Gambier.[98] Inasmuch as the financial help obtained in England was not sufficient for the college, Bishop Chase subsequently made an appeal also to his American brethren.[99]

---

[96] There were only five active Episcopal clergymen in the Diocese of Virginia in 1814, H. S. Burleson, *Conquest of the Continent*, 47.

[97] P. Chase, *Reminiscences*, I, 174-75.

[98] P. Chase, *Reminiscences*, I, 209 ff.

[99] P. Chase, *Plea for the West* (Philadelphia, 1826).

Bishop Chase, having intended Kenyon to be a Christian college, kept the control entirely in his own hands; it became so much of a "patriarchial despotism"[100] that dissatisfied members of the faculty tried to wrest some of the power from the Bishop. The instructors incited the students to rebellion; Bishop Chase was insulted as he went along the streets by boys shouting for "independence of episcopal tyranny."[101] In 1831 Bishop Chase gave up the fight, resigned his episcopate, and with it surrendered the control of the college.[102] In the following year he moved to Gilead in Michigan, and there he lived until he was elected Bishop of Illinois in 1836.[103] Doubtless Bishop Chase loved to rule —but he was a benevolent despot, and the Episcopal Church owes much to him for his work in the West.

DISCIPLES OF CHRIST

In the years covered in this chapter a new religious body was growing up in the West, the Disciples of Christ or "Christians," which, although not concerned with organized home missions at the outset, was, nevertheless, aggressively evangelistic. Its rapid spread in the West and the oft-expressed conviction among the older Protestant denominations that its teachings were subversive of the true principles of Christianity, led to determined efforts on their part to combat it. In the East, and in the West among rival religious leaders, it was regarded as another of the delusions of the frontier, but one of the most dangerous of all because, as they freely admitted, it had "the form of godliness."[104]

---

[100] B. C. Steiner, *Life of Henry Winter Davis* (Baltimore, 1916), 19.

[101] E. Waylen, *Ecclesiastical Reminiscences of the United States* (New York, 1846), 116-19.

[102] P. Chase, *Reminiscences*, II, 109.

[103] M. Randall, "Bishop Chase in Gilead, 1832-1836," *Michigan Pioneer Collections*, VII (Lansing, 1884), 358-65.

[104] The following comment on the teachings of the Disciples of Christ, or "Campbellites," as they were usually called, is typical of scores of criticisms made by Presbyterian and Congregational missionary pastors in their reports to the A.H.M.S. in the years when the Disciples or "Christians" were getting a foothold in the West: "I have no hesitation in saying that in my opinion Campbellism is the *great* curse of the West—more destructive & more injurious to the cause of religion than avowed Infidelity itself. There is evidence of wonderful cunning in the system, and in those who seek to carry it out. It presents something like a form of godliness, which may answer temporal purposes, and serve for those who cannot silence conscience without something in the semblance of religion." T. Eustace, Paris, Mo., Sept. 6, 1840, A.H.M.S. papers, C.T.S.

The Disciples Church was formed by the partial union of two religious movements, both of which took their origin in the West in the years of excitement which followed the Great Revival. In the preceding chapter a brief account was given of the origin and principles of the New Lights or "Christians."[105] A few years later a religious movement with similar aims took form in western Pennsylvania around Thomas Campbell and his son Alexander. Thomas Campbell had been the pastor of a Seceder Presbyterian Church in Ireland, but had become disgusted with the petty disputes which had split the Seceders into no fewer than four divisions.[106] Early in the nineteenth century he had come to America and settled in western Pennsylvania, where his liberal policy of inviting religiously homeless members of other denominations to share the communion of his Presbyterian Church brought down on him the censure of the Seceder Synod. The dominant note in Thomas Campbell's preaching had come to be a plea for Christian union on the basis of the Bible. He withdrew from the Synod and with a few followers formed the "Christian Association of Washington" in 1809. Campbell drew up a "Declaration and Address" in which the fundamental idea was the necessity for the rejection of all human opinions and the return to the Bible as the only basis upon which all Christians could unite. About this time Alexander Campbell, who had been a student in the University of Glasgow, came to America and joined heartily in the movement which his father had initiated; it was not long before he became the chief leader in what he and his followers have called the "Restoration Movement." The decision of the Campbells to take the Bible as the sole rule of faith and practice led them to reject infant baptism. Having adopted the views of the Baptists on that point, they naturally turned to that denomination and were admitted to the Redstone Association in western Pennsylvania in 1813.[107] This union did not last long, however, because there were important differences between the

---

[105] See above, page 129.

[106] In J. B. Schouller, *History of the United Presbyterian Church of North America (Amer. Ch. Hist. Ser.,* XI, New York, 1894), 146, there is a diagram which shows the division of the Seceder Church into four parts: Old Light Burgher, New Light Burgher, Old Light Anti-Burgher, and New Light Anti-Burgher.

[107] E. Gates, *Early Relation and Separation of Baptists and Disciples* (Chicago, 1904), 9-20.

Baptists and the Campbells, especially on the question of regeneration. The Baptists of western Pennsylvania were thoroughly Calvinistic, whereas the Campbells taught that any person who believed in Christ could obey him and receive the promise of salvation. By 1830 the difference between the Baptists and the "Reformers" had become so serious that there was no hope of reconciliation. Baptist associations in Virginia, Pennsylvania, Ohio, and Kentucky had been disrupted by the new doctrines; churches had been divided. By 1830 the "Reformers," who then numbered between twenty and thirty thousand, had quite generally been denied fellowship in the Baptist churches. Their exclusion from the Baptists had two results. The ministers of the Restoration movement were forced to organize churches in order that their adherents might have Christian fellowship—and thus did a movement for Christian union result in the birth of a new denomination. A second result of the separation from the Baptists was a movement for union with the New Lights.[108] Campbell's Restoration movement and Barton W. Stone's New Light movement had much in common; the essential idea in both had been the union of Christians on the basis of the Bible. Conferences between the leaders in 1832 led to a partial union between the two groups.[109] Complete union was never brought about, with the result that there were then two distinct denominations using the name "Christian Church." The larger of the two, often called the Disciples of Christ, traces its history back to the union of the followers of Alexander Campbell and Barton W. Stone, while the smaller denomination, sometimes known as the Christian Connexion, represented that branch of the New Lights which did not unite with the Campbell Restoration movement.[110]

The Disciples of Christ rapidly increased in numbers, especially in the Middle West. Before a hundred years had passed this religious movement had more than a million adherents, having outgrown some of the older denominations. The explanation is to be found in part in the fact

---

[108] W. W. Jennings, *Origin and Early History of the Disciples of Christ* (Cincinnati, 1919), 190.

[109] B. W. Stone, *Autobiography*, in J. R. Rogers, *Cane Ridge Meeting House*, 201-04.

[110] The Christian Church or Christian Connexion joined with the National Council of Congregational Churches in 1931 to form the General Council of Congregational and Christian Churches.

that Alexander Campbell and his associates taught a simple doctrine, free from the subtleties of Calvinistic theology. Campbell represented the "time-spirit (Zeitgeist) of the American Republic. He came in line with the great social and political movements of his day. He was the voice of democracy, of individualism in the religious sphere."[111] The Disciples of Christ did not establish a society for the prosecution of missionary work for several years; indeed, Campbell was for a time unfriendly to such un-Biblical organizations. The Restoration movement is of significance in the present connection, however, as an illustration of the spirit of the West and as a rival of the older Protestant churches whose missionaries came from the East to establish their systems on the frontier.

By 1820 the Mississippi Valley had become the center of home missionary activity in the United States. The number of people in this region was increasing so rapidly and it was so far removed from the principal base of missionary interest in New England and New York, that the old method of operation through small local societies which sent out preachers on short missionary tours was no longer adequate. The realization that the West was bound to play an increasingly important part in the life of the Nation added the element of patriotic interest to stimulate the spirit of disinterested benevolence and the religious zeal which were responsible for missionary activities. In keeping with the nationalistic tendencies of the period, general or national home missionary societies, either voluntary or denominational, were formed to supplant or to co-ordinate the activities of local organizations. Of these general and national societies the most important was the American Home Missionary Society, both because of its prestige and because for more than a quarter of a century it stood as an agency through which members of two great communions made an effort, while minimizing their own differences, to work together for a common cause in the West.

---

[111] H. Van Kirk, *History of the Theology of the Disciples of Christ* (St. Louis, 1907), 50-51.

CHAPTER VII

THE GREAT VALLEY, 1835-55

The religious and political destiny of our nation is to be decided in the West. There is the territory, and there will soon be the population, the wealth and the political power. . . .
It is equally clear, that the conflict which is to decide the destiny of the West, will be a conflict of institutions for the education of her sons, for purposes of superstition, or evangelical light; of despotism, or liberty.—*Lyman Beecher.*

THE WEST

By 1835 it was apparent that the Great Valley of the Mississippi was soon to become the heart of the United States, not only geographically but also politically and socially. The opportunities for settlement and economic development there were almost boundless, and only the surface of the natural resources had been scratched. In the northern parts of Indiana and Illinois, states since 1816 and 1818 respectively, there were still large tracts of unoccupied or sparsely settled lands. In Michigan, which was admitted to the Union in 1837, the frontier line did not extend more than one fifth of the way up the lower peninsula. West of the Great Lakes, Iowa and Wisconsin—and after them Minnesota—called for pioneers to settle on their fertile lands. Farther south there was plenty of new land for farms in Missouri and Arkansas and for plantations in Alabama and Mississippi. Even Texas, although not yet a part of the United States, was receiving its share of the westward-moving mass of humanity.

The rapid settlement of the West, the great increase in land values—at least on paper—and the habit into which everyone fell of reckoning wealth in terms of future worth contributed to the speculative mania which spread over the land in the thirties. The buying of land and the laying out of townsites, the projecting of railroads and the digging of canals, all became absorbing interests in the West. The number of paper towns multiplied so rapidly that wags

remarked that soon there would be no room left for farms.[1] In the West, Chicago became a center of speculation. Concerning the boom there about 1835 a famous foreign visitor, Harriet Martineau, wrote:

> I never saw a busier place than Chicago was at the time of our arrival. The streets were crowded with land speculators, hurrying from one sale to another. A negro, dressed up in scarlet, bearing a scarlet flag, and riding a white horse with housings of scarlet, announced the times of sales. At every street-corner where he stopped, the crowd flocked round him; and it seemed as if some prevalent mania infected the whole people. . . . As the gentlemen of our party walked the streets store-keepers hailed them from their doors, with offers of farms, and all manner of land-lots, advising them to speculate before the price of land rose higher.[2]

For men interested in home missions this state of affairs meant, on the one hand, that land was being taken up and settlers were pouring into the West so rapidly that it was almost impossible to plant religious and moral institutions as fast as material development demanded, and, on the other, that the missionaries had to perform their labors in the face of overwhelming indifference to spiritual concerns. There are many references in the reports of the missionaries to this discouraging aspect of their work. A man from Michigan reported in 1836 that

> Christians are well nigh consumed with ye "land fever" & speculation is the all in all.—Sometimes money may be loaned at 50 & 100 percent, & ye whole country round us is on tip-toe.[3]

From Indiana came the following note:

> . . . The extended system of internal improvements which has been adopted by our State Legislature has given an impulse to the spirit of worldly enterprise which seems like to engulph every other interest. There is great reason to fear that the cause of religion will suffer a sad decline.[4]

A warning about the necessity of laying up treasures in Heaven came from an Illinois preacher:

---

[1] Thomas Ford, *History of Illinois* (Chicago, 1854), 181-82.

[2] Harriet Martineau, *Society in America* (London, 1837), I, 350.

[3] Silas Woodbury, Bronson, Mich., May 5, 1836, in A.H.M.S. papers, C.T.S.

[4] S. G. Lowry, Crawfordsville, Ind., April 6, 1836, A.H.M.S. papers, C.T.S.

There has been a general decrease of interest [in religion] for a few weeks past, owing to the public lands in this region [Bureau County] being about to come into market. There is a great excitement on this subject—many are running "to and fro" to get money & prepare for the land sales. Some will have hard work to enter their land—others will enter their land here, but fail, I fear, to secure a title to any inheritance hereafter.[5]

After the storm had burst in the panic of 1837 a missionary in Ohio wrote:

A principal difficulty with which we have to encounter is the spirit of speculation, so characteristic of the times. The great majority of the original inhabitants of this section of our country were poor and were in debt for their farms. When the time came that they could sell these for advanced prices very many of them sold and went still [farther] west where land is cheaper. There are but very few left who occupied these farms a few years ago. But for this fact, instead of asking aid from you [American Home Missionary Society] we might now be affording it to you.[6]

The speculation of the thirties ended in a panic. The pretty bubbles of imaginary wealth burst. Banks failed, factories closed, work was suspended on canals and railroads, "paper" cities became memories, real towns stagnated. In the West as in the East the people felt the effects of the business depression, and the westward movement was temporarily retarded.

The West had been filling up so rapidly during these "boom" years with speculators and settlers that it was quite impossible for means of communication, houses, churches, and school buildings, and all the other signs of civilized life to keep pace with the pioneers. Everything was new, and he who went there to live or work needed to be patient and cheerful, not too squeamish about departures from the niceties of life, and prepared to make the best of uncomfortable experiences. If he had a sense of humor, so much the better. Experiences such as those of Jackson Kemper, missionary bishop of the Episcopal Church in the Northwest, were common. Kemper had a sense of humor; he was not complaining, but simply recording his experiences during the course of an episcopal visitation of Indiana (1837), when he made the following entries in his diary:

---

[5] Lucien Farnham, Princeton, Ill., April 15. 1835, in A.H.M.S. papers, C.T.S.

[6] S. W. Rose, Homer, Ohio, Nov. 1, 1837, A.H.M.S. papers, C.T.S.

31 May . . . rode 15 miles over the prairie [en route from St. Louis to Vincennes, Indiana] . . . a heavy rain came on when I stopt for dinner in a crowded cabin, no sash, & the rain beating in it . . . was told the rest of my way was in an open wagon. Had to walk through the mud to it—the common loose board placed for a seat was damp & muddy. Seated along side the driver we soon entered the swamps of the little Wabash & here commenced a night of great trial. We entered a wood—the rain fell rapidly & I was obliged to put down my umbrella. It became so dark that I could not see one of the four horses. . . . 3 times we were against stumps or trees. . . . Thus we went I think for 5 miles thro this tremendous swamp—we then entered a prairie & the rain increased. At one o'clock we stopt, having been 5 hours in progressing 13 miles. I went into the house where the drivers sleep—made a fire & found I was wet to the skin. . . .

2 June Started at 2 stage full—night dark. In consequence of the badness of the roads, or of bridges, &c had frequently to get out & walk. . . . We arrived near at 10 at Burton's inn in Terrehaute, where I got a dirty room to myself. . . .

12 June . . . B & I were put in the same room with the landlord, wife and 4 little children. . . .

July 15. [Visited a woman who had come from Ireland. In her excitement at seeing a bishop she called Kemper "my Lord."]

Aug. 5. I obtained a room to myself—and altho I made a dead set for clean sheets do not think I got them. . . .

Aug. 23 . . . [En route to Ft. Wayne] we stayed at a cabin where there was a large family. J & I slept in one bed—a sick woman in the other—& 2 men in the 3d. The other room was equally well filled. . . .

Sept. 8 . . . We are now on the Michigan road—& in consequence of the late rains it is described as almost impassable, and true enough we found it wonderfully bad. Several times we were obliged to get out and walk—& sometimes the water extended over the whole road. . . . About sunset, thank God, we arrived safely at Smith's, 9 miles. The supper was good—but everything else abominable. The stage from Indianapolis came in after 8 with 4 people. . . . The two very dirty men who acted as servants or assistants placed themselves on a perfect equality. The 2 married couple with Smith & his family in one room—& there too I suppose was a child sick with the dysentery, whose moanings during the early part of the evening were scarcely noticed by the parents. In the other room—I had a bed, & I believe some bugs—2 others were in another bed—a fourth passenger was on a cot—he represented himself as devoured by vermin—one or 2 stage drivers occupied a 4th on the floor. The air of the room was much contaminated before morning.[7]

Some of Kemper's further experiences in Indiana are related in the following letter to his daughter Elizabeth:

I arrived here [Logansport] last night after a journey that presented all the variety that a traveller thro' so new a country might have ex-

---

[7] Jackson Kemper, Diaries 5, 6, and 7 (Feb. to Sept., 1837), Kemper papers, Wisconsin Historical Society.

pected. How is it possible for a stage or wagon ever to get thro that place, is an exclamation which I frequently used notwithstanding my long experience in the West. We started on Wednesday afternoon, and as it became dark were told we had yet 9 miles to travel. At the distance of ½ a mile were fast in the mud. Having turned out to ascertain what was to be done, an irish couple who had their baby and all duds with them, missed a bed which had been tied to the top of the stage. The exclamations, particularly of the poor woman, were very strange and amazing. A party set off to hunt for the lost treasure—a selfish man determined to walk forward—while I & the irish couple were left to guard the horses & stage. It became very dark—musquitoes flocked around us—and presently the bellowing of a cow greatly alarmed Paddy. We had been standing near the horses; but instantly on hearing the terrific noise he mounted into the driver's seat to get out of the reach of the mad bull. After a time the hunters returned—the bed had been found in a nice muddy place—& the driver informed us he was now satisfied he could not get on that night, & therefore we must go back about ½ mile to a tavern to sleep. And what a tavern! however you may form some opinion of it from one circumstance. I told the landlord that if possible I would like a room to myself. I was therefore taken into another room which was a little better than the one I had left & which was full of very dirty wagoners. Here after a few minutes I went to sleep & was refreshed in the morning —altho I found that while I was in bed—the landlord, his wife & two children were in another—the maid of all work was in a third—while the irish woman & her young one were luxuriating on her own nice muddy bed on the floor. Her husband and his friend had wisely determined to repose in the stage for the safety of our trunks &c. which being in a mud hole in a swamp they were all but carried away and eated up by the musical & tormenting musquitoes. . . . [8]

Anyone who traveled in the West at this time had to be prepared to sleep in the same room, and often in the same bed, with persons he never saw before—or else sleep outside on the ground. But if frontier cabins were crowded with human sleepers, the latter often had to share their beds with the bugs. Again and again missionary travelers mention the difficulties they experienced in securing clean beds, free from vermin. Hamilton W. Pierson, who toured the Southwest before the Civil War for the American Tract Society, tells of one experience which illustrates the problem. Once, worn out from his labors, he was especially hopeful that he had found a place where he might enjoy the luxury of a good clean bed. The cabin was new and its owners were friendly, but, alas, to quote his own words:

---

[8] J. Kemper, Logansport, Ind., Aug. 5, 1837, to Elizabeth Kemper, Kemper papers, XVII, 125, Wisconsin Historical Society.

As I turned down the blankets and moved my pillow to adjust it, I saw what I at first thought was a drop of molasses dried on the sheet. I impulsively moved my finger toward the spot to ascertain what it was, and it ran! My pleasant dreams were all banished, and I plunged in, in desperation, to share my bed with such company as for months and years I had found in so many of the loghouses in the Brush. The mild climate and the habits of the people conspired to make the beds quite too populous and repulsive to be described ... the want of beds fit to be occupied by a human being after my long, hard days' rides, was by far the greatest of all my privations and trials in the Brush.[9]

A sense of humor was especially desirable when men from the East who had been accustomed to receiving deferential treatment because of their position or calling came up against Western equalitarianism. In the West preachers had to deal with men who respected ability rather than clerical garb or authority. Typical of the leveling, democratic spirit of the West, unabashed before rank or dignity, is the story of the Irishman who called at the home of George Upfold, Episcopal Bishop of Indiana. The Bishop himself answered the knock at the door. "Is Misther Upfold in?" "Sir, the Bishop of Indiana is before you." Instantly the visitor turned on his heel and called back over his shoulder: "Och, and now he's behoind me!"[10]

INTELLECTUAL FERMENT

The third and fourth decades of the last century were noteworthy as years of intellectual and religious ferment. New humanitarian and socialistic ideas were in the air. Societies were formed to remove all sorts of abuses, such as the intemperate use of intoxicating liquors and slavery; or to foster new methods of living, such as the wearing of bloomers by women and the eating of graham bread; or to explore the wonders of phrenology and mesmerism. In the realm of religion and philosophy, Transcendentalism had its vogue among Eastern intellectuals, while among humbler folk there were converts to Mormonism, which purported to be a new revelation of God's will, to Millerism, which taught its devotees to prepare for the immediate second coming of the Lord, to Perfectionism, which offered the abundant life without the restraints of the law, and to

[9] H. W. Pierson, *In the Brush*, 245.
[10] G. White, *Apostle of the Western Church*, 134.

Spiritualism, which strove anew to pierce the veil which hangs between Life and Death. Some earnest souls were so much disturbed over the abominations about them that they tried to obey literally the Biblical injunction that they should come out of Babylon and be no longer partakers of her sins.[11] These "come-outers," as they were called, saw in marriage, property, and the ordinary conventions of society nothing but shackles on human freedom—some of them even rebelled at clothes as being signs of bondage to which no philosopher could quietly submit. In the words of Professor John R. Commons this was "the golden age of the talk-fest, the lyceum, the brotherhood of man—the 'hot-air' period of American history."[12]

In such a time of intellectual disturbance people seemed quite as willing to rely on mob violence as on the ordered processes of law; to yield to emotion rather than to follow the dictates of reason; to find it hard to distinguish between fact and fancy. A writer in the *Knickerbocker Magazine* said in 1837:

One of the most striking characteristics of the present age is the highly excitable state of the public mind. From the Northeastern boundary line to the Mexican gulf, from the Atlantic to the "Far West" there comes rumor after rumor of riot, insurrection and tumult. A species of moral cholera seems everywhere prevailing; and no portion of our country is exempt from its visitation. The cold and calculating sons of New England are now as readily lighted up into these out-breakings against order as the hasty and inflammable spirits of the South. The passions of the populace are ever ready for explosion, and it matters not what is applied to the train—abolition, Grahamism, high prices of food, bank frauds, or gambling, anything, in fact, is made use of by the people as an opportunity for taking the law into their own hands....[13]

THE FEAR OF THE CATHOLICS

In no respect did public nervousness manifest itself more in the thirties and the forties than over the question of the spread of Roman Catholicism in the United States.[14]

---

[11] Rev. 18:4.

[12] John R. Commons *et al.*, *Documentary History of American Industrial Society* (Cleveland, 1910), VII, 20.

[13] *Knickerbocker Magazine*, IX, 488.

[14] The best and most recent treatment of this subject is R. A. Billington, *The Protestant Crusade, 1800-1860* (New York, 1938); see also Billington, "Anti-Catholic Propaganda and the Home Missionary Movement, 1800-1860," in *Mississippi Valley Historical Review*, XXII (1935), 361-84.

Before the Revolution there had been sporadic outbursts
of anti-Catholic feeling in the colonies, especially during
the wars between Protestant England and Catholic France,
but these had not been serious and had attracted little attention because there had been so few Romanists here.[15]
With the fall of the French empire in Canada, the American
Catholics were relieved from the suspicion of being in
sympathy with a neighboring hostile power or in league
with the Indians. During the Revolution the assistance
given by the Most Christian King of France to the new
Republic tended to suppress the fear of "Popery" which
was so ingrained in men whose traditions went back to the
England of the Spanish Armada and the Gunpowder Plot.
In 1790 John Carroll, of Maryland, was consecrated the
first Catholic Bishop in the United States, and no serious
outcry was raised. At that time the number of Catholics
was estimated at thirty thousand, more than half of whom
were in Maryland.[16] Within the next forty years the number of Catholics in the United States increased greatly as
the result of immigration. It has been estimated that the
average number of aliens entering the United States at
the beginning of the nineteenth century was only five or
six thousand a year. Between 1820 and 1826 the figures
ranged from six thousand to ten thousand annually. Then
they began to mount rapidly: twenty-three thousand in
1830; sixty-five thousand in 1834; eighty-four thousand in
1840; more than one hundred thousand in 1842; over two
hundred thousand in 1847; more than three hundred thousand in 1850; while the arrivals in 1854 were in excess of
four hundred thousand.[17] Never before in the history of
the world had so many people moved so far in so short a
time. Normally, and throughout most of the nineteenth
century, immigrants were welcomed in the United States,
because unskilled labor was in demand and there was an
abundance of cheap land. But some found cause for alarm
in the fact that so many of the newcomers were Roman
Catholics. Ireland, famine stricken, torn with civil and

---

[15] Cf. T. Hughes, "An Alleged Popish Plot in Pennsylvania, 1756-7,"
in *Records of the American Catholic Historical Society*, X (1899),
208-21.

[16] H. K. Carroll, *Religious Forces of the United States (Amer. Ch.
Hist. Ser.*, I, New York, 1893), 68.

[17] *Eighth Census, Population* (1860), Introduction, xviii-xix.

religious dissensions, burdened with absentee landlordism, was the chief source of our immigrants during these years. In the eighteenth century the bulk of the Irish immigrants to America had been North of Ireland Presbyterians; in the nineteenth century they were mainly Catholics from the middle and southern parts of Erin. The German immigrants were second to the Irish in point of numbers, and some of these, especially the South Germans, were also Romanists.

Politicians who placed party advantage above public welfare were quick to seize the opportunity presented by this large group of potential voters. The immigrants were naturalized in droves, sometimes immediately after they had left the ship that brought them here, and were voted at the behest of the party bosses under whose influence they so easily fell. In this unseemly scramble for the alien vote the Democratic Party was most successful, but politicians of all shades of opinion were guilty. When an English traveler, Lyell, suggested to a friend in New York in 1845 that it would be well to exclude the pigs from the streets of that city, he was told that it was not possible to do so because they all had votes—that is, their Irish owners had votes, and they turned the scales in the city elections.[18] Resentment against this foreign influence in politics led to the rise of the Native American movement and the Know-Nothing Party.[19]

Furthermore, it was generally thought that these foreigners, or newly made American citizens, many of whom were Roman Catholics, were largely under the influence of their priests. But the Catholic priests in America at this time were themselves for the most part foreign-born, and comparatively few of them had become naturalized. They were unmarried and had no home ties to bind them to this country; many of them had been sent here on missions by European monastic orders or congregations, and were subject to recall at any time. In describing the clergy of his diocese, Bishop Purcell of Cincinnati wrote in 1843 that of his fifty priests, there were nine Americans, twelve Germans, eleven Frenchmen, ten Irishmen, four Italians,

---

[18] C. Lyell, *Second Visit to the United States of America* (London, 1849), I, 249; cf. T. L. Nichols, *Forty Years of American Life* (London, 1844), II, 68-80.

[19] H. J. Desmond, *Know-Nothing Party* (Washington, 1905), 7-59.

three Belgians, and one Spaniard.[20] A few years later
Bishop Henni of Milwaukee made a similar report regarding his diocese, in which eighteen of his fifty-five priests
were from Austria.[21] Obviously there was no other way in
which the Roman Church could at the time minister to the
spiritual needs of its sons and daughters who had crossed
the ocean in such numbers, but this situation gave to its
enemies an opportunity to question the loyalty of its representatives to American institutions and ideals; as later the
ranks of the Catholic clergy filled up with American-born
priests that particular grievance against Rome lost its force.

In keeping with the spirit of the times wild stories about
Catholic atrocities and lewd conduct of priests and nuns
were circulated and believed. Books which purported to
tell the inside story of convent life, such as Maria Monk's
Awful Disclosures or Rebecca Reed's *Two Years in a Convent,* found a ready sale. Such tales are of historical significance because they served as fuel for the fires of religious bigotry, and help explain an attitude of mind that
revealed itself in such unwarranted acts of violence as the
destruction of the Ursuline Convent in Charleston, Massachusetts, in August, 1834.

In the development of this anti-Catholic agitation in
the United States, one of the most important factors was
the publication of a series of articles in the New York
Observer during the year 1834, in which an attempt was
made to show that by the establishment in Austria of a
missionary society known as the Leopoldine Stiftung a plot
had been hatched against the liberties of the United States.
Attention was drawn to the articles by the seriousness of
the charge and the predisposition of the masses to give
credence to any statement derogatory to the Catholic
Church; they were at once reprinted in book form and
widely circulated, seven editions having been issued by
1855. The original articles and the first editions of the book
were written under the pen name of Brutus.[22] Brutus was
none other than Samuel F. B. Morse, a man who would have

---

[20] *Annales de l'Association de la Propagation de la Foi,* XV, 365.

[21] Bishop Henni to Leopoldine Association, Milwaukee, Jan. 14,
1851, quoted by R. Payne, in *Catholic Historical Review,* I, 187.

[22] [S. F. B. Morse], *Foreign Conspiracy against the Liberties of
the United States: the Numbers of Brutus, originally published in
the New York Observer* (New York, 1835).

been remembered as a noteworthy American artist if his artistic achievements had not been overshadowed by his invention of a practical electric telegraph. Samuel Morse's father, Jedidiah Morse, sometime pastor of the First Congregational Church in Charleston, Massachusetts, had had his foreign scare too. The elder Morse took alarm at the Bavarian Illuminati, and in May, 1798, preached a sermon in which he called attention to the dangers threatening the country from this group of eighteenth-century radicals, whose object was believed to be the overthrow of all existing religious and social institutions.[23] The fears of Father Morse proved to be groundless, but he stirred up some excitement—and so did his son in his day.

While in Italy as a student in art in 1830-31, the younger Morse became convinced that European despots and leaders in the Catholic Church had formed a conspiracy to stamp out democracy and republican government in the United States. As a New Englander of the strictest sect Morse had gone to Italy with no love for Catholicism, and his experience in Rome on the day of the procession of Corpus Domini, when his hat was knocked from his head by an Italian soldier for his failure to uncover, probably increased his feeling of antipathy toward everything connected with the Roman Church.[24] Morse believed that the center of the plot was in Austria, then dominated by Metternich, prince of reactionaries, and that it had the support of Pope Gregory XVI, who had been known as the Austrian candidate for the Chair of St. Peter at the Conclave of 1831. The United States, said Morse, in the characteristic "spread-eagle" style of his generation, is the freest, the most prosperous and most enlightened country on the globe. From it ideas of liberty, freedom, and self-government have spread to the more backward countries of Europe. The despots of the Old World have taken alarm and desire to stifle the new ideas in the place of their birth. In support of this thesis he quoted from a series of lectures on the Philosophy of History delivered before the royal court in Vienna by Friedrich von Schlegel, in which, while discussing the evils of the French Revolution, the lecturer had said that North America had been for France and the rest of Europe the

[23] V. Stauffer, *New England and the Bavarian Illuminati*, 10-12.
[24] *Samuel F. B. Morse, His Letters and Journals*, ed. bv E. L. Morse (Boston and New York, 1914), I, 353.

real school and nursery of these revolutionary principles.[25] Shortly after this pronouncement was made there was formed under royal patronage in Vienna a society known as the Leopoldine Stiftung for the support of Catholic missionary activities in America. Putting these things together Morse thought he saw a plot against the liberties of the United States. The heart of his charge is to be found in the following excerpt from his *Foreign Conspiracy:*

> The great patron of this *apparently religious* scheme is no less a personage than the *Emperor of Austria.* The Society is called the *St. Leopold Foundation.* It is organized in Austria. The field of its operations is these United States. It meets and forms its plans in Vienna. Prince Metternich has it under his watchful care. The Pope has given it his apostolic benediction, and "His Royal Highness, Ferdinand V. King of Hungary, and Crown Prince of the other hereditary states, has been most graciously pleased, prompted by a piety worthy the exalted title of an apostolic king, to accept the office of Protector of the Leopold Foundation."[26]

It was Morse's contention that religion was used as a cloak to cover a political design. American Popery, he said, is entirely under foreign control. Austria's agents in this insidious attack on American institutions, he continued, are for the most part "Jesuits in the pay and employ of a despotic government"; they are "at work on the ignorance and passions of our community"; they are *"foreigners,* who have been schooled in foreign seminaries in the doctrine of passive obedience; they are foreigners under vows of *perpetual celibacy,* and having therefore, no deep and permanent interest in this country; they are foreigners bound by the strongest ties of *pecuniary interest* and ambition to the service of a foreign despot."[27] The tyrants of Europe, according to Morse, had seized on Catholicism as the most effective means for accomplishing their object. Liberty in the United States threatened despotism in Europe; principles and ideas are not bound by geographical limits. There was neither opportunity nor pretext for interfering with the liberties of the United States by force. Hence despots

---

25 F. Schlegel, *Philosophy of History,* trans. by J. G. Robertson (London, 1835), II, 298.

26 [S. F. B. Morse], *Foreign Conspiracy,* 22.

27 [S. F. B. Morse], *Foreign Conspiracy,* 47; the idea that Jesuit spies in the pay of the Leopoldine Association were at work in this country was further developed by Morse in his *Proscribed German Student* (New York, 1836).

had turned to insidious propaganda as a means of subverting the principles of freedom on which the great American Republic rested.

Morse's articles attracted attention and received commendatory comments from some of the leading Protestant journals in America. The New York *Commercial Advertiser* said: "When the author commenced his labors we frankly told him in repeated conversations, that we were incredulous of the fact that he was maintaining; but we are free to confess, that in the course of his labors he has brought forth a mass of direct and circumstantial testimony, documentary and otherwise, which has left a strong impression on our minds, that after all, the alarm may not have been sounded without cause." The Boston *Recorder* (Congregational) said: "The author maintains, that what is called the Roman Catholic Religion is in reality a political despotism, disguised under a religious name. We think he proves it; and also that the leading enemies of free institutions in Europe are engaged in organized efforts to give that despotism prevalence in the United States."[28] The theme that the United States was in danger was developed by Morse in other writings, such as the letters of "An American" to the New York *Journal of Commerce* in 1835 on "Imminent Dangers to the Free Institutions of the United States through Foreign Immigration,"[29] and in the *Confessions of a French Catholic Priest.*[30] Lyman Beecher gave the idea publicity in his widely read *Plea for the West.*[31] Memorials were sent to Congress asking for a revision of our naturalization laws and referring to the operations of the Leopoldine Society to prove that there was a Catholic menace.[32]

The organization that had aroused Morse's apprehension was one of several missionary societies which had been formed among European Catholics in the first third of the nineteenth century. The most important of these was the Society for the Propagation of the Faith, which was founded

---

[28] These and other comments of approval are printed in the 7th edition of the *Foreign Conspiracy* (New York, 1855).

[29] These were reprinted in pamphlet form, New York, 1854.

[30] *Confessions of a French Catholic Priest, to Which are Added Warnings to the People in the United States by the same author*, edited by S. F. B. Morse (New York, 1837).

[31] L. Beecher, *Plea for the West* (Cincinnati, 1835).

[32] *E.g., Ex. Doc.* No. 154, 25th Cong., 2nd Sess., Vol. VII; *Ex. Doc.* No. 70, 25th Cong., 2nd Sess., Vol. II.

ın Lyons in 1822. In that year Father Inglesi, the vicar general of the diocese of New Orleans, was sent to Lyons by his superior, Bishop DuBourg, to reanimate the zeal of friends in France who had already made small contributions for the work in America. Father Inglesi found in Lyons a small society whose members contributed a cent a week toward the support of the Seminary of Foreign Missions in Paris. These various missionary interests were merged in May, 1822, in a general society to which was given the name of the Association de la Propagation de la Foi dans les Deux-Mondes. It took for its field Protestant and heathen countries; it did not concern itself with Catholic states such as France, Italy, Spain, Portugal, and Austria. The chief source of income was the small weekly contributions of its members, each of whom was expected to recite every day one "Our Father" and a "Hail Mary," with the addition of the invocation: "St. Francis Xavier, pray for us."[33]

The receipts for the first year, which came mainly from the diocese of Lyons, amounted to about twenty thousand francs, or four thousand dollars. This sum was divided into three parts, one of which was sent to missions in the Orient, while the other two thirds were divided between the missions in Louisiana and Kentucky.[34] The amount sent to the United States increased rapidly each year; over ten thousand dollars were sent in 1825, more than twenty thousand dollars in 1827, nearly seventy thousand dollars in 1839, and more than one hundred and twenty-five thousand dollars in 1840. The first gift to the Society from the United States was the sum of six dollars in 1833; until 1852 the gifts from this country were insignificant, only twice amounting to more than one thousand dollars annually. But as Catholicism became more firmly established in the United States, the contributions increased in size. At the end of the first hundred years of its history the Society had sent to the United States about seven million dollars, but had received from American Catholics almost eleven million

---

[33] [J. Freri], *Society for the Propagation of the Faith and Catholic Missions, 1822-1900*, 5-8; E. J. Hickey, *Society for the Propagation of the Faith*, 10-32.

[34] *Annales de l'Association de la Propagation de la Foi*, I, No. 3 (1824), 28-29.

dollars.[35] The gifts to America had been made at a time when Catholicism was weak here, and Cardinal Gibbons doubtless did not exaggerate the importance of the work done when he wrote to the directors of the Society: "If the grain of mustard seed planted in the virgin soil of America has struck deep roots and grown into a gigantic tree with branches stretching from the shores of the Atlantic ocean to the coasts of the Pacific, it is mainly to the assistance rendered by your admirable society, Gentlemen, that we are indebted for this blessing."[36]

A second channel through which the gifts of European Catholics flowed to the United States was the Ludwigmissionsverein.[37] In 1827 Bishop Fenwick of Cincinnati sent the German-born Father Rese to Europe to secure financial assistance for the missions and schools in his diocese. In Bavaria the Father secured permission from King Louis I to found a society similar to that at Lyons for the purpose of assisting the missions in the United States and in the Orient. Practically all the funds collected during the first decade of this society's existence, about twenty-six thousand marks, were sent to the diocese of Cincinnati; prior to the American Civil War it sent more than three million marks to the United States.[38]

The formation of the Leopoldine Stiftung, the society which had so much disturbed Samuel F. B. Morse, was another result of the visit of Father Rese to Europe in 1827. The latter's description of the needs of the Catholic Church in the United States and the opportunities awaiting it there, attracted the attention of men high in the affairs of church and state in Austria. It was determined to organize a society similar to the French Society for the Propagation of the Faith. The Archbishop of Vienna brought the matter to the attention of the royal family; Father Rese was granted an audience with the emperor, whose brother, Archduke Rudolph, Cardinal Archbishop of Olmütz, assumed the protectorate of the new undertaking.[39]

---

[35] E. J. Hickey, *Society for the Propagation of the Faith*, 153.

[36] [J. Freri], *Society for the Propagation of the Faith*, 21-22.

[37] T. Roemer, *Ludwig-Missionsverein and the Church in the United States (1838-1918). Franciscan Studies*, No. 12 (New York, 1933).

[38] P. Guilday, *Life and Times of John England* (New York, 1927), II, 181-83.

[39] A. I. Rezek, in *Catholic Encyclopedia*, XVI, 52.

After the approval of the Pope had been secured, the statutes of the society were adopted in April, 1829. The Association, which was to be limited to Austria-Hungary, was named after the deceased Leopoldina, daughter of Francis I of Austria, and wife of Pedro I of Brazil. The chief source of income was to be the weekly gifts of its members, each of whom engaged to offer daily "one Pater and Ave, with the addition: St. Leopold, pray for us," and every week to contribute for missions five kreutzers, or about two cents. The members were organized in groups of ten, one of whom was appointed collector to receive the weekly gift, which was sent up through the various stages of the hierarchy until it reached the central office in Vienna.[40]

The first contributions of this society were sent to the Diocese of Cincinnati,[41] but practically all the bishoprics in the United States have received some help from it. In 1830 the amount sent to this country was 34,000 florins; from then until the American Civil War the amount sent usually ranged from 30,000 to 50,000 florins annually. In addition to gifts of money, there were also donations of Church utensils, paintings, and statuary. Between 1829 and 1846 the total amount sent to dioceses within the limits of the United States was about 667,000 florins, or $330,000,[42] of which the Diocese of Cincinnati had received 115,000 florins. In the same period the dioceses of Baltimore, Charleston, St. Louis, Vincennes, and Detroit each received sums varying between 43,000 and 61,000 florins, while to each of the dioceses of Philadelphia, Richmond, Pittsburgh, Louisville, Little Rock, Boston, New York, Mobile, New Orleans, Natchez, Nashville, and Dubuque were sent gifts ranging from 10,000 to 32,000 florins.[43] The money was used for the support of priests, the building of churches, and the maintenance of schools. In 1831 the Association began the publication of the Annual Reports of the missions in Amer-

---

[40] The constitution of the Leopoldine Association is printed in the *American Catholic Historical Researches*, N. S. I (1905), 314-16.

[41] R. Payne, "Annals of the Leopoldine Association," in *Catholic Historical Review*, I, 52.

[42] Payne, *op. cit.*, I, 179, Note 19, says that in 1846 the contribution to the United States had reached 687,000 florins, but this figure included small gifts to Canada and the Antilles.

[43] P. C. Verwyst, *Life and Labors of Rt. Rev. Frederick Baraga* (Milwaukee, 1900), 464-65.

ica under the title of *Berichte der Leopoldinen-Stiftung in Kaiserthume Oesterreich.*[44] The appeals made in Europe for support for these Catholic missionary undertakings in America varied from optimistic accounts of the spread of Catholicism to discouraging reports of persecution and Protestant calumnies. Some, like the Archbishop of Baltimore, reported that they had found everywhere a praiseworthy curiosity to understand the doctrines of the Catholic Church and that many converts would be secured if the necessary priests were sent.[45] Others were encouraged by the rapid growth of Catholic schools, whose excellence, they said, was attested by the large number of Protestant children enrolled in them. The Bishop of Cincinnati reported in 1843 that more than half of the students in the College of St. Francis Xavier belonged to Protestant families. In this school, he said, they were receiving a careful training in all the important branches of knowledge suited to their position by Jesuits who never forgot that their teaching was an apostleship and that their first duty was to train up these young hearts in piety.[46] The education of the young offered a promising opening for the introduction and strengthening of Catholicism in this country, and the alarm of the Protestants at the number and excellence of the Catholic schools indicates how fully the Catholic Church had seized the opportunity.[47]

From the point of view of a Catholic, America, with its many competing sects, was in a state of religious chaos.[48] It was reported in Europe that men and women in America, bewildered by the cries of false teachers all about them, were turning to the "one true faith."[49] The ignorance of

---

[44] A description of the *Berichte*, with extracts from some of the reports, is given in R. Payne, "Annals of the Leopoldine Association," in *Catholic Historical Review*, I, 51-63, 175-91.

[45] Mgr. Eccleston, Baltimore, Jan. 31, 1838, in *Annales de l'Association de la Propagation de la Foi*, X (1837), 498; S. T. Badin, St. Joseph River, Mich., Dec., 1830, quoted by R. Payne in *Catholic Historical Review*, I, 52.

[46] Bishop Purcell, Cincinnati, Feb. 10, 1843, in *Annales de l'Association de la Propagation de la Foi*, XV, 366.

[47] For further discussion of Catholic education, see Chapter XII.

[48] J. Salzbacher, *Meine Reise nach Nord-Amerika im Jahre 1842* (Wien, 1845), 88-89, lists thirty-one sects found in Philadelphia about 1842.

[49] *Annales de l'Association de la Propagation de la Foi*, III (1828), 211; IV (1831), 655.

the American clergy, especially those ministering to the more popular denominations in the West, was emphasized as further evidence of the superiority of the Catholic Church.[50] The class distinctions in American churches received unfavorable comment. The Americans were reported to regard religion as a matter of convenience and fashion. There were sects for all the grades of society. The Negroes were reported to be Methodists, while men of property, education, and high official rank were Episcopalians, or at least Presbyterians, Quakers, or Unitarians. It was no more seemly for a poor man to join one of the sects reserved for the aristocracy of Protestantism than it was for him to have a coach and footman.[51] Of course such statements were exaggerations, but that there was a kernel of truth in them no one familiar with religious conditions in the United States could deny.

The poverty of American Catholics was given as an additional reason that they should receive aid from their brethren in Europe. They belonged mainly to the immigrant class and were usually poor. They had to contend with racial prejudice and religious bigotry. They were accused of disloyalty and of owing allegiance to foreign rulers. The amount and purpose of the financial assistance sent to them from Europe were misrepresented. Indeed, the outcry raised over European gifts to Catholic missions in the United States had been so great and had so stimulated Protestant activity, said Bishop England, that unless the assistance should be continued it would be questionable whether the former generosity would not prove in its results more injurious to Catholicism in America than it had been beneficial.[52]

Just as the Catholics appealed to their supporters in Europe for additional help on account of the activities of the Protestant sects, so the Protestant home missionary societies asked their constituents for larger offerings in order that the Romanists might not be permitted to gain control of the religious and educational life of the West.[53]

---

[50] *Ibid.*, IV (1831), 654.

[51] *Ibid.*, IV (1831), 653.

[52] John England to Central Council for the Propagation of the Faith, Rome, Sept., 1836, in *Works* (Baltimore, 1849), III, 245.

[53] H. C. Kingsley, "Roman Catholic Contributions and Missions," in *The New Englander*, XVII (1859), 93-110.

Their periodicals devoted much space in the thirties, the forties, and the fifties to the activities in the West of what some were pleased to call the "Man of Sin" and others the "Scarlet Woman." In the *Annual Report* of the American Home Missionary Society for 1842, for example, the question was discussed at length, and tables were given showing the number of Catholic priests and schools in the United States.[54] The presence of this large body of Catholics was at once a problem and an opportunity. Some Protestants saw there the unfolding of a divine purpose. The ignorant and superstitious masses of Europe who had been kept in intellectual bondage and made to bow down before false gods had been brought, they said, to the land of enlightenment and liberty in order that they might the more easily be shown the light of Protestantism. "Such an extensive migration of the subjects of false religion to this land of light and civil liberty," to quote from one of the *Reports* of the American Home Missionary Society, "is one of the most striking events of the age; and one that unfolds another leaf in our country's eventful destiny."[55]

Whether the Catholic population was regarded as a menace or an opportunity, the method of dealing with it which commended itself to men of sober judgment interested in home missions was the same—Protestant preaching and teaching.[56] They did not advocate mob violence; they did not desire that this country should renounce its principles of religious freedom. With sounder judgment than he had shown when he scented a plot in the formation of the Leopoldine Stiftung, Morse, the author of the *Foreign Conspiracy,* had indicated the only proper course for those to follow who were opposed to Roman Catholicism. He said:

We must make an immediate and a vigorous, a united, a persevering effort to spread religious and intellectual cultivation through every part of the country. Not a village, not a log-hut of the land should be overlooked. Where Popery has put darkness, we must put light. Where Popery has planted its crosses, its colleges, its churches, its chapels, its nunneries, Protestant patriotism must put side by side college for college, seminary for seminary, church for church.[57]

---

55 A.H.M.S., *Sixteenth Report* (1842), 84.
56 R. W. Clark, *Popery and the United States* (Boston, 1847), 18.
57 [S. F. B. Morse], *Foreign Conspiracy,* 101.

The significance of the contest between Catholicism and Protestantism for the dominant position in the West was not minimized by the participants. The President of Wabash College, an institution born and bred in the home missionary tradition, waxed eloquent as he looked over the West—"this battle-field grander than a thousand Waterloos, these hosts, which Milton's pen could not describe, that consumation in victory, more joyful or woeful, than ever perched on a conqueror's standard, these invest the West with solemn sublimity."[58]

The fight was on for the control of the West; and, judging from the attention it received in the Eastern religious periodicals during the period, it might have been expected that the reports from the Protestant minutemen on the frontiers—the home missionaries—would have been filled with stirring accounts of skirmishes with the enemy. It was not so; at least, it was not so with respect to the representatives of the American Home Missionary Society. In their letters references to Catholic activities were comparatively few in number and were written usually from the vicinity of such centers of Catholic strength as Dubuque in Iowa or St. Louis in Missouri. Most Presbyterian and Congregational missionaries in the small towns and farming communities in the Middle West in the 1840's knew about the Catholic problem only indirectly; in their letters during these years they deplored the teachings of the "Campbellites" and the practices of the Mormons (especially in the case of the Illinois, Iowa, and Missouri correspondents) about as often as they expressed alarm over the Catholic menace. Fear of "Popery" was a powerful motive for Protestant home missions, but it was a fear based more on the fancies of the Eastern religious leaders than on the actual experiences of the majority of the missionaries in the West.[59]

---

[58] J. F. Tuttle, "The West and Western Eloquence," in *Biblical Repository*, 3rd Series, No. 4 (1845), 669.

[59] An analysis of the contents of 940 A.H.M.S. reports from Indiana, Illinois, Wisconsin, Iowa, Missouri, and Kentucky for the years 1840, 1842, 1844, and 1846—years in which the *Home Missionary* played up the Catholic menace—shows that (omitting merely casual references) there were 55 letters (about 6%) in which the writer made unfavorable comments on Catholic activities or manifested alarm. If the 15 additional letters in which there are casual references to Catholics be added, the total is 70 (less than 8%). Of course, it does not follow that the other letters were pro-Catholic; they were not. These figures

OTHER MOTIVES FOR HOME MISSIONS

In addition to the general motives for missionary activity which were pointed out in the first chapter, and the rivalry between Catholicism and Protestantism which became acute in the generation preceding the Civil War, certain other motives closely associated with the political and economic conditions of the time appeared. In a previous chapter[60] it was shown that after the War of 1812 far-sighted men in the East predicted that political power would soon pass to the West and made that the basis of an appeal for missionary work in that area. In the quarter of a century preceding the Civil War this prophecy began to be realized. Between 1830 and 1860 the frontier line had been pushed out in the Middle West until it included most of Wisconsin, southern Minnesota, Iowa, the eastern part of Kansas, all of Arkansas, and eastern and southern Texas. By 1860 there were two states, California and Oregon, on the Pacific Coast. Nevada was added to the Union in 1864. Political power was passing to the West. Following the Census of 1840, the *Home Missionary* published a table showing that in the next reapportionment of seats in the Congress the representation of the Eastern states would drop from 164 to 134, while the Western states would find their representation increased from 81 to 93.[61] After the Census of 1850 this periodical took occasion again to call attention to the phenomenal growth of population in the West. Between

---

simply mean that when these missionaries listed their difficulties and problems, as they did again and again, most of them did not think of Catholicism.

One of these letters and its treatment by the editor of the *Home Missionary* illustrates the way in which Eastern religious leaders made the most of such anti-Catholic sentiment as did exist. Lucien Foote, writing from St. Charles, Ill., Dec. 2, 1842 (A.H.M.S. papers, C.T.S.), made an appreciative comment on an anti-Catholic article that had previously appeared in the *Home Missionary*. Then the editor took this comment out of its context in the letter and printed it, without a note about its origin, as further evidence of the Catholic peril in the West. See *Home Missionary*, XV (1843), 227-28.

Local conditions determined largely the extent of the anti-Catholic bias in the letters. For example, in the Oregon letters of the 1850's the attack on Catholics was often bitter. (Evah I. Ostrander, "The American Home Missionary Society in Oregon, 1849-1870," MS. thesis, School of Divinity, University of Chicago, *passim.*) This was due largely to the belief that the Catholics were ultimately responsible for the Whitman Massacre.

[60] See above, page 170.
[61] *Home Missionary*, XIV (1842), 277.

1840 and 1850 the population of Vermont had increased only 7.59 per cent and that of Massachusetts 34.81 per cent, while the ratio of increase in Wisconsin had been 345.84 per cent and in California 890.48 per cent. In politics the West now held the balance of power. How was it to be used? A man who believed that the safety of the nation and the salvation of the West depended upon the introduction of Christian principles said: "If the West is filled with the Gospel; if every town and neighborhood is pervaded by the doctrine which came down from heaven, and whose effect is to strengthen the authority of law, to teach men industry, temperance and justice and to lead quiet and peaceable lives in godliness and honesty, then every town and neighborhood will send forth a wholesome political influence and western representatives will be, by choice or by constraint of a virtuous public sentiment, the advocates of righteousness."[62]

Closely akin to this was the plea that home missions be supported in order that the United States might be made safe for democracy. Political democracy was coming in the United States no matter how much the conservatives dreaded its approach. The West was committed to the principle of universal white manhood suffrage. The East held back, but it too had to fall in line. But just at the time the right to vote was being bestowed generally on all white men, the number of foreign-born began to increase notably. It was bad enough for men of the old school to contemplate a republic run by Tom, Dick, and Harry, but positively appalling to think that now Pat, and Mike, and Ludwig were also about to go to the polls. In his well-known *Plea for the West*, Lyman Beecher, one of the outstanding Protestant preachers of America, wrote:

The great experiment is now making in the West, whether the perpetuity of our republican institutions can be reconciled with universal suffrage. Without the education of the head and the heart of the nation, they cannot be; the question to be decided is, can the nation, or the vast balance power of it be so imbued with intelligence and virtue, as to bring out, in laws, and their administration, a perpetual self-preserving energy?[63]

Passing from vague to more specific perils Beecher went on to say:

---

[62] *Home Missionary*, XI (1839), 209.
[63] L. Beecher, *Plea for the West*, 40-41.

This danger from uneducated mind is augmenting daily by the rapid influx of foreign emigrants, the greater part unacquainted with our institutions, unaccustomed to self-government, inaccessible to education, and easily accessible to prepossession, and inveterate credulity, and intrigue, and easily embodied and wielded by sinister design.[64]

Other preachers took up the theme; from pulpit after pulpit ministers warned their hearers of the dangers confronting the republic and suggested remedies. Said John Thompson, of Poughkeepsie: "I do not believe any nation can endure on the basis of democratic equality and universal suffrage, unless through the influence of pervading Protestant Christianity."[65] "The Church Essential to the Republic" was the subject of a sermon preached in New York and Brooklyn in 1848 by one of the friends of the home missionary movement, and then printed for general distribution.[66] There was, of course, nothing new in the contention that religion was essential to the welfare of the state—that was an old doctrine when the colonies were young; it was now simply redressed to apply to the growth of democracy.

Again and again the sponsors of Protestant home missions insisted that their movement represented the highest type of patriotism. It was held up as the means through which American institutions were to be preserved; its humble soldiers of the Cross on remote frontiers were the minutemen of democracy. At the successive annual meetings of the American Home Missionary Society sentiments such as the following were set forth again and again in resolutions, elaborated upon in sermons, and applauded by those present:

Resolved, That the influence which the Protestant Missionary exerts for the proper organization, regulation and general welfare of society at the West, entitles him to the confidence and support, not only of the Christian, but also of the patriot.[67]

Resolved, That the thorough evangelization of the masses of the people is the only guaranty of Representative Democracy.[68]

---

[64] Ibid., 51.

[65] Home Missionary, XXI (1848), 114.

[66] E. N. Kirk, The Church Essential to the Republic (New York, 1848).

[67] Joseph P. Thompson, N. Y., in A.H.M.S., Nineteenth Report (1845), 110.

[68] John Thompson, Poughkeepsie, N. Y., A.H.M.S., Twenty-second Report (1848), 101.

Resolved, That the Gospel of Christ, brought into contact with the mind and heart of our entire population, is the only influence to which we can safely entrust the destiny of this country.[69]

When so viewed the home missionary movement was lifted above the petty bickerings of rival denominations. It had to do not only with the welfare of individual souls, but also with the destiny of a nation.

THE PRESBYTERIANS

As was pointed out in the preceding chapter, Presbyterians had shared with Congregationalists in the formation of the American Home Missionary Society in 1826. The new society and the General Assembly's Board of Missions both appealed to Presbyterian churches for aid, with the result that friction developed and finally schism came. The conservative "Old School" Presbyterians believed that the Church should have complete control of its missionary operations, and that the Board of Missions of the General Assembly was the proper agency. They argued that the Church itself is a missionary society and that it cannot delegate its prime function to any other body; they questioned the Biblical authority for missionary societies distinct from the Church itself. The liberal "New School" Presbyterians favored the use of voluntary, as opposed to ecclesiastical, missionary societies, and desired to continue co-operation with the Congregationalists through the American Home Missionary Society. Behind the controversy over the best method of conducting missions lay doctrinal disputes. Since the eighteenth century American Presbyterianism had embraced both a High Church and a Low Church party. Presbyterianism was originally established in America by men from England who had been acting in harmony with the English Independents under the Heads of Agreement of 1691.[70] From the outset close relations had been maintained with the New England Calvinists. With the coming of the Scotch-Irish in the eighteenth century a less liberal and more dogmatic spirit had been added

---

[69] Andrew L. Stowe, Boston, A.H.M.S., *Twenty-fourth Report* (1850), 108.

[70] H. Woods, *History of the Presbyterian Controversy,* 25-26; H. W. Clark, *History of English Nonconformity* (London, 1913), II, 160-62.

to American Presbyterianism.[71] In 1741 this dichotomy had been revealed by the split into Old Side and New Side; but this schism was of short duration. Under the operation of the Plan of Union many men trained in New England Congregationalism, some of whom departed from traditional Calvinism in their greater emphasis on man's responsibility for his own salvation, had been introduced into western Presbyterian churches, especially in western New York, northern Ohio, Michigan, and Illinois. Questions about the orthodoxy of the New Englanders were raised at about the same time that the controversy over the proper method of conducting missions became heated. These controversies directly involved the American Home Missionary Society in that it was accused of having introduced heresy into the Presbyterian Church through its appointees from New England.[72] Antislavery feeling was also stronger among Congregationalists and New School Presbyterians than among their Old School brethren.[73]

The Board of Missions of the Presbyterian Church was ten years older than the American Home Missionary Society, or a quarter of a century older if one counts from the establishment of the Standing Committee on Missions in 1802. The growth of the work sponsored by the Board had been slow because so many Presbyterians had preferred the voluntary societies.[74] The American Home Missionary Society, on the contrary, grew rapidly in the years immediately following its organization, and from the outset seemed to overshadow its older rival. The failure of a scheme of union in 1828 drove the wedge still deeper between the two organizations.[75] The Board rejected the proposal for union on the ground that it had absolutely no authority from the General Assembly to make such an arrangement; most

---

[71] Cf. W. Riley, *American Thought from Puritanism to Pragmatism* (New York, 1915), 119-21.

[72] For a statement of these charges and reply, see [Asa Mahan, D. W. Lathrop, James Gallaher], *Report of the Minority in the Convention on Domestic Missions, Held in Cincinnati, November, 1831* (Cincinnati, 1831), 20-36.

[73] On the connection between the antislavery agitation and the Presbyterian schism, see W. W. Sweet, *Religion on the American Frontier.... The Presbyterians*, 111-20.

[74] The receipts of the Board of Missions were less than $5,000 in 1816; they dropped to less than $3,000 in 1828. S. J. Baird, *History of the New School* (Philadelphia, 1868), 311.

[75] See above, page 199.

members of the Board had an honest preference for a missionary organization wholly under control of the Church; in the minds of some there may have been the feeling that to suggest a plan of union which would have made the Board of Missions of the Presbyterian Church auxiliary to a nonecclesiastical society less than three years old was presumptuous. Under the circumstances the most the American Home Missionary Society could expect was toleration in the Presbyterian Church, and as late as 1829 the General Assembly granted that by the adoption of a resolution to the effect that the individual churches were to be allowed to choose freely between the two rival missionary agencies.[76] As time passed the controversy between the adherents of the two missionary systems became more acrimonious.[77] The conservatives soon came to the point where they were no longer willing to tolerate the voluntary society within the bounds of Presbyterianism, and the presbyteries and synods began to pass resolutions pledging their support to the Assembly's Board of Missions and calling upon the rival society to cease its activities within their limits.[78]

From 1830 to 1836 the problem of the American Home Missionary Society was before the General Assembly in one form or another, but no action openly hostile to it was taken because the New School party was in the majority at practically all of the meetings of the Assembly held during these years. Among the Old School men the feeling was growing that the situation was serious, and so long as they were outnumbered in the General Assembly there was no hope of action from within to save the Church. The opportunity to act came unexpectedly when the General Assembly met in 1837, and it was realized that the majority of those present were adherents of the Old School. Declaring that the Plan of Union, which since 1801 had been

---

[76] *Extracts from Minutes of the General Assembly of the Presbyterian Church*, VI, 374.

[77] Letters on both sides of the controversy may be found in A. Peters, *Brief Answer to an Official Reply of the Board of Missions of the General Assembly to Six Letters of the Rev. Absalom Peters.*

[78] *E.g.*, Presbytery of Indianapolis passed a resolution in 1833 censuring the American Home Missionary Society. S. Hurd, Greensburg, Ind., Dec. 26, 1833, A.H.M.S. papers, C.T.S. Similar action by the West Lexington Presbytery was reported by J. Lane, Lexington, Ky., Oct. 1, 1836, in C.H.M.S. (11th year, No. 776); not found in A.H.M.S. papers, C.T.S.

accepted as binding by both Presbyterians and Congregationalists, was contrary to the Constitution of the Presbyterian Church, and hence had been null and void from the beginning, a resolution was adopted excluding from the Church the four synods which had been built up under this plan, and in which the New School party was mainly located. These four synods were Utica, Geneva, and Genesee in western New York, and Western Reserve in Ohio. Five other synods were ordered to root out heretical doctrines from certain of their presbyteries. The American Home Missionary Society and the American Education Society, the latter a voluntary organization whose function was to subsidize young men preparing themselves for the ministry, were asked to cease their operations within the Presbyterian Church.[79] Delegates from the New School appeared at the General Assembly of 1838, but their efforts to secure recognition were of no avail; they accordingly withdrew and organized a General Assembly of their own. Thus was the Presbyterian Church divided into two parts, both of which used practically the same name and claimed to be the real Presbyterian Church in the United States. Over five hundred churches, with about one hundred thousand members, went with the New School Assembly; the constituency of the Old School was slightly larger.

The unedifying story of the disruption of the Presbyterian Church has been told because the occasion for the break was a dispute over the methods of conducting home missions, and because it is indicative of the tendency in the generation preceding the Civil War to strengthen denominational distinctions. The home missionary movement has never lacked the element of sectarian propaganda; during this period it seemed too often to be the dominant motive.

It is interesting to note that at the time the Old School Presbyterians expressed the fear that the American Home Missionary Society was endangering their faith and polity, men trained in New England were complaining that this same society was hostile to Congregationalism in the West. One missionary in Illinois reported that he had found many people in that state prejudiced against the American

---

[79] R. E. Thompson, *History of the Presbyterian Churches in the United States (Amer. Ch. Hist. Ser.,* VI, New York, 1895), 117; A. Green, *Historical Sketch or Compendious View of Domestic and Foreign Missions in the Presbyterian Church,* 29.

Home Missionary Society, because of their feeling that it was trying to build up Presbyterianism at the expense of Congregationalism in the West.[80] Another wrote from Michigan that on account of the efforts of some of the agents of the Society to injure Congregationalism in his state, he thought of laying the matter before the churches of New England; the fact that the major portion of the funds of the Society came from New England made its action, he thought, all the more unfair.[81]

After the disruption of 1837 the Assembly's Board of Missions had a free hand within the Old School Church. Its receipts for the year ending in 1835 were less than thirty thousand dollars;[82] by 1840 the balance on hand and the receipts amounted to a little more than forty thousand dollars;[83] by the end of the forties the annual receipts were twice as much as they had been ten years earlier, while in 1859 they amounted to about $120,000, or approximately two thirds as much as those of the American Home Missionary Society at the same time.[84] But judged by the number of states and territories in which its representatives were working, the Board of Missions covered the United States more completely, and on the eve of the Civil War had more reason to claim to be a "national" organization, than the American Home Missionary Society; the latter, as will be pointed out below, had practically abandoned the South and the Southwest by the end of the fifties, whereas the Old School Board of Missions had increased its missionary activities in the slave states by that time. Another difference between the work of the American Home Missionary Society and the Board of Missions was that the latter made much more use of the itinerant system of preaching. The report of the Board for 1839 stated that pastors living in the vicinity of destitute places had been urged to devote six or eight weeks each year to this form of missionary labor,[85]

---

[80] T. Baldwin, Jacksonville, Ill., Jan. 31, 1834, in C.H.M.S. (8th year, No. 1266) ; not found in A.H.M.S. papers, C.T.S.

[81] J. D. Pierce, Marshall, Mich., May 1, 1837, in A.H.M.S. papers, C.T.S.

[82] [Presbyterian] Board of Domestic Missions of the General Assembly, *Report* (1835), 22.

[83] *Ibid.* (1840), 27.

[84] *Ibid.* (1849), 36, 40; (1859), 83.

[85] *Ibid.* (1839), 25.

and the letters printed in the *Missionary Chronicle*, the official publication of the Board of Missions, indicate not only that this had been done, but that there were several missionaries who had organized regular circuits.[86]

THE AMERICAN HOME MISSIONARY SOCIETY

The New School Presbyterians and the Congregationalists continued to co-operate in their home missionary activities through the American Home Missionary Society. This organization, as was pointed out above, grew rapidly in its first decade (1826-36). This was a period of great activity in the West, and the Society increased the number of its representatives on the frontier in order to keep up with the westward movement. At its tenth anniversary meeting (1836) it was reported that the annual receipts of the Society had reached one hundred thousand dollars and that there were 755 missionaries on its rolls. Then came the panic of 1837. The revenues dropped to $85,000 in 1837 and to $78,000 in 1840.[87] It was a time of worry for the officers of the Society and of hardship for the missionaries. Gifts in the East fell off, while the people in the West, who also felt the pinch of hard times, reduced their contributions to the support of the missionary pastors. The latter found themselves in a precarious position. For some time complaints had been coming in from the West that the missionaries were underpaid and that the basic salary of $400 a year was entirely inadequate for the support of a man and family even in the small country towns.[88] Some went so far as to express the opinion that no more missionaries should be sent out until adequate provision had been made for those already in the field. Farming and other secular pursuits, except occasionally schoolteaching, to which the preachers of some of the denominations had recourse, were practically closed to the representatives of the American Home Missionary Society by its rules. All the factors in the situation combined to place the missionaries in an embarrassing position.

---

[86] *Missionary Chronicle*, X (1842), 29; XI (1843), 380; XIV (1846), 250; XVI (1848), 222.

[87] *Home Missionary*, LXIV (1891), 114.

[88] T. Baldwin, Jacksonville, Ill., Dec. 14, 1836, in A.H.M.S. papers, C.T.S.; N. Cooke, Bloomfield, Mich., June 3, 1836, *ibid*.

When the financial crash occurred in 1837 the American Home Missionary Society found itself at one time without funds; it was forced to send out a circular letter to its missionaries asking them not to draw upon the Society until the crisis passed. The men in the field generally accepted the situation without complaint, although some pathetic letters were sent in by men to whom the cutting off of pecuniary aid had brought hardship and suffering. One missionary, who had not received the circular letter until after he had disposed of his draft for his quarter's salary,[89] wrote to explain his action:

> I received your circular the 21st instant and am sorry to say that my draft on you was paid away on the 2c instant. I had no cow and scarcely any bread for my family, and the distress under which our country groans is so severely felt in this region that my people were unable to assist me in any manner—having only received to the amount of eight Dollars from them for the last five months. Nevertheless if I had received your letter earlier I would have withheld my draft and subsisted in the best way we could. . . . [90]

As late as November, 1837, the situation was still acute. One of the officials of the Society wrote at this time:

> . . . Our missionaries are in distressing need. We should get a loan for one or two thousand dollars, to give a few crumbs of comfort to each if the banks here were not drawing in, probably with a view to being prepared for the resumption of specie payments. . . . There are 220 missionaries who have recd no payments during 6 months, & many of them not under 12 months past.[91]

Nor did the effects of the panic quickly disappear. For fully five years the reports of the missionaries contain references to hard times in the West. Occasionally they moralized, seeing in the situation the Hand of God. One man wrote that the West had been "saved by adversity." Recalling the spirit of speculation which dominated the West during the days of temporal prosperity, he said: "You might as well undertake to lay the foundation of a house

---

[89] At this time it was customary for each missionary to write out and sell his draft on the Society for the amount of money to which he was entitled for his services. These drafts were ordinarily sold to local merchants or other businessmen who had financial dealings in New York.

[90] W. Waith, Burton, N. Y., June 24, 1837, A.H.M.S. papers, C.T.S.

[91] C. Hall to John Murray, Nov. 22, 1837, A.H.M.S. Letter Bk. K, 212, C.T.S.

amid the rushing over-flow of a river as to have attempted the founding of the spiritual temple here had not those floods abated which in 1837 were bringing the worshippers of mammon from every quarter of the globe."[92]

MISSIONARY BOXES

As a method of alleviating the sufferings of the missionaries it became customary about this time to send to them boxes of clothing, books, and other useful articles. In the case of the American Home Missionary Society the impetus appears to have come from two appeals from Michigan which were printed in the *Home Missionary* in the year 1841. One was from the wife of a missionary who asked if there were some way in which her husband could be supplied with a few helpful books. Her letter, which gives us an insight into one phase of the privations missionaries endured, ran as follows:

> We have been in the West seven years; and all the time except one year, have been engaged in the service of your Society. It has been a scene of constant toil and privation of every luxury.... Often have we tried to do without the comforts of life in order to lay up a fund for the purchase of a small library; and as often have we been defeated. Our only hope, under God, is in the effort that we now make in writing to you—that you would kindly intercede for us with your wealthy clergymen and lay brethren—or pursue any other method that you may judge proper. Perhaps you may think that this is too great a demand upon you; but you would not, if you could see the dejected countenance and hear the half suppressed sigh of your brother in Christ, as he sits down before his empty shelves to handle over his pamphlets and few periodicals, to store his mind with new thoughts for the Sabbath. Your missionaries are not in heathen lands; but in the midst of enlightened and often well educated communities, and surrounded by unbelievers ready to take advantage of every point where in a minister fails. What can your Society do without a well informed ministry? Its energies will be crippled, and its funds in a great measure thrown away.[93]

The second appeal, which was from the Presbytery of Marshall, asked for donations of clothing as well as books. It pointed out that sheep were scarce in that part of the West, and that woolen goods and other articles of wearing apparel were expensive. Again attention was called to the scarcity of books in the homes of missionaries in frontier

---

[92] A. Donaldson, Dover, Ill., Feb. 8, 1842, in A.H.M.S. papers, C.T.S.
[93] *Home Missionary*, XIV (1841), 12.

communities and to the serious consequences of that particular deprivation. "Deprived of books," so ran the appeal, "good books, standard works, the means of a severe and advancing discipline, the most pious and sensible men in our profession, will soon run down intellectually, and then brethren, what will become of the churches and the community? They will be flooded with fatal errors."[94] The response was generous; so many boxes of miscellaneous supplies were sent to the office of the Society in New York or forwarded directly to Michigan, that after the immediate needs of the members of the Marshall Presbytery had been met, there were still many boxes left for distribution among other missionaries who were equally needy but who had made no appeal for assistance of this kind.[95] It is also noteworthy that in the preparation of these boxes the women shared largely.[96]

The boxes usually contained serviceable clothing, and sometimes were "made to order" in the sense that they had been packed with respect to the needs of a particular family. The following letter to the pastor of a church in Orange, New Jersey, which was preparing a box for a missionary's family in Illinois, gives an idea of the specific needs of persons living in new communities in a state as old even as Illinois was in 1843:

[94] *Home Missionary*, XIV (1841), 112. The officers of the A.H.M.S. had some doubts about the advisability of publishing the appeal for fear it would deter men from offering themselves for service in the West; one of the corresponding secretaries wrote: "There is prevailing at the East, a sort of panic in respect to the prospects of the West. Ministers are absolutely afraid to go there lest themselves, & those dearer to them than their own flesh, shall be in danger of perishing for lack of food and raiment." C. Hall to John P. Cleveland, July 8, 1841, A.H.M.S. Letter Bk. O, 56, C.T.S.

[95] The officers of the Society had to be fair in their distribution of the boxes, not only with reference to the needs of the recipients but also with respect to their denominational affiliations. Mr. Hall, a corresponding secretary, said in a letter in September, 1841, "Suspicions are already springing up that the Presbytery of Marshall, or at least *Presbyterians* will receive an undue share of the contents of these boxes. We have had so many hints & even letters, that I published a card stating that all Presbyterian & Congregational missionaries [? word blurred] whose need could be ascertained should share in the distribution." C. Hall to J. P. Cleveland, Sept. 30, 1841, A.H.M.S. Letter Bk. O, 148, C.T.S.

[96] Some of the women believed that in packing their boxes they were doing their tiny bit to help save the West from the Pope and the kings of Europe. Mrs. N. E. Moody, Sec'y. of the Ladies' Sewing Society of Plainville, Conn., Aug 27, 1845, A.H.M.S. correspondence, 1845-46, No. 1726, A.H.M.S. papers, C.T.S.

His [the missionary's] family consists of his wife, a young lady living with them, & six daughters from the age of 18 years down to 14 months, in all 9 persons. Of course, almost any kind of wearing apparel or bedding will find a welcome place in such a family; but the following is more particularly needful viz.

Calico, or dresses
Apron stuffs
Shoes & stocking yarn
Bed ticking
Material for cloak for Mrs. S.
Cheap plaid shawls wd be of great use
School books for primary instruction—Stationary

Mr. Smally is wearing his last suit of clothes for the 4th year. He needs pilot cloth or similar material for an over-coat ... [he has now? (words blurred)] no overcoat whatever.—cloth for a suit of clothes— A fur cap—middling size, for use in travelling over the prairies in Winter—Leather for shoes & boots—blk. [? indistinct] cravats, or stocks, or materials.

Nothing but plain, strong articles are wanted by them; & the sooner they have them the better.

To the above remark I would add the general remark, that it is more difficult for missionary families to procure woollen fabrics than almost any other. Flannel of any description is therefore a very acceptable article in a Missy box....

I will only say further that the kind benefactresses in this case may ply their needles without any secret misgivings as to the possibility that their aid will be misapplied. Let them imagine a mother with 6 girls—far removed from all facilities of education, ... in the middle of a wide prairie, in a house built in 12 hours by the axes of a few friends, with as yet no chimney or glass windows.[97]

Well-meaning people, however, sometimes used very poor judgment in their choice of articles for missionary boxes. We cannot help sympathizing with the disappointed minister in Michigan who wrote as follows after he had opened the box of books sent to his Sunday school:

Ye Books we expected ... were rec'd—But on opening ye box & looking over its contents we sat down & literally wept—Instead of *Library* Bks: behold, 196 vols: of ye *Union Question Bks;*; & 15 or 20 vols of a similar character!!! not worth as much to a school in ye interior of Mich: as so much brown paper—Then besides these, there was a quantity of old newspapers, Eng: Grammars, Arithmetics, Dutch Ch: Magazines, National Preachers &c &c &c—ye money we paid for freight (which was collected at that season of ye year with much difficulty) I verily believe would have purchased new Bks: of *greater value* to our Library, than *all our Committees judged it proper to put into ye Library from ye box.*[98]

---

[97] C. Hall to J. S. Gallagher, June 10, 1843, A.H.M.S. Letter Bk. Q, No. 64, C.T.S.

[98] S. Woodbury, Manchester, Mich., Dec. 13, 1841, A.H.M.S. papers, C.T.S.

Missionary boxes no doubt helped make life more endurable for the missionaries and their families,[99] and the anticipation of what the box might contain probably surpassed occasional disappointment over its actual contents.

MISSIONARIES IN IOWA

Serious as was the panic of 1837, recovery finally came; the whole country soon went to new heights of optimism and prosperity. Meanwhile a new frontier territory, Iowa, was attracting settlers, whose spiritual needs were the concern of the various missionary agencies. The Black Hawk Purchase of 1832 had opened to white settlement land just west of the Mississippi River, but the occupation of Iowa had not gone far when the panic hit the country. Hard times in the East drove off to the West a certain number of the unemployed and dissatisfied; so during the long, lean years of recovery eastern Iowa was filling up with farms and small towns. The people were poor, but they were in no danger of starvation because food was plentiful and cheap—so cheap that farmers had no market for their surplus crops. Money was extremely scarce. Julius A. Reed, one of the pioneer preachers of Iowa, in looking back at his experiences in the early days, said:

> The present inhabitants of Iowa [this was written about 1883] know nothing of the poverty of its first settlers. They know what a poor man is, but a community of poor men they never saw. In this Fairfield, in 1840 and onward, corn was worth ten cents a bushel, dressed pork one and a half cents per pound, a cow about eight dollars, *all in trade*. There were men in this vicinity who had good claims, good cabins and teams, who wore through the winter straw hats, padded; some wore two pairs of summer pants, and clothing could not be so patched as to attract attention on the streets. They could *dicker* for the products of the country, but it was exceedingly difficult to obtain money so as to purchase any goods and groceries. Mr. [Asa] Turner once, about this time, rode nearly half a day to borrow money so as to take his letters from the post office. Postage on eastern letters was then twenty-five cents.[100]

---

[99] One missionary wrote that he had made a trip of 120 miles in December in order to get from one of the boxes some "comfortable & decent" clothes for his family: L. Humphrey, Edwardsburg, Mich., Jan. 20, 1842, in C.H.M.S. (16th year, No. 1497) ; not found in A.H. M.S. papers, C.T.S.

[100] Julius A. Reed, *Reminiscences of Early Congregationalism in Iowa* (Grinnell, 1885), 7.

Representatives of the American Home Missionary Society arrived early in Iowa. In 1831 Aratus Kent, of Galena, Illinois, preached west of the Mississippi. In 1834 Cyrus Watson began work at Dubuque, and in 1838 Asa Turner, a member of the Yale Illinois Band, moved to Iowa and established the first Congregational church west of the Mississippi River at Denmark.[101] By 1842 the Congregational ministers in Iowa were sufficiently numerous to warrant them in forming an association for that territory. Then came a great impetus to religious work there through the arrival of the Iowa Band. This organization was formed at Andover Theological Seminary by a group of young men who were looking for a field where they might work together as the Yale Band had done in Illinois. Various Western states and territories were considered: Missouri was rejected because it was a slave state; Ohio and Michigan were partly occupied and were no longer typical of the frontier; Iowa was still in its infancy, and to it they decided to go.

For several years Asa Turner had been urging the American Home Missionary Society to send more men to Iowa, but he did not want those who came to be disappointed in what they might find or in what was expected of them. In 1840, for example, he had written:

I hope in the spring you will send us on a fresh supply [of missionaries]. But let all understand that in Iowa they will not find towering steeples pointing to heaven—nor parsonages all fitted for their reception—nor a people that will come round a minister and ask him what he wants.—If he is cold he may be obliged to put his axe into the root or stump of the tree; if he is hungry to lay his corn onto his "criture" and [? illegible] "git" [it] cracked, for even *money* will not always supply all his wants. The people are all at work and hard at it too—and those who have any standard above a log cabin and a "corn patch" have many weary months before them of hard labor, before houses and barns and walls will make comforts abound as in the land of our Fathers.[102]

The American Home Missionary Society had promised to commission the members of the Iowa Band, so the young preachers naturally turned to Asa Turner, the Society's

---

[101] Asa Turner's description of Iowa appeared in the *Home Missionary*, XIII (1840), 99 and 123.

[102] Asa Turner, Denmark, Iowa, Dec. 14, 1840, A.H.M.S. papers, C.T.S.

agent in Iowa, for suggestions and information. To them he gave homely advice concerning the preparations they should make for the journey and sage counsel as to what to expect:

> Come prepared to expect small things, rough things. Lay aside all your dandy whims boys learn in college, and take a few lessons of your grandmothers, before you come. Get clothes, firm, durable, something that will go through the hazel brush without tearing. Don't be afraid of a good, hard hand, or of a tanned face. If you keep free from a hard heart, you will do well. Get wives of the old Puritan stamp, such as honored the distaff and the loom, those who can pail a cow, and churn the butter, and be proud of a jean dress or a checked apron.
>
> Tell those two or three who think of leading out a sister this fall, we will try to find homes as good as Keokuk, the high chief and his lady live in, and my wife will have the kettle of mush and the johnny-cake ready by some cold night in November.[103]

In another letter he wrote to one of the members of the Band:

> Don't come here expecting a paradise. Our climate will permit men to live long enough, if they do their duty. If they do not, no matter how soon they die.
>
> Chances for health, if one is inclined to pulmonary complaints, I think are greater than in New England. I have known many persons improved by a residence here. We have some two hundred people connected with our society here. I doubt whether one in fifty has ever had fever and ague. I never knew so much good health for so long a time.
>
> Office and station are but little regarded here. People will not speak of you or to you, as the Rev. Mr. So-and-so, but will call you simply by your name, and your wife Peggy or Polly, or whatever her name may be.[104]

The eleven members of the Iowa Band,[105] two of whom had followed "Father" Turner's advice about "wives of the Puritan stamp," assembled in Buffalo in October, 1843, en route to the "Far West." By their numbers they attracted attention to themselves and their mission. A Buffalo news-

---

[103] Quoted by T. O. Douglass, *Pilgrims of Iowa* (Boston, c. 1911), 55-56.

[104] *Ibid.*, 55.

[105] Their names and places of birth were: Harvey Adams (N. H.), Edwin B. Turner (Mass.), Daniel Lane (Me.), Erastus Ripley (Conn.), James J. Hill (Me.), Ebenezer Alden (Mass.), Benjamin A. Spalding (Mass.), Alden B. Robbins (Mass.), Horace Hutchinson (Mass.), Ephraim Adams (N. H.), William Salter (N. Y.). *Ibid.*, 51.

paper printed the following comment: "We have seldom seen so many banded together in an enterprise, who seemed to possess such sterling good sense, and humble quiet characters, coupled with firmness and decision, as did these young men."[106] They were firm also in their purpose of remaining in the West; they went to Iowa with the intention of making permanent homes there. A few months before they left New England, one of the Band wrote:

The men who are going to Iowa have but one feeling: "It is to go and spend our days beyond the Mississippi—there to labor in the cause of Christ, till he shall call us to mansions of rest.... The understanding is among us all, that we go West not for a *temporary* purpose, unless the Great Head of the Church shall make it so—We go to remain *permanently—to live and die there*—and God grant us grace to carry out this purpose, in the most effectual way for securing his glory and the good of the people where we shall labor."[107]

In November, 1843, the members of the Band met at Asa Turner's home in Denmark, probably ate mush and johnnycake, sang and prayed together, gave careful consideration to the place to which each one should go, and then parted "sad, yet hopeful." The posts selected for the mission stations were mainly in southeastern Iowa. It was, and still is, a beautiful farming country, but it was new then. There were almost no roads or bridges; there were not enough houses and cabins to shelter all the people properly, and even a single room for an unmarried man was hard to find. A month after the members of the Band had separated to go to their respective posts, one of them made this entry in his diary:

Am somewhat troubled for a room. Cannot study—there is no lumber to make or stove to warm, or room to be had—have no opportunity for secret communion with God unless it be when I am walking or riding alone over the country when the constant necessity of resulting [*sic*] to expedient to keep warm prevents any steady devotion of the mind to Divine things....[108]

---

[106] Buffalo *Gazette*, quoted by E. Adams, *Iowa Band* (Boston, 1870), 20-21. A Burlington, Iowa, paper copied the notice from the *Gazette* and expressed the hope that the missionaries would soon learn by a short residence in Iowa that the people were not the heathens that the American Home Missionary Society, by sending so many missionaries at once, seemed to think that they were. J. A. Reed, Fairfield, Iowa, Nov. 28, 1843, A.H.M.S. papers, C.T.S.

[107] Daniel Lane, Andover Theol. Sem., Mass., to Sec'y. of A.H.M.S., July 13, 1843, A.H.M.S. papers, C.T.S.

[108] P. D. Jordan, ed., "William Salter's 'My Ministry in Iowa, 1843-1846,'" in *Annals of Iowa*, 3rd Ser., XIX (1935), 549.

From the diary of another comes this fragment of frontier experience:

> In the afternoon yesterday [Aug. 11, 1844], by invitation, preached for the Baptists. In the course of the sermon was a little vexed as I noticed two ladies smiling at some holes in my coat sleeve, revealed by my gesturing. Drew down my arms, and their faces, too, by preaching straight at them. Perhaps on this account, I preached with more point and earnestness than usual; for after meeting an Old School Presbyterian said he would give five dollars if I would stop and preach a year in the place. Felt it quite a compliment, considering the source.[109]

But after all a few holes in coat sleeves were of little moment. Mr. Adams added that the trials of the missionary are not

> that he has to wear a seedy coat, as good perhaps as his brother Christians about him wear; nor that, in his travels in a wet season, he occasionally gets "sloughed," or has to swim the stream. That is just what his neighbors do, and is nothing in a new country. But if he takes a paper, he reads of books which he can never see. He thinks of minister's meetings, and the culture of a literary fellowship among his brother ministers, which he can never enjoy.

But he knew there were compensations. If books were scarce, there were plenty of men to sharpen his wits; so he continued:

> Men are to be studied, as well as books; and the contact of mind with mind is a vigorous mental stimulus. Place now a young minister in some new Western settlement, where, in his line, nothing yet is established, nothing even started; where everybody and everything about him is on the quick, earnest move; where are commingled from all quarters every shade of prejudice, opinion and belief; and where all, with the trammels off are free to speak out just what they think, and he must have some earnest mental work. Every inch he gains here he must get by a sort of conquest.[110]

The Iowa Band is of significance also in relation to the development of Congregationalism in the West. In the early part of the nineteenth century, as was pointed out above,[111] it had been customary for Congregationalists who moved west from New England to affiliate themselves with Presbyterian churches; those who refused or neglected to do so might even find their orthodoxy questioned. But by the

---

109 E. Adams, *Iowa Band* (new and rev. ed., 1902), 49.

110 E. Adams. *Iowa Band* (new and rev. ed., 1902), 170-71.

111 See above, page 150 f.

thirties and forties throughout western New York, Ohio, Michigan, and Illinois, it was observed that erstwhile Congregationalists who were united with the Presbyterians under the Plan of Union were becoming dissatisfied. The reason for the change in attitude, as expressed by a missionary pastor in Michigan, was simple and natural. "Many of us," he said, "have spent our time, and talents, and property for years, in building up the cause of religion in this new country under a Presbyterian form of government, because we thought it best for the time being; but now, when there are enough of us, ... we wish to have things a little New England fashion, and no longer keep under the Presbyterian wing."[112] The members of the Oberlin colony,[113] which was founded in 1832, set up a Congregational Church—and were adversely criticized for so doing; yet four years later a Congregational Association was formed in the Western Reserve. In 1834 a similar association had been formed in western New York by Congregationalists who had broken away from their Presbyterian associates. It was evident that as Congregationalists became more numerous in the West during these years when sectarian differences were being generally emphasized, they too developed a stronger feeling of denominational loyalty.

There was a like tendency in Iowa where a Congregational Association was formed in 1840. When Asa Turner was in correspondence with the members of the Iowa Band before they left Andover, he had expressed the hope that they would retain their Congregational affiliations. He said:

Come on, brethren, come with the spirit of your Pilgrim Fathers, and plant their principles in this rich soil. Don't be ashamed of your mother as soon as you cross the Alleghanies, as many of our good brethren are, even some on whom she has put honorary titles. The principles of church government planted on Plymouth Rock are in my opinion the same as taught by our Saviour and his Apostles, and I am free to wish they might spread over this great valley. ... [114]

The members of the Iowa Band not only retained their Congregational connections and greatly augmented Congregational forces west of the Mississippi, but they also

---

[112] A. S. Arms, Milford, Mich., March 21, 1844, A.H.M.S. papers, C.T.S.

[113] On the Oberlin colony and the founding of Oberlin College, see below, page 379 f.

[114] Quoted by T. O. Douglass, *Pilgrims of Iowa*, 55.

helped make Western Congregationalism respectable in the East. The significance of their decision to stand by the church polity under which they had been trained was pointed out by one of their number as follows:

... They settled the question that Congregationalism was to become a power in Iowa, and indeed in the West, and was to enjoy the sympathy and aid of Eastern churches. It was claimed that Western Congregationalists who refused to become Presbyterian were unsound in the faith, or were "radicals," a synonym for everything bad. ...

But this Band represented six states and eight colleges; graduates of Andover, whose soundness in the faith, at that time none questioned, ... Their orthodoxy could not be assailed. It was dangerous to call them cranks, and a good share of New England at once gave their confidence and sympathy to Iowa Congregationalism.[115]

After 1840 New England Congregationalists who went into the West tended more and more to form churches of their own order, with the result that in Iowa and Wisconsin, for example, Congregationalism secured a stronger foothold than it had obtained in some older frontier regions where the New England element was just as numerous. It is especially significant that the development of a denominational self-consciousness among Western Congregationalists helped create a like feeling in New England—an illustration, although intangible, of the influence of the frontier on the coastal regions.[116]

WISCONSIN AND MINNESOTA

At the same time that representatives of the American Home Missionary Society were planting churches in Iowa, other men bearing its commissions were at work in Wisconsin. The removal of the Indians from the southern part of this territory following the Black Hawk War (1832) had opened the country to settlement. Stephen Peet, formerly a missionary in Michigan, had spied out the land in the late thirties; his favorable report, together with a map of the territory, was published in the *Home Missionary* in

---

115 Statement by Julius Reed, quoted by T. O. Douglass, *Pilgrims of Iowa*, 61.

116 L. K. Mathews, "Some Activities of the Congregational Church West of the Mississippi," in *Essays in American History dedicated to Frederick Jackson Turner* (New York, 1910), 10-11; [H. D. Kitchel], "The Congregational Convention," in *The New Englander*, XI (1853), 72-92.

1839.[117] The American Home Missionary Society announced its intention to send men to Wisconsin at once. Here was a chance to begin at the beginning. In many of the western territories missionary activities had not been undertaken until the population had assumed such a character that the efforts were remedial rather than preventive.

At the outset the representatives of the American Home Missionary Society were optimistic about the opportunities for Christian work in Wisconsin because of the high level of intelligence and culture that seemed to exist there. Mr. Peet said in 1839 that "a large portion of the population of the Territory are of the best class of emigrants from the eastern states—intelligent, enterprising, and decidedly in favor of education and religious institutions." But Wisconsin, like every other missionary field, presented its own peculiar problems; in this case the foreign-born, who came in such numbers in the 1840's, seemed to cause the Presbyterian and Congregational preachers the most difficulty. In the official report of the American Home Missionary Society for 1853 we read that

... A larger proportion of the population than in most other western States is composed of foreigners. Of these, the Germans are the most numerous and influential. Refugees from civil and religious despotism, they associate all forms of church organization with the instruments of oppression in the old world, from which they have fled, and which they hold in intense abhorence. The refined Pantheism, which they have learned in Germany here degenerates into downright Atheism, which manifests itself in avowed hostility to the Church, the Sabbath, the Bible, the cause of Temperance, and the institution of marriage. Not less than five newspapers, published in the German language, are of decidedly infidel character.[118]

In Wisconsin the Plan of Union of 1801 was not applied. This territory was being settled at a time when the Plan was breaking down; consequently a different scheme of co-operation between the two affiliated denominations was tried. An arrangement known as the "Presbyterian and Congregational Convention in Wisconsin" was worked out in 1840. It did not provide for composite churches as in

---

[117] *Home Missionary*, XII (1839), 102-10; this report gave so favorable a picture of Wisconsin and its people that one of the missionaries in Illinois protested that the men who were attracted there by it would be disappointed. A. Hale, Springfield, Ill., Jan. 29, 1840, A.H. M.S. papers, C.T.S.

[118] A.H.M.S., *Twenty-seventh Report* (1853), 83.

the old Plan of Union; there was instead a federation of churches, each congregation retaining its distinctive polity and principles. The Wisconsin Convention was not therefore "an amalgamation of Presbyterianism and Congregationalism, but a cordial union of *brethren* of both these denominations, who, agreeing in doctrinal belief, mode of worship, and the prosecution of the same missionary work, do [did] not consider the difference between them upon the mode of church government so great as to make it either necessary or expedient that they should walk apart."[119] By 1850 there were thirty-three Presbyterian ministers and thirty-one Presbyterian churches in Wisconsin, and fifty-eight Congregational ministers and eighty-three Congregational churches; nearly all of these churches were either organized by missionaries of the American Home Missionary Society or were aided in the support of their ministers by its funds.[120]

In the neighboring territory of Minnesota representatives of the American Home Missionary Society began work in 1849. When Mr. E. D. Neill "landed" in St. Paul on April 4, 1849, it was, to quote his words, "a village of 300 inhabitants, mostly illiterate French Canadians attached to the Church of Rome. The largest building was a rude log chapel in which French Services were performed by the priest."[121] Early in September of that year the first legislative assembly of Minnesota convened "in a building which answered the double purpose of Capitol and Hotel. As the flag was run up the staff, a number of Winnebago Indians sat on a rocky bluff in the vicinity & gazed at what to them was a novel and no doubt saddening scene; for if the tide of emigration sweeps inward from the Pacific Coast, as it has done from the Atlantic, it will not be many years before the Red Man will become extinct."[122]

---

119 Dexter Clary, *History of the Churches and Ministers Connected with the Presbyterian and Congregational Convention of Wisconsin* (Beloit, 1861), 12; see also Stephen Peet, *History of the Presbyterian and Congregational Churches and Ministers in Wisconsin* (Milwaukee, 1851), 26-37.

120 Stephen Peet, *History of the Presbyterian and Congregational Churches*, 190-91, 197.

121 E. D. Neill, St. Paul, Minn., Feb. 23, 1850, in A.H.M.S. papers, C.T.S.

122 E. D. Neill, St. Paul, Minn., Sept. 12, 1849, A.H.M.S. papers, C.T.S.

It happened that the first representatives of the American Home Missionary Society sent to Minnesota were Presbyterians; in 1850 the founders of Congregationalism in that territory appeared in the persons of Richard Hall and Charles Seccombe. Between them and their Presbyterian colleagues there was unfortunately some misunderstanding and bickering about the denominational affiliations of the churches organized.[123] The old Plan of Union was now so discredited that it could be of little service; however, a temporary compromise was reached at one point of tension, St. Anthony (site of Minneapolis), by forming a "Plan of Union Church."[124] In general the churches organized in Minnesota were of the one order or the other; the rivalry between New School Presbyterians and Congregationalists was becoming too keen to make it easy for them to worship the Lord together in the same congregation. Of the forty-three Congregational churches established in Minnesota between 1850 and 1860 nearly all received assistance from the American Home Missionary Society.[125]

THE BAPTISTS

The formation of the American Baptist Home Mission Society in 1832 was an indication not only of a growing sense of denominational consciousness, but also of a greater interest in missions among the more progressive elements among the Baptists. The work of the Baptist society did not expand rapidly. The funds available for its use before the Civil War were scanty, because the antimissionary spirit was still strong among certain groups in the Baptist brotherhood; indeed, the "anti-means, anti-mission" movement within this denomination probably reached its climax in the thirties and forties. Baptist Associations were divided on the question of missions: in the Miami Association nineteen out of twenty-five churches withdrew and formed

---

[123] Messrs. Hall and Seccombe resented what they thought was a premature attempt to organize a presbytery which they were importuned to enter. The A.H.M.S. Minnesota correspondence for 1851 and 1852 is largely taken up with the controversy.

[124] C. Seccombe, St. Anthony, Minn., Aug. 27, 1852, A.H.M.S. papers, C.T.S.

[125] A. Hadden, *Congregationalism in Minnesota, 1851-1891* (Minneapolis, 1891), 11.

a separate antimissionary organization;[126] in the Chemung Association of New York and Pennsylvania, a resolution was adopted in 1835 declaring that fellowship would no longer be continued with churches that united themselves "with the world and what are falsely called benevolent societies founded upon a monied basis."[127] Those who withdrew from the main body of the Baptists about this time are usually called "Primitive" or "Old School" or "Anti-Mission" Baptists; their strength was and still is in the southern and southwestern states. Such conditions, combined with the fact that Baptists generally had not been educated in giving, explain why the annual receipts of the American Baptist Home Mission Society amounted only to about thirty thousand dollars in its fifteenth year (1847); in 1859 the receipts were approximately fifty thousand dollars.

As in the case of the other missionary societies, men were sent into new territories as they were opened to settlement. Michigan was the first field cultivated by the American Baptist Home Mission Society; Thomas W. Merrill, who was already a pioneer preacher in that territory, received a commission in 1832, the year of the Society's organization. Merrill desired appointment by the Society in order that he might use his small salary to purchase a site for an institution of learning under Baptist influence, an aspiration which resulted ultimately in the founding of Kalamazoo College.[128] In 1838 the Society began work in Iowa and Wisconsin, both of which were then in an early stage of development; one of the missionaries in Wisconsin reported instances in which people had come nine miles with ox teams to hear preaching.[129]

In 1839 an "exploring missionary" was sent to Texas. The early Baptist churches in Texas were antimissionary or "hardshell." In 1837 the first missionary Baptist church in Texas was organized at Washington. A committee of this church sent a letter to the Baptist Board of Foreign Missions—Texas was then a foreign country—pointing out the religious destitution of Texas and asking for missionaries.

---

[126] A. S. Carman, "Baptists of Central Western States," in A. H. Newman, *Century of Baptist Achievement*, 93.

[127] H. K. Carroll, *Religious Forces of the United States*, 45.

[128] A.B.H.M.S., *Sixty-eighth Report* (1900), 66.

[129] *Baptist Home Mission Monthly*, VIII (1886), 2.

"Perhaps one-half of our fellow-citizens do not hear preaching once in six months," they said, "and many of them have never heard a gospel sermon since they have been in Texas." The matter was referred to the Home Mission Society, which collected money in the South, mainly in Georgia, for the Texas mission. The growing estrangement between the North and the South interfered with the intersectional aspects of the work. An agent of the Baptist Home Mission Society, who was soliciting in Georgia for the new mission in Texas, authorized a statement in a local religious periodical (1840) that "any moneys which may be contributed for this object will be deposited in the hands of some gentleman or in some bank in this state, subject to the order of Brother Huckins [missionary in Texas]. It will not be sent to the North at all."[130]

THE METHODISTS

Methodism grew so rapidly in the United States that before it was old enough to celebrate the diamond anniversary of its introduction into America its adherents were more numerous than those of any other Protestant denomination. The itinerant preacher riding the circuit continued to be the principal missionary agency of this Church, but it was noticeable, however, as time passed that there was a growing tendency for the circuit riders to become settled pastors; furthermore, as Methodism grew in strength and popularity it lost some of its early fervor. Bishops sounded the warning against these changes and declared that Methodism would lose its power unless it retained the methods and institutions under which it had made such rapid progress.[131] The Methodist Missionary Society, which was formed in 1819, continued to support and supervise missionary work in those places where circuits could not be otherwise formed or where conditions were unusual. Its work among the English-speaking population of the United States was mainly in the new states and territories and in the suburbs of the large cities.

One of the most important phases of the work of the Methodist Society in the period here under consideration

---

[130] Quotation from J. M. Carroll, *History of the Texas Baptists* (Dallas, 1923), 159.

[131] "Address of the Bishops to the General Conference of the Methodist Church, 1844," in *Journal of the General Conference* (1844), 157.

was that carried on among the foreign-born in the United States, and especially among the Germans in the Mississippi Valley states. In 1835 William Nast, a native of Germany who had come to America a few years earlier to make a fortune, was converted and became a Methodist local preacher in Ohio. He was assigned by the Ohio Conference to work among the German population in Cincinnati.[132] This was the beginning of a work which grew so rapidly that in less than ten years there were German Methodist missions in the principal German communities in western Pennsylvania, Ohio, Indiana, Illinois, and Missouri. In 1858 it was reported that the Methodists had 245 missionaries and 170 assistants working among the Germans in this country, and that there were about sixteen thousand members in the German Methodist churches.[133] Although most of the Germans in the United States in the period preceding the Civil War were to be found in the West, not all of them were in frontier communities; many were located in such cities as Cincinnati and St. Louis, and in states which were rapidly leaving the pioneer stage of development. Home missionary work among the Germans was carried on in the face of considerable opposition and ridicule. Some of them were Catholics; many of them were steeped in rationalism and were opposed to any form of revealed religion; others were unwilling to break with their Lutheran traditions; Methodist rules of conduct and German conviviality were often incompatible. It is not strange then that some German Methodists met with ridicule and even ostracism from those of their own race and tongue.

The Texan victory in the battle of San Jacinto (1836) suggested that the time was ripe for the advance of Protestant missionaries into that foreign country, and so three were sent in by the Methodists in 1837. Although there had been some Methodists among the early American settlers in Texas, neither law nor circumstance had left much opportunity for the public observance of Methodism or any other form of Protestantism.[134] There were few churches or

---

132 A. Miller, *Origin and Progress of the German Missions in the Methodist Episcopal Church* (Cincinnati, 1843), 13 ff.

133 D. D. Lore, "Missions in America," in *Methodist Quarterly Review*, XL (1858), 601.

134 M. Phelan, *History of Methodism in Texas* (Nashville, [1924]), 10.

ministers. Sunday was a day for hunting, fishing, breaking wild horses, and, occasionally, elections. One of the early Methodist missionaries in Texas described the inhabitants of one of the towns as "recklessly wicked," and another, who acted for a time as chaplain of the Texas Senate, characterized a boat on which he had traveled in company with several of the political leaders of the state as a "floating hell."[135] Obviously the Methodists had a mission to perform in Texas, which was organized as a separate conference in 1840. At the division of the Methodist Church in 1844 the work in Texas was turned over to the Southern branch.[136]

THE EPISCOPALIANS

On account of two fundamental changes in missionary policy the year 1835 marks a turning point in the history of the Protestant Episcopal Church. In the first place, the Domestic and Foreign Missionary Society, which had been formed in 1821, was reorganized so as to include all members of the Church. Hitherto it had been a society distinct from the Church, membership in which was secured by the payment of dues or the contribution of money for missions. At the General Convention of 1835 a new principle was announced, namely, that the Church is a missionary society and that all Churchmen are *ipso facto* members of the society. This announcement, however, was not enough to arouse the interest of the members in their society; ten years later the *Spirit of Missions*, the official missionary organ of the Protestant Episcopal Church, complained because the gifts for the work were so insignificant. Estimating the number of persons in the United States who had been baptized into the Episcopal Church at one and a half million, their average contributions for domestic missions amounted to about one cent a year. The moral was obvious: "Missions in the West will never flourish as they ought till Eastern piety can be warmed to a self-denial, which shall measure itself by some larger offering than 1 cent per annum."[137]

Much more productive of immediate results was the

---

[135] D. F. Arthur, "Jottings from the Old Journal of Littleton Fowler," in *Texas Hist. Asso. Quarterly*, II (1898), 82.

[136] M.S.M.E.Ch., *Twenty-seventh Annual Report* (1846), 17.

[137] *Spirit of Missions*, IX (1844), 343.

second innovation of 1835, the election of missionary bishops. This action involved a revolution in the theory of the organization of the Protestant Episcopal Church as well as in missionary methods. Hitherto the Episcopal Church in the United States had been a federation of autonomous state churches. Whenever the clergy in a state became sufficiently numerous they met, organized a diocese, and elected a bishop. It was in this way that Philander Chase was elected Bishop of Ohio in 1818 by a "so-called convention of two clergymen and nine laymen," and was later chosen Bishop of Illinois (1835) in "a diocese which had, in all, four presbyters, one church building, and thirty-nine communicants."[138] The disadvantages in such an arrangement were obvious. There was no bishop to supervise the clergy of a frontier state or territory, or to plant new churches, or to gather the scattered members of the Church together, until after the clergy of the state or territory met and elected one. But after they chose a bishop there was still the question of his support. How was that to be provided in a new frontier diocese? Under the old arrangement the Church as a whole assumed no responsibility for the selection of bishops in the new states or for their maintenance. In 1835 the General Convention of the Episcopal Church abandoned this method of procedure, which had been so largely responsible for the failure of the Church to conduct an aggressive campaign in the West, and decided thereafter to send missionary bishops to the new settlements. The Church as a whole now took over the responsibility for supporting bishops on the frontier until conditions warranted the organization of dioceses. By this change "Episcopacy passed from the idea of a Federation of constituent State Churches to that of a National Church with component dioceses."[139]

Two missionary bishops were chosen in 1835, Francis Hawks for the Southwest and Jackson Kemper for the Northwest. Hawks declined election, but Kemper began his work at once in his vast northwestern diocese which included what is now Indiana, Missouri, Wisconsin, and Iowa. Illinois was not included because in 1835 Philander Chase, formerly Bishop of Ohio (1818-31), had been made head of

---

[138] H. L. Burleson, *Conquest of the Continent*, 52-54.

[139] S. D. McConnell, *History of the American Episcopal Church* (rev. ed., Milwaukee, 1916), 310.

a newly created diocese in that state.[140] As the frontier moved west Kemper's bishopric expanded to include Kansas, Nebraska, and Minnesota, but at the same time it was being contracted in the older settlements by the erection of new episcopates in Missouri (1844), Indiana (1849), and Iowa (1854). A missionary bishop had the frontier continually as his diocese. Through it he traveled, exercising supervision over the missionary priests sent out by the Board of Missions, visiting the scattered Churchmen, gathering them into congregations, making arrangements for the erection of church buildings, and preparing the way generally for the establishment of independent bishoprics when the time was ripe.

For almost a quarter of a century and in the face of difficulties which seemed insurmountable—the vastness of the bishopric, inadequate means of transportation, lack of helpers and money, and indifference on the part of the great mass of Westerners towards the Episcopal Church and its ritual—Bishop Kemper worked and traveled, talked and prayed for the cause to which he had devoted his life. When he resigned as missionary bishop in 1859 to become the diocesan bishop of Wisconsin the Committee on Domestic Missions gave the following summary of what he had accomplished in the Northwest in the preceding twenty-four years:

When Bishop Kemper was appointed Missionary Bishop, in 1835, with jurisdiction over Missouri, Indiana, Wisconsin, and Iowa, neither of which was an organized Diocese, there was but one of our clergy and one church in Missouri, one clergyman and one church in

---

[140] In 1835 Chase was invited by the Episcopal clergy in Illinois to become the bishop of a feeble diocese which they had just erected. As in Ohio, there was a struggle to secure a living for the bishop and to raise money for churches and schools. Again Bishop Chase planned to found a college and again he turned to friends overseas for help. In October, 1835, he sailed for England, and despite the fact that some of his former patrons were dead, he was able to return in the following year with money and pledges amounting to about ten thousand dollars with which he laid the foundations for Jubilee College in Illinois. See P. Chase, *Appeal by Bishop Chase, in behalf of a Protestant Episcopal Theological Seminary for the Diocese of Illinois* ([London], n.d.) ; and Samuel Chase, *Review of Jubilee College* ([Peoria], 1843). But Bishop Chase was growing old, the task of traveling about his bishopric was burdensome, some of his clergy were rebellious under his iron rule, and so his closing days in the diocese of Illinois were stormy. See Samuel Chase, *Malignity Exposed; or a Vindication of Bishop Chase* (Peoria, 1847). In the midst of his troubles Bishop Chase died in 1852.

Indiana, and neither church nor clergyman in Wisconsin or Iowa. Twenty-four years have passed away, and by God's blessing on the Church, he now sees Missouri a Diocese with its Bishop and twenty-seven clergy; Indiana a Diocese, with its Bishop and twenty-five clergy; Wisconsin, his own Diocese with fifty-five clergy; Iowa, a Diocese, with its Bishop and thirty-one clergy; Minnesota an organized Diocese, with twenty clergy. Kansas but just organized as a Diocese, with ten clergy; and the territory of Nebraska, not yet organized as a Diocese, with four clergy; in all six Dioceses, where he began with none, and one hundred and seventy-two clergymen where he was at first sustained by only two.[141]

When this "Napoleon of a spiritual empire" died in 1870 the *Spirit of Missions* paid him this well-deserved tribute:

> In the prosecution of his work, he [Bishop Kemper] travelled three hundred thousand miles, many thousands of them on horseback, hundreds of them on foot, through snow and mud, under cold and burning skies, exposed to all vicissitudes of weather. So vast was his field, and so constantly was he in motion to visit even the most important places, that, for the first twelve years of his Episcopate, he could hardly be said to have had a home. He claimed but one day in the year for himself. Christmas Day he always tried to spend with his family.... Bishop Kemper lived to see seven Dioceses formed within the limits of what was once his great field.... Within these limits, mainly, he consecrated nearly one hundred churches, ordained more than two hundred Priests and Deacons and confirmed not far from ten thousand persons.[142]

In 1838 the Protestant Episcopal Church found a missionary bishop for the Southwest, by which was then meant Arkansas, Indian Territory, Mississippi, Louisiana, Alabama, and the Republic of Texas. The man chosen was Leonidas Polk, member of a distinguished Southern family, who had been converted while a student at West Point, and who had entered the ministry after his graduation from the Military Academy. His first missionary tour was made in 1839 through Alabama, Mississippi, Arkansas, Louisiana, and southern Texas. Texas then had the reputation of being the place to which fled insolvent debtors and fugitives from justice. Even the Bishop was suspected of belonging to one or the other of these classes. A Texan, happening to hear that he was one of the Polks of Tennessee, sat for a time in silence and then said: "Well, stranger, if it is a fair question, I would give a *heap* to know what brought *you* here." When

---

[141] Quoted by Greenough White, *Apostle of the Western Church*, 176.
[142] *Spirit of Missions*, XXXV (1870), 394-95.

the Bishop told him his mission, the Texan replied: "Oh, my friend, go back, go back; we are not worth saving."[143] In 1841 Polk resigned his missionary bishopric to become the Bishop of Louisiana, which post he held until he laid aside his ecclesiastical vestments to put on the uniform of the Confederacy.

For three years after Bishop Polk's resignation James Hervey Otey, first Protestant Episcopal Bishop of Tennessee, was given jurisdiction over the missionary diocese of the Southwest. The magnitude of the task laid upon him is indicated by his statement that at one time the limits of his spiritual jurisdiction were from "Kentucky and Missouri on the North to the Gulf of Mexico on the South, and stretching between the eastern shores of Florida and the Pacific."[144]

Another indefatigable missionary pioneer of the Episcopal Church was James Lloyd Breck, who is remembered for his plan of associate missions. In 1841 while Bishop Kemper was in the East seeking missionaries for Wisconsin he met at the General Theological Seminary several young men who had been contemplating the establishment in the West of a mission along monastic lines.[145] According to Breck, who was a leader in the movement, the basic principles were: (1) the unity of the Church must be restored; (2) the West must be saved from Romanism and sectarianism; (3) there must be concert of action. He suggested a method of procedure and set forth the advantages of the plan as follows:

... Let a certain number from every class ... deeply imbued with Catholic principles devote themselves to the West. Let them band together, & as co-workers in *one* cause, recognize before God & each other (without assuming the vows of a Religious House) the solemn obligation resting upon them as thus devoted, to give up themselves unreservedly to the work of establishing the Chh in the West, & consequently to forego every thing that could possibly interfere in any manner with such entire devotion:—as for instance, all idea of *any right* to marry—at least until they shall have seen the work *so far* progressed that *less entire, constant, laborious personal devotion* to it, may seem necessary. Let them go forth *as one* (not to scatter their forces) but to act together as one compact, organized missionary body.

---

[143] W. M. Polk, *Leonidas Polk, Bishop and General* (New York and London, 1915), I, 161.

[144] W. M. Green, *Memoir of Rt. Rev. James Hervey Otey* (New York, 1885), 89.

[145] Jackson Kemper, St. Louis, April 2, 1841, to S. R. Johnson, Kemper papers, XXIV, No. 67, Wisconsin Historical Society.

... Let them ... consider themselves as devoted to a life of *self denial* in every form—as to food, sleep, clothes, rest, self control, & even as far as the common interest of his brethren of the body may be subserved, *private property.* ... Let them at such point as the Bishop shall command, establish a Mission College or Religious House: where they shall teach freely, faithfully & in so far as practicable gratuitously, all who will be taught, and let them with all quietness, prudence, humble faithful diligence, seek to minister continually to the spiritual, intellectual & other wants of those in the country around. ... This would unite what in both cases have been eminently successful, the itinerating of the Methodists & the Chh education of the Romanists. ... [146]

Nashotah, Wisconsin, was selected as the place for the experiment, and there in 1842 the "associate mission" was opened. Inasmuch as Breck, the soul of the movement, was only twenty-two years old, Bishop Kemper selected as "Father Superior" Richard F. Cadle, chaplain at Fort Crawford. The "brethren" adopted as their uniform a cassock of coarse cloth for winter and one made of lighter material for summer. From Nashotah missionary journeys were made into the surrounding country to preach to the people and to organize churches. A school for the training of preachers was an essential part of the plan, and at Nashotah prospective candidates for the Episcopal ministry were assembled and subjected to a discipline that was almost military in character. When Father Superior Cadle withdrew shortly after the venture was started, the youthful Breck was put in charge. The money for the support of the mission and school came from the Board of Missions, supplemented by voluntary contributions made by friends in the East;[147] but there was so little of it that even young men devoted to asceticism felt pinched and cramped. One of them wrote to the Bishop:

... May I not say then that it is absolutely necessary that we should have at least 4 or 5 hundred dollars? How can we get along without it? We can indeed live on potatoes,—roasted in our stove, dwell in a scant furnished room, wear one shirt a week, walk to our several

---

[146] J. L. Breck, Nashotah, Wis., March 16, 1843, to Jackson Kemper, Kemper papers, XXVII, No. 58, Wisconsin Historical Society.

[147] The Nashotah experiment attracted attention in England as well as in the East. Henry Caswall wrote to Bishop Kemper from Market Lavington, Wilts., Eng., Dec. 27, 1842, "the eyes of a large & influential portion of the clergy in England, of both schools of theology, look with deep interest on the Wisconsin mission." Kemper papers, XXVII, No. 26, Wisconsin Historical Society.

stations and depend on our missionary stipend. But a few hundred dollars will furnish our room plainly—purchase us one or two horses and keep them—& assure us of independence of the people here, themselves pinched for means—& enable us to go about the fulfilment of our plan with minds unburdened with such worldly cares—able to look schimatics, heretics, infidels & all men in the face with the assurance which the possession of money, let them cry it down as they will—certainly gives.... [148]

A movement which approached so closely certain practices ordinarily associated with the Roman Catholic Church received a good deal of criticism from some Episcopalians. Breck was accused of being a "papist" at heart, and, indeed, it was pointed out that six of the Nashotah students did go over to the Roman Church and that at one time the leader himself was on the point of doing just this.[149] The plan for a semimonastic mission failed; the students did not like Breck's arbitrary rule over them; there was dissension among the associates, and one of them, William Adams, married Bishop Kemper's daughter, thus helping undermine the ascetic principles on which so much store had been set. In 1850 Breck abandoned the Nashotah project, leaving it in the hands of able but more practical men, and set out for a new frontier, Minnesota, there to try again to work out his theories. A new mission was established at St. Paul. From a letter written by Breck about this time we get an idea of his plans and methods. He said that his associates at St. Paul had

joined the Mission understandingly, that is, they have come to it as a *Religious House* or *Brotherhood*, such as Nashotah in its integrity was meant to be.... We wish to establish a system that will be complete in itself for the extension of the Church, without other machinery, such as the General Missionary Society. Let *it* do what it can,... but for those for whom this system is fitted, let it be an instrument in itself for the work unto which it is sent.

We wish to raise up parishes at proper distances in every part of our land. Already we number twelve points at which we officiate, and when we shall have gone over the country intervening between this and the Sauk Rapids, a distance of eighty miles,... then shall we have traversed and fixed stations for Divine Service in every part where the white man has as yet settled. We desire to make these stations self-supporting before they pass from our hands into those of another.[150]

---

[148] J. H. Hobart, Prairieville, Wis., Oct. 4, 1841, to Jackson Kemper, Kemper papers, XXV, No. 48, Wisconsin Historical Society.

[149] G. White, *Apostle of the Western Church*, 122-23.

[150] Quoted in Charles Breck, *Life of the Reverend James Lloyd Breck*, 150.

Breck was a high churchman. The Bishop wrote while on a visit to the St. Paul mission in 1851:

> The pecularities of B[reck] continue. I see some Oxford caps hanging up but I have not yet seen them used.... The service of the Ch is at 6 & 6—& even I must be surpliced if I am only to pronounce the absolution. There is a Litany every day at noon—then the brethren are clothed in their cassocks & sashes. On Thursday we have Eucharist at 6—Prayers at 9—Litany at noon—& prayers again at 6.... And the bell is perfectly Nashotah in its most palmy days—& then B rings it with much gusto—to get up—to pray—to come to meals —7 times a day at least—& often more.[151]

As to the expediency of Breck's methods there might be an honest difference of opinion. He himself abandoned the ideal of a celibate life and married in 1855. But there can be no question about his sincerity and his implicit confidence that he was doing God's work and that the necessary physical means for carrying it on would be provided. In Minnesota, as in Wisconsin, he was instrumental in laying the foundations for Episcopal schools, but that phase of his work, together with his latter activities in California will be discussed in the chapter on Education.[152]

The three decades preceding the Civil War were marked by an intensification of denominational feeling in the United States. The desire for sectarian aggrandizement had become a powerful motive in home missions. Co-operative missionary enterprises broke down. The churches of America were in competition with one another for vantage points in the West. In this contest all had an equal opportunity so far as the state was concerned. Except for occasional extralegal interference with some cult of real or supposed immoral or antisocial tendencies, there was complete freedom of religion. No sect or party could use force. The weapons in the contest were intellectual and spiritual, rather than physical. One writer summed up this contest between ideas, principles, and systems in the West in the following words:

> The action and reaction of colliding elements in the Ohio Valley struck out much intellectual heat and light. Civilized races met with savage, Christianity met Judaism, Protestant challenged Catholic,

---

[151] Jackson Kemper, St. Paul, Aug. 1, 1851, to Elizabeth Kemper Adams, Kemper papers, XXXIV, No. 91, Wisconsin Historical Society.

[152] See below, page 398.

Calvinist encountered anti-Calvinist, Unitarian opposed Trinitarian, old denominations split by contention projected new sects into being, and each new sect criticized all the others. Antagonizing churches in general, and even assaulting the bulwarks of religion itself, the agnostics, the skeptics, and the avowed atheists joined the thick combat. Extremes grappled.[153]

[153] W. H. Venable, *Beginnings of Literary Culture in the Ohio Valley*, 225.

CHAPTER VIII

THE PACIFIC COAST

We feel that we [of the American Home Missionary Society] are working in coincidence with the divine plan.—*Reverend E. L. Cleaveland.*

T HE WEST UP TO 1840 had not extended far beyond the woodland area east of the Mississippi; it had been mainly the abode of hunters, traders, small farmers, and petty merchants who had roamed over or lived in a forested region where innumerable trees had to be cut down before the work of civilization could proceed very far. In general, except for early settlements in Kentucky, Tennessee, and Ohio, each successive frontier had been contiguous to, or at least not far removed from, the area already reclaimed from the wilderness. The West of any given time and place had been another new stratum of society laid down irregularly just beyond those already in existence. Although the settlement of the new lands had been far from compact or orderly, there had usually been no great gaps between the settled and the unsettled regions. Up to 1840 this normal process of pushing on to fairly adjacent new frontiers had taken the pioneers not only out to the western edge of Missouri but even across the southwestern boundary of the United States into Texas.

After 1840 pioneering took on new characteristics. Beyond the western edge of Missouri lay a vast region which had long been known as the Great American Desert. From about the one hundredth meridian to the Rocky Mountains rainfall was scanty and timber scarce. As the pioneers approached this section of the Great Plains in the thirties it seemed so barren and uninviting that they did not venture into it in search of homes; and since it was a "desert" it was graciously set aside as a permanent abode for Indians. But the momentum behind the westward-moving mass of Americans was sufficiently great to carry the restless home seekers over the so-called desert and across the mountains

to Oregon, Utah, and California. In the case of Oregon a combination of motives, economic, political, and religious, set several thousand middle western farmers in motion towards the Far Northwest in the forties. So far as Utah is concerned, the desire of the Mormons to find a remote and isolated spot—and one outside the United States—where they might be free to practice their religion without molestation, explains their trek into the Valley of the Great Salt Lake. But even while the Latter-day Saints were setting the stakes of their new Zion, the termination of the War with Mexico and the cession of the whole Southwest to the United States (1848) brought them back under the jurisdiction of the country from which they had just fled. To the West of Utah lay California, the land of gold and romance and adventure. No wonder that the Forty-niners were counted by the tens of thousands.

MANIFEST DESTINY

An intangible but very real motive for American advance into the Far West was the notion of Manifest Destiny, the belief that it was the will of God that the United States of America should occupy all, or at least the best parts of, North America. The doctrine had religious connotations also; it signified the triumph of Protestantism over Catholicism. Manifest Destiny was used to explain and justify the conquest of territory in the Southwest at the expense of Mexico, a Catholic country. And in the succession of events leading up to the outcome of the Mexican War preachers and moralists saw the unfolding of a divine plan. God had reserved America for Protestantism and Democracy. More than that, the delay in the discovery of gold in California until after that land had passed from a Catholic to a Protestant power was taken by some to be an indication that God intended to use the new Protestant settlements on the Pacific Coast as a means for the conversion of the teeming heathen lands that lay on the other side of the ocean. The following is a typical exposition of the theories of those who saw the Hand of God at work in American history:

Why, Sir, did God preserve this whole country more than a century after its discovery, for the English race, turning the foot of the Spaniard to the sunny regions of the tropics? Why did he induce Columbus, just before making land, to veer a few points southward, so that instead of striking the coast of Florida, as he would have done,

had he adhered to his original purpose of sailing due west, he struck the West India Islands? Why did God keep this great country from the English until they had renounced the supremacy of the Roman Pontiff? And why did he keep it from the Protestants until they had purified the reformed faith from its still remaining Romish tendencies? ... Why did he blast every attempt of the Spaniards to colonize the Valley of the Mississippi? Why, when La Salle, upwards of one hundred and seventy years ago, had taken possession of the whole country from the mouth of the Illinois to the Gulf of Mexico, politically in the name of Louis the Great, and spiritually in the name of the Church of Rome; and when, a few years after, the French attempted to realize the design of La Salle, by erecting a chain of forts through Peoria and Vincennes, towards the Southwest, building chapels and celebrating mass in the same—why did God drive them from every one of those posts and defeat their well-laid scheme? ... In fine, why were the immense treasures of California hidden from all the world, even from the keen-scented Spaniard, until she was annexed to this Republic? And tell me, if any one can, why it was that the title deed of transference had no sooner passed into our hands, than she gave up her mighty secret, and unlocked her golden gates? Is it possible not to see the hand of God in all this?[1]

Far fetched as all this seems to the critical student of history, and vulnerable as it is to the attacks of the scoffers who ask embarrassing questions, it furnished, nevertheless, a powerful motive for missionary work. The man who believed that God had reserved a portion of the earth for his sect or creed had the agreeable feeling that he was working in harmony with the Divine Purpose when he tried to establish his Faith there, and not unlikely he felt too that he would be held accountable for delay and negligence in carrying out the will of the Almighty.

AMERICAN HOME MISSIONARY SOCIETY AND OREGON

Ministers of the gospel were among the earliest pioneer settlers in Oregon, but since they were interested primarily in Indians they were regarded as foreign and not home missionaries. In this instance foreign missions helped open the way for white settlement, and white settlement called for home missions.[2] The Lees, who went to Oregon in 1834 for

---

[1] E. L. Cleaveland, in *Home Missionary*, XXVI (1853), 61.

[2] For example, Dr. Marcus Whitman, missionary to the Indians in the Northwest, looked forward to the time when foreign missions to the Indians in that region would decrease and home missions to the white settlers would increase in importance. Cf. A. B. and D. P. Hulbert, *Marcus Whitman, Crusader*, Part Two *(Overland to the Pacific*, VII, [Colorado Springs and Denver, 1938]), 329-30; C. M. Drury, *Marcus Whitman, M.D.* (Caldwell, Idaho, 1937), 346, 352.

the Methodist Episcopal Church, and the Whitman-Spalding party (1836) for the American Board of Commissioners for Foreign Missions (Presbyterian and Congregational) were among the most potent influences in attracting American settlers to Oregon. Between 1840 and 1850 several thousand persons from the East and the Middle West sought homes "where rolls the Oregon." Their motives were first of all economic, but political and religious considerations were also of importance. In the Mississippi Valley states and territories the home market for agricultural produce had so completely broken down by 1840 that farmers could not sell what they raised; in Oregon they hoped to find a market for their crops among the fur traders and whalers. The ownership of Oregon was in dispute with Great Britain; it was thought that settlers would strengthen the claims of the United States.[3] And then there were the heathen, some of whom, so the story went, had gone to St. Louis in search of the white man's Book to Heaven;[4] a few of the men and women bound for Oregon may have had rather vaguely in mind the presumptive salutary effect of their presence upon the benighted inhabitants of the region.[5] In addition, Oregon, with its mild climate, its rich soil, its pleasant streams, and its stately trees, was pictured as an earthly paradise. So the "Oregon fever" swept over the Middle West and carried off its hopeful, and often fortunate, victims to the valleys of the Columbia and the Willamette.

Where the settlers went the church must go too. The flag was there also, since by treaty with Great Britain in 1846 the United States secured Oregon as far north as the forty-ninth parallel. The first missionary sent to Oregon by the American Home Missionary Society was George A. Atkinson, who, with his wife, reached Oregon City in June, 1848, after a nine-months' trip around the Horn.

Moving from New England to Oregon in 1847-48 by way of the tip of South America was no light undertaking. There were supplies for the mission and household to be

---

[3] On the relationship of the American pioneers to the settlement of the boundary dispute in 1846 see F. Merk, "The Oregon Pioneers and the Boundary," in *American Historical Review*, XXIX (1924), 681-99.

[4] A. B. and D. P. Hulbert, *The Oregon Crusade (Overland to the Pacific*, V, [Colorado Springs and] Denver, c. 1935), 85-131.

[5] Cf. A. B. Hulbert, "Undeveloped Factors in the Life of Marcus Whitman," in J. F. Willard and C. B. Goodykoontz, eds., *The Trans-Mississippi West* (Boulder, 1930), 97.

assembled;[6] some food for the journey, eight or nine months in length, must be secured;[7] a supply of medicines must not be forgotten; insurance must be arranged for—all these and many other details occupied Mr. Atkinson's time as he made preparations for a voyage which involved about as many problems and uncertainties as a trip to Africa or India.[8]

In one very important respect Mr. Atkinson was prepared for his Oregon mission when he offered his services to the American Home Missionary Society: he had a wife. His classmate at Andover, Horace Lyman, who had planned to go to Oregon with him, was not married but had been strongly advised by his friends not to go to a region so distant without a helpmeet. But to find and "fall in love" with a young woman with the proper qualifications who was willing to go to Oregon on short notice as the wife of a missionary was not an easy task, as anyone may see who reads the letters written by this prospective missionary in the autumn of 1847 as the time for the departure of the Atkinsons drew near. The basic cause of his difficulty was that perforce he had to be a hasty wooer if he were to find a wife before the boat sailed. Missionaries were not impersonal objects who moved about the earth entirely indifferent to mundane affairs with their minds and hearts set only on the life beyond the grave. They were human beings, with all the emotions of other men and women, and the missionary movement loses its full significance unless the personal element is taken into account. With this in mind, let us take this unusual opportunity to look over Mr. Lyman's shoulder as he takes his pen in hand to explain his plight to the officers of the Society. In September, 1847, with the date of the Atkinsons' departure set for October, he wrote:

---

[6] Mr. Atkinson took six tons of freight with him (books, household supplies, etc.). N. A. Peirce, Boston, Oct. 6, 1847, to M. Badger, A.H.M.S. papers, C.T.S.

[7] Atkinson laid in a supply of "crackers, lemons, sugar &c" to the value of $15 before going on board ship; his friends furnished "apples, vinegar, pickles, & hard ginger bread & cake & jellies." G. H. Atkinson, Boston, Oct. 16, 1847, A.H.M.S. papers, C.T.S.

[8] Atkinson had intended to go to Africa under the American Board of Commissioners for Foreign Missions, but shifted to the Oregon mission on the advice of a physician. G. H. Atkinson, Boston, Oct. 15, 1847, A.H.M.S. papers, C.T.S.

...I indulged the hope sometime since, that ere this I should have had my preparation chiefly completed; but I have not yet been able to make any definite arrangement in the matter of securing a companion to go with me. My friends with great earnestness advise me not to go, till I have done so. If I follow their advice, I cannot now definitely tell when I shall be ready to sail.[9]

A month passed and Lyman, still unprepared "in this particular," sent a fuller explanation of his difficulties:

...I did confidently expect in the Spring that I should be ready ere this time: and I have very little doubt, that I should have been had I known then that bro. A would not sail till the 20th of Oct. Supposing in the first place, that he might sail in June, and then afterwards in Sept. I felt it necessary to *press* forward my preparation in a *certain particular* with a good deal of haste. This *haste* no doubt defeated itself.... It was not till I changed my course in respect to *urging* forward my preparations in *this particular* that I had any prospect of being *fully* prepared as bro. A is, and as *all* my friends tell me every missionary should be. I think I have some prospect now of being thus prepared, but *haste* would *defeat* me *at once*. Now if it be necessary that missionaries destined to such *distant* fields, in order to their highest usefulness should go out married, they must surely have *time* given them, that they may [make] a union of this kind with worthy individuals. Those of a different character may possibly be obtained in a very short time; but *such* cannot usually be as speedily secured.[10]

Two weeks later Lyman wrote to admit another defeat: "Since I wrote you before," he said, "I have been disappointed *unexpectedly* in regard to my expectations of securing the lady to whom I have before referred, as my companion. The difficulties of my field seem to have dissuaded her from acceding to my proposals. The question, and one of great moment to me now is, what *ought* I to do under these circumstances? Ought I to make ready to sail next month, in the vessel then going, or ought I to delay till Spring, & make still further efforts for securing one to go with me?"[11] Fortunately for Horace Lyman he took his time and found a suitable "companion," with whom he arrived in Oregon in 1849. Good wives were so important to the missionaries— and so often taken for granted or overlooked in the accounts

[9] H. Lyman, East Hampton, Mass., Sept. 3, 1847, A.H.M.S. papers, C.T.S.

[10] H. Lyman, East Hampton, Mass., Oct. 12, 1847, A.H.M.S. papers, C.T.S.

[11] H. Lyman, East Hampton, Mass., Oct. 27, 1847, A.H.M.S. papers, C.T.S.

of their husbands' labors and achievements—that it is worth our while to turn aside for a moment to this bit of personal experience in the career of a faithful missionary.

Messrs. Atkinson and Lyman began their work in Oregon under trying circumstances. As a result of the Whitman Massacre[12] of 1847 the white settlers and the Indians were in a state of excitement. Religious animosities had been intensified because of the charges made by Henry H. Spalding, one of the pioneer American Board missionaries in Oregon, and other rabid foes of Rome that Catholics had stirred up the Indians to attack the Protestant missionaries.[13] Oregon was in a state of transition from provisional to regular territorial government. The California gold fever, which broke out shortly after Atkinson's arrival in Oregon, occupied men's minds to the exclusion of religious considerations. On September 14, 1848, Atkinson wrote:

During the last two weeks our town and our territory have been in a state of high excitement. Our lawyers are going or gone. Our mechanics left their shops in many cases: our three physicians decided to leave. Some of our merchants hastened to dispose of their merchandise or to close business and leave. Several Ministers (preachers) left camp meetings and religious duties to follow their fleeing people.... We are left with women and children. Families are moving into town from fear of the Indians who may make incursions upon the out settlements. Several hundred men will have left our valley ere the end of the month. I am sorry to hear that a few have left their wives and children in open dwellings with little provision for the long rainy winter.... Some gray haired men have tottered on with the large company to the El Dorado.[14]

Although the gold excitement interfered with his work, the missionary found a crumb of comfort in it, for he saw the Hand of God directing human affairs. In one of his letters he asked and answered the questions:

Why has this immense treasure been stored in one region [California], and that far away from the civilized portions of the world? and why has it been reserved for our nation? How will it affect this Territory and the nation ... ? But one answer can be given

12 A discussion of the work and services of Dr. Marcus Whitman, who was primarily a missionary to the Indians, does not fall within the scope of this book.

13 C. M. Drury, *Henry Harmon Spalding* (Caldwell, Idaho. 1936), 354-59.

14 G. H. Atkinson, Oregon City, Sept. 14, 1848 (Atkinson wrote two letters to the A.H.M.S. on Sept. 14; this one was given the office number 4363), A.H.M.S. papers, C.T.S.

as to the design & ultimate effect. God does all things and he will promote his own glory by it. . . . Already we see this in checking the Papal influence. By their wealth in this Territory they [Catholics] were holding men in bondage. Money has made them independent and free. . . . They are striving hard to possess the land. But that same kind Providence is sending or inviting an American population to this coast. We might have urged in vain for Eastern emigrants but God, seeing the necessity of peopling this whole region with a Saxon and Protestant race, hath, by one of those simple yet mighty agencies, which have always marked his works, poured a vast living stream over our whole land.[15]

In addition to the usual difficulties of carrying on religious work in the midst of many men who were given to intemperance, gambling, and profanity, the representatives of the American Home Missionary Society, some of whom were Congregationalists from New England, faced special problems. One grew out of a local practice of taking up mile-square claims, which separated neighbors so much that it was difficult for them to assemble for public worship, while at the same time the uncertainty regarding land titles made the people hesitate to make permanent improvements.[16] Another difficulty was found in the nature of the population. It was not only heterogeneous,[17] but there was also a considerable number of persons of Southern background or sympathies who were prejudiced against New Englanders.[18] In pre-Civil War days there were sharp clashes in Oregon between the foes and friends of slavery. The uncompromising stand of the New England men rendered them unpopular with certain groups who denounced them as abolitionists, "black Republicans," "grannies," and the "beneficiaries of Old Women's Sewing Circles."[19] According to Henry H. Spalding, who served for a few years under the American Home Missionary Society after the American Board closed the Lapwai mission following the Whitman Massacre, the

---

[15] G. H. Atkinson, Oregon City, July 31, 1849, A.H.M.S. papers, C.T.S.

[16] G. H. Atkinson, Oregon City, Sept. 14, 1848 (office No. 419), A.H.M.S. papers, C.T.S.; A.H.M.S., *Twenty-sixth Report* (1852), 89.

[17] Gustavus Hines, *Voyage Round the World* (Buffalo, 1850), 412.

[18] Milton B. Storr wrote from Corvallis, Ore., April 26, 1861, A.H.M.S. papers, C.T.S., "The great majority of our citizens are Southern sympathizers. Their angry countenances betray their special hostility to those 'Poor trays' who are 'caught in the bad company' of New England Republicans."

[19] O. Dickinson, Salem, Ore., March 2, 1857, A.H.M.S. papers, C.T.S.

failure of the Presbyterian and Congregational churches to reach more people was due to the long period of preparation demanded of ministers and their use of written sermons. There is, he said, in Oregon "a deep rooted prejudice against written sermons." Another reason, he continued, is the fact that the more popular churches pushed young men into the ministry with little preparation. "Hence they will get ten into the ministry while we do one, & obtain hearers in about the same proportion. As to the amount of good accomplished, none of us have any thing to brag of."[20]

A homely phase of missionary life in Oregon involved household supplies and articles of wearing apparel. To the officers of the Society in New York City came requests from time to time that such purchases as these be made on account of some particular missionary: "3 pairs best French kid walking shoes for Mrs. L. sise 4½ & 2 pairs of good pegged boots (calf) & 2 pegged shoes, sise smallish No. 9s for myself. 2 good hats, circumference (I do not know No.) at the band on the outside 22¾ inches & 1 cloth cap. 1 good Summer straw bonnet good sise, lined and trimmed;"[21] or "1 Thick, well lined overcoat, loose fit, dark, pilot cloth if not too coarse. 1 India Rubber overcoat with leggins & cap, not a comical one. I wish this to wear over others but to button, in surtout form. . . . 4 pairs of shoes for a little boy, 1, 2, & 3 years old. 4 pairs of shoes for a girl 9 and 10 years old—small size."[22] Specifications so indefinite as to size and style must have raised some questions in the mind of the person delegated to make the purchases. What a boon to these remote frontiersmen a Montgomery Ward or Sears-Roebuck catalogue would have been!

CALIFORNIA

As soon as California passed into the possession of the United States with the signing of the Treaty of Guadalupe Hidalgo (1848), and before knowledge of the discovery of gold at Sutter's ranch reached the East, the American Home Missionary Society made arrangements to send two men to

---

[20] H. H. Spalding, Kalapooya, Ore., Jan. 2, 1857, A.H.M.S. papers, C.T.S.

[21] H. Lyman, Portland, Ore., Jan. 4, 1850, A.H.M.S. papers, C.T.S.

[22] G. H. Atkinson, Oregon City, Jan. 7, 1850, A.H.M.S. papers, C.T.S.

that remote region. It was known that for several years Americans had been moving into California in small parties, that the climate was salubrious and the soil fertile, and it was naturally expected that the Anglo-American population would increase in numbers rapidly. Furthermore, so far as was known to the officers of the Society, there was not a single Protestant minister in all of California. To make a beginning in this field Samuel H. Willey and John W. Douglas were sent out in December, 1848.[23] They went by way of Panama, and when their ship touched at New Orleans they learned of the discovery of gold in the country to which they were bound. They realized at once that they were faced with new and unexpected problems. Should they preach in the towns as they had planned or should they follow the men to the mines? How long would the excitement last? What kind of society would develop? How could they meet their expenses in a mining territory on an allowance based on prevailing prices in a pastoral and farming region? These and other questions about the mission were also in the minds of the officers of the Society, who wrote to the men on the way that they would be taken care of financially under the changed conditions, and also that they should not be discouraged with the thought that only gamblers and reckless adventurers, "the bowie knife & Colt's revolver gentlemen," were on their way to the land of gold; a respectable portion were "from the bone & muscle of our old settlements," young men of ability who would eventually give tone and character to the population.[24] But no matter who went, it was especially important under the circumstances that missionaries be on the ground "to hold up the standard of the Gospel in all its purity & strictness—to plead for the Sabbath & for temperance & to minister to the dying, to warn & reclaim backsliders."[25]

Early in 1849 Messrs. Willey[26] and Douglas reached

[23] *Home Missionary*, XXI (1849), 193.

[24] M. Badger, N. Y., Jan. 31, 1849, to S. H. Willey, A.H.M.S. Letter Bk. V, 1513, C.T.S.

[25] C. Hall, N. Y., Jan. 31, 1849, to J. W. Douglas, A.H.M.S. Letter Bk. V, 1515, C.T.S.

[26] Mr. Willey chose to labor at Monterey, then the capital of the territory and the place at which the constitution of the state of California was framed. As chaplain of the constitutional convention he observed carefully its proceedings, with the result that his *Transition Period of California* (San Francisco, 1901) is an important source of

California.[27] In addition to the difficulties usually encountered by missionaries in frontier communities there were problems that were peculiar to the time and place. The heterogeneous population was thirsting for gold. Avarice was the consuming passion. Men had no time to waste in Sabbath observance; while the godly stopped for prayer, the ungodly might pick up the shining nuggets. Everyone lived in the midst of an overruling excitement. Lucky strikes, speculation in land and town lots, uncertainty about claims and land titles, deeds of violence, and "vigilante justice," all claimed more interest than religion. The whole spirit of the mining camp encouraged gambling; mining itself was a gamble when no one knew when or where the stroke of a pick would uncover a fortune. Exposure in the placer mines furnished excuse, if one were needed, for daily brandy drinking as a health measure. The men were generally without their families, and lacked the restraining and civilizing influence of good women. The miners had as yet no permanent interest in the community. Their chief aim was to get as much gold as quickly as possible in order that they might return to their homes to enjoy their new-found wealth. They did not respond readily to appeals for gifts to introduce or to sustain religious or educational institutions in the land of their temporary abode. To secure unity of action among the few who cared for spiritual concerns was difficult because of the absence of those social ties and bonds of relationship that unite families and individuals in the older communities and cement them together in interest and affection.[28]

After the first rush of excitement had passed it became apparent that permanent towns and cities would exist not only in mining districts but also in the agricultural valleys; many men who had come to California to dig gold remained

---

information for this phase of California history. Cardinal Goodwin, *Establishment of State Government in California, 1846-1850* (New York, 1914), 86.

[27] T. Dwight Hunt, who came from the Hawaiian Islands to California about this time, organized the First Congregational Church in San Francisco in July, 1849. H. H. Bancroft, *History of California* (*Works*, XXIV), VII, 727, Note 79.

[28] There is a succinct statement of the difficulties of missionary work in California in S. H. Willey, *Decade Sermon* (San Francisco, 1859), 29-46. The letters to A.H.M.S. contain elaborate and specific statements of difficulties, *e.g.*, T. Dwight Hunt, San Francisco, Aug. 1, 1849, A.H.M.S. papers, C.T.S.

to enjoy and praise the state. As the population became stabilized the opportunities for religious work improved, but through the decade of the fifties the missionary reports put much more emphasis on discouraging than on encouraging features. Widespread desecration of the Lord's Day was especially trying to the preachers. One of them wrote from a town in a mining county in 1853:

> The Sabbath in Sonora is awfully desecrated. It is the great day of business & pleasure. Every store & shop is open & filled with purchasers & idlers. On my way to church I pass three large gambling saloons in full blast each containing three times the number that are found in any church in town. Stages are constantly arriving crowded with miners from adjacent camps to spend the day in business, debauchery, roit [sic], or dissipation. Enormous trains of freight wagons, are constantly arriving from Stockton. The teamsters make it a point to get here on the Sabbath, for they are then paid off & they have a chance to revel with the excited multitude already congregated. The merchants are also interested in their arrival on this day, for unloading their goods in the sight of the crowd is a good & cheap way of advertising. All these things together with dog, bear & bull-fights are the order of the day on the Sabbath in Sonora.[29]

Another commented on the prevailing indifference to religion:

> One thing can be said that is good. There is less religious hypocrisy here than at home; every man is above gain or loss in reputation, so if he is a devil he acts the devil. He that for years was concealed under "garments of light" at home, now stalks thro community just as he is. ... A prevailing stubborn sentiment is that this is not a place for religion; men came here to get money, not religion; that stands right in their way; when they get home, then they will hear preaching & think of eternity.[30]

Until after the Civil War most of the people who went to California from the eastern and central parts of the United States settled in the northern and central sections of that state; that was where the mining camps and supply towns were located. Southern California was left for a time much as it had been under its Spanish and Mexican rulers. Protestant missionaries regarded the lower part of California with its Catholic population as a hard and uninviting field. One of them who paid a visit to Los Angeles in 1851

---

[29] S. S. Harmon, Sonora, Tuolumne Co., Calif., July 1, 1853, A.H. M.S. papers, C.T.S.

[30] E. S. Lacy, Crescent City, Calif., Feb. 12, 1855, A.H.M.S. papers, C.T.S.

said it was a community so debased that it ought to be called Los Diablos![31] Another said it was "just as destitute of the gospel as the villages in Turkey," and that any missionary who went there should go "with exactly the same anticipations that he would have in going into any South American city."[32] The attitude of Protestant missionaries towards southern California changed when it became the land of promise for tens of thousands of people from the Middle West after the Civil War.

In spite of meager returns and the heavy expenses in the California mission, the American Home Missionary Society added to its staff of workers there as fast as funds would permit. A party of eight missionaries, six of them destined to California and two to Oregon, was sent to the Pacific Coast in one ship in the winter of 1852-53.[33] There were those who thought that after the days of wild excitement had passed and California had settled down to a more sober existence, it would no longer present any unusual problems to those concerned about the spiritual welfare of its people. To combat that idea a committee of Congregational and Presbyterian ministers sent in 1854 an appeal for more missionaries. They said in support of their request:

> Let no one think that California is safe. She is *not safe*. If you were here you would see it so. With a heathen population rushing in upon us; with a recklessness of old restraints a chief characteristic of our people; with all forms of old error from the four quarters of the globe germinating rapidly or towering high, giants already in stature while young in years; and a ready soil for the production of new errors; with a general disregard of the Sabbath; with a public press corrupt & profligate; and finally in our isolation from all established Christian states, California is not safe.[34]

At the end of the first ten years there were twenty-eight New School Presbyterian and Congregational ministers in California, nearly all of whom had been sent there by the American Home Missionary Society.

---

[31] J. W. Douglas, quoted by S. H. Willey, San Francisco, Jan. 30, 1851, A.H.M.S. papers, C.T.S.

[32] S. H. Willey, San Francisco, March 5, 1857, A.H.M.S. papers, C.T.S.

[33] *Home Missionary*, XXV (1852), 195.

[34] W. C. Pond, S. S. Harmon, and J. G. Hale, San Francisco, Jan. 31, 1854, A.H.M.S. papers, C.T.S.

OLD SCHOOL PRESBYTERIANS

The General Assembly's Board of Missions, like the other major missionary organizations, sent representatives to the Pacific Coast shortly after the United States acquired territory there. In 1848 the Board announced that four appointments had been made for Oregon, and that one representative was already there.[35] In 1849 it announced that four men of ability and experience had been sent to California;[36] one of them, Sylvester Woodbridge, reported that he had organized at Benicia the first Protestant church in that territory.[37] In 1859 the number of Old School missionaries reported for Oregon was five; for California, seven.[38]

THE BAPTISTS

In 1845 Ezra Fisher and Hezekiah Johnson, who had already been missionaries in Iowa, went overland to Oregon as the first Baptist emissaries to that territory.[39] Fisher was a Yankee who had preached successively in Indiana and Illinois. While in Illinois he had written: "I feel that I am a frontiersman, and when God in his providence shall indicate to me that this place demands another than a frontier man, if my health and that of my family admit, I hope once more to take a frontier post."[40] His wish was gratified twice, first in Iowa and then in Oregon. Fisher was a practical man who had long experience on the frontier; he naturally became one of the recognized leaders in his emigration company, which consisted of more than two hundred persons with fifty wagons. After his arrival in Oregon in December, 1845, Fisher wrote concerning the journey: "When you learn that I walked further than would cover the whole distance of the journey, bearing my full proportional part of the services of the company, and that neither myself nor family laid off our clothing more than four or five nights

---

[35] Board of Domestic Missions ... Presbyterian Church, *Report* (1848), 34.

[36] Board of Domestic Missions, *Report* (1849), 34.

[37] *Missionary Chronicle*, XVII (1849), 251.

[38] Board of Domestic Missions, *Report* (1859), 20.

[39] *American Baptist Register, 1852* (Philadelphia, 1853), 293.

[40] Letter from Quincy, Ill., May 14, 1838, in *Correspondence of the Reverend Ezra Fisher*, ed. by S. F. Henderson, N. E. Latourette, and K. S. Latourette (n.p., n.d.), 60.

during the whole journey, always sleeping on the ground, you will not be surprised that we were worn down with protracted fatigue and care."[41] Fisher's letters from Oregon give an interesting description of life in that territory in the early days. Concerning living accommodations for himself and family during the first winter in Oregon, he wrote:

> On our arrival, although we were greeted with kindness by the few brethren we met, we did not find our lot cast in the midst of wealthy churches who were participating in the fruits of centuries of labours in civilization and Christianity. We were, however, kindly received into the cabin of Br. Lenox, where we have resided up to the present, and, although his house contains but one room about 18 feet by 22, without a single pane of glass, and his family consists of 13 souls, besides, almost every night, one, two, or three travelers, and my family consists of six souls, we have passed the winter thus far quite as pleasantly as you would imagine in view of the circumstances, and probably more so than a large portion of the last emigration, although perhaps a little more straightened for room.[42]

During the gold excitement Fisher went to California where he dug about a thousand dollars worth of the yellow metal,[43] all of which and more too he invested in Baptist educational projects in Oregon.

Fisher's companion in the Oregon mission, Hezekiah Johnson, a native of Maryland, and an enthusiast for missions, had begun his ministry by preaching in country schoolhouses; it is said that he was once locked out of one in Ohio on account of a fervent missionary sermon he had preached. His success as a pioneer preacher in Iowa, where he made use of an itinerant system, led to his appointment to Oregon. He built the first Baptist meetinghouse on the Pacific Coast at Oregon City in 1848, on land donated by Dr. John McLoughlin, well-known factor of the Hudson's Bay Company.[44]

In 1848, before news of the discovery of gold in California had reached the Atlantic Coast, the American Baptist Home Mission Society sent a missionary, O. C. Wheeler, to that new possession of the United States.[45] He reached San

---

[41] *Correspondence of the Reverend Ezra Fisher,* 166.

[42] *Ibid.,* 166.

[43] *Ibid.,* 260.

[44] A.B.H.M.S., *Seventy-seventh Report* in *Annual of Northern Baptist Convention, 1909,* 2; H. B. Grose, *Frontier Sketches* (New York, n.d.), 4-9; M. R. Seebach, *Missionary Milestones* (New York, [1917]), 155.

[45] A.B.H.M.S., *Seventeenth Report* (1849), 68.

Francisco late in February, 1849. In the summer of that year he organized a Baptist church, for the use of which was erected the first Protestant house of worship in California. The building was made of the plainest materials—scantling, rough siding, roof of ship's sails, ceiling of cotton cloth—and put together in the cheapest manner possible, yet its cost exceeded six thousand dollars; it was erected on a lot which cost ten thousand dollars. In accordance with the prevailing scale of prices the pastor's salary was set at ten thousand dollars a year.[46]

THE METHODISTS

Methodist home missions in Oregon grew out of a mission intended for the Indians. When Jason and Daniel Lee arrived in Oregon in the autumn of 1834 to work among the Flatheads they soon decided that those natives were too few in number and too migratory in their habits to warrant carrying out the original plans. Hence they established their mission on the Willamette River, sixty miles south of Ft. Vancouver.[47] There they engaged in farming, operated a sawmill, and carried on other secular occupations. They had not lost sight of their original object—Indian missions—but in a short time they found themselves surrounded by white settlers as the latter arrived in Oregon in the 1840's and took up farms in the Willamette Valley. Indian troubles, as reflected by the Whitman Massacre (1847), combined with the need and opportunity for home missionary work among the whites resulted in shifting the labors of the Methodist missionaries principally, if not wholly, to the white population in Oregon.[48] The mission flourished in numbers and temporalities. In 1840 the staff was augmented by the arrival of a party of about fifty persons: five additional missionaries, one physician, six mechanics, four farmers, and one missionary steward, with their wives and children. However, the secular character of the mission soon became a source of embarrassment. The time of the missionaries was so taken up with worldly duties that they did

---

[46] C. A. Woody, "Baptists of the Pacific Slope," in A. H. Newman, *Century of Baptist Achievement*, 108; *American Baptist Register*, *1852*, 38.

[47] A. B. and D. P. Hulbert, *Oregon Crusade (Overland to the Pacific*, V), 181.

[48] M.S.M.E.Ch., *Thirtieth Report* (1849), 20-24.

not have sufficient time for spiritual affairs, and the size
and prosperity of the mission and the multiplicity of its
business activities aroused jealousies among the other settlers in Oregon. By 1846 the mission was disencumbered of
its secular character, and the official report of the Methodist
Missionary Society, while admitting that a mistake had been
made, took comfort in the contributions that had been made
to the temporal development of Oregon:

> But it should be kept in mind that, however burdened and clogged
> in its operations the mission may have been, on account of its con-
> nections with worldly concerns, and however injurious this state of
> things may have been to its spiritual advancement, it has, on account of
> this very connection, conferred great temporal benefits on the terri-
> tory. Indeed, it is not too much to say, that the importance this
> territory has assumed in the estimation of the American Republic
> is attributable more to the influence exerted by our mission than to
> any other cause. Whether we regard its colonization civilization, or
> evangelization, the Methodist missionaries have been its most influen-
> tial and successful pioneers. And though the immigrants, on account
> of the secular character of the mission, were disposed to look on
> them with a suspicious eye, and in some instances to impute to them
> motives of avarice and ambition; yet, upon the organization of a
> territorial government, one of these lay missionaries was elected to
> the office of Governor, and another to that of Judge of the Probate and
> Circuit Courts.[49] These facts speak volumes, and show conclusively
> that we have not entirely forfeited the public confidence in Oregon;
> and when first impressions, founded on suspicion and jealousy, shall
> be subjected to the tests of candor and truth, the indebtedness of the
> colony to our mission will, we doubt not, be generally acknowledged.[50]

Both Southern and Northern Methodists sent missionaries to California. In 1848, on recommendation of the
Board of Missions of the Northern Church, two representatives were sent to that land of gold; the work developed so
rapidly that in the year ending in May, 1852, eighteen additional men were sent to this difficult field. California, not
having been included in the Plan of Separation agreed upon
by the Methodists in 1844—the date of their division over
slavery—the Southern branch also sent in its missionaries.
To support this mission the "Thousand Dollar" plan was
proposed; under this each of the Annual Conferences was

---

[49] Dr. Ira L. Babcock was elected judge in 1841; the first governor,
George Abernethy, who was also of the Methodist mission, was not
chosen until 1845. H. H. Bancroft, *History of Oregon (Works*, XIX,
San Francisco, 1886), I, 292, 472.

[50] M.S.M.E.Ch., *Twenty-seventh Annual Report* (1846), 38-39.

expected to raise one thousand dollars and send one of its members to California. When the Southern Methodist Annual Conference was organized in San Francisco in 1852 there were twenty charges and three hundred members. Both before and during the Civil War these preachers of Southern origin and sympathies were accused of being propagandists for slavery and secession.[51]

THE EPISCOPALIANS

An Episcopal missionary, the Reverend J. L. H. Ver Mehr, arrived in San Francisco in September, 1849, "after a most tedious voyage of seven months."[52] In 1850 it was announced that the Board of Missions had decided to plant a mission in Oregon.[53] But both California and Oregon needed the services of a directing head; hence in 1853 the system of missionary bishoprics was extended to the Pacific Coast, William I. Kip being chosen for California and T. F. Scott for Oregon and Washington. When Bishop Kip reached San Francisco in January, 1854, he found that life in California, although not so hectic as it had been three or four years earlier, was still full of excitement. He wrote:

A gentleman described [life in California] truly when he said: "Everything here is hurry-skurry. It is like living on curry...." The active and energetic have thronged hither from all parts of the world, and there is a rush and hurry to grasp sudden fortunes. Blanks in the lottery are of course innumerable, yet they are seldom heard of, while the prizes are published, and are sufficient to keep alive the hopes of all.[54]

To combat the idea prevalent in the East that there was no need to spend money for missions to the "land of gold," Bishop Kip wrote in one of his letters:

The mistake at the East had been to consider California a land of gold, and therefore aid from without is not needed. There is, indeed, wealth here (and so there is in China), but it is not yet available for Church purposes. A contest is first to be fought with the intense worldliness of the land. The religious element is first to be created,

[51] James Cannon, III, *History of the Southern Methodist Missions* (Nashville, 1926), 282-84.

[52] *Spirit of Missions*, XV (1850), 10.

[53] *Ibid.*, 75.

[54] W. I. Kip, *Early Days of My Episcopate* (New York, 1892), 77.

before the Church here can be self-supporting. And to call this into being, we who are the laborers in this distant region must, for some time to come, look to our friends in the East for aid.[55]

Most of the people who have shared in the westward movement have hoped to gain something for themselves; this was especially true in the great rush to the Pacific Coast. It is noteworthy that at least a few of those who ran the risks of the journey were more interested in giving than in getting; such were a valuable leaven in frontier society.

---

[55] *Spirit of Missions*, XX (1855), 606.

CHAPTER IX

SLAVERY AND THE CIVIL WAR

We cross the prairie as of old
The pilgrims crossed the sea,
To make the West, as they the East
The homestead of the free!
—*John Greenleaf Whittier.*

HE HOME MISSIONARY movement, like practically all other human activities in the United States, felt the effect of the dispute over slavery and the shock of the Civil War. Even Christian churches split because of their differences of opinion about human bondage. As Calhoun pointed out in his last public address (1850), the spiritual ties that had united the North and the South were being severed.

SLAVERY AND THE AMERICAN HOME MISSIONARY SOCIETY

The American Home Missionary Society, an organization which professed to be national in scope and to represent no faction, avoided the slavery question as long as possible. Although it finally took a stand against slavery as an evil system, it was far from being an abolitionist institution. In response to a specific inquiry on this point the Corresponding Secretary wrote in 1837 that there was nothing in the principles of the Society nor its rules of operation that had anything to do with abolitionism. Its single and sole business was to send the gospel to the desolate and to aid feeble congregations in all parts of the United States without respect to political institutions.[1] From Lewis Tappan, prominent antislavery leader in New York, came a series of questions in 1844 about the relation of the American Home Missionary Society to slavery. Did it solicit funds from slaveholders? Did it accept money from slaveholders

---

[1] A. Peters, N. Y., [date illegible], to S. W. Magill, A.H.M.S. Letter Bk. K (1837-1838), 176, C.T.S.

without rebuke? Have its missionaries in slave states been instructed to preach against the sin of slaveholding? Has the Society ever refused assistance to a church because it had a slaveholding minister or member? In reply Milton Badger, who was then the Secretary, said the Society had no soliciting agents in slave states and that only a small part of its funds came from them; he did not know what portion, if any, came from the slaveholders. The instructions to the missionaries were of a general character; it had no special instructions for those living in slave states. The Society had never denied assistance to a church on the ground that its members held slaves, nor had any church been denied help because its members had opposed slavery. The Society, in brief, sustained the character only of an eleemosynary institution; it had no ecclesiastical power and hence could not prescribe terms of church or ministerial fellowship.[2] In other words, the American Home Missionary Society as late as 1844 tried to wash its hands of the slavery question.

But it was becoming more and more apparent that an organization which was largely dependent on the North for financial support would have to take a definite stand. Step by step it was led or forced towards an antislavery position. In 1847 it declared slavery to be an evil and a serious hindrance to the spread of the gospel;[3] in 1850 it insisted that its missionaries should be allowed to preach against the "peculiar institution" of the South if they felt that to be their duty;[4] and by 1853 it was denying missionary commissions to slaveholders.[5] On the other hand, it refused to deny Christian status to slaveholders, and it continued to send missionaries into slave states until the outbreak of the Civil War. Believing that the teachings of Christ, if properly presented, would tend to remove evil, the Society took

---

[2] M. Badger, N. Y., July 27, 1844, to L. Tappan, A.H.M.S. Letter Bk. R, 312, C.T.S. The Presbyterian Synod of Kentucky protested because the A.H.M.S., against its recommendation, had renewed the commission of J. G. Fee, antislavery minister who refused to admit slaveholders to his church. A. C. Dickerson, Bowling Green, Ky., Dec. 3, 1846, A.H.M.S. papers, C.T.S. On the other hand, Reverend O. Emerson of DeWitt, Iowa, resigned his commission from the A.H.M.S. on Aug. 16, 1844, because he felt that the Society countenanced slavery by receiving funds from slaveholders. A.H.M.S. papers, C.T.S.

[3] *Home Missionary*, XX (1847), 1.

[4] *Home Missionary*, XXIII (1850), 160.

[5] *Home Missionary*, XXV (1853), 266.

the position that it was its duty to support missionary work in the section cursed with slavery, particularly in those parts of the South where the system had the slightest hold and where it might be expected soonest to yield to moral influences.[6]

Until the middle of the decade of the 1850's the position of the American Home Missionary Society on the slavery question was conservative. Its missionaries on the whole appear to have been opposed to violent antislavery agitation, although there were some abolitionists among them. Of these perhaps the most famous was Elisha P. Lovejoy, who held a commission from the Society while he was the editor of the *Observer* in St. Louis;[7] this connection appears to have been severed after Lovejoy moved in 1836 to Alton, Illinois, the place where he met his death in the riot of 1837.

As the antislavery sentiment grew in the North the American Home Missionary Society began to take a stronger stand on the question, but it was not until 1857 that it took a position that was at all in keeping with the wishes of the radical antislavery party. In that year it announced that thereafter it would not "grant aid to churches containing slaveholding members, unless evidence be furnished that the relation is such as, in the judgment of the Committee, is justifiable, for the time being, in the peculiar circumstances in which it exists."[8] That pronouncement, although mild, was a reversal of the previous policy, and appears to have been forced on the Society by a memorial sent in by the Congregational Association of Iowa, recommending that all appropriations be withheld from churches containing slave owners. In justification of its action the Society called attention to the growth of antislavery sentiment among the people of the North and West from whom it drew its support and to the equally significant fact that the Southern churches had withdrawn their support from the Society, its receipts from the slave states having fallen to less than two thousand

---

[6] *Home Missionary*, XXV (1853), 267.

[7] E. P. Lovejoy, St. Louis, March 11, 1835, A.H.M.S. papers, C.T.S. Lovejoy's letters to the officers of the A.H.M.S. in 1835 regarding a delay in the renewal of his commission throw light on his impulsive nature and the difficulties under which he was working in the West, *e.g.*, E. P. Lovejoy, St. Louis, Apr. 29, 1835; St. Louis, Feb. 22, 1836; Alton, Ill., Aug. 24, 1836, A.H.M.S. papers, C.T.S.

[8] A.H.M.S., *Thirty-first Report* (1857), 57.

dollars a year.[9] Withdrawal from the South had been in progress for several years. It had been hard to get men from the North and Northeast to go into the slave states,[10] and probably most of those who did go were not welcome. In 1835 the American Home Missionary Society had fifty-two representatives south of Mason and Dixon's line and the Ohio River, including Missouri. In 1845 there were thirty-six there, seven of whom were in Kentucky and twenty in Missouri. In 1860 there were only three, one in Delaware and two in Kentucky. The national society had become sectional.

The delay of the American Home Missionary Society in taking a strong antislavery stand led to sharp criticism of its course by the abolitionists. Some of its missionaries resigned their commissions because they thought it was winking at iniquity. An antislavery missionary society was formed in 1846 under the name of the American Missionary Association by the merging of four organizations which had been formed to work among or protect the Negroes and the Indians. One was the Amistad Committee, which had been formed in 1839 to protect the rights of the blacks involved in the Amistad case;[11] another was the Union Missionary Society, which was established about 1841 to discountenance slavery and to send missionaries to Africa; a third was the Western Evangelical Society formed on the Western Reserve to conduct missionary operations among the Indians; the fourth was the Committee for West India Missions. In 1846 a convention of the supporters of these various missionary enterprises was held in New York, and a new union society was established on "Bible principles." The American Board of Commissioners for Foreign Missions was condemned because it was thought to tolerate slavery at home and polygamy, idolatry, and caste in heathen lands. The American Home Missionary Society was denounced for its failure to declare that no slaveholder could be a Christian. The American Missionary Association, which was to engage in both foreign and home missions, announced that in the collection

---

[9] *Ibid.*, 128.

[10] W. M. King, Woodford Co., Ky., Jan. 2, 1845, protested against this attitude: "If Paul had declined to go into any provence [*sic*] of the Roman Empire until slavery was abolished, ... he would not probably have had half as many stars in that crown. ... " A.H.M.S. papers, C.T.S.

[11] *United States* v. *Schooner Amistad*, 15 Peters, 518.

of funds, in the selection of missionary fields, and in the appointment of its officers, agents, and missionaries, it would endeavor to discountenance slavery by refusing to receive the known fruits of unrequited toil, or to welcome to its employment those who held their fellow human beings as slaves.[12] One of the aims of this Association was to aid ministers who had been dismissed from their churches on account of their antislavery principles. The American Missionary Association was nonsectarian, but its support came mainly from Congregationalists who did not approve the moderate policy of the American Home Missionary Society on the slavery issue. By 1855 it had 103 home missionaries located mainly in Ohio, Indiana, Michigan, Illinois, Iowa, Wisconsin, Minnesota, Kentucky, North Carolina, Kansas, and California.[13] After the Civil War, as a recognized agency of the Congregational Church, it took the care of the freedmen as its special task.

The American Home Missionary Society was on the whole more representative of the sentiment of the church people of the North than was the radical American Missionary Association. The religious leaders of the country were conservative and opposed to violent antislavery agitation. They did not take the leadership in this moral crisis. That duty was left to humbler folk in the churches and even to men who were indifferent to the claims of organized Christianity. Concerning the failure of the Church to stand out clearly against the injustice of slavery Henry Wilson said that it is a humiliating fact that "while the churches of America furnished many able and earnest advocates and valiant defenders of the great doctrines of liberty, equality, fraternity, their leading men and influences (at the South entirely, at the North largely), the great organizations, ecclesiastical and missionary, the colleges and seminaries of learning, though almost exclusively under religious and even clerical control, were not thus true. In that great trial of their faith and test of their principles they faltered and failed."[14] This stern criticism is fair if the slavery question

---

[12] L. Tappan, *History of the American Missionary Association* (New York, 1855), 3-24.

[13] *Ibid.*, 52.

[14] H. Wilson, *History of the Rise and Fall of the Slave Power in America* (7th ed., Boston, 1887), III, 723; cf. W. E. Dodd, "Profitable Fields of Investigation in American History, 1815-1860," in *American Historical Review*, XVIII (1913), 530-34.

be regarded only as an abstract moral issue. It was a moral issue, but it was also a political question with social and economic bearings so important that they could not be lightly dismissed. There was something to be said for the point of view of the man who believed that since the North was guilty along with the South it should be patient; that the social readjustment which the abolition of slavery would entail could not be accomplished in a day; and that compromise was justifiable as a means of preserving the Union.

THE KANSAS QUESTION

While some men talked about slavery, others acted. Kansas appeared on the western horizon in 1854 as a territory where momentous decisions about the future of slavery were to be made. If it became a slave territory and later a slave state, the "peculiar institution" would take a new lease on life. If the South failed to win Kansas, which lay directly west of the slave state of Missouri, what hope was there for it to capture any one of the remaining territories? Not all of those who went to Kansas, however, were interested primarily in the slavery controversy; there were some who obviously cared more about farms, town lots, and political careers. Although it was an agricultural territory, the early days in Kansas were anything but quiet and peaceful. A representative of the Protestant Episcopal Board of Missions, who spent a month in the border town of Weston, Missouri, in the autumn of 1854, wrote an entertaining description of the speculative spirit of the time and place. The town was filled with lawyers, speculators in Kansas lands, and politicians. In the chief hotel, he says, might have been seen

a knot of some half-dozen persons, eagerly listening to a very fluent Dr. F.——, discanting on the many advantages of situation and resources connected with Marysville, one hundred and fifty miles interior, on the Big Blue, Kansas; a rude pen-and-ink draft of the future city was displayed by him, and small portions of copper ore exhibited, and declared to abound close by the city-limits. Shares in the town held at $100 each. In like manner the praises of Leavenworth were cried aloud. Four hundred dollars a share, but no title guaranteed. Every share-holder must enter into bonds to help secure the title, i.e., to help rob the Delaware Indians of their land!

Bills announcing the completion of the survey at Kickapoo City, were thrown in at the door—a sale would at once be made. Wonderful advantages at Kickapoo City—"Fortunes ahead!" *"Fortes Fortuna*

juvat," Coal-beds underlie the city! The deepest water of the Missouri
is at this place! It will become the outlet of Salt Creek Valley! No
humbug about the title! Hurrah for the future Emporium of Kansas!
"Walk up, gentlemen, John Ellis' flat-boat will be waiting to take
parties across at 11 o'clock."[15]

Atchison, Pawnee, and fifty other paper towns also had
their advocates and agents, all armed with rolls of foolscap
and charcoal sketches. Meanwhile, a few poor straggling
Kickapoo Indians looked on in amazement "at the white men
violently gesticulating and pointing with their rolls of paper
towards the Territory, lying in its primitive state."

But speculators were not the only men who had an
interest in Kansas. In the autumn of 1854 Mr. S. Y. Lum
was sent out to the newly opened territory by the American
Home Missionary Society. He began preaching at Wakarusa,
a settlement laid out by the Emigrant Aid Society. From a
church in Worcester, Massachusetts, where there was a
keen interest in the effort to populate Kansas with free-
state men, came a gift of five hundred dollars for the support
of Christian ministers in this border-line frontier territory.[16]
Mr. Lum soon reported that he had founded at Lawrence a
church with twenty members. Conditions were primitive,
and services were held in an old hay tent, "consisting of two
rows of poles brought together at the top, and the sides
thatched with prairie hay. The room was also used as a
general sleeping apartment, the trunks, bunks, and boxes
of the lodgers serving for seats on Sunday." The minister
had to build his own house of "shakes." "These were split
from logs and nailed to a frame, covering sides and roof. It
was well ventilated, but not blizzard proof. A blanket of
snow on the bed and a carpet of snow on the floor were no
unusual thing in the morning."[17]

At the outset Mr. Lum, his attention fixed primarily on
his own free-state group, was enthusiastic about the character of the new settlers in Kansas:

The population, if what is already here be a fair criterion of the
whole, will compare favorably with that of any State or Territory in
the Union. For firmness of purpose, indomitable courage, and execu-

---

[15] [J. McNamara], *Three Years on the Kansas Border* (New York
and Auburn, 1856), 22-23.

[16] *Home Missionary*, XXVII (1854), 172, 197-98.

[17] R. Cordley, in *Home Missionary*, LXXII (1900), 221.

tive talent, they will equal the emigration to California; while in intelligence and moral worth, they will be surpassed by none. A holy purpose has called them to this western world.[18]

In "The Kansas Emigrants" Whittier represented the free-state pioneers as singing:

> We cross the prairie as of old
> The pilgrims crossed the sea,
> To make the West, as they the East
> The homestead of the free!
>
> We go to rear a wall of men
> On Freedom's southern line
> And plant beside the cotton-tree
> The rugged Northern pine!

In spite of a certain amount of earnestness among the settlers it was not an easy task to plant churches in "Bleeding Kansas." Mr. Lum himself was soon disillusioned with respect to the moral goodness of the population. Late in 1854 he wrote as follows:

In reference to the character of the emigration as a whole I hardly know what to think. Many there are who come here with a noble purpose—they are willing to be martyrs in the cause of Religion & Liberty & yet I am compelled to think that the number of such is small in comparison to those who have some selfish or mercenary end to gain. I must confess that my mind has changed on this subject & I do not think so highly of the aggregate emigration, as at first. I find many, perhaps a majority, without any settled moral principles as a basis of action & when come outside the restraints of eastern society, they act out the native depravity of the human heart....[19]

A few months later he wrote:

All kinds of radical ideas are pretty fully represented here, and I have almost thought, at times, that all this class of persons from the entire Union, are flowing hither, in the hope of realizing their wildest schemes. Time after time, have they made their boast, that they would crowd orthodoxy out of Kansas.[20]

One of the chief difficulties, of course, grew out of the fact that for months there was a state of civil war in Kansas. The people were excited and angry. In June, 1856, Mr. Lum said:

---

[18] *Home Missionary*, XXVII (1855), 217; on the moral tone of Kansas, see Carl Becker, "Kansas," in *Essays in American History dedicated to Frederick Jackson Turner*, 85-111.

[19] S. Y. Lum, Lawrence, Kan., Dec. 6, 1854, A.H.M.S. papers, C.T.S.

[20] *Home Missionary*, XXVIII (1855), 55.

Bands of armed men have been & are still arresting travellers, all about us, taking whatever they find upon them of value, & if they are at all obnoxious putting them out of the way. Every day accounts are brought in of persons robbed & murdered & for no offence, except of holding opinions not corresponding with those of the ruling powers. We are truly experiencing the reign of terror.[21]

About the same time he complained that "it has seemed as though the Sabbath was selected as the day for special excitements; and not infrequently have the members of my congregation and even members of my church, been called from the morning service to go to the rescue of their brethren, attacked by the banditti who surround us."[22] In short, to quote the words of another missionary, "The camp, the battlefield & such scenes as have been witnessed at the polls have been anything but favorable to religion. Scarcely a month has passed since the first settlers arrived, after the passage of the 'Nebraska Act,' without something occurring to excite them & not infrequently arouse the worst passions of the heart."[23]

In the summer of 1856 a Kansas Band, similar to the Illinois Band and the Iowa Band, was formed in Andover Theological Seminary. The original members were four in number: Sylvester D. Storrs, Grosvenor C. Morse, Roswell D. Parker, and Richard Cordley. They met weekly to hold a Kansas prayer meeting and to study reports from that scene of conflict. As conditions in Kansas became more serious the Band expanded until its membership reached sixteen. But by the time the men were ready to go out with commissions from the American Home Missionary Society, the situation in Kansas was less ominous for the free-state party, and only the original four members went to that territory in the autumn of 1857. Storrs began work at Quindaro, the "port of entry" for Kansas; Morse, who organized a Congregational church in Emporia, later acted as County Superintendent of Schools and was interested in the State Normal School. Parker went to Leavenworth, the largest town in the territory, while Cordley took over the work of Mr. Lum at Lawrence.[24]

---

[21] S. Y. Lum, Lawrence, Kan., June, 1856, A.H.M.S. papers, C.T.S.

[22] *Home Missionary*, XXIX (1856), 95.

[23] S. D. Storrs, Quindaro, Kan., Feb. 9, 1858, A.H.M.S. papers, C.T.S.

[24] Richard Cordley, *Pioneer Days in Kansas* (New York, c. 1903), 8-60.

NEBRASKA

Inasmuch as Kansas was on the border line between freedom and slavery and was a prize eagerly sought by both sides, it attracted vastly more attention in these years than did the neighboring territory of Nebraska; the latter was counted lost to the South and safe for the North under the operation of popular sovereignty. But even though the slavery disputants were content to let Nebraska wait, the speculators in land and town lots were not. They early picked on the plateaus and hills on the west bank of the Missouri opposite Council Bluffs as a likely site for a city, and there the foundations of Omaha were laid in the summer of 1854. Anticipating a rapid rush of settlers to Nebraska, and desiring to pre-empt ground for his own organization as soon as possible, the Reverend Reuben Gaylord, a representative of the American Home Missionary Society who had gone from Connecticut to Illinois and then to Iowa, moved his family from southeastern Iowa to Omaha in the winter of 1855-56. It was a trying trip: the weather was bitter cold, the streams in western Iowa were unbridged and had high, steep, icy banks. They crossed the Missouri River on the ice, Mr. Gaylord carrying the baggage over by hand.[25] There were the usual difficulties of beginning religious work in a new community, but the missionary was hopeful. In May, 1856, he wrote from Omaha:

... It is evident that in and about this place is to be gathered, at no distant day, a vast amount of enterprise, wealth and population. Such is the influx of strangers coming here for permanent settlement, that although many houses were vacated on the return of spring by persons going out upon their claims, yet already every house is filled, the hotels and boarding houses are full to overflowing, and every day there are new arrivals....

The growth of many years in the eastern part of Iowa will here be crowded into a comparatively small compass. The rail road from Davenport to Iowa City, now completed, has just been let to Fort Des Moines and the general conviction is that it will reach the Missouri River opposite this place in three or four years. Then there will be nothing to check that mighty tide of emigration that is flowing in this direction with constantly augmenting strength.

Our work is beset with difficulties. A spirit of worldliness is

---

[25] R. Gaylord, Omaha City, N. T., Jan. 4, 1856, A.H.M.S. papers, C.T.S.; [Mrs. R. Gaylord], *Life and Labors of Rev. Reuben Gaylord* (Omaha, 1889), 177-81.

strongly excited by the great increase in the value of property caused by the rapid growth of the place. Men think and labor for the objects of the present life and it is hard to interest them in any thing else....[26]

In the following statement, Mr. Gaylord was more specific as to some of his problems:

A large proportion of the citizens are from New England, and yet a smaller proportion are professors of religion than in any community I have ever known. The Sabbath, to a great extent, is a day of pleasure or business. The first boat from St. Louis reached here on Sunday, and, in consequence, the day seemed more like a week day than the Sabbath. A correct moral sentiment is yet to be created, and there are but few to aid in doing it. Did we not feel that the Lord is on our side, we might well give up in despair. But, trusting in Him for success, we are seeking to put in operation those gospel influences that, when brought constantly to bear, never fail to secure good results.... Last Sabbath, May 4, I organized a Congregational church in this place, the first fruits of the home missionary enterprise in Nebraska.... [27]

One of Mr. Gaylord's chief interests during his early years in Nebraska was Fontenelle College,[28] which he helped found. When the cornerstone of the building for the preparatory department was laid in July, 1858, Mr. Gaylord reviewed the humble origins of Puritan education in New England, and continued:

We are gathered here, many of us of New England birth and ancestry, to transplant from the Puritan nursery a young and healthful tree, expecting it to receive that care and culture which will insure its future growth. Our work to-day may seem small, but when viewed in its true design and relations is worthy to enlist our largest energies and most persevering efforts.[29]

NEW SCHOOL PRESBYTERIANS AND CONGREGATIONALISTS PART COMPANY

Until 1861 the American Home Missionary Society was the joint agency of the Congregationalists and New School Presbyterians. But after 1850 the relations between the two partners in the missionary enterprise were becoming more

[26] R. Gaylord, Omaha, May 6, 1856, A.H.M.S. papers, C.T.S.

[27] [Mrs. R. Gaylord], *Life and Labors of Rev. Reuben Gaylord*, 186-87.

[28] For a fuller statement regarding Fontenelle College, out of which grew Doane College, see below, page 391.

[29] [Mrs. R. Gaylord], *Life and Labors of Rev. Reuben Gaylord*, 425.

strained every year. Within the local churches set up under the Plan of Union there was dissension. Complaints were made by both sides regarding the conduct of the American Home Missionary Society, and by each the Society was accused of favoring the other. From an angry Presbyterian in Missouri came a letter in 1847 charging that the American Home Missionary Society was neglecting that state, that it had falsely attributed its failure to send men to Missouri to its inability to find men who were willing to go to a slave state, whereas it had really diverted to other states men who had expressed a desire to go to Missouri. This was interpreted by the writer as an attempt to build up Congregationalism in the Northwest at the expense of Presbyterianism in the Southwest. The letter ended with a threat of an appeal to the New School General Assembly to form a missionary society of its own unless a different policy were adopted. Something must be done, this irate correspondent concluded, to save Illinois, Indiana, and Ohio "from Congregationalism entire."[30] At the same time the Society was receiving complaints from Western Congregationalists that it was not fair to them. One man wrote from Michigan to complain because one of the agents of the Society was casting aspersions on Western Congregationalists by his statement that there was as much difference between Eastern and Western Congregationalism as there was between good New England currency and the paper put out by one of the broken-down wildcat banks of the West. In view of the fact that the larger part of the receipts of the Society came from New England, the writer thought that this was not fair; and he expressed the belief that if it continued some other channel would be provided through which the contributions of New England churches could flow to the West.[31] Inasmuch as it was under fire from both sides it would seem that the Society was pursuing a policy of impartiality, but it was useless to continue union activities which were causing more ill than good will between the two denominations.

One of the first direct moves to bring about a separation

---

[30] A. Bullard, St. Louis, Aug. 19, 1847, A.H.M.S. papers, C.T.S.

[31] A. S. Arms, Milford, Mich., March 21, 1844, A.H.M.S. papers, C.T.S.; similar ideas were expressed by I. T. Holmes, Greggsville, Ill., Oct. 17, 1844, J. W. Whipple, Knox Co., Ohio, Jan. 7, 1843, and J. D. Pierce, Marshall, Mich., May 1, 1837, A.H.M.S. papers, C.T.S.

came from the West. In 1846 a Congregational Convention which was held at Michigan City, Indiana, called for the abrogation of the Plan of Union of 1801 on the ground that it was a cause of discord.[32] Six years later the Plan was renounced by a convention of Congregational Churches held at Albany, New York. For nearly ten years more the New School Presbyterians continued to carry on their missionary activities through the American Home Missionary Society, but the receipts from the New School churches dwindled each year, thus indicating their growing dislike for the Society. In 1855 out of $125,000 received by the American Home Missionary Society, only 32 per cent came from New School sources; in 1859 the proportion had dropped to 23 per cent, and in 1860 to 19 per cent.[33] In 1861 the New School Presbyterians withdrew from the American Home Missionary Society, but its name was not changed to the Congregational Home Missionary Society until 1893.

SOUTHERN BAPTISTS

The slavery quarrel led to the formation of the Southern Baptist Convention in 1845. Up to this point Baptists in the South had not taken an active part in organized home missions, partly because of the prevalence among them of anti-mission sentiment, and partly because the chief missionary agency of their denomination was located in the North. The new Southern Baptist Convention created two mission boards, one for foreign and one for home missions. From 1846 to 1861 the Southern Baptists responded with considerable enthusiasm to the call for home missions. During these years they contributed about $300,000 to missions, or approximately seven times as much as they had given for this purpose through the American Baptist Home Mission Society in the preceding thirteen years.[34] As the sec-

---

[32] C. Clark, Kalamazoo, Mich., Aug. 8, 1846, A.H.M.S. papers, C.T.S.

[33] Each side issued in 1860 a pamphlet in defense of its position: *Relations of the Presbyterian Church to the Work of Home Missions* (New York, 1860); A.H.M.S., *Reply of the Executive Committee of the American Home Missionary Society to ... the General Assembly* (n.p., 1860).

[34] I. T. Tichenor, "The Home Mission Board of the Southern Baptist Convention," in A.H. Newman, *Century of Baptist Achievement,* 218-20; A. H. Newman, *History of Baptist Churches in the United States (Amer. Ch. Hist. Ser.,* II, New York, 1894), 449-55.

tional conflict became more acute the Northern Baptists gave up their home missionary work in the slave states.[35]

DIVISION IN THE METHODIST CHURCH

The split in the Methodist Episcopal Church over slavery (1844) led to the formation of a new missionary organization, the Missionary Society of the Methodist Episcopal Church, South. To it went the contributions of the Southern and Southwestern conferences, and to it was assigned responsibility for missions in that region. The officials of the Northern society, trying to make the best of "the lamented division of the Church," expressed the belief that the separation would not have disastrous effects upon missions, since each party might now be expected to vie with the other in benevolence.[36] The receipts did increase, but that was a poor apology for division in the Church.

THE CIVIL WAR

That the Civil War should interfere with home missionary operations was to be expected. In general the contributions to the various societies declined in the early months of the War; the number of men sent out decreased; the noise and excitement of battle turned men's minds from spiritual to worldly struggles. Some of the missionaries enlisted as soldiers or went into the armies as chaplains. In the new border states and territories work that had already been begun was sometimes disrupted and congregations were broken up. Kansas, Bleeding Kansas, probably suffered most in this respect. The letters from missionary pastors stationed there during the War contain many references to alarms and excursions. Concerning the results of Quantrill's raid on his church and work, one preacher wrote from Lawrence:

... Our Church here was weakened far more than appeared on the surface. Three members only were killed; but we have already dismissed four others who leave on account of the raid. Twelve members of the congregation were killed but more than fifty have left from the same cause. ... Now we have a company of soldiers stationed here —six cannon frowning from the hill above us—every able bodied man enrolled in the militia & compelled to come out to weekly drill. Every

[35] A.B.H.M.S., *Twentieth Report* (1852), 26.
[36] M.S.M.E.Ch., *Twenty-seventh Annual Report* (1846). 10.

man is supplied with a musket. Besides this every shop & store has
from three to six Sharpe's rifles & revolvers conveniently hanging by
the wall. Most men carry their revolvers round with them. I never
either carried or owned any arms before, but now I keep a Colt's Navy
on my study table & thirty rounds of cartridges in the drawer with
my sermon paper.[37]

Another missionary wrote from Wyandotte:

... Quantril's bloody band have been proceeding like beasts of prey
along the Border. We have often seen the fires of union homes kindled
by them. Like my neighbors, I have slept with arms by my side, and
beneath my pillow, and have taken my turn in standing guard nights.
I have been repeatedly called out to defend the town from threatened
attacks, sometimes at the midnight hour. Once the danger signal of
the Union League struck upon my church bell, and the terror of the
people, especially of the blacks, brought vividly to mind the massacre
at Lawrence. Like most of our people we have kept a few articles of
indispensable wearing apparel packed ready for a hasty flight, and
in my absence, my sermons, as combustible, and of chief value, have
slept out of doors.[38]

The remarkable thing about the effect of the Civil War
on the home missionary movement is not that it interfered
with it, but that it interfered with it to so slight an extent.
Before the War the main burden of carrying the gospel to the
frontiers had been assumed by the churches in the North,
the part of the country that suffered least from the conflict
so far as the destruction of property was concerned. Furthermore, the exceptional demands for benevolence for the
Army Christian and Sanitary Commissions trained the
people for more liberal giving. In the first year of the War
the receipts of the American Home Missionary Society
dropped to $163,000, a loss of about $20,000 in one year.
But two years later, in the heart of the conflict (1863-64),
they mounted to $195,000, the highest point reached in the
Society's history up to that time. In the year immediately
following the end of the War (1865-66) the annual receipts
for the first time passed two hundred thousand dollars
($221,000).[39] The decline in revenues in 1861 was also due,
in small part, to the fact that this was the first year after the

---

[37] R. Cordley, Lawrence, Kan., Feb. 29, 1864, A.H.M.S. papers,
C.T.S.

[38] R. D. Parker, Wyandotte, Kan., Nov. 2, 1863, A.H.M.S. papers,
C.T.S.

[39] *Home Missionary*, LXIV (1891), 114.

withdrawal of the New School Presbyterians from the American Home Missionary Society, leaving it entirely a Congregational organization.

During the Civil War the leaders of Congregational home missionary activities pointed with pride to the loyalty of the Northwest to the Union, for they saw in it one result of their labors. More than once they raised the question as to why the Northwest had not gone with the South when the Union was disrupted. Again and again they found the answer in the moral ties that home missionaries had drawn between the Northeast and the Northwest. They insisted that the preaching of the "pure gospel" and the encouragement of education by their representatives had beneficial political as well as religious results. The Reverend William W. Patton, of Chicago, in an address before the American Home Missionary Society in 1864 in support of the resolution "that the marked loyalty of the West in our present national conflict is largely due to moral causes connected with the influence of Home Missions," developed this theme at length. He admitted that the loyalty of the West was the result of many influences, geographic, ethnic, political, historic, and commercial, but he stressed the moral. The missionaries of the great American society, he said, had carried a religion based on intelligence; they had laid foundations of loyalty deep in the consciences of men by teaching the scriptural doctrine of government; they had prepared the people for the present crisis by showing them the dangers that threatened the country; and they promoted loyalty by their connection with a national society which emphasized union between East and West.[40] In 1862 the Secretary of the Vermont Home Missionary Society wrote in a similar vein:

The work of Home Missions has been one powerful agency for preparing the nation successfully to resist and put down this wicked insurrection. And while the friends of Home Missions have been prosecuting the work with a direct aim at the conversion and salvation of souls, and the uplifting of Christ's kingdom, and that, for the most part, without a thought of any political result whatsoever, they have yet, at the same time, been using the most sure and effectual means of perpetuating our civil institutions and promoting our national well-being.... Had the work of Home Missions been prosecuted

---

[40] A.H.M.S., *Thirty-eighth Report* (1864), 83-85.

throughout the South as thoroughly and as successfully as it has
been at the North and Northwest, it is morally certain that this
rebellion would have not occurred. . . . [41]

In spite of the exaggeration in the above statement and
the difficulty of proof, it can be safely asserted that religious
ties between the East and the West were of some significance
when the test of the Union came.

---

[41] J. F. Stone, in *Home Missionary*, XXXV (1862), 201.

CHAPTER X

THE ROCKIES AND INTERMONTANE PLATEAUS

There are limits to the ascendancy of extreme wickedness in frontier towns. The worst characters kill each other off and kill themselves off rapidly. The righteous outlive the wicked two to one, and righteousness will outlive wickedness in any community in our land. You may take any new town or territory in this New West, and I care not how gross and defiant may be its wickedness at first, nor how much the laws of God and of man are trampled under foot,... I care not how weak may be the hands of the first Christian workers, nor how feeble their knees; such is the persistent staying power of that force in the world which makes for righteousness, such is the evangelizing, transforming power of Christ's Gospel, that I know and am sure that by and by that community will be a Christian community, and sometime it may be a very 'saint's rest.'

The frontier in our country, ever since it crossed the Hudson, and even before, has been except in spots a wicked frontier. As a rule, organized Christianity has always been weak on the frontier; but behind its weakness there has been an organized Christian power in the land that has all along been strengthening the weak hands and confirming the feeble knees of frontier Christianity.—*R. T. Cross.*

MINING CAMPS

*E*XPLORERS, TRAPPERS, AND traders from the Eastern states had been penetrating the Western cordilleras ever since the opening of the nineteenth century; tens of thousands of settlers and adventurers had crossed the mountains to Oregon and California before the Civil War, but except for the Mormons almost none of the Anglo-Americans had thought of settling in the midst of the Far Western mountains and deserts. Why should they? This region was remote and relatively inaccessible; it had no obvious economic resources of immediate value except furs, and furs did not attract settlers; its lofty heights and arctic snows gave warning of winter hardships. But the discovery of gold in the Pikes Peak country in 1858 and the finding of both gold and silver in the Washoe district on the eastern side of the Sierra Nevadas caused a change in attitude. Men

could endure any hardship and run any risk for gold, and so into the mountains they went in the sixties as one new Eldorado followed another—Colorado, Nevada, Idaho, Montana, Arizona, and the Black Hills. There was a double movement of prospectors and settlers into the Rockies: from the West came men trained in the California mines looking for new worlds to conquer; from the East came thousands of restless, inexperienced gold seekers, fresh from farms, stores, or factories. They were eager to dig for gold—or to pick it up off the ground. There were some in the throng who saw the possibility of securing a livelihood and perhaps wealth by ministering to the needs or pandering the passions of the miners. For still others there was a romance, a glamour, about the West that lured them there with no particular objective. In following the setting sun they were doing what their fathers and grandfathers before them had done—but with the shout of Gold! Gold! ringing in their ears.

In the Rocky Mountains the typical settlement of the sixties and seventies was the mining camp, and even after farming and ranching had come to surpass mining in economic importance, it remained one of the symbols of the romance of the West. To people in the East mining camps suggested the wild and lawless abodes of desperadoes, gamblers, and harlots. Actually, most of the inhabitants of most of the camps, especially after the excitement of the first few years had passed, were ordinary men and women. The people as a whole were intelligent, but so absorbed in the pursuit of riches, or just food and shelter, that they devoted little thought to spiritual concerns. Young men predominated; the refining influence of good women was often lacking. To be sure there were virtuous women— faithful wives and devoted mothers—in mining camps, but the "painted ladies" were frequently more conspicuous in the early days.

Everything about an early mining camp indicated haste, excitement, and lack of permanence. It grew up almost overnight, hence it was a town or "city" of wooden shacks and tents. If the "strike" proved to be especially important, more pretentious frame and brick buildings were erected; but if, as more often happened, the gold "played out" the camp was soon deserted by most of its inhabitants. The shifting nature of the population made it difficult to build

up and maintain a church even when a sufficient number of the faithful could be found. Placer mining normally came first; in this there was a chance for the poor man, because the tools were few and simple, and for the inexperienced, because Lady Luck might bestow her favors on the tenderfoot. But when, after a few months or years, the gold in the creek bed or near the surface of the ground had been picked up and quartz mining with its elaborate metallurgical processes and expensive machinery had been introduced, the character of the mining camp changed. Outside capital was brought in; gulch miners and prospectors gave way to mine laborers. This change meant that the camp had attained a greater degree of permanence; men sent for their families; schools and churches were started. But even so the mining town was likely to stand in need of outside assistance in establishing religious institutions. It might be turning out a "mint of money," but much of it went to the Eastern capitalists who controlled the mines. In its later as in its early stages a mining camp was a hard place in which to plant and maintain a church.

In traveling through the mountains to isolated mining camps missionaries had their full share of danger and hardship. As an illustration, consider the experience of the Reverend George M. Darley, Presbyterian pioneer in southwestern Colorado, in a journey through the San Juan Mountains in the early spring of 1877. From a new mining town a call had come for a minister. Mr. Darley, who agreed to go, set out with one companion. The story of the trip, as told by Dr. Sheldon Jackson is, in part, as follows:

... They procured a burro to carry their blankets and provisions, and started out on foot, March 20. The snow was from one to five feet deep, and the distance of 125 miles through a wilderness without an inhabitant except at the Ute Indian Agency. The first day they walked twenty-five miles, reaching a deserted log-cabin. During the day the tin-plates and coffee-pot were lost from the burro. And the third day, the bread by constant jolting upon the burro had become so fine as to necessitate eating with a spoon, while the snow storms were so continuous, that much of the way they could not find any wood dry enough to make a fire. After a couple of hours of sleep, they were up and on their way at 5 A. M. All that long day they tramped through the snow in the face of a snow storm so severe that they made only fifteen miles. That night they lay down in the snow in a roofless cabin. Unable to sleep in their wet clothes, they arose at mid-night and at 3 A. M. started on, making by night thirty-four miles. Lying down in the mud and slush, they were kept awake by the wolves, scenting the

provisions, and coming so near that the snap of their teeth in the darkness had a most ominous sound. The fourth night, in the midst of a severe snow storm, they reached the Indian Agency, having had altogether only about three hours' sleep in three nights. Four days and three nights their clothes had been soaking wet and part of the time frozen. Their feet and legs had swollen to twice their natural size, and they were in danger of being permanently crippled.

While bathing their limbs with whisky, an old frontiersman, looking on, thought it was a great waste of the whisky. He would have taken it internally and rubbed the limbs with the bottle.

And now comes the last and hardest day of all. It is twenty-five miles to Ouray, every step of which will be acute pain and torture. In that twenty-five miles the Uncompahgre River, a rushing mountain torrent of ice-water, is to be waded twenty-one times. . . .

Coming to the river, seizing hold of the ears and tail of the burro, they would throw him off the steep snow-bank into the stream, and then plunge in after him. Placing a pole in the rocks below them, they were kept from being swept down by the swift current and thus, waist-deep, they waded through the ice-water to the farther shore. Another mile through the snow and then another ice-bath and thus snow and ice-water until 8 P. M., when he arrived in Ouray, the first minister of the gospel.[1]

RAILROAD TOWNS

The acquisition of California and Oregon, along with the opening up of mining camps and other settlements in the Far West, made necessary for both political and economic reasons the building of railroads into and through the Rockies. The construction of the Union Pacific and other Western roads, built as they were so largely through unsettled territory, created on the frontier what were known as railroad towns. Located at or near the end o' track, their first function was to serve as supply stations for the construction gangs. As the rails were laid, the town of shacks that had housed the workers and the parasites who lived off them was periodically moved out towards the frontier. These jerry-built towns were as raw and as blatant in their wickedness as the wildest mining camp of the time. "Hell-on-Wheels" was the title appropriately bestowed on one migratory city. Occasionally one of these towns survived the exodus of the workers and gamblers as they followed the engines over the newly laid track: perhaps it was made into a division point with railroad yards, a big red water tank, and roundhouses for locomotives; perhaps it became a coun-

---

[1] S. Jackson, "Pioneering for Christ in the Rocky Mountains," in *Rocky Mountain Presbyterian*, VI, No. 8 (1877), 2.

ty seat with a courthouse, a grain elevator, a hotel, and several stores; perhaps it remained an insignificant station with a tiny depot, a general store, and a cluster of houses. Whatever the future had in store for it one might be sure that for many years to come it would be another prospective or actual mission station.

INDIAN WARS

One important consequence of the building of the railways in the West and the planting of mining camps and other towns in or near the mountains was the outbreak of a series of Indian wars, the last of magnitude in the line of sanguinary conflicts that stretched back to the beginning of English settlement in America. Except for the relatively unimportant disturbances known as the Seminole War and the Black Hawk War, Indian relations had not been especially hostile from 1815 to 1861. Homes had been found for the Eastern tribes in Indian Territory and elsewhere to the west of the Missouri, in and on the edge of the "desert." There, in land not then desired by the stronger race, the weaker was left unmolested, except for the traffic over the great trails to Santa Fé, Salt Lake, Oregon, and California. The Plains Indians did not like this, but at the time they could still exist. The discovery of gold and the establishment of towns in the Rocky Mountains, the building of railroads, and the erection of long lines of telegraph poles changed the whole situation. Settlements had been made on lands closed to whites by treaties; the game on which the aborigines depended for a livelihood was driven off or exterminated; stagecoaches, railway trains, and telegraph lines presaged the coming in of ever-increasing hordes of settlers. The Indians fought savagely against the invaders during and after the Civil War, and on the Great Plains made their last futile stand against the white man and his civilization.

THE SPANISH-AMERICANS

But American gold seekers and railroad builders were not the first white settlers in the Rockies and intermontane plateaus. In the Southwest the presence of hundreds of Spanish-Americans presented another and a very different missionary problem. These people were the original white settlers in their communities. Santa Fé in New Mexico is

as old as Jamestown in Virginia. The Spanish-speaking people of the Southwest were in the United States as the result of the conquest of their territory. By birth they were adherents of the Roman Catholic Church. Why send missionaries among these Christians? At least two reasons could be given by any Protestant apologist. In the first place, Anglo-Americans had begun to settle among the Mexicans of the Southwest, and there was the same reason for sending missionaries to them as to all the other men and women on the frontiers. In the second place, the backwardness of the white inhabitants when the United States occupied the Southwest was regarded as an indication of the inferiority of the Roman religious system. The Spanish-speaking population in the Mexican Cession, although within the territorial limits of the United States, was regarded as essentially a field for foreign missions. But missionary work among them met with little encouragement. Their Catholic religious leaders were naturally hostile; the people themselves were indifferent. A Methodist missionary in reflecting on his problem asked rhetorically:

> What can I do, a lone missionary in this vast field, unacquainted with the language and customs of the people, except a few American men, and they nearly all married to Mexican women, apparently going back into the dark ages, morally and religiously.... I am almost the only republican in the neighborhood. Mrs. Harwood [my wife] and I, so far as we can see, are the only ones who dare speak a word against Sabbath breaking, intemperance, gambling, or the dance. Mixed marriages and no marriages seem to be largely the custom of the country, so far as the most of the American men with whom we have met are concerned. Hardly two families in the whole neighborhood can agree on any one thing. The Americans had come from the different sections of the country with their different notions of religion, education, morality, etc., and there was only one thing upon which it seemed that the people could unite, and that was a school in their midst, and even in that it required much patience and effort and aggression upon the part of the missionary and his wife to bring the people together.[2]

From a Baptist observer came a similar comment on religious and moral conditions in New Mexico:

> ... Most of the American population seem to be entirely apathetic on the subject of religion. Government officials seem to have left all, or nearly all, of their respect for religious matters "in the States" to be

---

[2] Thomas Harwood, *History of New Mexico Spanish and English Missions of the Methodist Episcopal Church* (Albuquerque, 1908), I, 76-77.

resumed, perhaps at the close of their probation here. The common soldier seems to have no ambition above whiskey. There are, of course, a few honorable exceptions; very few, however. As for the Mexicans, who comprise nineteenth-twentieths of the population, they are very well supplied with their Catholic churches, as [in] every little village and hamlet, whether Mexican or Pueblo, the inevitable church, always the most commodious building, is always to be found.[3]

THE MORMONS

From those interested in the religious life of the West, no group of people in that region received so much unfavorable criticism as did the Mormons or Latter-day Saints. Mormonism originated in western New York about 1830 at a time when that region was the center of a violent religious controversy. At first it was dismissed lightly as an unimportant religious vagary. Who would have dreamed in 1830 that from an inconspicuous family on the New York frontier there would come a religious movement which in a hundred years would have half a million Americans among its adherents? Even when the Mormons settled at Nauvoo, Illinois, after their unfortunate experiences in Ohio and Missouri, there were few outward manifestations of the heights of power and influence to which this persecuted people were soon to rise. The unjustifiable murder of Joseph Smith and his brother Hyrum by a mob at Carthage, Illinois, was followed by the emergence to power of Brigham Young, one of the most remarkable men in American history. Young, who led the Mormons to Utah and who there directed their activities with great skill, was of the type from which our captains of industry have come—bold, shrewd, indomitable, and practical. He encouraged the Mormons to think of themselves as a distinct people who were in the fullness of time to inherit the earth. They alone were to be saved. They were the chosen people, and all others were "Gentiles"; Salt Lake City, according to one unfriendly wag, was the place where "all the Jews are Gentiles, and all the saints are sinners." Their sense of distinctness was encouraged by their attempt to get as far away as possible from other people; when the Mormons set out for Salt Lake in 1846 it was outside the limits of the United States and was as inaccessible as any region in the West. But above all, the teaching and practice of polygamy, although not essen-

---

[3] A.B.H.M.S., *Forty-third Report* (1875), 27.

tial to their system, came to be their distinguishing characteristic; it was their point of sharpest deviation from the
accepted moral standards of the country. Since it was with
them a matter of religion, public and political attacks on
the institution made them feel that they were being persecuted for their religion—and no one can endure so much
suffering as the martyr.

In spite of such an anachronism in modern society as
polygamy, in spite of an anthropomorphic theology, and in
spite of the ridicule heaped on Joseph Smith's alleged revela-
tions, Mormonism grew. Nor were the reasons hard to
find. The Mormons were sincere and fired with missionary
zeal. Bishop J. C. Talbot of the Episcopal Church said, "I
have never yet conversed with a lay Mormon whom I believed to be a hypocrite."[4] Hundreds of missionaries were
and still are sent out annually. Any young man with the
requisite qualifications might be called upon to go out as a
missionary for two years. He went at his own expense.
That he had been thought worthy to go was an honor to his
family, and to his community, as well as to himself. "The
missionary's outfit," said Bishop Talbot many years ago,
"consists of a Prince Albert coat, a white necktie, a Mormon
compendium of Ready Reference Scriptural Texts, a great
deal of courage and self-assurance, tempered with enough
religious zeal to arouse the attention of the most careless."[5]
The missionary not only won converts—he strengthened his
own faith by his efforts to convert others.

A second reason for the success of Mormon missionaries
in winning converts was that they could point to the material blessings that God had showered upon His chosen
people in Zion. Thanks to the various co-operative undertakings of the Mormons, to their industry and thrift, and
to skillful leadership, quite apart from any miraculous
favors from the Deity, they have become prosperous. It is
a trite saying that they have made Utah to blossom as the
rose.

Once the convert had been won, he and his family were
enmeshed in an efficient and elaborate organization. The
average person enjoys responsibility, the holding of office,
and the feeling that he is the custodian of mysteries and

---

[4] G. White, *Apostle of the Western Church*, 178.

[5] Quoted by H. L. Burleson, *Conquest of the Continent*, 129.

secrets—hence the secret and fraternal societies that flourish so mightily in our "sweet land of secrecy." By its secret initiatory ceremonies Mormonism has tapped the deep well of human wonder; in its elaborate hierarchy there are places of responsibility and honor for a large number of the male members; and with some four hundred bishops in the organization, that dignity does not appear remote and unattainable. There were so many bishops in Salt Lake City and among the Mormons generally that the Protestant Episcopal missionary bishop in Utah was sometimes confused with his numerous episcopal brothers. Bishop D. S. Tuttle told about a man who came to his door in Salt Lake City and asked, "Is the bishop in?" "No." "Is the bishop's wife in?" "No." "Well, are *any* of his wives in?"[6]

In the generation following the Civil War, when the boys and girls born in Utah were growing into manhood and womanhood, and before the isolation of the Mormons had been broken down by the coming in of many Gentiles, Mormonism had another element of strength in the fact that this rising generation believed implicitly that the moral standards of the Mormons were infinitely superior to those of other people. And it must be admitted that there was much in the conduct of the average Gentile who appeared among the Mormons to justify them in their notion. Bishop Daniel S. Tuttle of the Protestant Episcopal Church insisted that one of the ways in which the Gentiles in Utah could weaken the power of Mormonism was simply by living exemplary Christian lives. In a letter written from Salt Lake City in 1867 he mentioned the fact that the Mormons had been in Utah for twenty years, and added:

> There are, therefore, young men and young women here who have never seen aught of the outside world, who have never witnessed Christian worship of any kind whatever, who have been taught (and from specimens here may well believe) that all Gentiles are a cheating, blasphemous, licentious set of men. One great duty we have to do is, with God's help and blessing, to show these young Mormons by our lives and conversation that we are the pure, just, peaceable, and loving people, that, if we are Christ's true disciples, we ought to be. Meanwhile, be it said, there seems to be less profanity, rowdyism, rampant and noisy wickedness among the young Mormons than among the youth of any other town or city where I've been. Drunkenness is a crime almost unknown among them.[7]

[6] H. L. Burleson, *Conquest of the Continent*, 132.

[7] D. S. Tuttle, *Reminiscences of a Missionary Bishop* (New York, [1906]), 110.

Bishop J. C. Talbot is another who adds his testimony as to the good order and soberness of Mormon communities. In 1864 he wrote:

> The state of society in Salt Lake presents the most remarkable contrast anywhere to be found. Outwardly, it is the most moral, orderly and quiet city I have ever seen. Containing a population of at least fifteen thousand souls, it is absolutely free from those enticements to immorality, which abound in all other places of its size. So far as I could ascertain, there is not a single drinking-saloon, or gambling establishment, or house of ill-fame within its limits. There is no drunkenness or rioting in its streets. Good order prevails. Yet its inner life is most shocking to the Christian sense. The most flagrant and open violations of the Christian law of marriage abound.[8]

But to the "Gentile" missionaries the good features in the system by whitening the sepulchre made it all the worse. By one of them Mormonism was characterized as "a strange compound of Christianity, Judaism, and Mohammedanism; of saintliness, sensuality, and superstition; of the devout and the diabolical." This observer continued: "It is not all evil. A system all evil couldn't have the power and the hold this has. There is enough of good with the evil to make it a masterpiece of the deceiver."[9]

The direct results of mission work in Utah as measured by converts from Mormonism were so slight as to be almost negligible; the indirect results as shown by modifications in the teachings and practices of the Latter-day Saints and in the improvement of the educational facilities of the territory were much more apparent.

AMERICAN HOME MISSIONARY SOCIETY IN COLORADO AND UTAH

As new fields were opened in the West the American Home Missionary Society sent in representatives, not always the first but usually early, because the administration of the Society was aggressive and denominational rivalries were still strong.

In the case of Colorado the first missionary was sent in 1863, four years after the great gold rush of 1859. By 1863 it was apparent that many Colorado mining camps and

---

[8] *Spirit of Missions*, XXIX (1864), 362.

[9] S. Graves, "The Gospel for Utah," in *Baptist Home Mission Monthly*, VI (1884), 271.

other towns were there to stay indefinitely; churches might then be organized with some prospect of permanence. William Crawford, of Massachusetts, went to the Rocky Mountains to reconnoiter for the Society as well as to perform the usual function of a missionary. He settled at Central City, the chief mining center in the Territory, and organized there the first Congregational Church in Colorado. Although a frontier mining camp, Central City was not so wild and lawless as he had imagined it would be. Shortly after his arrival he wrote back,

... Perhaps there are some who think our Society is so rude and wicked that there is no living here in comfort. Wicked enough, and rough enough it is, but not wholly so. In few places will one meet with more well-informed and cultivated people, or with pleasanter families. Our people demand and can appreciate good preaching. Many of them have been accustomed to the best.[10]

It should not be inferred from this, however, that missionaries found it easy to carry on their work in Colorado mining camps. The speculative spirit dominated life, and the men shifted from place to place as new strikes were made. In November, 1863, Mr. Crawford described some of his difficulties as follows:

It is impossible to make a contract with a church here as on most mission fields. In the first place, ministerial contracts in the West don't generally amount to much. Our churches have no conscience in respect to their obligations to the minister. The salary is first fixed at the lowest possible figure, the contract fails, and the rest the minister must make up in economy. In the second place, no one can tell where *this* church will be in a week hence. They may be in the States or at the new mines, they may have become rich or poor. We depend on nothing but uncertainty. Hence our subscription runs so much a *month* instead of so much a year.[11]

Some time in 1864 the President of Wheaton College in Illinois made inquiry of Brigadier General Connor, of Camp Douglas, Utah, as to the practicability of attempting to establish an orthodox church in the territory of the Mor-

---

[10] William Crawford, Central City, Sept. 18, 1863, A.H.M.S. papers, C.T.S. Dr. Lynn Perrigo has shown in his "Social History of Central City, Colorado" (MS. Ph.D. thesis, University of Colorado Library), that Central City, even in the early days, was not a town of unusual lawlessness and violence.

[11] William Crawford, Central City, Nov. 12, 1863, A.H.M.S. papers, C.T.S.

mons. In reply General Connor stated that there were enough Gentiles in Salt Lake City and soldiers in the near-by camp to provide a non-Mormon preacher with a clientele, not to mention the Mormons themselves, who had "greater need for missionary labor than any other people or community on the face of the earth." Moreover, added the General, "so long, at least, as the troops remain here, freedom of opinion and the expression of it, in its broadest American sense, will be protected, and a church could be established here without any apprehension of interference from the Mormon authorities."[12] Following the suggestion that the time was ripe to invade the stronghold of the Latter-day Saints, Norman McLeod, who was already engaged in missionary work in Denver, was sent to Salt Lake City in January, 1865, by the American Home Missionary Society; he was the first Protestant missionary to attempt to make Utah a permanent field of labor. In spite of the support of the commander of the army post in the vicinity of Salt Lake City, Mr. McLeod reported that his life was in danger and that an attempt had been made to assassinate him. "I am doged and stoned by the spies of the tyrant" [Brigham Young], he said, "even under the folds of the old flag."[13] Having established a Congregational church in Salt Lake City, McLeod returned to the East to raise money for a better church building and to give information on conditions in Utah to a Congressional investigating committee. On his way back to Salt Lake he was informed that one of the leading members of his congregation had been assassinated, presumably by order, or at least with the connivance, of the Mormon hierarchy. Believing that his own life would be in danger if he returned to Utah, McLeod changed his plans and the mission was abandoned.[14] In 1872 McLeod returned to Salt Lake City, but left again after a year. By that time several other Protestant churches had sent missionaries into Utah, but it soon became apparent to all that these preachers were making little progress in their efforts to convert the Mormons. Mindful of the unfair treatment they had received in the Middle West in the thirties and forties, and

---

[12] P. E. Connor, Camp Douglas, Utah, Oct. 25, 1864, to I. Blanchard, A.H.M.S. papers, C.T.S.

[13] Norman McLeod, Salt Lake City, Aug. 2, 1865, A.H.M.S. papers, C.T.S.

[14] A.H.M.S., *Forty-first Report* (1867), 75.

their trek across the plains to establish an asylum, the Latter-day Saints felt a strong dislike for their non-Mormon neighbors. Believing as they did that their brand of Christianity was a fuller and more perfect revelation of God's will than that of the orthodox churches, and that their moral standards were higher than those of the Gentiles, they resented the coming of missionaries to Utah and regarded it as an impertinence if not an insult. Certainly preaching did not shake the Mormon system, and the Congregationalists along with the other denominations turned their time and money more and more into educational channels.[15]

THE BLACK HILLS

The discovery of gold in the Black Hills corner of Dakota in the middle of the seventies was followed in 1876 by the sending in of a representative of the American Home Missionary Society, Mr. Lanson P. Norcross. He found that conditions were similar to those that existed in other Western mining camps: there were the usual vices of intemperance, gambling, and prostitution; there was the usual haste and excitement; only makeshift facilities were available for the exercises of public worship. In describing his difficulties he wrote:

> We have the present use of the Inter-Ocean Hotel, free of rent. It is a fearfully cold place, which the best efforts of a powerful stove cannot make comfortable on a moderately cold day....
> We have the use of an organ—the only one in town, I believe. It does duty every night at a concert and faro hall. We go and get it Sunday morning and carry it back before dark. Thus you see it does duty for God and Mammon both—not quite scriptural, I fear.[16]

The story is told of another missionary, B. F. Perkins, that once when riding in the Black Hills he came by chance upon some rich pieces of ore, which he naturally picked up and put away carefully in his handkerchief. Then as he found his mind coming back to those bits of rock—to their probable value and to a possible mining claim—he realized that his thoughts were being distracted from his great mission. At once he untied his handkerchief, shook it to the winds, and then, dropping on his knees in prayer, rededicated himself to his spiritual task.[17]

---

15 See below, page 401.
16 *Home Missionary*, XLIX (1877), 256-57.
17 J. B. Clark, *Leavening the Nation* (New York, [1903]), 159.

THE PRESBYTERIANS

In the direction of their work in the West the Presbyterians made much use of district secretaries or superintendents of missions, men who exercised some of the functions of the missionary bishop in the Episcopal Church. The duties were arduous and called for men who could "expatiate," to quote from a missionary report, over a vast territory. A study of the career of Sheldon Jackson shows something of the problems that confronted them and the methods that were used by one of the most successful of these superintendents.

Mr. Jackson, who had been forced by ill-health to abandon his plan of going out as a foreign missionary, began his missionary labors among the Choctaw Indians in 1858. Continued ill-health forced him to abandon the Indian Territory, and so he turned to the Home Board (Old School) and in 1859 became a missionary to the white population of Minnesota. His commission was to two specified towns and "vicinity," which he interpreted to mean every needy community within reach. His field in Minnesota at one time included nineteen preaching places, the extremes of which were a hundred miles apart. His report for the period from July to December, 1859, shows that he had traveled over a thousand miles, more than four hundred of them on foot, had met seventy appointments, and organized three churches. In the following quarter (January to April, 1860) he traveled over a thousand miles, of which he walked 233, and met sixty-four appointments. For ten years, except for a brief service as chaplain in the Union Army, he continued this active missionary life in Minnesota, during which time he organized or assisted in the organization of twenty-three churches, secured by letter or by visit to Eastern theological schools twenty-eight ministers, and collected funds for missionary work to the amount of $13,500.[18]

In 1869 Mr. Jackson's attention was turned towards the Rocky Mountains and Great Plains region into which new settlers were then pouring. In April of that year the Des Moines Presbytery appointed him its district missionary in central and western Iowa. In May the Missouri River Presbytery in session in Sioux City, more ambitious still, appointed him "superintendent of missions for western Iowa,

---

18 R. L. Stewart, *Sheldon Jackson* (New York, [1908]), 36-91.

Nebraska, Dakota, Idaho, Montana, Wyoming and Utah." Thus began the "Iowa Movement" for home missions; but the word "Iowa" should not mislead us as to the scope of the movement, for it was national, not local, in its objectives. Mr. Jackson accepted these appointments, although the presbyteries had no money to pay either the superintendent or the missionaries whom he proposed to plant at strategic places in the West. Within one week after the Missouri Presbytery acted, Jackson had posted three men along the line of the new Union Pacific railway: to one was assigned the territory between Omaha and Julesburg; to a second, eastern Wyoming; to the third, the region between Green River, Wyoming, and Corinne, Utah. Before eight months had passed the new superintendent of missions had put ten new missionaries at work in Iowa, Nebraska, Wyoming, Colorado, and Utah.[19] For the first year the salaries of these men were largely dependent on voluntary offerings that came as a result of Jackson's personal appeals for money. From May 1, 1869, to December 31, 1870, he received from private sources about ten thousand dollars for this work.[20] The Board of Home Missions, realizing the importance of the work Jackson had begun, then assumed the financial responsibility. Jackson made one of his flying visits into and through the Rocky Mountains in the summer of 1869. Between the 15th of July and the 17th of August he traveled 2300 miles by rail and 1200 by stagecoach and organized eight Presbyterian churches, including those at Grand Island in Nebraska, Cheyenne, Laramie, and Rawlins in Wyoming, and Helena in Montana. In Wyoming and Montana he was the pioneer for Presbyterianism; in Colorado, which he entered in January, 1870, Presbyterian activity dated back to the gold rush of 1859, but to Jackson fell the task of organizing the work. New Mexico, Arizona, and Utah also came within the scope of his boundless activities; into them he made various journeys of missionary reconnaissance. From his headquarters in Denver he viewed the West as a general views the field of battle. His aggres-

---

19 R. L. Stewart, "Mission Work in the Rocky Mountains," in *Rocky Mountain Presbyterian*, VI, No. 6 (1877), 2.

20 R. L. Stewart, *Sheldon Jackson*, 101-03; Sheldon Jackson, "Iowa Movement for Home Missions," in J. F. Hinkhouse and W. M. Evans, eds., *One Hundred Years of the Iowa Presbyterian Church* (Cedar Rapids, 1932), 359-69.

siveness was sometimes annoying to his religious neighbors, who charged that he planted some of his new Presbyterian churches in places where they were not needed and probably could not survive, thus weakening still further the already too much divided Protestant forces of small Western communities.[21]   Perhaps Mr. Jackson was no worse than his critics in this regard; he was probably more successful. In the midst of his busy life he found time also to edit a magazine, *The Rocky Mountain Presbyterian*,[22] in the interest of the home missionary movement.

It is mainly for his work in Alaska that Sheldon Jackson is remembered, but the story cannot be told adequately here because it belongs to Indian missions rather than to "home missions." As early as 1875 his attention was drawn to the needs of the natives in Alaska, and from then until his death he was continually concerned about the educational, religious, and economic development of that remote province. There, as in the Rocky Mountain region, he planted mission stations and missionaries, and helped establish schools. He was the first Commissioner of Education in Alaska; he conceived and executed the plan of bringing reindeer into Alaska from Siberia in order to alleviate the suffering and to improve the economic condition of the natives. Fitting indeed was it for the Presbyterian Church in the United States of America to confer on this tireless Western missionary leader its highest honor by electing him Moderator of the General Assembly in 1897.

To Sheldon Jackson, more than to any other man, was due the credit for the organization of a home missionary society among the women of his denomination. In almost every number of his *Rocky Mountain Presbyterian* he called attention to what he characterized as the degraded condition of the women and children among the Indians, the Mexicans, and the Mormons in the Southwest, and the need for greater efforts to educate and evangelize them. In 1878 his agitation

---

[21] An A.H.M.S. Secretary wrote in 1872: "Neither the Treasury nor our consciences will permit us to employ a man at large expense to compete with Mr. Jackson in gathering churches where the ground is already occupied & where they only can be sustained by extravagant outlay and by weakening other evangelical churches." A.H.M.S. Letter Bk., 1871-72, No. 1260, C.T.S. On denominational comity, see below, page 351.

[22] For a time this paper was sent free to all Presbyterian ministers; *Rocky Mountain Presbyterian*, V, No. 12 (1876), 2.

bore fruit in the formation of the Woman's Executive Committee of Home Missions. Its object was to co-operate with the Presbyterian Board of Home Missions, and especially to diffuse missionary information, to raise money for the maintenance of mission schools and for general missionary purposes.[23] In general it has not been the policy of the Presbyterians to establish primary schools or academies under ecclesiastical control. They have preferred to support the public schools. In the Southwest, and especially in Utah and New Mexico, they regarded conditions as unusual, and there they established elementary schools and academies.[24] In common with the other Protestant churches working in that field, they were convinced that only through the children could they make any impression on the Spanish-Americans or the Mormons.

THE EPISCOPALIANS

It was not until after the Civil War that the Protestant Episcopal Church fully awoke to its opportunities in the West. True, in the quarter of a century preceding the War, a good beginning had been made, but the work of this Church in the West had not thus far been conspicuously successful. By some observers its indifferent success was attributed to the fact that frontiersmen preferred a service less formal and less ritualistic than that so dear to the heart of the Churchman.[25] By others it was explained by the lack of missionary fervor and zeal in the Church. Whatever the reason was, a change was noticeable after the War. The old prejudice against the Episcopal Church had largely disappeared, partly perhaps because the Church had become less Anglican and more American in its outlook, less passive and more active in its methods, less aristocratic and more democratic in its appeal. One indication of this new period of vigor was in the increase in the annual contributions for the support of missions. From the reorganization of the

23 *Historical Sketch of the Board of Home Missions of the Presbyterian Church* (New York, 1888), 18-21.

24 See below, page 402.

25 Bishop George M. Randall denied this. He said: "My own observation in this Jurisdiction [Colorado and Wyoming] has confirmed me in the opinion that no form of worship and no ecclesiastical polity are better suited to successful missionary work in a new country than that of the Protestant Episcopal Church." *Spirit of Missions*, XXXIV (1869), 459.

Missionary Society of the Episcopal Church in 1835 until 1855 there had been no appreciable increase in the annual contributions for domestic missions; the amounts had ranged annually from approximately twenty to forty thousand dollars.[26] In the fifties there were signs of a more liberal spirit, and in 1860 the amount had risen to more than sixty thousand dollars. The receipts fell off during the War, but after 1865 they began to mount more rapidly, passing the hundred thousand dollar mark in 1867, and exceeding two hundred thousand dollars for the first time in 1881; four years later they came to more than a quarter of a million dollars.[27] Even that amount may have been a small contribution from a people whose ranks included so many of the socially elite of the North and East, but it does represent a tremendous increase over the trifle given annually before the War.

Another sign of a more vigorous life was the appointment of several new missionary bishops for the West. In 1860 there were only four missionary bishops. Jackson Kemper, the first and one of the greatest of the line, had just become bishop of Wisconsin after nearly a quarter of a century's service as missionary bishop of the Northwest. That title then passed to Bishop Joseph C. Talbot. There were three other missionary bishops: Henry C. Lay for the Southwest, William I. Kip for California, and Thomas F. Scott for Oregon. Each of these men was charged with the oversight of a region greater than he could adequately supervise under the circumstances, but of all Talbot was by far the most overburdened. His jurisdiction included all the land between the western limits of Wisconsin, Iowa, and Missouri on the one side and the rather indefinite bishoprics of California and Oregon on the other; it stretched from Nebraska to Arizona, from Minnesota to Nevada. Altogether he had a diocese of about one million square miles— little wonder that he sometimes referred to himself as the Bishop of All-out-doors![28] In 1863 Bishop Talbot made an

---

[26] *Spirit of Missions*, XIX (1854), 423.

[27] *Ibid.*, L (1885), 546.

[28] In his report for 1862 Bishop Talbot said: "I have been Bishop of Nevada Territory for more than two years and a half, and have never seen it. . . . And this without any fault of mine; I have earnestly desired to go. I have not thought of shrinking from the weary journey of more than half a month, night and day, necessary in order to reach Nevada. Nor have I been unwilling to take my life in my hands, and face the positive perils which, in times like these, I knew I must encounter." *Spirit of Missions*, XXVII (1862), 361.

episcopal visitation that necessitated traveling between three and four thousand miles "in wagons, in stages, in ambulances—guarded through hostile tribes of Indians by escorts of armed men—sleeping in tents, in coaches and by the wayside; sometimes performing himself the offices of cook and groom; sometimes, for weeks, night and day, tossed in the most indifferent coaches over routes which are made roads only by travel—in the earlier period encountering the heat of the plains, in the later period, the deep snows of the mountains."[29] After a jump from Denver to Salt Lake City he made the comment: "Think of a jurisdiction requiring two weeks, night and day, in a crowded coach, to go from one of its stations to another, and you will form a pretty good idea of the size and labor of my own."[30] In his report for 1865 he pointed out that to get from Nebraska to the populated sections of Colorado he had to ride through six hundred miles of wilderness; to Montana was a thousand miles farther; and thence another thousand miles from Montana through Utah to Nevada. Everywhere the personal presence of the Bishop was required if the Church were to be established. "It would be as reasonable," he said, "to expect efficient Episcopal oversight and administration of the Diocese of Massachusetts or New York from a Bishop resident in London."[31]

In 1865 Bishop Talbot's protests against the size of his diocese led to the appointment of two new missionary bishops—Robert H. Clarkson for Nebraska and Dakota, and George M. Randall for Colorado and parts adjacent. In the following year a considerable slice of the "parts adjacent"—Montana, Idaho, and Utah—was entrusted to Bishop Tuttle, concerning whose work in Utah mention was made in an earlier portion of this chapter. In Colorado, Bishop Randall enhanced materially the influence of his Church and left tangible monuments not only in religious institutions but also in such educational foundations as Jarvis Hall at Golden and Wolfe Hall in Denver.

THE METHODISTS

Methodist preachers were usually among the very first Protestant ministers to appear in new frontier communities.

---

[29] *Spirit of Missions*, XXIX (1864), 1.
[30] *Spirit of Missions*, XXIX (1864), 6.
[31] *Spirit of Missions*, XXX (1865), 491.

In 1850, two years after the acquisition of the territory, the
Methodist Church, North, sent its first missionary, E. G.
Nicholson, to New Mexico.[32] He made his headquarters in
Santa Fé and organized a small church composed wholly of
"Americans," as distinguished from the natives of the
country. The conditions were so discouraging for Protestants that the mission was soon abandoned; it was reopened
in 1853 and closed again in 1855. The work was not established on a permanent basis until 1869, when Thomas
Harwood began missionary operations there. One of the
difficulties, and it was felt especially by Methodists, who had
been accustomed to the itinerant system, was the sparseness
of the population. Missionaries were compelled to spread
their energies over a vast area. When Mr. Harwood appeared in New Mexico he inquired of his presiding elder,
"Father" J. L. Dyer, where his field of labor was to be. The
answer was:

> Get your pony shod, then start out northward via Fort Union,
> Ocate, Elizabethtown, Cimarron, Vermejo and Red River until you
> meet a Methodist preacher coming this way, then come back on some
> other road and rest up a little; thence go south via Las Vegas, etc.
> until you meet another Methodist preacher coming this way; thence
> home again and rest a little; thence westward and eastward until
> you meet other Methodist preachers coming this way. All this will be
> your work.[33]

Obviously the itinerant system was not designed for such
conditions. It had worked in agricultural regions where the
houses and settlements were relatively close together. But
when there were perhaps fifty thousand people spread over
an area of more than one hundred thousand square miles
and "separated by mountain chains lifting their snowy
summits to altitudes of from ten to thirteen thousand feet,"
circuits were impracticable;[34] it became the part of wisdom
to concentrate effort in the more populous centers.

In the case of Colorado at least two Methodist ministers
went out with the Fifty-niners to explore the Pikes Peak
country for their Church. They visited the principal camps
in the mountains and organized two missions. By 1861 the

---

[32] M.S.M.E.Ch., *Thirty-fifth Report* (1854), 86-89, contains an account of the origin of this mission.

[33] T. Harwood, *History of the New Mexico ... Missions*, I, 59-60.

[34] M.S.M.E.Ch., *Seventy-seventh Report* (1895), 280.

Rocky Mountain District of the Kansas-Nebraska Conference had been formed with six appointments besides a presiding elder.[35] At Virginia City in Montana there was a Methodist Church with 90 members by 1866. The minister in charge, A. M. Hough, said he liked that country because it was free from that first-of-all church pests, "a godly formal saint"; men who were irreligious made no pretense about it, so that one could be sure of the sincerity of those who did lend their support. Unfortunately, since at least half of the people in the community were backsliders, there were not many who were willing to help.[36] The problems in Idaho, another mining region, were similar to those in Colorado and Montana. The population was unstable. As one man put it: "The least trouble growing out of this is the fact that you know not where to put a church or parsonage. Your hopeful mining camp is crowded to-day with eager thousands, and the next season it is well-nigh deserted."[37]

In Arizona, where physical and social problems were similar to those in New Mexico, missionary work was carried on under great difficulties. The Reverend G. H. Adams, a Methodist superintendent of missions in that territory, commented as follows on some of his problems and troubles:

> Traveling throughout this mission as superintendent is very fatiguing. Of all the charges in the Territory, Tucson is the only one on a line of railroad. In every other case it requires the most exhausting methods of travel to reach the different towns where our churches are located. The roads are, many of them, about as bad as they can be, and allow for the passage of a vehicle at all. I doubt if a worse road can be found on the face of the globe for the passage of wheels than the one to Prescott. And be it remembered that during my four years' residence there I passed over its whole length to the railroad, 140 miles, not far from thirty times.[38]

In addition to these difficulties, the Indian situation was serious in the seventies and eighties. In his report for 1883 Superintendent Adams said:

> The past two years have been times of trial and test of faith and endurance for the Arizona Mission. Throughout the whole of this

---

[35] M.S.M.E.Ch., *Forty-first Report* (1860), 67-68; *Forty-second Report* (1861), 77; for experiences of a Methodist preacher in the Colorado mining camps in 1861, see J. L. Dyer, *Snow-Shoe Itinerant* (Cincinnati, 1890).

[36] M.S.M.E.Ch., *Forty-seventh Report* (1866), 162.

[37] M.S.M.E.Ch., *Forty-ninth Report* (1868), 130.

[38] M.S.M.E.Ch., *Sixty-sixth Report* (1884), 219-20.

period the Territory has not been free from the depredations of Indians. Some of our ministers have stood as sentinels all the night long, with gun in hand, until the break of day guarding against slaughter the people to whom on the following Sabbath they preached the word of life. Others fled with their families to places of safety, and in one case a camp-meeting was abandoned, the worshipers traveled by the light of the stars to escape the fury of the hostile savages, who were only a few miles in their rear.[39]

The Methodists, like the other principal Protestant groups, found it desirable to shift the emphasis from preaching to education in the Southwest, and especially among the Mormons. This phase of home missions will be discussed more fully in a later chapter.

---

[39] M.S.M.E.Ch., *Sixty-fifth Report* (1883), 215.

CHAPTER XI

THE LAST AMERICAN FRONTIER

In 1869 I went to Kansas ... to a new part of the State ... to a town that had no existence except on paper.... During that first summer people came there in their prairie schooners from all directions. They selected their lands and then went to work to turn over the prairie sod, ... It is no easy task to turn over this sod, and thus disturb the prairie's thousand-centuried sleep. The roots of the grasses are matted together so closely that it requires more than one yoke of oxen or more than one span of horses to send the plow through it. When turned over it is good for nothing the first year except to raise a few stalks of sod corn, and that has to be planted with an ax. After having chopped in their corn, the pioneers go to work to provide some shelter for the approaching winter. Lumber is high and money is scarce. Rude shanties or sod houses are all that many are able to provide for their families at first. Think of the number of things these new settlers have to do. The land must be broken up, houses and barns built, orchards planted, roads and bridges constructed, farm machinery purchased. Then remember that most of these settlers ran in debt for their farms.... Do the best they can, it is with great difficulty that they are able to raise enough to keep soul and body together, and make their annual payments on their lands.

You can well imagine that there will be little or no surplus that can be devoted to securing religious or educational privileges. This is a time when people appreciate a little help. This is the time they must have it, if they are to be kept in Christian ways.—*W. M. Barrows.*

AS THE NINETEENTH century was drawing to a close a home missionary publication declared that there never had been a more urgent call than there was then for new workers and enlarged outlay for Western missions. "From almost every part of the great West," said the editor of the *Home Missionary,* "come to us eloquent and piteous appeals for missionary help. Everywhere there are opportunities presented now for successful work, and everywhere the day of advantage is rapidly passing." This statement is typical of the many appeals for money and men that were then being issued by all the home missionary societies in the United States. After three centuries of Christian preaching in America and after one hundred years of organized home

missionary endeavor, the task of converting the country and establishing Christian institutions was still unfinished. That it was so did not mean that the home missionary movement had failed; it did mean rather that the needs and opportunities had grown as fast as, or perhaps even faster than, the agencies created by the various churches for ministering to those needs. But the appeals for larger contributions for this unfinished task were made optimistically as the twentieth century drew near. They were made by men who took pride in the rapid material development of the country, but who were sobered by the lag in spiritual progress; by men who looked forward to even better days and greater deeds; by men who exulted in the speedy and signal victory of the United States over Spain and who interpreted that conflict as "the last struggle between the Middle Ages and the Declaration of Independence, between the Inquisition and the common school, between intolerance and tyranny and the compact in the Mayflower;"[1] by men who seized upon and magnified such idealism as there was in that war, attributing it in no small part to the inculcation in the people of Protestant principles by missionaries and other preachers of the gospel; by men who saw the United States stand forth among the nations as a world power, young, strong, and vigorous, not perfect, but perfectible. Such men renewed their appeals for the West at the close of the nineteenth century in a spirit of thankfulness for what had been accomplished in the past and with a sense of responsibility for the future.

Nor is it surprising that as these religious leaders stood at the turn of the century and looked back into the recent past—into the period since the Civil War—they should have felt an honest pride in what had been accomplished. The third of a century following the War between the States was a period of rapid expansion in home missionary activities. Never before had the expenditures for missions been so great, the workers so numerous, the area occupied so vast, or the interests so varied.

THE WEST AFTER THE WAR

The close of the Civil War was followed by a period of rapid material development, especially in the North and the

---

[1] J. H. Barrows, in *Home Missionary*, LXXII (1899), 25.

West. To what extent the reason for this was psychological, so far as the North was concerned, it is impossible to say, but it is not improbable that the successful outcome of the war for the preservation of the Union stimulated a feeling of optimism and buoyancy in the victorious section of the country. More tangible forces may be found in increased business activity, the rapid exploitation of natural resources, and the coming in of hundreds of thousands of immigrants who by their toil added more than they consumed to the stock of national wealth.

The quarter of a century following the Civil War is the period of the most rapid occupation of the unsettled parts of the United States—an occupation so complete, superficially at least, by the close of the century that the frontier had practically disappeared. There are several reasons for the speedy overrunning of what remained of the West in these years. The close of the Brothers' War was followed by the return to civil life of more than a million men who had to find places for themselves in the economic order; thousands of them turned to the farm lands of the West. By the Homestead Law of 1862 the National Government indicated its willingness to give a farm to the loyal, landless citizen of proper age who would live on it and use it for five years. Much of the available land was of the best quality, land on which a man might expect to raise bumper crops. Moreover, the prices of agricultural products were high at the end of the War; temporarily, farming appeared to be a profitable industry.

The construction of the various new Western railroads, and especially the completion of the Union Pacific in 1869, greatly stimulated the settlement of the land west of the Missouri River. The railroads not only made the land more accessible, but their promoters assiduously advertised the wonders of the region to the land-hungry folk at home and abroad. Several of the Western railways had received subsidies of Government land along their tracks. It was to their interest to sell a part of this land—some of it they might hold back for an enhanced price—not only to get money to pay for the cost of construction, but also to create a clientele for themselves in the new towns and counties through which they passed. However, much of this land lay in the old "Great American Desert." True, the notion of the existence of a desert in the High Plains region was breaking

down but it had not entirely disappeared. As late as 1867 General John Pope, who was in command of the Department of Missouri, which then extended as far west as Colorado, stated in one of his reports that there was a belt of land never less than five hundred miles wide stretching from Canada to Mexico along the eastern base of the Rockies which was "beyond the reach of agriculture, and which must always remain a great uninhabited desert."[2] The land-grant railroads worked earnestly to correct this impression: they explained the advantages of irrigation; they described the enormous crops that had actually been grown on irrigated lands; they pointed out the excellence of the market for farm produce in the Western mining camps. The Northern Pacific, which opened up to settlement a vast region in the Northwest that had hitherto been little known,[3] used in its advertising propaganda terms so glowing—its line if carried far enough East on the forty-fifth parallel would cross northern Italy—that it was called in derision the Banana Route. But it brought in settlers by the trainload, many of them from Europe. Thus a class of pioneers gathered together by railroads, transported to the frontier by railroads, and largely dependent on the railroads came into existence.

Another industry associated with the "wild West" of the postbellum period was the raising of cattle on the Great Plains. Stockraising on unoccupied land has always represented a stage of frontier development, and such place names as Cowpens of Revolutionary fame in northwestern South Carolina and the title of "Porkopolis," which was applied to Cincinnati early in the nineteenth century, are significant of the time and region. After the Civil War the cattle industry rose to new heights of importance. In the absence of a market for Texas cattle during the War, their numbers had increased enormously. The discovery by experience that cattle could live on the northern plains in the winter opened a new feeding ground. The extinction of the bison, hitherto the chief source of food for the tribes of the plains, not only made room for the cattle but imposed on the Federal

---

[2] *House Exec. Doc.*, 39th Cong., 1st Sess., No. 76, 2.

[3] L. P. Brockett, writing in the *Baptist Home Mission Monthly*, V (1883), 234-35, said that while the Union Pacific Railway had been important, it had opened up a country that was well known and fairly accessible; but the Northern Pacific had opened "as veritable a new world as that which Columbus gave to the Spanish Crown."

Government the necessity of providing meat for the Indians, who were now being placed on reservations. The segregation of the latter, incidentally, is of significance in that it made it safer on the plains for the cattle and their attendants. The growth of cities in the East and Middle West provided another market for the meat; the building of the railroads into the West made it easier to get the cattle to market, while the invention of the refrigerator car and the tin can made it possible to preserve the meat and to transport it longer distances. The result of this combination of circumstances was the growth of the cattle business on a large scale on the Great Plains. The "long drive" was developed from the breeding grounds in Texas to the "cow towns" on the railroads in western Kansas and Nebraska, to the northern feeding ranches in Dakota, Montana, and Wyoming, and to the Indian reservations. The Great Plains from Texas to Montana soon became a vast cattle ranch. The cowboy was even more picturesque than the miner. He was often honest, generous, friendly, and chivalrous, but the cow town with its many saloons, bawdy houses, and gambling dens took its place alongside the mining camp and "Hell-on-Wheels" as another symbol of Western wickedness. The cattlemen presented a difficult problem to missionaries, and one that was never fully solved. They were too hard to locate; there were too few in one place; and they represented a passing phase of Western development. Close behind the cowboy came the "nester," whose barbed wire fence meant the ultimate extinction of the open range pasturage on which the cattle industry had flourished in the seventies and eighties.

Land-hungry pioneer farmers, whose predecessors a generation earlier had either turned back at the "Great American Desert" or had jumped it to land in California or Oregon, now entered it confidently, equipped with new tools and weapons and bolstered by new hopes and ideas. Colt's revolver made them more than a match for mounted Indians; barbed wire solved the problem of fencing; better and cheaper windmills assured water for man and beast; new farming machinery and methods, supplemented by drought-resistant seeds, gave promise of a harvest in a dry land.[4]

---

[4] Walter P. Webb, *Great Plains* (Boston, c. 1931), has shown in convincing manner the effect of the industrial revolution on the settlement of the plains region.

The advance into the plains area, however, was made at the cost of a good deal of suffering. People were led to believe that the character of the climate had changed and that thereafter there would be enough rainfall to bring crops to maturity. Eastern Colorado, for example, was advertised after 1880 as being in the "rain belt." The claim was set up that the moisture taken up into the sky from the irrigated lands near the mountains would now descend as rain in eastern Colorado and make that part of the state suitable for agriculture.[5] There were a few years in the eighties when the rainfall in the plains region was abnormally high; but by the end of the decade climatic conditions became normal, with the result that disappointed, disillusioned people were forced to leave or to cling to submarginal lands that produced hardly enough to keep their occupants alive.

Another problem for the people who took up homesteads or bought railroad lands in Kansas, Nebraska, and the Dakotas in the 1870's was the plague of "grasshoppers" that came upon them for several years. A missionary from Brookings County, on the eastern line of Dakota Territory, sent in this description of the coming of these unwelcome visitors:

Two weeks ago the swarm of locusts . . . called grasshoppers, came down on this whole valley, and in a few hours the fruits of weeks and months of labor were swept away. I never saw such devastation. Their descent was like the falling of a snow storm. They covered the fields of grain, and the blade and ear melted away before them. . . . Many families, in the loss of their crops, have lost all their living. . . . On the morning of the third day the wind came from the north; about nine o'clock they began to rise; and from grain fields and prairies they went up in clouds that darkened the air. It seemed to be a simultaneous movement, and all day long the swarms were continuous, filling the sky as thickly driving snow. But they had completely devastated the region before they left. Fields of corn were left stripped to the stalk like bean poles.[6]

Serious as this was, it was only a temporary phase of Western life. People lived in hope that the 'hoppers would depart, and so optimistic pioneers kept coming in and taking

---

[5] *Baptist Home Mission Monthly*, I (1879), 269, pointed out that there was more rainfall on the Plains as a result of the cultivation and irrigation of land along the eastern base of the Rockies. "The climatic changes on the Plains have opened this entire country into a missionary field."

[6] G. S. Codington, in *Home Missionary*, XLVII (1874), 139.

up Government land. Between 1862 and 1882, 86,936 original homestead entries were made in Kansas for a total of nearly twelve million acres of land. In this same twenty year period, the final entries were 34,055 in number for more than 4,600,000 acres. In the neighboring state of Nebraska the original entries between 1862 and 1882 were 64,328 for about eight million acres; final entries were 29,-140 for 3,566,477 acres.[7] The difference between the figures on original and final entries is explained partly by the fact that some who took up land had abandoned it, but it must also be borne in mind that some who had entered land had not had time by 1882 to "prove up." Whether they stayed or whether they left, the fact that they had come is significant in the home missionary story because, as was pointed out again and again by the various missionary societies, here was a vast missionary field that was crying for attention.

The rush of land seekers into Dakota Territory started in the main later than the invasion of Kansas and Nebraska. It was at its height in eastern and southern Dakota in the 1880's. In the year ending on June 30, 1883, about 22,000 original homestead entries for a total of nearly 3,500,000 acres of land were filed in the land offices of that territory. New settlements were springing up almost as if by magic, wrote a missionary as he watched the throngs that poured into South Dakota in 1883. "The railroads much of the time," he said, "had two passenger trains a day each way, with from seven to nine coaches full of new-comers, while there were nine or ten freight trains a day taking their goods, and yet they could not get them fast enough." At almost every station goods were piled up promiscuously in every direction, waiting to be moved out to the new homes.[8]

In the near-by Northwest, in northern Michigan, northern Wisconsin, and Minnesota, and in the Far Northwest, or in Oregon and Washington, the lumber camps represent another passing phase of Western development, although one not so transitory as the cattle industry of the Great Plains. The growth of the great cities of the East, the removal of the forests of the Ohio Valley, the demand for lumber on the treeless prairies of the West, and the voracious appetites of the great newspaper presses for wood-

---

7 T. Donaldson, *Public Domain* (Washington, 1884), 1284.

8 From the report of Stewart Sheldon, A.H.M.S., *Fifty-eighth Report* (1884), 46-47.

pulp paper, all levied heavy toll on the northwestern forests. The typical town that grew up in the pineries had in its early days all the vices and few of the virtues of modern urban life. It was reported that one new lumber town in northern Minnesota with a population of fifteen hundred had between forty and fifty saloons, twenty gambling halls, and many—perhaps no one knew how many—houses of ill-fame. Northern Wisconsin, said a preacher in the heyday of the boom there in lumbering and mining, was "fearful in wickedness." Vice was so rampant that "the very air on the train passing through seems blue with the fumes of hell."[9] The seasonal character of the work in the pineries of Michigan, Wisconsin, and Minnesota added to the difficulties of reaching the men; when summer came many of them found employment in the wheat fields or with the railroad construction gangs of the Northwest. For these men as for the cowboys comparatively little was done by the organized forces of Christianity, although here and there a lumberjack sky pilot fought almost single-handedly against debasing influences in the logging towns.

Farther south a new frontier was being opened up in the Indian Territory. By the end of the 1880's the prairies and plains west of the ninety-fifth meridian had been for the most part occupied by settlers. With land-hungry pioneers pushing out into the dry lands of western Kansas and Nebraska, into eastern Colorado and northern Texas—into a region where it was appropriate for a discouraged and disgusted homesteader to put up this sign on his farm when he abandoned it: "250 miles to a Post Office; 100 miles to Water; 6 inches to Hell; Gone back East to live with the Wife's folks"—it was inevitable that pressure should be put on the National Government to dispossess the red men of their lands in present-day Oklahoma. Beginning in 1889 and continuing at intervals for the next thirteen years the Government opened first one section and then another in the Indian Territory to white settlement. Here was good farming land right between eastern Kansas and northern Texas. It was to be offered on the principle of first come, first served; the result was one of the most spectacular events in the entire history of the occupation of the West. In the first great rush, that of April 22, 1889, at least

---

[9] G. A. Hood, "The New North," in *Home Missionary*, LX (1887), 294.

one hundred thousand persons are said to have entered Oklahoma in one afternoon. At twelve o'clock noon on that day the site of Oklahoma City was still waving prairie; by sunset it was a canvas city with ten or fifteen thousand inhabitants. An eyewitness of this run for land, writing from one of the boom towns, said:

... As I rode into this place on the cars, I could see on either side the wild riders hastening with all speed to some favorite claim, which they had marked out in advance, and over the prairie following at less speed, but with no less frantic eagerness, were scores upon scores of wagons and buggies filled with boomers seeking homes in the new land.

In that mad race wheels were broken, horses disabled, wagons overset, occupants spilled upon the ground, and those who witnessed such mishaps swept on, rejoicing, perhaps, at the misfortunes which removed some of the claimants from the race to the limited homesteads of the promised land. ...

At Guthrie, 15,000 people were poured out like swarms of bees from successive railroad trains, in three hours' time. Imagine, if you can, the wild scramble for lots. Confusion reigned supreme; claims were mixed up in almost inextricable entanglement.

Men ran from the trains with all speed to the places they thought vacant land, and marked out town-lots, only, perhaps to leave them in a few moments for what they considered more choice locations. Even women and children were in the scramble. ...[10]

Even more thrilling was the rush into the Cherokee strip in September, 1893, in which, according to some estimates, one hundred and fifty thousand persons participated. A home missionary who joined in the race in order to get a choice building lot in a new town for his denomination has left a graphic description of this wild scramble for land. According to this writer:

On Saturday, September 16th, at twelve o'clock, I presume from 100,000 to 150,000 people witnessed and took part in the occupancy of this new land. Such a wild, reckless scramble for dirt was never known, and I hope may never be repeated. I drove to the line four miles north of Hennessey and witnessed the rush from that point. ... Fully 10,000 entered the Strip from this point. Besides horsemen and footmen, men and women in vehicles of every description awaited the signal from the United States soldiers to start into the promised land. The horsemen and those in light vehicles were lined within a hundred-feet strip along the border for miles, and the heavier teams, loaded with merchandise of all sorts—lumber, household goods, tents, buildings fitted and ready to be put together, barrels of water, stacks of cooked food, etc. etc.—were arranged in the rear to follow the owners

10 R. W. Hill, Presbyterian Superintendent of Home Missions in Indian Territory, quoted in *Spirit of Missions*, LIV (1889), 311.

who were to race for claims and town lots. On the railway there were forty palace stock cars attached to three engines. As this train moved into position it was literally filled and covered, sides and top, with living humanity as fast as men and women impelled by the wildest frenzy could scramble into place. I could hardly see a foot of the wooden slats as the multitudes went up the sides to the top like so many squirrels or monkeys. Every part of the cow-catchers and of the engines was covered with men anxious to be near the front to jump and get a little advantage of the other fellows. Eleven minutes before twelve o'clock a false signal was given, and in less time than I can pen it the prairie was covered with the myriad racers. The few soldiers were utterly powerless to stop the rush, and away in the distance went the wild crowd. The rush and roar of the thousands, the whistle of the engines and the rumbling of the immense train, the shouts of the excited drivers, the noise of the moving wheels of the lighter and heavier wagons, the rearing and tossing and neighing of excited horses, the discharge of firearms in every direction, and the clouds and clouds of dust raised by this moving mass, all conspired to make impressions upon those who witnessed the grand and awful scene, never to be erased.[11]

"A nation is being born in a day," said the missionaries again and again as they recounted their experiences in this big and busy West, and as they asked for more and more helpers in their fight against irreligion and sin.

THE FOREIGN-BORN

Surely a West so vast and so complex presented problems sufficiently great to call forth the best endeavors of Christian statesmen. But the problem was even more complicated than has thus far been indicated. The great increase in the number of foreign-born in the United States, both East and West, after 1865 provided still another incentive for home missions. There were several reasons for the rising tide of immigration into this country after the Civil War. The outcome of that struggle had enhanced the prestige of the United States, and the abolition of slavery made it appear as a country where conditions favorable to free labor prevailed. America was prosperous, wages were high, work was plentiful, and land was cheap; it was still the land of opportunity. Until 1890 our immigrants were coming mainly from the north of Europe. Between 1860 and 1890 nearly three and a half millions of English, Irish, and Scotch from the United Kingdom and about three hun-

---

[11] J. H. Parker, in *Home Missionary*, LXVI (1894), 449-51.

dred thousand Scandinavians came to the United States. Although the number of immigrants from Italy and Austria-Hungary increased rapidly between 1880 and 1890, the total was as yet unimpressive, amounting to less than half a million from the dual monarchy and fewer than four hundred thousand from Italy in the thirty years ending in 1890. Before 1890 the immigrants on the whole were more easily assimilated and less prone to congregate in the cities than the bulk of those who came after that date. A large number of the Germans and the majority of the Scandinavians went to Western farm lands. The coming of so many industrious and thrifty settlers was generally a matter for national pride. America was the melting pot out of which it was thought would come a new and higher type of mankind. Fear was expressed occasionally, however, in religious periodicals that continental habits of Sunday observance would overthrow the Puritan Sabbath, and that German rationalism and infidelity would undermine revealed religion. In a report to the Presbyterian General Assembly in 1876, for example, it was pointed out that German education "in its higher forms and in the common rudiments is confessedly higher than our own," and that the Germans regarded America as being in its formative stage and hoped to modify its institutions by their influence. "The force of their subtle philosophy, materialistic and rationalistic," so runs the report, "permeates even beyond the German mind into hundreds and thousands of our young Americans. The determination of many of them to pull down by definite organization the Sunday civil law, the Church of God, the authority and inspiration of the Scriptures, and the foundations of belief in immortality and the divine existence, is as bold and constant as the unscrupulous advocacy of the anti-Christian press. In short, they not only aim to be, but they are already, a powerful controlling mind in America."[12] The danger to American institutions may have been exaggerated in this statement, but it is true that the home missionary often was a potent agency in the Americanization of foreigners and did help them bridge the gap between the old life and the new. As President Theodore Roosevelt put it, "It is a serious and dangerous thing for any man to tear loose from the soil, from the region in

---

[12] *Minutes of General Assembly Presbyterian Church in U.S.A.* (1876), N.S., IV, 46.

which he and his forebears have taken root, and to be transplanted into a new land. He should receive all possible aid in that new land, and the aid can be tendered him most effectively by those who can appeal to him on the grounds of spiritual kinship."[13]

The Roman Catholic Church was the one that could claim spiritual kinship with the largest number of immigrants, but with its activities we are not here concerned. Second to the Roman Catholic and first of the Protestants in this regard stood the various Lutheran bodies. Lutheranism in the United States because of linguistic differences and doctrinal disputes has been and still is characterized by divisions into a number of independent and sometimes antagonistic synods and councils. As late as 1860 there was a "General Synod" which embraced about two thirds of the Lutherans in this country, but in that year the Swedes and Norwegians withdrew and developed their own Augustana Synod; in 1862 the Southern synods set up the General Synod of the Confederate States, and in 1867 the conservatives under the lead of the Ministerium of Pennsylvania erected their own General Council; independent of all of these was the Synod of Missouri. Home missionary work among the Lutherans has been marked by rivalry between synods as well as with other churches. The Missouri Synod, until 1918 the largest unit among American Lutherans, was zealous in the maintenance of pure Lutheran doctrines and active in missionary work. Its churches were to be found in every state in the Union and all over Canada. Most of its home missionary operations were conducted by District Boards, but there was also a general home missionary treasury to which all the churches contributed and from which money was drawn to supplement the work of such districts as could not raise enough for their own missionary work. Both the General Synod and the General Council engaged in missionary work in the West. The representatives of the Synod went west from Ohio, Indiana, and Illinois into Kansas and Nebraska; the Council turned more to the Northwest, to Wisconsin, Minnesota, the Dakotas, and Washington. The General Synod operated through a Board of Home Missions which spent more than a million and a half dollars and organized over six hundred churches be-

---

[13] Quoted by J. R. E. Hunt, *Lutheran Home Missions* (Rock Island, 1913), 58.

tween 1870 and 1910. The Augustana Synod, organized in
1860, was divided into a Swedish and a Norwegian Synod
in 1870. The Swedish Augustana Synod has carried on its
missionary work among the Swedes of the West and the
Northwest through a Missionary Committee. This Synod
has gathered together about a quarter of a million members. The Norwegians have been more successful than the
Swedes in reaching their fellow countrymen; in 1890 the
Norwegian Augustana Synod and the Norwegian-Danish
Conference united to form the United Norwegian Church.[14]
Altogether the Lutherans numbered approximately four
million communicants in the United States and took rank
as the third most numerous Protestant group. The various
Lutheran Synods have felt that the German and Scandi-
navian immigrants were their special field of work and have
resented somewhat the efforts of other Protestant churches
to win converts among them. The latter, however, felt
that they had a duty to perform and started or enlarged
their departments devoted to work among the foreign-born.

At this point another motive for home missions should
be noted, missions among the immigrants to lessen industrial warfare and safeguard American social and economic
institutions. In the thirties and forties fear had been expressed for the safety of the American political system because of the work of the Roman Catholic Church among the
aliens in the West. In the seventies and eighties conservatives in economics and politics were alarmed over the frequent and serious labor disturbances of those years; the
terroristic methods of the Molly Maguires, the secrecy of
the Knights of Labor, the destruction of property in the
railroad strikes, and the May Day disturbances in Chicago,
which culminated in the Haymarket Square riot (1886), all
indicated that the workers were seething with unrest. So-
cialism, anarchism, and other notions of European origin,
it was feared, were undermining American institutions.
The advocates of these subversive principles, it was pointed
out, were aliens, and their pernicious doctrines found lodgment especially among the foreign-born. What to do, was
a serious question in the minds of many. The proponents
of home missions came forward to claim that they had the
best solution for the problem: it was to spread Christi-

---

[14] A. R. Wentz, *Lutheran Church in American History* (Philadelphia, [1923]), 222-23.

anity of the standard American Protestant type among the immigrants. To be sure, the seat of the difficulty was more and more in the Eastern cities and other industrial centers —and to that extent falls outside the scope of this study of missions on the frontier—but any agency that in any way helped hold the foreign-born in any part of the land to the conventional way of life in America was regarded as something to be encouraged. Hence we find in a report of a Baptist committee on work among the immigrants the following:

Closely joined with the problem of political assimilation is the problem of industrial peace and prosperity. The wide-spread industrial agitation under which the country is now suffering, is in large part caused, and certainly is greatly intensified by the presence of vast numbers of foreign laborers, nearly all of whom are imperfectly acquainted with our laws and social customs, and many of whom are ruled by ideas and prejudices that are distinctly hostile to Christian civilization. Some, indeed, have received from unscrupulous immigration-agents and other sources, ideas of liberty in this country that would be grotesque were they not fraught with such serious results to society. The *dangerous* leaders of the workingmen in their strife with capital are almost exclusively foreigners. This is especially true of the revolutionary and incendiary men, who, in the name of labor, and to the limitless damage of honest labor, are enacting bloody tragedies in the streets of our cities. The loudest-voiced denouncers and opposers of wholesome legislation are foreigners, many of whom, despite the facility with which political parties manufacture voters, have not been in the country long enough to become citizens. The Home Mission Society by its work among foreigners strikes at the roots of anarchy and industrial war.... [15]

Such was the West of the post-Civil War decades—a vast area swarming with thousands of eager, busy, restless pioneers, some of whom had not yet been assimilated in the American population, but all of whom were thirsting for wealth. This was the "wild and woolly" West of cowboys and tenderfoots, of miners and stagecoach robbers, of railroad builders and small farmers, of lumberjacks and gamblers. In none of the previous "Wests" had the problem of home missions been so complex and so vast.

THE AMERICAN HOME MISSIONARY SOCIETY

On the withdrawal of the New School Presbyterians in 1861 the American Home Missionary Society became a

---

[15] A.B.H.M.S., *Fifty-fourth Report* (1886), 30-31.

Congregational organization. But so loath were Congregationalists to abandon the ideal of co-operation in home missions by kindred religious bodies, and so reluctant were they to admit that by the dissolution of the partnership the national or American society had lost its broad characteristics and become denominational, that they clung to the old name for more than thirty years after it had ceased to be entirely appropriate. Finally the logic of facts, when reinforced by a gift of $150,000 on condition that the word "Congregational" be substituted for "American," was strong enough to bring about the change in name to Congregational Home Missionary Society in 1893.[16]

The policy of the Congregationalists in their home missionary work remained essentially the same as in the earlier period. They regarded it as their chief business to organize and support churches; they encouraged a settled rather than an itinerant ministry, although they did at times depart from this rule in sending out students from theological seminaries to engage in mission work in Western states during their summer vacations; they gave support only to ministers who refrained from secular employment; they encouraged self-help by making their grants in inverse proportion to the ability of a congregation to contribute to the support of its pastor. Although the number of workers in the Southern states increased after the War, the Society still confined its efforts mainly to the West and the Northwest, and especially to those parts of the West where the New England element was most numerous. In reply to criticism on this point the officers stated that since men and money were limited, it seemed wise Christian economy to use both where they would be most likely to reach those who were predisposed toward Congregational principles.[17]

In mitigation of the evils of denominational rivalry it is sometimes claimed that competition has had the effect of increasing the amount of money given for religious purposes. Such would appear to have been one of the results of the withdrawal of the New School Presbyterians from the American Home Missionary Society. The receipts in the first year following the severing of the old relationship fell off only twenty thousand dollars, and this too in the

---

[16] A.H.M.S., *Sixty-seventh Report* (1893), 15; A.H.M.S., *Minutes of Executive Committee*, Vol. LXVII (1892-93), 454, in C.H.M.S.

[17] *Home Missionary*, LXVIII (1895), 344-47.

first year of the Civil War. Four years later, and for the
first time in the history of the Society, the annual income
exceeded $200,000; it was more than $300,000 in 1875, more
than 450,000 in 1885, over $600,000 in 1890, and in excess
of $750,000 in 1896.[18]

In proportion to their numbers (about 600,000 in 1895),
the gifts of Congregationalists for organized home missions exceeded those of any other major Protestant body
in the generation following the Civil War.

AMERICAN HOME MISSIONARY SOCIETY ON NORTHERN PRAIRIES

As the pioneers pushed first into central and then into
western Kansas and Nebraska after the Civil War, missionaries followed them as best they could. It was hard to
keep up. According to a superintendent of missions in
Kansas, the combined efforts of the State Immigration
Commission, the railroad companies with land to sell, and
the real-estate agents had induced an immigration unparalleled in the history of any agricultural state.[19] The
people were too poor after making payments on their lands,
erecting houses and other necessary buildings, and paying
interest on railroad bonds to contribute much to the support of religion; they were too excited about railroad construction, the laying out of towns, and the prospective increase in land values to give much thought to religion. "Everything here is feverish and uncertain," wrote a missionary from Coffey County, Kansas, in 1870. Railroad promoters had appeared with offers to bring in the rails in
exchange for bond subsidies. "These ideal railroads seem
to be scattered over our prairies ready to wind around a
town, almost in any numbers, for a consideration in the
way of bonds."[20] New towns, some of them of the "fever
and ague" variety in which growth and stagnation alter-
nated, were laid out along the lines that were actually built;
unfortunately, according to the preachers, they were often
pre-empted by the agents of the Devil. From Nemaha County, Kansas, came this complaint in 1870:

---

[18] C.H.M.S., *Seventieth Report* (1896), 92.

[19] J. G. Merrill, Topeka, Kan., March 23, 1871, A.H.M.S. papers,
C.T.S.

[20] J. D. Parker, Burlington, Kan., Oct. 1, 1870, A.H.M.S. papers,
C.T.S.

The Railroad from Saint Joseph to Denver City is now constructed for seventy five miles west from St. Jo, passing within two miles of us. ... At the point where the Road passes nearest to us a new town has been laid out during the last month.... Building has commenced on the new site.... But wickedness is there. The first building put up in anticipation of the location of the town site there was a *Whiskey Shop*.[21]

Conditions in Nebraska were similar to those in Kansas: in both the poverty of the people hindered the establishment of churches and the maintenance of preachers. Here is a letter from Hamilton County, in central Nebraska, on conditions there in 1876:

Prospects had been good but the 'hoppers came in greater numbers than ever before known....[22] Most of the people in this region of country are involved in debt from the effects of the scourge two years ago, so that they have to sell what little grain they have, scarcely holding enough for bread...and to satisfy the merchant as far as possible who has been long waiting upon them so that clothing is out of the question altogether and it is for the want of even common clothing that many are kept away from the means of grace....I felt cut to the heart three weeks ago when I visited a poor earnest Christian Brother who is struggling with eight in the family to build up a home. He had just had his team taken from him on a chattel mortgage which he could not meet on account of failure in his crops, and three of his children were crying to go to Sunday School but could not because they had nothing but rags to cover their nakedness....[23]

In the summer of 1876 the American Home Missionary Society sent eighteen theological students from Yale, Hartford, and Chicago to Nebraska; they spent their time visiting the people, organizing churches and Sunday schools, and learning at firsthand some of the problems of the home missionary. One who spent the summer in Red Willow County emphasized in his report the poverty of the people:

... The settlements here are largely composed of men who have been unfortunate in the east and have come here without means to procure a home.... The grasshoppers have so frequently destroyed their crops

---

[21] O. A. Thomas, Albany, Kan., Sept. 1, 1870, A.H.M.S. papers, C.T.S.

[22] H. N. Gates, Omaha, Neb., Mar. 17, 1877, made the observation that the depressing effect of the grasshoppers on the people was often out of proportion to the damage they actually did to crops. A.H.M.S. papers, C.T.S.

[23] W. Woolman, Aurora, Neb., Oct. 2, 1876, A.H.M.S. papers, C.T.S.

that the people are still very poor, in many instances poorer than when they first came, and really suffering for want of the comforts of life. . . . [24]

But still the people came, and in 1878 a correspondent to the *Home Missionary* wrote that the emigration to Nebraska was "perfectly tremendous." "Our railroads are crowded," he said; "our villages are overflowing with newcomers till they actually find it difficult to get places to sleep."[25]

In the southern and eastern parts of Dakota Territory, also a plains region, the home missionary was confronted with problems similar to those to be found in Kansas and Nebraska. So great was the rush of homeseekers into the region north of Nebraska and west of Minnesota that contemporary observers seemed to feel that even such adjectives as "amazing" and "stupendous" were hardly strong enough to do justice to the situation. The southeastern corner of Dakota, according to a missionary agent in 1882, was being settled at the rate of a thousand homesteads a day. "At a single land office," he said, "for two days in succession, a short time since, 16,000 acres were entered. Today, you drive your team over the broad prairies till you are out of sight of all human habitations. A few days more, and the railroad has come, and towns spring up in every direction."[26] In the following year the same man wrote:

> The rapid settlement of this Territory has no parallel in the history of the nation. Not far from 4,000,000 acres of land have been entered in all, and about two-thirds of this, by the most reliable accounts in Southeastern Dakota. 100,500 acres were entered at one land-office in a single day. During a portion of the season the average has been a thousand homestead entries a day—from 2,000 to 4,000 newcomers every twenty-four hours! Scores if not hundreds of new towns are springing up and the whole country has been under a big 'boom.' The trains on four trunk lines (which, with their intersections, make some 11,000 miles of road where, three years ago, there were only sixty miles,) have been crowded. . . . One hundred and thirty-seven new post-offices have been established.[27]

The success and fame of the Illinois Band, the Iowa Band, and the Kansas Band suggested that a similar plan

---

[24] W. A. Beecher, New Haven, Conn., Sept. 1, 1876 (filed with Nebraska letters), A.H.M.S. papers, C.T.S.

[25] *Home Missionary*, LI (1878), 15.

[26] S. Sheldon, in *Home Missionary*, LV (1882), 152, 207-08.

[27] S. Sheldon, in A.H.M.S., *Fifty-seventh Report* (1883), 90.

be tried in the Dakotas. The organization of the Dakota Band at Yale followed a visit to that territory one summer of a student, Mr. A. B. Case, of Illinois. Several members of his class in the seminary joined him in a decision to go to Dakota.[28] In the summer of 1881 the young bachelors of divinity took up their work at various towns in the territory.[29] In October of that year several of them came together at a little prairie station for the first time since they had parted under the Yale elms. Hours of waiting were before them until train time. The prairie stretched around them uninhabited. Feeling that they were unobserved, they cast aside the ministerial dignity which had so recently been put upon them; they talked and sang, and were college boys again. When application for half-fare ministerial tickets was made to the local ticket agent, who, unbeknown, had been watching them, he replied: "I may look awful green, but I ain't green enough yet to believe that fellers that has been carrying on as yous has, are ministers." When on the arrival of the local pastor the agent was assured that they were all preachers in good standing, he remarked: "It may be so, but they're the queerest lot of preachers that ever struck this Territory."[30] The youthful energy and enthusiasm of the members of the Band stood them in good stead as they made their way over the Dakota prairies, sometimes through blinding blizzards, to preach to the people and to plant churches. And they had their troubles. The land was new, most of the people poor, and all absorbed in making money. One of the Band wrote after a year in Dakota:

I lived in hotels for seven months. Every train brought such a crowd that I had neither study nor sleeping room to myself.... Every train brings to us land-hunters, and I am tired of listening to their plans. Every new specimen of them tells the people that he is coming here to live; is going to start a bank, or to start a twenty-thousand-dollar lumber yard, or to erect a mill, and so on. All mere lies, told to secure respect for themselves among the "natives."... Every Western pastor would greatly like to have the words of the Colorado brother

[28] American College and Education Society, *Seventh Annual Report* (1881), 14.

[29] W. H. Thrall went to Webster; J. R. Reitzel to Mitchell; A. B. Case to Madison; C. W. Shelton to Dell Rapids; P. E. Holp to Plankinton; W. B. Hubbard to Chamberlain. *Home Missionary*, LV (1882), 29-34.

[30] C. W. Shelton, in *Home Missionary*, LXXIII (1901), 192.

in *The Congregationalist* ... thundered in the ears of every minister
in the States whose people came West: "Wind up your church-
members so that they will not run down in crossing the Mississippi
River."[31]

AMERICAN HOME MISSIONARY SOCIETY ON THE LOGGING
FRONTIER

In the 1880's the northern parts of Michigan, Wisconsin,
and Minnesota also were busy frontier regions. The chief
economic interests there then were lumbering and mining.
As elsewhere in the West the people were absorbed in secular pursuits. "They talk business," complained one missionary, "till you are sick of it. Your ear grows weary of
pine land, mineral land, filings, entries and acres, corner-
lots, additions, plots, plans and contracts, building associations, loans, and interest. Or, in *mining,* of fee simple, ore
and docks, options, drills, pumps, shafts, and drifting."
The moral situation he described as appalling, and he made
the observation that since most of the inhabitants of the
new towns were young men, they were like college boys in
that they sometimes did things together that they would
not think of doing at home. "So common," he added, "are
the low amusements that I have been invited to smoke,
dance, play cards and drink."[32]

But if the new lumber camps and mining towns had all
the vices of Eastern cities, the isolated settlers in the little
clearings in the woods were living under conditions about
as simple as those that had characterized the backwoods of
Virginia and the Carolinas a century earlier. A missionary
in the Upper Peninsula of Michigan tells of an experience
with a couple who lived in "the most primitive log-house"
he ever saw:

But these people have great hearts—bigger than their houses.
When a brother minister was trying to find a place for me to stay, a
man said: "Let him come with me." "Have you room?" "Lots of it."
So I went. In a little clearing I found the most primitive log-house I
ever saw; but the "lots of room"—that was out-of-doors.... There
was only one room and one bed; but they took off the top of the
bedding and put one tick on the floor. "That's for me," I thought.
Not a bit of it. I was to have the place of honor. So, hanging some
sheets on strings stretched across the room, they soon partitioned

[31] P. E. Holp, in *Home Missionary*, LV (1882), 33.

[32] G. A. Hood, "The New North," in *Home Missionary*, LX (1887),
293-94.

off the bed for me. Then, after reading and prayers, the man said: "Now any time you are ready for bed, elder, you can take that bed." But how to get there? First I went out and gave them a chance; but they did not take it. I thought, perhaps they will go and give me a chance; but they did not. So I begun to disrobe. I took a long while taking off coat and vest; then slowly came to the collar and necktie; next came off my boots and stockings. Now, I thought, they will surely step out; but no; they talked and laughed away like two children. Slipping behind the sheet, and fancying I was in another room, I balanced myself as well as I could on the feather bed, and managed to get off the rest of my clothes, got into bed, and lay looking at the moonbeams as they glanced through the chinks of the logs and thinking of New England with her silk bed-quilts and bath-rooms, till, as I mused, sleep weighed down my drowsy eyelids, and New England mansions and Michigan log-huts melted into one; and they both became one Bethel with the angels of God ascending and descending. . . . [33]

NEW FIELDS ON PACIFIC COAST

On the Pacific Coast two new regions, southern California and Washington, were being opened by settlers, town builders, and other speculators about this same time. In gold-rush days and even until after the Civil War the northern and central parts of California had been the mecca for emigrants from all corners of the earth, while the southern end of the state had been left mainly to its Spanish-American population. After the War, and especially in the last two decades of the century, southern California came into prominence as a place for settlement, for pleasure, and for money-making. The old Spanish grants were split up into ten-acre tracts for fruit farms. The newly constructed railroads brought in tourists and excursionists, some of whom came to look but remained to praise. Everyone felt that the population was bound to grow because, among other reasons, in the words of the old Kansas farmer, "people are going to live where they can live warm."[34] Whether the Kansas—and Iowa—farmers who moved into southern California to get warm rented or sold their old farms in the Middle West, they usually had some savings to take with them. But even though southern California was not a typical frontier region, the Eastern societies regarded it as a missionary field. If for no other reason, denominational rivalries demanded that each try to plant and support its

---

[33] W. G. Puddefoot, in *Home Missionary*, LVI (1883), 321.
[34] *Home Missionary*, LX (1887), 215.

own type of church organization in all of the promising new towns.

The territory of Washington, which, because of the heavy stand of large trees, did not settle up so fast as Oregon, was still a frontier region as late as 1880. To it in 1890, the year following its admission to the Union, went six young men from the Yale Divinity School, who were loosely organized in the Washington Band.[35] They selected eastern Washington as their general field. Each took a church; from time to time they joined forces in evangelistic campaigns, all or part of them coming together for several days of special religious services at designated places. Fifteen such special meetings were held by the members of the Band during their first two years in Washington.[36]

AMERICAN HOME MISSIONARY SOCIETY IN OKLAHOMA

By the time Oklahoma was opened to settlement the officers of the various missionary societies were well aware of the importance of an early start in a new territory. Congregational missionaries did not participate in the first Oklahoma rush (April, 1889), but they were on the ground by August of that year. Within two years fifteen Congregational churches had been organized. However, when the time came for the greatest of all land rushes in our history, that into the Cherokee strip in September, 1893, at least six representatives of the American Home Missionary Society[37] participated in an effort to secure choice building lots for churches in the new towns.[38] Mr. W. C. McCune, who made "the run" to Pond Creek, relates his experiences in these words:

With my certificate I got aboard one of the cattle cars provided by the railroad to convey the home seekers into the Strip. At noon September 16th, the signal gun was fired and the train started. On

[35] The six members of this Band were: L. O. Baird, William Davies, G. E. Hooker, J. T. Nichols, S. B. L. Penrose, and Edward L. Smith.

[36] *Home Missionary*, LXIII (1890), 279-81; LXV (1893), 553; LXXIII (1901), 194-95.

[37] The change of name from American to Congregational Home Missionary Society took effect Oct. 1, 1893, *Home Missionary*, LXVI (1893), 333-34.

[38] Enid and Pond Creek on the Rock Island, Santa Fé and Perry on the Santa Fé, Woodward on the Kansas Southern, and Pawnee in the northeastern part of the Territory, *Home Missionary*, LXVI (1894), 453.

the right and left, as far as the eye could reach, were horsemen, and men and women in buggies, carriages, spring wagons, road wagons, and on bicycles, all making the highest possible speed to obtain a valuable corner lot or fertile quarter section in the "Strip." Some teams ran away, some vehicles broke down, and some exhausted horses lay down and died. Now and then some one with flag and hatchet, leaping from the moving train, would run and drive his flagged stake on a quarter section.

About 1.50 o'clock we reached Pond Creek, the county seat of "L" County, but the train never stopped; it only slowed up. With some 1200 or 1500 others, some of them women, and one of them with a babe in her arms, I jumped from the moving train.

The next forenoon (Sabbath), standing in a spring wagon in the public square in a blinding dust storm, I preached to an attentive audience, and have preached in Pond Creek regularly every Sabbath since.[39]

On the same afternoon Mr. R. T. Marlow staked out a claim for Congregationalism in the town of Perry. In his report he said:

... The first Sabbath after the opening the wind blew a gale, and the dust formed impenetrable clouds, driving into the skin and blinding the eyes. There was no possible chance to speak to the people. But the second Sabbath Brother Platt, our worthy superintendent of Sunday-school work in the Territory, and myself held meetings in the forenoon and in the afternoon. Congregationalists have the honor of doing the first missionary work in Perry, and we did it from a lumber pile in the street. Three other Sabbaths I either preached on street corners or in unfurnished store buildings. Then Brother Parker ... sent me a large tent, sixty by forty feet, which I erected on a vacant lot, and the wild wind leveled it with the ground. As it lay prostrate that night, some thief stole the wall canvas, and cut enough off one end to make a good-sized tent. Then I went to one of our lumbermen, who generously gave enough lumber to make a wall five feet high and a room thirty by forty. This I built, and covered it with the canvas left by the thief. Here we organized the First Congregational Church of Perry, and the first church of any order....[40]

Oklahoma was a country of sharp contrasts. Almost overnight the towns acquired the signs of well-developed urban life—banks, newspapers, brick and stone store buildings with plate-glass fronts, and electric lights. A few miles out in the country the people were living in sod houses, or tents, or shacks with canvas roofs. The poverty of the people in the country, their hardships, and their hunger for

[39] *Home Missionary*, LXVI (1894), 472-73.
[40] *Home Missionary*, LXVI (1894), 465-66.

preaching were touchingly described by an agent of the Congregational Home Missionary Society who made a tour through the Territory in 1895. After having told about interesting sights and experiences on the trains and in some of the new towns, he wrote:

Our next trip was 100 miles westward in the strip. After riding about twenty miles we helped dedicate a new church. The little building stood out on the prairie all alone, the farmhouses being scattered a half-mile from each other. I thought, There won't be much of a turn-out here; but hot as it was the church was packed; the wagon seats and all the chairs for miles were brought in and filled. The communion season was touching. The people were very poor, but woman's hands here lit up the poverty of the little deal table with wreaths of wild flowers. The wine was in an old catchup bottle, and two common tumblers and an old plate was all their table furniture.

Next came another dedication, fourteen miles farther on. The church stood on a hill—nothing else in sight but a blacksmith's shop, opened two days in the week, a little grocery, and one house.... After tea I said to myself, There won't be much of a crowd here; but I was wrong again. By eight o'clock I saw people coming from all directions, as they came in Ian Maclaren's "The Mourning in the Glen." Why, I said, they seem to be coming out of the ground, as I saw their forms gradually rising above the horizon. "Well," said the man, "most of them are."... Never had I seen people so hungry for the Gospel.... Women wept—and so did strong men—as the old hymns were sung, and fond memories came up of home and mother. Oh the loneliness of these prairie homes, hundreds of them without the common necessaries of life, even such as flour and milk! Men were cutting wood and carrying it twenty miles for fifty cents, and sometimes having to beg for it at that.... I met faces in these audiences I shall never forget. They haunt me. Soul-hungry, and many of them, alas! body-hungry too. ... Others showed signs of better times long ago—the old silk dress well kept, a hat many seasons out of style; but a respectable face bright and happy today, for they had come with the multitude to the house of God to keep holy day....

Never was there a more truly Macedonian cry going up than that which comes from the lonely sod houses and dugouts of Oklahoma. Thousands of these people were poor when they came, after battling with drought for years in western Kansas and other states. They came because, as they said, they could not be worse off.... [41]

DENOMINATIONAL COMITY

One phase of home missionary activity to which an increasing amount of thought was given in the period after the Civil War was the duplication of effort and the planting of many small churches in the same community by the vari-

[41] W. G. Puddefoot, "An Oklahoma Trip," in *Home Missionary*, LXVIII (1895), 288-91.

ous denominations.[42] Each of the great national churches naturally felt that its existence was justified, that it had the Truth, and that it ought to do everything within its power to establish local congregations in as many places as possible in the West. The result oftentimes was to divide the religious forces of a community to such an extent that no one of the churches could expect soon to attain to a position of independence. There would thus be an unending demand for Eastern money to support home mission churches in the West. The first attempt at a solution, after the failure of the Plan of Union (1801-52), seems to have come from the Congregationalists and the Presbyterians, who, in spite of many disputes, probably had more in common than any other two of the major Protestant denominations. In 1874 the secretaries of the Presbyterian Board of Missions and the American Home Missionary Society adopted a statement in favor of co-operation. After reciting the evils of unnecessary competition, they made the following plea:

... We therefore most earnestly recommend to all Presbyterians and all Congregationalists, especially to all our brethren in the ministry, and more particularly to all missionaries, ... to study first of all the things that make for peace; ... to be careful so as to advise and act with respect to all unorganized communities that, if possible, there may be but one strong and harmonious church organization at first, whether it be Congregational or Presbyterian; to avoid the wicked waste of funds in the support of two feeble churches, both of which must be weak, and which might become involved in bitter, protracted and unholy strife.... [43]

In 1892 an effort was made to secure a conference of representatives of the Methodist, Baptist, Episcopal, Reformed, Presbyterian, and Congregational home missionary organizations with a view to adopting such methods of common action as would avoid unwise duplication of evangelical churches on missionary ground. The conference was attended by members of the Presbyterian, Congregational, and Reformed churches, the others having declined to participate. A statement of principles similar to those of 1874

---

[42] J. Scotford wrote from Louisville, Kan., March 1, 1877: "... in our small villages here, three or four different sects will erect each its separate standard ... where there is not room for more than one good church,—the effect is jealousies—with a loss of brotherly love and fellowship, and so a loss of moral power for good on all sides." A.H.M.S. papers, C.T.S.

[43] *Home Missionary*, XLVII (1874), 162.

was announced, and committees of conference were provided to deal with specific conflicts as they arose in the field. The American Home Missionary Society announced that its invariable rule was "not to plant a Congregational Church, or mission, on ground which, in the proper sense of the word, is cared for by other evangelical denominations."[44] There might be a difference of opinion as to when that point had been reached, but, of course, the Society was free to make its own decision. Some possible contingencies were considered by the officers of this organization. Suppose there were already an Episcopal Church in a given place; should one of the Congregational order be established? Yes, answered the Congregational Society, if it were a growing community, because it was impossible to work out a union service that would satisfy those who liked and those who disliked a liturgical order of worship. What about Baptists? Union presented no great difficulties until Communion Sunday came around, but then a gulf as wide as that between the East and West opened up; the Baptists would insist that only those who had been baptized by immersion might partake, while Congregationalists would regard that attitude as illiberal and unchristian. Was union with Methodists feasible? Perhaps, but the Methodists would not find in the quiet and orderly devotional exercises of the Congregationalists the means of grace their souls craved, while the New England-born Congregationalists would chafe in spirit against the extravagancies of Methodist worship, especially as they appeared in many western communities. The conclusion was that there was no common ground of union as a permanent arrangement between Congregationalists and Episcopalians, Baptists, or Methodists. However, in a small community where there was no prospect that two or more churches could be supported, a union of divergent elements might be both wise and necessary. But in a growing community where there was a fair assurance of future strength the American Home Missionary Society regarded it as its business "to plant Congregational Churches where they will live and grow to self-support, illustrating to coming times the Gospel of Christ and that peculiar pattern of the Gospel which the Pilgrims brought to New England. For this its funds are given, that all over the country, wherever needed,

---

[44] *Home Missionary*, LXV (1892), 366.

the Congregational Church may rise, whether alone or by the side of other churches, without rivalry and without weakness to them; may rise with such help of ours as shall be needed for a while, and then stand alone for all coming time, testifying to the grace of God and to that faith and polity which first conquered America, and which we believe essential to its future well-being."[45] As already explained, relations between Congregationalists and Presbyterians, were on a somewhat different basis; similiarities in theology and methods of worship furnished a basis for union or at least co-operation on the mission field. In spite of strong denominational loyalties efforts were made to avoid conflicts. An analysis of 2100 mission fields occupied by one or both of these two denominations indicated that in only 133 cases, or six per cent, were both churches present. In 91 of these 133 fields there was a population ranging from 2500 to 25,000, and, presumably in towns of that size there was room for both.[46] The comity arrangements with the Presbyterians did not always work out, however, and the reports of missionaries and even the columns of the church papers occasionally contain charges of unwarranted intrusion.

In conclusion of the discussion at this point (1892), the American Home Missionary Society declared its readiness to enter into any arrangement with other missionary societies "for the promotion of a true inter-denominational comity whereby the waste of consecrated gifts may be stopped, our broad missionary field may be equitably divided and the unholy strife of sects may cease."[47]

THE PRESBYTERIANS

By 1861 what had been in 1837 the main body of Presbyterians in the United States had split into four factions— Old School North, Old School South, New School North, and New School South. The division into Old School and New School had come in 1837; shortly before the Civil War the slavery question became so acute as to result in the separation of the New School group into its Northern and Southern elements; in 1861 the Southern Presbyterians in the Old School withdrew and set up their own Church, because the

---

45 *Home Missionary*, LXV (1892), 368.

46 *Ibid.*, 369.

47 *Ibid.*, 370.

General Assembly of that year had made a declaration of loyalty to the Union and the Constitution of the United States. The antagonism created by the conflict between North and South was so great and the bonds of union between comrades in arms so strong that new alignments took place during and shortly after the War. Old and New School South now discovered that they had so much in common that they could unite, which they did in 1864; Old and New School North now felt that the "vital" differences which had led to division in 1837 were not so important as they had then appeared, so they came together in 1870.

One of the reasons for the division into Old and New School in 1837 had been the desire of the New School party to conduct home missionary work through the voluntary American Home Missionary Society in conjunction with the Congregationalists. When the Civil War ended, that bone of contention had been buried for several years. In 1861 the New School North withdrew from this union society and set up their own denominational Committee of Home Missions, thus admitting tacitly the superior wisdom on that point of their more conservative brethren. The union of the Northern Old and New Schools resulted in the merging of the Old School Board of Domestic Missions and the New School Committee of Home Missions in a new Board of Home Missions. The result of this was not only economy in administration and the elimination of a certain amount of unwholesome competition, but also the growth of a new interest in missions. The united Northern Presbyterians faced the task of carrying the gospel to the frontiers with new zeal and hope. The combined contributions of the two branches for home missions in 1869, the last year of division, had been $347,000; in 1872 the amount given by the reunited Church passed the four-hundred-thousand-dollar mark; in 1875, it exceeded half a million dollars. Then followed several lean years, a time of slow recovery from the panic of 1873. About 1880 the receipts began to mount again, exceeding six hundred thousand dollars in 1884, eight hundred thousand in 1888, and a million dollars in 1893. In volume of contributions for home missions the Northern Presbyterians took first place among the Protestant churches.[48]

---

[48] H. C. Weber, *Presbyterian Statistics* (n.p., 1927), 15-25.

THE EPISCOPALIANS

Missionary bishops, as has already been pointed out, were largely instrumental in the introduction of the Episcopal Church into the trans-Mississippi West and in the enhancement of its prestige there. The roll of missionary bishops is a list of honor, but the scope of this study does not permit the recording of their names or the summarizing of their achievements. They were necessarily men of affairs as well as spiritual leaders. Although they varied greatly in their methods, their problems were essentially the same. Some, of whom Bishop Leigh R. Brewer of Montana may be taken as an example, conceived of their mission as primarily spiritual. Bishop Brewer regarded himself as the chief missionary of his diocese and he announced that, valuable as were schools, hospitals, and church buildings, he would not assume responsibility for their erection. In other words, he did not intend to allow material concerns to divert his attention from what he regarded as his principal function—preaching the gospel himself and finding others to preach it in his diocese.[49] Others, of whom Bishop Alexander Garrett of northern Texas may be taken as a type, regarded it as their function to "lay foundations"—to establish schools, erect churches, organize parishes, quite as much as to provide preaching. Indeed, Bishop Garrett went so far as to suggest that it would be better to spend money on church schools than on missionary preachers—"men of the wandering foot."[50]

Although a particular bishop might stress either the temporal or the spiritual phase of his work, he was necessarily expected to be a leader in both. Ordinarily he went in advance of his Church. When he entered his diocese there might not be a single Episcopal Church in it. With regard to his own financial support he was relieved from care because that was paid by the Board of Missions; in addition he had an appropriation from the Board which he could spend as he pleased for missionary service. One of his first tasks was to find the Churchmen in his diocese and those friendly to the Episcopal Church, to organize them in local congregations, and to find ministers for them, pledging to the minister as much of a small appropriation at his disposal

---

[49] *Spirit of Missions*, LI (1886), 410.
[50] *Spirit of Missions*, XLIX (1884), 560.

as seemed wise or necessary. And the minister must be suited to the field if he were to succeed. Once Bishop Garrett, as he thought of the vast region of the Panhandle of Texas into which no missionary of his Church had ever gone, cried out: "Oh, for a man who can ride like a cow-boy, pray like a saint, preach like an apostle, and having food and raiment be therewith content."[51] Once the local congregation was organized, it required supervision; and from time to time the Bishop was expected to visit it. Communities where there was no Episcopal Church were also visited by the missionary bishop, who ministered to the spiritual needs of the people, married them, baptized the children, and buried the dead. Usually he was also interested in the establishment of an academy, a college, or a seminary within his diocese; he might help found a hospital; and he would be expected to help raise money for church buildings. Ordinarily much of the money for schools and similar institutions had to be obtained in the East. If the bishop concerned himself with such matters he might be compelled to spend several months each year in the East, interviewing prospective benefactors or addressing gatherings of people on the West and its needs. Unfortunately there was a tendency among some to judge the bishop's success by his skill in raising money.

On the whole the Episcopal Church was fortunate in its missionary bishops, both in respect to the system itself and in the incumbents of the office. Other denominations had missionary superintendents or agents who did many of the things a missionary bishop did, but they lacked the prestige that went with the bishop's title and robes. His position guaranteed to him a respectful hearing, and curiosity, if nothing else, would ordinarily secure for him an audience. His visit to a frontier community usually attracted wide attention.[52]

---

[51] *Spirit of Missions*, XLIX (1884), 562.

[52] Bishop Ethelbert Talbot, whose diocese included Wyoming and Idaho, says that once when he visited Wallace, a new mining camp in the Coeur d'Alene country, he was handed a large green circular which had been widely distributed and was posted on stumps, logs, and shacks in every direction. It read as follows: "The Bishop is coming. Let all turn out and hear the Bishop. Services in George and Human's Hall to-morrow, Sunday, at 11 A. M. and 8 P. M. Please leave your guns with the usher." E. Talbot, *My People of the Plains* (New York, 1906), 87-88.

THE BAPTISTS

Among the Baptists home missionary work during and after the Civil War was prosecuted by both the Northern and Southern branches, and occasionally both tried to gain a foothold in the same community.[53] In 1859 the Southern Baptist Convention had in its employ 104 missionaries who were distributed through all the Southern and Southwestern states, including California. One effect of the War was to disrupt this work; from 1861 to 1865 the emphasis was placed by Southern Baptists on Confederate Army missions. After the War home missionary work was revived but was conducted on a small scale until the eighties. After 1882, as the reconstruction period was drawing to a close, there came a time of more rapid development. In 1892 it was reported that in the preceding ten years more had been accomplished in Southern Baptist Home Missions than in the whole thirty-seven years of the previous history of the Convention. Texas and Florida, and later Oklahoma and New Mexico, were among the fields occupied by the representatives of this denomination.[54]

The Northern Baptists, drawing their support from a more prosperous part of the country, had more money to spend for missions. The income of the American Baptist Home Mission Society in 1860 was about $45,000; it exceeded $100,000 in 1866, and $200,000 in 1873. Then for several years the effects of economic depression were reflected in materially lowered receipts. In 1882, the fiftieth anniversary of the founding of the Society, more than $300,000 was contributed for the cause. The number of missionaries was also increasing; there were 281 on the list of the American Baptist Home Mission Society in 1880, 695 in 1885, and 1053 in 1892.[55]

As was true of the other societies during the same period an effort was made to follow the frontiersmen and especially to occupy strategic places in the new states and territories. For example, in accordance with this policy,

---

[53] See, for example, A.B.H.M.S., *Seventy-seventh Report* (1909), 18-19, for comments on the conflicts between the Baptists North and South in mission fields in New Mexico.

[54] M. E. Wright, *Missionary Work of the Southern Baptist Convention* (Philadelphia, [1902]), 292-310.

[55] *Baptist Home Mission Monthly,* VIII (1886), 1-7; *ibid.,* IX (1887), 183; A.B.H.M.S., *Sixtieth Report* (1892), 36-37.

it was reported in 1882 that the Northern Baptist missionaries had just occupied the following towns: Grand Forks, Jamestown, Bismarck, and Mandan in Upper or North Dakota; Miles City and Butte City in Montana; El Paso, Ysleta, and Laredo in Texas; Tucson in Arizona; Boise City in Idaho; and Los Angeles in California.[56] Wherever possible the Society worked in co-operation with the local state conventions. By such an arrangement, which was in keeping with the traditional Baptist dislike for excessive centralization, the Mission Board was relieved of many details in the supervision of missionaries, self-help was encouraged in the states, while the resources and strength of the national society gave steadiness to missionary enterprises.[57] In order to spread a small amount of money and to distribute a limited number of men over as large a territory as possible, extensive use was made by the Baptists of "general missionaries," men who roved over large sections of frontier states and territories somewhat after the fashion of the Methodist itinerants. One of these exploring agents, as they were sometimes called, had a parish sixty miles long out on the Great Plains. These men, who prepared the way for settled pastors, were likened by one writer to "living shuttles in the loom of frontier life, moving hither and thither all along the advancing borders of civilization, introducing into the former texture of society, of morals, and of religion, the strong white linen cords of Gospel righteousness."[58]

In 1877 two home missionary societies for Baptist women were organized. The Women's Baptist Home Mission Society, with offices in Chicago, emphasized evangelism;[59] the Woman's American Baptist Home Mission Society, with headquarters in Boston, paid especial attention to education. For more than thirty years the two societies worked independently; in 1909 they were united as the Woman's Baptist Home Mission Society.[60]

---

[56] A.B.H.M.S., *Fiftieth Report* (1882), 50.

[57] *Ibid.*, 48.

[58] A.B.H.M.S., *Fifty-first Report* (1883), 37.

[59] A.B.H.M.S., *Forty-fifth Report* (1877), 24.

[60] A.B.H.M.S., *Seventy-seventh Report* (1909), 33; B. G. Judd, *Fifty Golden Years* (New York, c. 1927), 252.

THE CHANGING NATURE OF HOME MISSIONS

In 1890 the Superintendent of the Census announced that the frontier of settlement had practically disappeared. The unsettled area had been so broken into by isolated bodies of settlement that there could hardly be said to be a frontier line any longer. "This brief official statement," wrote the late Professor Frederick J. Turner, "marks the closing of a great historic movement. Up to our own day American history has been in large degree the history of the colonization of the Great West."[61] With the passing of the frontier the story of home missions on the frontier naturally comes to an end. The home missionary movement continued, but the problems and methods changed. First of all, the various societies began to realize that in their haste and competition they had planted too many small churches in some parts of the West; they began to work out comity arrangements, such as the division of the field or priority agreements. In the second place, the great city with its large unassimilated alien population now presented the main challenge to the home missionary. Furthermore, the magnitude of the problem of Christian work and education among the Negroes of the South was being more fully appreciated than ever before. Up to 1880 home missions had meant largely the relatively simple but important task of following American families as they moved from the East into the successive Wests and of aiding them in the establishment and maintenance of the institutions of religion. After 1880 home missions came to mean more and more city missions, missions for the foreign-born, and support for weak churches in all parts of the country. There was still the West, but now an erstwhile mission church "way out West" might make its contribution to the support of a mission in East Side New York—perhaps the money might even go to help pay the preacher in a region of abandoned farms in New England! If and when such gifts came from the West, some church was only paying off a part of its debt.

---

[61] F. J. Turner, *Frontier in American History* (New York, 1920), 1.

CHAPTER XII

HOME MISSIONS AND EDUCATION

After God had carried us safe to New-England, and wee had builded our houses, provided necessaries for our livelihood, rear'd convenient places for God's worship, and setled the Civill Government: One of the next things we longed for, and we looked after was to advance learning and perpetuate it to Posterity; dreading to leave an illiterate Ministry to the Churches, when our present Ministers shall lie in the Dust. —*New England's First Fruits.*

*I*N THE COLONIAL PERIOD religion had been the dominant motive in education. Even under Calvinistic theology the responsibility for the welfare of a man's soul rested upon the man himself, and it was his duty to go directly to the source of authority, the Bible, for instruction and guidance. To do this he must be able to read. It is probably more than a coincidence that of all the countries of Europe in the eighteenth century, Scotland, the stronghold of Presbyterianism, was the most literate. The first generation of Puritan clergy in New England were men who had been trained in the great English universities. In order that an educated ministry might be prepared to take their places in the new land a college was necessary. And so Harvard College was founded in 1636. Similarly, the ministers who met at New Haven in 1700 and agreed to establish a college there were moved by a desire to uphold their faith by a succession of learned and orthodox preachers. Likewise, the College of New Jersey, or Princeton, was founded by the Synod of New York for the purpose of supplying the Presbyterian churches of the colonies with educated and able clerics.

As religious zeal declined in the eighteenth century and ministerial authority grew weaker, education deteriorated also. An educational revival began in the East after the War of 1812, but the religious motive, once so powerful, had been largely supplanted by new impulses resulting from the industrial revolution with its growth of cities and fac-

tories, from the extension of suffrage, from humanitarianism, and from the nascent labor movement.[1] In the West, however, and among Eastern men interested in the religious development of the West, religion continued to be a strong motive in education. Just as seventeenth-century Puritans had founded Harvard College in order that an educated ministry might be created in New England, so the missionaries in the West in the nineteenth century founded colleges in order that young men from the West might be trained on the ground for service in the Western churches. In no other way could there be obtained either a sufficient supply of ministers or men so well adapted to the work. Many Easterners who contributed to the advancement of education in the West did it from a religious motive. The same spirit which led them to send preachers to the West moved them to send schoolteachers or to give money to found colleges. Teachers and schools stand alongside preachers and churches as agencies of control.

FEAR OF THE CATHOLICS

The growth of Roman Catholicism was just as much an incentive for the establishment of Protestant schools and colleges in the West as for the erection of Protestant churches. The educational activities of the Catholics in the West were a challenge to Protestantism. The schools in the West conducted by the Catholics, mainly primary schools and academies, were numerous. The children of Protestant parents frequently attended them either because there was no other school available or because of their excellence. More than one half of the students of the College of St. Francis Xavier in Cincinnati in 1843 were of Protestant parentage.[2] Indeed, according to some Protestant alarmists, the Catholic schools were built for no other purpose than the instruction of Protestant children,[3] because, they said,

---

[1] F. T. Carlton, *Economic Influences upon Educational Progress in the United States, 1820-1850* (Madison, 1908), 18-44; E. C. Moore, *Fifty Years of American Education* (Boston, [1917]), 12-13.

[2] Bishop Purcell to Conseil Central de Lyon in *Annal. de l'Asso. de la Prop. de la Foi*, XV, 366; cf. M. Rese, N. Y., May 20, 1832, *ibid.*, VI, 182.

[3] J. R. Barnes, Evansville, Ind., May 3, 1842, wrote that he intended to start a good female seminary since the Catholics had the entire control of all the schools for females in the vicinity and held out every inducement to get Protestants in their schools; "and they succeed to an alarming extent," he added. A.H.M.S. papers, C.T.S.

there was no demand for education among the ignorant constituency of the Roman Church. Protestant periodicals kept their readers informed about the spread of "Papist schools." The *Home Missionary* for April, 1842, gave a detailed statement of the number and size of the schools, academies, and orphan asylums in the West conducted by the Catholic Church. In the Diocese of Detroit, which comprised Michigan and Wisconsin, there were eleven such institutions. In addition to the college conducted by the Jesuits in Cincinnati, to which reference has already been made, there was in that city an academy of the Sisters of Notre Dame. Three schools were listed in the Diocese of Vincennes. In the Diocese of Dubuque there were academies for boys at Davenport and similar institutions for girls at Dubuque and Burlington. A summary of Catholic educational forces in these and other Western and Southern dioceses showed that there were twenty-three institutions for boys and men, and thirty-four for girls and women, besides many orphan asylums; in the higher seminaries there were nearly three thousand students.[4] Another well-known Catholic school in the West was Sinsinawa Mound College, which was founded about 1846 by Father Mazzuchelli, an Italian who had come to America to engage in missionary work among the Indians; his interest in education was shown by the fact that he always erected a schoolhouse in connection with the twenty-five or more churches he established.[5]

Sinister motives were frequently attributed to these laudable efforts in behalf of education. The teachers were referred to as "Jesuits," and no doubt many of them did belong to the order that has concerned itself especially with education. The notion that there was a Catholic plot against the United States bobbed up again. In 1847 a Boston clergyman made an address in which he quoted the words of a Catholic who was reported to have said: "Our plan is to build schoolhouses, academies and colleges, and place in these institutions first-rate men. *We mean to take the coun-*

---

[4] *Home Missionary*, XIV (1842), 278-82.

[5] J. D. Butler, "Fr. Samuel Mazzuchelli," in *Wisconsin Historical Collections*, XIV (1898), 155-56. J. C. Holbrook, Dubuque, Iowa, June 22, 1846, complained about the "popish" lack of regard for the Sabbath, since that was the day selected for the laying of the cornerstone of the college. "A vast concourse of spectators assembled, cannons were fired, ... refreshments were served." A.H.M.S. papers, C.T.S.

try by seizing on the rising population."[6] The great attention paid by Catholics to the education of girls was a matter for comment; by some it was interpreted as an insidious attempt to give future generations of Americans "Romish mothers."[7] A typical statement of such fears was made by the learned Leonard Bacon who said: "To us then the Jesuit comes, as the teacher—the educator—the man of learning, smooth, polished, accomplished, gliding with sinuous motion to what he, with the wisdom of the serpent, recognizes as the true seat of power in such a country."[8] It was his conclusion that the best means of defense was to found better schools and colleges than the Jesuits could establish.

MINISTERIAL EDUCATION

It is evident then that the relationship between the home missionary movement and education has been exceedingly close. Early in the nineteenth century this relationship was indicated clearly by the formation in the East of societies, both local and national, designed to assist young men in the preparation for the ministry. From the point of view of men trained in the Eastern colleges and seminaries, there was an appalling dearth of educated ministers in the United States. According to one estimate made in 1818 there were then in this country only about twenty-five hundred educated ministers, or one out of thirty-six hundred souls. In contrast to this it was pointed out that in New England in the middle of the eighteenth century the ratio had been one liberally educated minister to 628 persons.[9] The writer of this report, of course, did not recognize as "educated" the thousands of Baptist preachers and Methodist circuit riders in the West and South; otherwise he would not have stated that in the states and territories then comprising the frontier there were not more than seventeen "competent and stated"

---

[6] J. H. Towne, in *First Report of the Ladies' Society for Promoting Education at the West* (1847), 29.

[7] Cf. E. Beecher, "Address," in *History of the Formation of the Ladies' Society for the Promotion of Education at the West* (Boston, 1846), 7-9; J. Dixon, *Personal Narrative of a Tour through a Part of the United States and Canada* (3rd ed., New York, 1850), 383-84.

[8] L. Bacon, "Address," in *Second Report of the Society for the Promotion of Collegiate and Theological Education at the West* (1845), 23.

[9] American Society for Educating Pious Youth, *Third Report* (1818), 11.

preachers of the gospel for a population of 350,000. Even if
one assumed, as this writer apparently did, that only Presbyterian and Congregational preachers were "educated," the
figures he gave were inaccurate; but a much more serious
error was involved in his assumption that only a man who
had a particular kind of training was fitted to be a spiritual
leader. The acceptance of an uneducated ministry probably
made it easier for charlatans to acquire a following, but if
the West had been forced to wait for salvation until ministers bearing college diplomas appeared, its chance of salvation would have been very slight.

Attention was also called to the fact that fewer educated
men were entering the ministry than formerly. From college catalogues it appeared that before 1720 more than half
of the graduates became ministers; from 1720 to 1770 one
out of three went into the ministry; between 1770 and 1810,
one out of five, while between 1800 and 1810 the ratio was
one to six.[10] To remedy this state of affairs efforts were
made to help pious young men obtain a ministerial education.
The connection between this and missions is obvious—a
plentiful supply of preachers would make it easier to get
missionaries; more ministers in the East would presumably
result in more converts, and the latter might be expected
to give more money to support missions.

During the year 1815 two small societies were formed in
Boston to help young men prepare for the ministry. The
interest in the work grew, and a call was issued by Jedidiah
Morse, father of the author of the "Brutus Letters"[11] and
pastor of the First Congregational Church in Charlestown,
for a meeting to consider the formation of a general education society. This preliminary meeting was held in the Park
Street Church,[12] center of Congregational orthodoxy and
missionary zeal for Boston, in July, 1815. At the same place
a month later a constitution was adopted for the new organization which was to be known as the American Society

---

[10] American Society for Educating Pious Youth, *Third Report*
(1818), 11.

[11] See above, page 224.

[12] For the origin of the Park Street Church and its connection
with the reform, benevolent, and missionary movements of the nineteenth century, see *Semi-Centennial Celebration of Park Street Church*
(Boston, 1861), 132-34; and *Preservation of Park Street Church*
(Boston, 1903), 7-9.

for Educating Pious Youth for the Gospel Ministry.[13] The American Education Society, as it was soon called, was intended to be national in scope and sufficiently catholic in principle to embrace the standard, orthodox Protestant sects, but practically all of its funds came from Congregationalists and Presbyterians, and its beneficiaries were usually men who were preparing for the ministry of one or the other of these churches. Inasmuch as it was a voluntary society not under direct ecclesiastical control, it fell, along with the American Home Missionary Society, under the disapprobation of the conservative wing of the Presbyterian Church, and was one of the causes of the disruption of that body in 1837.

The Old School Presbyterians gave their support to the General Assembly's Board of Education, which was formally organized in May, 1819. Within the next fifteen years at least four other similar societies were formed, such as the Baptist Education Society of New York, the Northern Baptist Education Society, the Education Society of the Protestant Episcopal Church, and the Connecticut Church Scholarship Society; their methods and objects were similar to those of the American Education Society, except that they were the agencies of particular denominations.

Another illustration of the close relationship between ministerial education and home missions appears in connection with the founding of the Chicago Theological Seminary by the Congregationalists in 1855. While on the one hand this action reflected the growing feeling of denominational loyalty among Congregationalists as they began to diverge more and more from their New School Presbyterian associates in the West, on the other hand it showed some of the results of the home missionary movement since the impetus came largely from the home mission churches that had but recently been planted in the Northwest. "Who have established this seminary; already so vigorous and promising," asked a contemporary, "who but the churches fathered and nourished by our noble Home Missionary Society?"[14]

---

[13] American Education Society, *Eighteenth Report* (1834), 71; *Twentieth Report* (1836), 71.

[14] H. N. Eggleston, "Chicago Theological Seminary," in *The New Englander*, XVII 1859), 356.

PRIMARY AND SECONDARY EDUCATION

Of the more important Protestant denominations it seems that the Congregationalists, the Presbyterians, and the Episcopalians maintained throughout the first half of the nineteenth century the highest standards for the education of their clergy. Their missionaries were naturally much concerned about the lack of satisfactory educational advantages in the West and were often active in improving conditions. Their reports contain frequent references to the crying needs for books and schools in the new settlements. Messrs. Mills and Smith, representatives of the Massachusetts Missionary Society, writing from the Mississippi River below New Madrid, Missouri, in 1815 said:

> This country is almost wholly new ground. Many institutions that conduce to the benefit of Society, and to the advancement of religion, are not yet established. Much good might be done by exerting an influence in favour of schools, and of the education of children. An inhabitant of the Eastern States can have no adequate conception of the want of schools in this country. It is very common to find men of considerable property, whose children cannot read a word.[15]

The Reverend John M. Ellis, writing from Kaskaskia, Illinois, in 1826 to the Secretary of the American Home Missionary Society, said:

> You can have little hope of seeing a radical, permanent change in the character of the people . . . without giving them a taste for reading and the means of improving it. This you know cannot be done without books—but books they have not. I speak now of the vast majority— when they came to this country they were careless of preserving what books they had. . . . All or most that is done for several years in the way of establishing libraries—or furnishing the opportunity of reading —must be done by the beneficence of our eastern friends—for I have before said that though there is corn enough & meat enough, yet there is almost no money among the people generally. Thus their children do not learn to read. . . . Besides I am fully convinced that the profanation of the Sabbath will not cease until employment can be given to the mind, that is, by reading. But while the Sabbath is profaned as it is now, a most heart sickening and deadly obstacle will lie in the way of the success of your missionaries. . . .[16]

Concerning the frontier of 1820-30, which in this respect was typical of the whole, Professor Frederick Jackson Tur-

---

[15] Mills and Smith, *Report of a Missionary Tour*, 20.

[16] John M. Ellis, Kaskaskia, Ill., Aug. 7, 1826, in C.H.M.S. (box 1, bundle 1); I have not found this letter in A.H.M.S. papers, C.T.S.

ner has said: "The West was too new a section to have developed educational facilities to any large extent. The pioneers' poverty, as well as the traditions of the southern interior from which they so largely came, discouraged extensive expenditures for public schools."[17] The settlers on the frontiers were generally comparatively young people with large families; hence schools were greatly needed. Obviously the missionary had boundless opportunities in the field of education.

The services rendered were various, sometimes direct, sometimes indirect. Some missionaries taught school, although the American Home Missionary Society discouraged this on the ground that its representatives should give all of their time to religious work. Some were put in positions of responsibility in the West and helped mold the educational systems of new territories or states. To John D. Pierce, who went to Michigan in 1831 under the auspices of the American Home Missionary Society, was entrusted in 1836 the task of organizing the public-school system of that new state. Through his influence the control of the school lands was taken from the townships and given to the state; as Superintendent of Public Instruction he vetoed a plan, thoroughly in keeping with the speculative spirit of the time, to spend half a million dollars for the first building of the University of Michigan, because of his fear that so large an expenditure of money for buildings at that time would cripple the academic work of the new college.[18] In Indiana Caleb Mills of Wabash College probably did more than any other man to put the public-school system of that state on a sound basis. Through his addresses to the State Legislature and to the Constitutional Convention of 1851 he aroused interest in an improved school system, and later as Superintendent of Public Instruction he did much to introduce such reforms as the use of better textbooks, normal schools to train teachers, and increased expenditures for schools.[19] In Illinois likewise home missionaries rendered

17 F. J. Turner, "The Colonization of the West," in *American Historical Review*, XI (1906), 326.

18 C. O. Hoyt and R. C. Ford, *John D. Pierce Founder of the Michigan School System* (Ypsilanti, 1905), 66-86.

19 J. F. Tuttle, "Caleb Mills and the Indiana Common Schools," in C. W. Moores, "Caleb Mills and the Indiana School System," in *Indiana Historical Society Publications*, III (Indianapolis, 1905), 380-96.

valuable services to the cause of public education; Professor J. B. Turner of Illinois College traveled through that state in the interest of public schools, and at Jacksonville *The Common School Advocate* was published in 1837.[20] The list of missionaries who rendered notable services to the cause of education in their several states and communities might be continued indefinitely; enough has been said to indicate their interest in the public school.

SCHOOLTEACHERS FOR THE WEST

One of the difficulties in establishing good schools in the West was the lack of competent teachers. To meet this need societies were formed in the East for the purpose of sending teachers to the West. To Catherine Beecher, distinguished daughter of a distinguished family, belongs the credit for inaugurating this movement. On account of the prominence of her father, Lyman Beecher, her own books and lectures on the subject of education for women,[21] and her share in the establishment of the Western Female Institute in Cincinnati, she was a national figure. At the same time that she received letters from people in the West asking if she could recommend schoolteachers to them, she received other letters from women in New England who wanted her to help them find schools in the West. It occurred to her that a society should be created to do what she had been doing informally. She made a journey through New England in which she discussed the matter with many men and women interested in educational and missionary activities in the West, and she published anonymously in 1845 a book entitled *The Duty of American Women to their Country*. One of the results of the publication of this small volume, which called attention to the great need for schools and teachers in the West, was the establishment in Boston of the Ladies' Society for the Promotion of Education at the West.[22]

---

[20] M. T. Carriel, *Life of Jonathan Baldwin Turner* (n.p., 1911), 70-73; C. P. Kofoid, "Puritan Influences in the Formative Years of Illinois History," in *Transactions of the Illinois Historical Society* (1905), 332.

[21] C. E. Beecher, *Essay on the Education of Female Teachers* (New York, 1835).

[22] C. E. Beecher, *True Remedy for the Wrongs of Woman* (Boston, 1851), 96-100; C. E. Beecher, *Educational Reminiscences and Suggestions* (New York, 1874), 90-105.

The Ladies' Society was formed in the Mount Vernon Congregational Church on February 4, 1846, for the purpose of sending to the Western states "competent female teachers, of unquestioned piety, belonging to the Congregational Churches in New England."[23] The missionary motive was dominant, but at the same time it was believed that such an organization could render a real service to young women who desired to go West. It was pointed out that there was in New England, as a result of commerce and the emigration of the men, a surplus of nearly twenty thousand women who could never become the "heads of families" if this disproportion of the sexes continued. The Ladies' Society and similar organizations that made it easier for the women to find employment in the West was characterized as "a merciful provision for hundreds of well-educated Christian young women, whose sex forbids their adventuring as their brothers do, and yet who, if such a Society will encourage them, and send them forth, may go cheerfully and understandingly right to the best spot for them in all that wide region."[24] The young women who were to participate in this unusual phase of the westward movement were to be between the ages of seventeen and thirty-six. They were expected to furnish testimonials of their piety, energy, and discretion. The Ladies' Society acted as an agency; it supplied teachers for places in the West that applied for them. It also defrayed the traveling expenses to the field of labor of those candidates who were unable to do this for themselves, and if necessary assisted them to procure outfits. During the first year (1846-47) nineteen teachers were sent out. They all came from New England, and places were found for them in eight Mississippi Valley states.[25] When, in 1854, the Ladies' Society was merged with the Board of National Popular Education, it was announced that since its organization in 1846 it had sent 109 teachers to the West.[26] The method used by the Ladies' Society was open

---

[23] *History of the Formation of the Ladies' Society for the Promotion of Education at the West*, 3-5; Sarah Tuttle letter, A.H.M.S. Correspondence, 1845-46, No. 2601, in A.H.M.S. papers, C.T.S.

[24] E. N. Kirk, "Address," in *History of the Formation of the Ladies' Society for the Promotion of Education at the West*, 15.

[25] Ladies' Society for the Promotion of Education at the West, *First Report* (1847), 9-22.

[26] Board of National Popular Education (abbreviated hereafter as B.N.P.E.), *Seventh Report* (1854), 21.

to criticism in that it gave the prospective teachers no training for their duties in the West, and also because the officers had little opportunity to gain firsthand information about the character and ability of the women whom they sent out. Generally they seem to have given satisfaction, but one missionary complained that the teacher who was sent to his town "used her tongue without regard to subject, time or place."[27]

Catherine Beecher's activities in behalf of education led also to the formation of the Board of National Popular Education. To promote common-school education in the Western states there was formed about 1846 a preliminary organization called the Central Committee for Promoting National Education with Catherine Beecher's brother-in-law—Harriet's husband—Professor Calvin E. Stowe, as chairman. Governor William Slade of Vermont, who had become interested in the movement, agreed to become its director on the expiration of his term as governor. Under his direction there was formed at Cleveland, in 1847, the Board of National Popular Education.[28] The object of this society was to prepare schoolteachers and send them to the West. Unlike the Ladies' Society of Boston, which was strictly Congregational, it was nonsectarian; it chose its teachers from various Protestant denominations.[29] The religious motive was strong, and the constitution of the society provided that "all teachers to be received under the patronage of the Board, shall be of unexceptionable moral and religious character. It expects from them the daily use of the Bible in their several schools, as the basis of that sound Christian education, to the support and extension of which, it is . . . solemnly pledged."[30] The women for whom places were found by this society were constantly reminded that they were missionaries just as truly as the men sent out to preach the gospel. The burden of sin and irreligion in the crude Western communities weighed heavily on some of them. Miss Harriet E. Bishop, a pioneer teacher in St. Paul, Minnesota, unburdened herself to the Secretary of the American Baptist Home Mission Society as follows:

---

[27] E. B. Turner, Colony, Iowa, Nov. 1, 1847, A.H.M.S. papers, C.T.S.

[28] B.N.P.E., *First Report* (1848), 7; C. E. Beecher, *True Remedy for the Wrongs of Woman*, 100; C. E. Beecher, *Educational Reminiscences*, 106-20.

[29] B.N.P.E., *Fifth Report* (1852), 15.

[30] B.N.P.E., *First Report* (1848), 3.

I address you with reference to the spiritual conditions of this country, and to make the enquiry, can any thing be done for its benefit? ...I came out to this region under the patronage of the "Board of National Popular Education," and for a year and a half have been doing the duties of my calling as a teacher, though in much weakness, and, in view of the surrounding wickedness, have truly felt to say, "Who is sufficient for these things?"

For nearly a year I was the only professor of Christianity in town. The weight of responsibility resting upon me has at times pressed sorely.... I sometimes felt all the anxieties of minister, sabbath-school teacher, superintendent, and teacher of day school combined; but now, I confidently believe the time of greatest darkness is past.[31]

The lady teachers often had their full share of hardships and inconvenience too when they left their comfortable homes in the East to share the privations of overcrowded Western cabins. We get a glimpse of some of the disagreeable features of such a life in the following letter written from an unnamed place out West:

The inhabitants here are chiefly from North Carolina, Tennessee and Germany. All are farmers and their chief object is to make money. They seem desirous to have their children educated, but they differed so much about almost everything, that they could not build a school-house.... I commence school every day with reading the Bible and prayer; this was new to them but they made no objections.... I have commenced a Sabbath School.... I board where there are eight children and the parents, and only two rooms in the house. I must do as the family do about washing, as there is but one basin and no place to go to wash but out the door. I have not enjoyed the luxury of either lamp or candle, their only light being a cup of grease with a rag for a wick. Evening is my only time to write, but this kind of light makes such a disagreeable smoke and smell I cannot bear it, and do without light except the fire. I occupy a room with three of the children and a niece who boards here. The other room serves as a kitchen, parlor, and bedroom for the rest of the family.[32]

In addition to finding teachers for the Western schools, the Board of National Popular Education gave them a short training, usually six weeks in length, to prepare them for their duties. The prospective teachers were gathered together and given instruction on such subjects as Methods of Organizing Schools, School Government, Methods of Teach-

---

[31] H. E. Bishop, St. Paul's, Nov. 25, 1848, in A.B.H.M.S., *Sixteenth Report* (1848), 65-66.

[32] Quoted by C. E. Beecher, *Educational Reminiscences*, 121. Other excerpts from reports of the teachers may be found in [S. W. S. Dutton], "Popular Education in the West by Female Teachers from the East," in *The New Englander*, VII (1849), 593-610.

ing Reading, Writing, and Arithmetic, Calisthenic Exercises, Hygiene and Physiology, and Moral and Religious Instruction. They were given practical advice on problems of discipline, on the proper method of opening a school, and on how to behave in the community. One of the prospective teachers noted in her diary during the course of the training period: "We assembled this morning [March 27, 1850] to listen to instructions in regard to our habits as boarders. We were cautioned against disturbing the family with whom we are stopping by talking late, or making any noise; we were to remember that our life was constantly subject to the inspection of those around us."[33]

From the viewpoint of the society this brief period of preparation was valuable because it gave the managers an opportunity to become acquainted with the prospective teachers and thus better able to send them to the places for which they were best fitted. Moreover it helped to build up an *esprit de corps* among the women and to cause them to realize that they were a part of a great patriotic movement designed to advance the interests of their country and to spread and protect Protestantism.[34] Religious principles were kept constantly before the girls; on the third day after the class of 1850 assembled its members were asked to write out their views on regeneration and to state the reasons why they thought that they had undergone that change.[35] The missionary impulse behind the movement should not be forgotten; although the society was actually formed in the West, it was essentially a New England organization. The idea originated in a New England family whose missionary zeal had been quickened by residence in the West; the financial support came mainly from New England, and it was there that most of the teachers were secured.

After a class had been trained in some Eastern city, usually New Haven or Hartford, it was ordinarily taken to Buffalo and divided into groups, which, whenever possible, were escorted to Western centers of population, such as Chicago, Cincinnati, or St. Louis, by reliable gentlemen traveling in that direction. To act as escort to the West was

---

[33] Fanny Warner Diary, entry for March 27, 1850, original MS. in the possession of Miss Martha Morrison, Denver, Colorado.

[34] B.N.P.E., *First Report* (1848), 10-11; *Fifth Report* (1852), 12.

[35] Fanny Warner Diary, entry for March 21, 1850, Morrison MS.

sometimes one of the duties of the general agent of the society, and in one of his reports Governor Slade commented as follows on this phase of his work:

It may have surprised some, and amused others, to see the undersigned periodically conducting large companies of ladies through the great thoroughfares, on their way to the West. But it has seemed to him nearly indispensable. If experience is necessary to the proper conducting of any part of this enterprise, it is eminently needed here, as any one would soon learn, who should for the first time undertake this part of the work.[36]

At the close of the tenth year of its history it was announced that the Board of National Popular Education had sent 452 teachers to the West, all but twenty-five of whom had come from New England. Their destinations had been mainly the states of the Old Northwest, but many had crossed the Mississippi into Iowa and Missouri, and eleven had gone to the Pacific Coast.[37] These figures do not represent the whole of the society's achievement, because the women it sent to the West frequently found places there for their friends who went out without reference to the Board; moreover, the interest aroused by its work had the effect of increasing the number of teachers who went into the West on their own initiative. The teachers sent out were generally successful, and one observer remarked that "the young women of New England succeeded in the West better than the men."[38] History is silent on the important question of how many of them became "heads of families" in the West. But it is known that many of "Slade's girls," as they were often called, did marry and help make homes in the region to which they had gone. We can be sure that any Christian young woman who challenged the accepted notions about "woman's place" and who ran the risks involved in a trip from New England to a more or less uncertain destination in the Far West in the middle of the nineteenth century was possessed of more initiative and self-reliance than the average of her sex. She probably had a strong personality and was conscious of a mission in life. It is not unreasonable to suppose then that after marriage she became, if she were not already, a leader in the community, and that she im-

---

[36] B.N.P.E., *Ninth Report* (1856), 6.

[37] B.N.P.E., *Tenth Report* (1857), 6.

[38] B.N.P.E., *Ninth Report* (1856), 10.

pressed her characteristics upon her children. Her sons might be approaching manhood when the Civil War broke out; and it would have been strange if they had not shared their mother's probable devotion to the Union and dislike for slavery. It is said that once when General McPherson's Army of the Tennessee was fighting its way from Chattanooga to Atlanta in the Sherman Campaign of 1864, McPherson was especially impressed by the extraordinary fighting qualities of one regiment. On inquiry he was informed that it was an Iowa regiment made up of young fellows who had been a short time in the service; some of the men in it, we are told, were Slade's girls' boys.[39]

Governor Slade and Miss Beecher did not agree regarding the management of the Board of National Popular Education, and the latter severed her connection with it the year after it was started. Miss Beecher thought that too large a portion of the receipts, which were never large, was spent for administrative purposes, and that sufficient care was not taken to look after the teachers after they had been placed in the West.[40] Her most serious criticism, however, was that the Board, except for the short period of training which it gave the teachers, was little more than an intelligence office. It found teachers for the places that wanted them and were willing to pay them, but it did little in what Miss Beecher regarded as the missionary work of education, that is, sustaining teachers in the towns and villages of the West which, by reason of poverty or dissensions, could not support a teacher, or which cared so little about education that they would not.[41] It was not until the home missionary frontier came into contact with the Mormons and the Mexicans of the Southwest after the Civil War that attempts were made generally to provide elementary schools and teachers as a part of a regular missionary program; that phase of the work will be discussed in the latter part of this chapter.[42]

---

[39] J. L. Hill, *Yankees* (Boston, [1923]), 29.

[40] C. E. Beecher, *Educational Reminiscences*, 118-21.

[41] C. E. Beecher, *True Remedy for the Wrongs of Woman*, 175-80; C. E. Beecher, *To the Board of National Popular Education* (printed, not published; n.p., n.d., pamphlet in Harvard Library).

[42] See below, page 401 ff.

EARLY CONGREGATIONAL AND PRESBYTERIAN COLLEGES
IN THE WEST

One way to provide teachers for Western schools was to train the young men and women of the West in the West, but to do this colleges and academies must be established near at hand.[43] These institutions of higher education might also train Western preachers for Western churches, and, indeed, that was the chief reason for the establishment of many, perhaps most, of the colleges founded in the West under denominational auspices. One of the chief results of the missionary impulse when applied to education was the founding of more than one hundred colleges and academies west of the Alleghenies. President Charles F. Thwing of Western Reserve University once said:

> The great majority of all the colleges founded in the last eighty years [prior to 1906], have been founded with the religious motive; the larger share, too, of this great number have been endowed and their prosperity promoted through denominational zeal. They represent an agency created, not only for the members of their own church for its prosperity, but also they represent the offering which that church makes to general humanity for its development.[44]

As the head of another of these colleges, President Tuttle of Wabash, said: "The Christian College is the grand power in moulding the civilization and institutions of a new country."[45] Scores of these Christian colleges, most of them denominational, have been established in the United States. Throughout the West the leading denominations usually have at least one in each state. Our concern is not with the denominational colleges as such, but only with those institutions which in their origin have been connected with the home missionary movement; it is not with religion as a motive in higher education, but with Eastern benevolence and leadership as applied to the West. This is the reason for the greater emphasis placed upon Presbyterian, Congregational, and Episcopalian colleges in this discussion than

---

[43] E. W. Baldwin, Address ... on Occasion of his Inauguration as President of Wabash College (Cincinnati, 1836), 14.

[44] C. F. Thwing, History of Higher Education in America (New York, 1906), 231; the origin of denominational colleges is treated fully in D. G. Tewksbury, Founding of American Colleges and Universities Before the Civil War (New York, 1932), 55-132.

[45] J. F. Tuttle, Baccalaureate Sermon: The Christian College in its Relations to the Institutions of a New Country (New York, 1865).

upon Methodist and Baptist schools, although the latter may be fully as important as the former. In the one case the impulse and much of the financial support can often be traced to Eastern missionary zeal; in the other, the promoters of colleges were usually forced to rely more upon their own efforts and ability. In so far as they were independent of the East, it was an independence born of necessity rather than choice; for colleges were, are, and ever will be hopeful beggars. Fortunate were those that because of Eastern connections could draw upon the store of wealth of the older and more prosperous part of the country.

Many of the better known of the Christian colleges of the West were formed by the Presbyterians and Congregationalists in the period when they were acting together in their missionary operations. Some are classed now as Congregational in their origins, others as Presbyterian, but here they will be treated together because of the close relationship maintained in the West by these two Calvinistic bodies under the Plan of Union.

In the planting of Christian academies and colleges in the West in the latter part of the eighteenth and the early years of the nineteenth centuries first place unquestionably belongs to the Presbyterians. Their ministers, who were generally college-trained men, often founded academies in their frontier communities in the hope that from these "log-colleges" would go forth new recruits for the Lord's service. Thus in 1777 the Reverend Samuel Doak, who had been educated at Princeton, carried a sackful of books on his horse when he crossed the mountains to begin his ministerial labors in the Holston settlements. He not only founded a church, but also an academy which later grew into Washington College, "the first institution of the kind west of the Alleghanies."[46] In western Pennsylvania a short time later the name of the Father of his Country was attached to another frontier school, Washington Academy; it owed its origin largely to the educational interests of such Presbyterian preachers as John McMillan and Thaddeus Dod. McMillan was also one of the founders of the near-by Cannonsburg Academy, out of which ultimately came Jefferson College. In Kentucky the Transylvania Presbytery launched Kentucky Academy in the last decade of the

---

[46] T. Roosevelt, *Winning of the West*, II, 223.

eighteenth century.[47]   When two of their members, Dr.
Blyth and David Rice, were sent to the General Assembly
in 1795, they were instructed also to solicit funds in the
East for the new school. They obtained about ten thousand
dollars, of which President Washington and Vice-President
John Adams contributed one hundred dollars each and
Aaron Burr fifty dollars. This academy was merged in 1798
with the University of Transylvania.[48] About the same time
the New Englanders who settled in and around Marietta,
Ohio, under the leadership of Manasseh Cutler were making
plans for a college. It was the day of small beginnings; their
Muskingum Academy, organized in 1797 and opened in
1800, was the first institution of higher learning in the
Northwest Territory; it was not until 1832 that it developed
into the Marietta Collegiate Institute.[49] As will be pointed
out presently, it was one of the colleges that looked to New
England and the Northeast for financial and moral support.

A few years before the institution at Marietta attained
collegiate dignity, Western Reserve College was founded in
northern Ohio by the members of the Grand River Presbytery (1827). The object of these men, missionaries all, was
to create an instrument which would provide "an able,
learned, and pious ministry" for the infant churches which
they had gathered in the wilderness. Just as in the case of
Harvard College, and as was to be the case with so many
Western schools and seminaries, the object of the founders
was to secure a "native" educated ministry. Nearly all of
the ministers who co-operated in the establishment of
Western Reserve College had been sent out originally by
the Missionary Society of Connecticut, but had affiliated
themselves with the Presbyterians in the West.[50] Five years
after the establishment of Western Reserve College, Lane
Seminary, a product of Baptist generosity and Presbyterian
initiative, was founded at Cincinnati. Dr. Lyman Beecher,
who said in 1830 that the greatest thought that ever entered
his mind was the idea of educating ministers in the West

---

[47] W. W. Sweet, *Religion on the American Frontier... The Presbyterians*, 583-89.

[48] R. Davidson, *History of the Presbyterian Church in the State of
Kentucky*, 124.

[49] G. N. Knight and J. R. Commons, *History of Higher Education
in Ohio* (Washington, 1891), 101.

[50] W. S. Kennedy, *Plan of Union*, 236-44; G. W. Knight and J. R.
Commons, *History of Higher Education in Ohio*, 116 ff.

for the West, became the Professor of Theology when the new school opened its doors in 1832. It was primarily in behalf of this seminary that Dr. Beecher wrote and delivered his famous "Plea for the West." In this he not only pointed out the educational needs of the West and the necessity for training preachers in the West, but he also rang the changes on the Catholic menace. "The religious and political destiny of our nation is to be decided in the West," he said, and the struggle will be "a conflict of institutions for the education of her sons, for purposes of superstition or evangelical light; of despotism or liberty."[51]

Oberlin, the second missionary college to be founded in the Western Reserve, as the northern part of Ohio was called, was the very embodiment of New England conscience. It was founded by John J. Shipherd, who had gone from Vermont to Ohio bearing a commission from the American Home Missionary Society, and by his friend, Philo P. Stewart, who had been a missionary of the American Board of Commissioners for Foreign Missions to the Choctaw Indians. In a letter written in 1832, Shipherd outlined his plan: "I propose," he said, "to plant a colony somewhere in this region, whose chief aim shall be to glorify God, and do good to men." The establishment of "schools of the first order, from the infant school up to an academic school" was essential to the plan, because "these schools will also educate school-teachers for our desolate Valley, and many ministers for our dying world." To make the beginning Shipherd stated that he wanted twenty-five or more good families and a two-thousand-dollar outfit for the school. The foundations of the town and the college were laid together in 1833 by several families of New England ancestry, whose attitude toward life was shown in the covenant they signed. It began as follows: "Lamenting the degeneracy of the Church and the deplorable condition of our perishing world, and ardently desirous of bringing both under the influence of the blessed Gospel of peace; and viewing with peculiar interest the influence which the Valley of the Mississippi must exert over our nation and the nations of the earth ... the undersigned covenant together under the name of the Oberlin Colony." The covenanters agreed to hold no more property than they could manage as profitable

---

[51] L. Beecher, *Plea for the West*, 11-12.

stewards of God; what they obtained by their industry and economy above necessary personal and family expenses was to be spent for the spread of the gospel; in order that they might have time and health for the Lord's service, they agreed to eat only plain and wholesome food; they promised to deny themselves "all strong and unnecessary drinks, even tea and coffee, as far as practicable, and everything expensive that is simply calculated to gratify the palate;" they renounced all bad habits, "especially the smoking and chewing of tobacco, unless it is necessary as medicine," and "all the world's expensive and unwholesome fashions of dress, particularly tight dressing and ornamental attire."[52]

At the outset the manual-labor system was introduced at Oberlin. This plan of combining literary study with manual labor in order that the students might earn all or part of their expenses was a manifestation of the growing industrialism of the country, and had been tried in several Eastern academies in the preceding ten years.[53] At Oberlin a farm of eight hundred acres was secured, and a steam engine, with mills and other machinery, was put in operation. The girls—Oberlin was co-educational from the beginning—were to perform domestic labor in the boarding halls. The manual-labor system proved to be unsuccessful. Student labor was found to require too much supervision and to be unsuited to the management of a farm. It was stated that the wheat and corn raised at Oberlin under this system, even when there was a good crop, cost twice as much as the market price.[54]

Oberlin was definitely Congregational in its sympathies and affiliations. By the Presbyterians and those Congregationalists who favored joint action with the Presbyterian Church under the Plan of Union, it was looked upon as an intruder in the Western Reserve, because Western Reserve College antedated it by several years. The Oberlin people were looked upon by some of their neighbors as fanatics, as persons who were unstable in the faith and prone to take up such heresies as "Perfectionism," while their abolitionism

[52] J. H. Fairchild, *Oberlin: the Colony and the College* (Oberlin, 1883), 25-27.

[53] R. G. Boone, *Education in the United States* (New York, 1894), 223-24.

[54] J. H. Fairchild, *Oberlin, Its Origin, Progress and Results* (Oberlin, 1871), 48-51.

brought down upon them the wrath of all opposed to anti-slavery agitation.[55] In spite of the opposition, or perhaps because of it, Oberlin throve, and became a missionary center from which both preachers and teachers were sent out over the "desolate Valley of the Mississippi" as the founders had intended. Oberlin was also a mother of colleges: Olivet and Hillsdale in Michigan, Tabor in Iowa, Ripon in Wisconsin, and Carleton in Minnesota were among those that owed their origin directly or indirectly to the efforts of men and women who had caught the Oberlin spirit. Olivet, indeed, was founded by John J. Shipherd himself. In February, 1844, this earnest man of God led a little colony of thirty-nine persons out of Oberlin to repeat in Michigan the Oberlin experiment. As before, the colony and the college were to grow up together. The new college was opened in December, 1844, under the name of the Olivet Institute; it did not secure a charter from the state and become Olivet College until 1859.[56]

The origin of Illinois College has already been described briefly in connection with the work of the Illinois Band.[57] Mr. John M. Ellis, who planned the school, was a missionary of the American Home Missionary Society, and it was under the auspices of this organization that the Illinois Band went West. The establishment of a college was as much a part of the program of the Illinois Band as the establishment of churches. The reason for this as stated by one of the members of the group was their hope that the college would provide a center of intellectual and spiritual stimulus:

The band was organized on the principle that education and religion must go hand in hand to the world's conversion. It had been noticed too that individual missionaries often went West, and by being compelled to labor single-handed, found themselves at last borne down by adverse influences, and instead of maintaining an elevated standard as ministers, and lifting the community, they were cut off from the means of improvement, and gradually sunk down as intel-

---

[55] Cf. H. Cowles, *Defence of Ohio Congregationalism and of Oberlin College*, [Oberlin, 1856?].

[56] For several years Michigan discouraged the founding of small colleges which might interfere with the development of the State University. See Willis Dunbar, "Public Versus Private Control of Higher Education in Michigan, 1817-1855," in *Mississippi Valley Historical Review*, XXII (1935), 385-406. There is a brief sketch of the early history of Olivet College in *Michigan Pioneer Collections*, III (reprint, Lansing, 1903), 408-14.

[57] See above, page 195.

lectual men. The philosophy of this movement was to secure such a combination, and set in motion such *agencies* as would enable them to *create* a literary atmosphere whose vital power all should feel. Hence a college was to be the center of the system.[58]

Before they left New England in 1829 the members of the Illinois Band had raised ten thousand dollars for Illinois College, and in January, 1830,[59] the doors of the College were opened with J. M. Sturtevant as sole instructor. The first president was Edward Beecher, son of Lyman Beecher and brother to Catherine, Henry Ward, and Harriet. In 1835 Reuben Gaylord, a young alumnus of Yale, arrived to act as tutor in the preparatory department;[60] this was the beginning of Gaylord's missionary career, the influence of which was to be felt all the way from the prairies of Illinois to the mountains of Colorado. Illinois College at Jacksonville became a center for Puritan influences in the state of Illinois; the labors of various members of its faculty in behalf of a better school system were mentioned in an earlier part of this chapter; its antislavery bias was so strong that it probably hindered the growth of the college by alienating students from families of southern sympathies.[61]

Wabash College was founded by four pioneer Presbyterian missionaries, John Thomson, John Steele Thomson, Edward O. Hovey, and James Carnahan. They had appealed in vain for additional laborers in their field in Indiana, but at the same time there were in the churches in the Wabash Valley ten or twelve promising young men who stood ready to devote themselves to the ministry if they could secure the necessary training. Another school for preachers was needed. At a meeting held in Crawfordsville, Indiana, it was decided to found a college. Before the men who had made this high resolution separated, they proceeded in a body to the intended location in the forest and there, kneeling in the snow, dedicated the ground to Christian edu-

---

58 M. Grosvenor, "Summary of Addresses," in J. M. Sturtevant, *Historical Discourse*, 42-43.

59 John M. Peck, *Guide for Emigrants*, 249-52.

60 [Mrs. R. Gaylord], *Life and Letters of Rev. Reuben Gaylord*, 39.

61 C. H. Rammelkamp, "Illinois College and the Anti-Slavery Movement," in *Transactions of the Illinois State Historical Society* (1908), 193; C. P. Kofoid, "Puritan Influences in the Formative Years of Illinois History," *ibid.* (1905), 311.

cation.[62] The Wabash Manual Labor College and Teachers' Seminary was opened in 1833 with Professor Caleb Mills in charge. The men who labored at Wabash College in the early years did it through the missionary spirit. As Caleb Mills said: "We can build the Institution only by the aid of men who possess a missionary spirit & are willing to live on a missionary's salary, for we have not the funds to pay the customary salary of Professors in the old Institutions."[63]

Knox College was the outgrowth of a plan of Christian benevolence that originated with George W. Gale, Presbyterian minister of Whitestown, New York. He gathered a company of people who agreed to buy a tract of land in Illinois and found there a Christian colony and college. Before they left New York state the college was christened Prairie College, but after they had settled at Galesburg it received a charter from the State of Illinois (1837) under the name of Knox Manual College. Although most of its founders were Presbyterians, Congregationalists later came to dominate the Board of Trustees; it was Christian but not sectarian.[64]

THE "COLLEGE SOCIETY"

The colleges that have been considered thus far had much in common: they were the results of the labors and prayers of missionaries, the majority of whom, whether Presbyterians or Congregationalists, were under commission from the American Home Missionary Society; they all looked to the same constituency in the East for support and sent their representatives there to ask for help. Following the panic of 1837 practically all of these new Western colleges were in financial difficulties. People who had made pledges to them were unable to pay. Property valued at thousands of dollars would be lost unless help could be secured. Their cries for help were redoubled, but the repeated

---

[62] J. Thomson, Cincinnati, Dec. 3, 1832, in A.H.M.S. papers, C.T.S.; Society for the Promotion of Collegiate and Theological Education at the West (abbreviated hereafter to S.P.C.T.E.W.), *Fifth Report* (1848), 33; J. F. Tuttle, *Origin and Growth of Wabash College* (Logansport, Ind., 1876); J. H. Johnston, *Ministry of Forty Years in Indiana* (Indianapolis, 1865).

[63] C. Mills, Crawfordsville, Ind., May 10, 1834, in A.H.M.S. papers, C.T.S.

[64] J. W. Bailey, *Knox College, by whom Founded and Endowed* (Chicago, 1860), 51-56.

and conflicting appeals wearied the people of the East. A pooling of interests was suggested as the way out of the difficulty. This idea seems to have occurred first to Theron Baldwin, whose interest as a member of the Illinois Band was primarily in Illinois College. In 1842, following a conference of New School Presbyterians and Congregationalists in Cincinnati, in which the effect of the Presbyterian schism of 1837 on their Western churches and colleges was discussed, Baldwin set out for the East to solicit help for the Monticello Female Seminary of which he was president. It was while he was engaged in this work that he conceived the idea of establishing a society to conduct a united campaign in behalf of needy Western colleges. About the same time President Edward Beecher of Illinois College, who was in the East on a similar mission for his institution, came to the same conclusion independently. The idea met with the approval of the religious leaders of New England who were broached on the subject, because they saw the need for some organization which would prevent rivalry such as that which led a member of the staff of Wabash College, who was then begging for money in New Hampshire, to announce his intention of hurrying down to Connecticut in order that he might make his appeal there ahead of President Beecher. Out of this situation grew a conference in March, 1843, at the home of Dr. Lyman Beecher in Cincinnati, with representatives present from Lane Seminary, Marietta College, Wabash College, and Illinois College. Within a few months the organization of the Society for the Promotion of Collegiate and Theological Education at the West had been completed. In addition to the four colleges just named, Western Reserve College was a member of the group when the first united appeal was made to the East.[65]

This organization, the name of which was shortened in common usage to the "College Society," was not for the benefit of the original colleges alone; others were admitted to the privileges of membership from time to time, and as the older members grew in strength they dropped out. The Society quickly acquired a commanding position among those

---

[65] S.P.C.T.E.W., *First Report* (1844), 5-7; *Fifth Report* (1848), 8; *Twenty-fifth Report* (1868), 38-57. It is noteworthy that Oberlin College, which at the time was regarded by some as a black sheep in the Presbyterian-Congregational flock, was not in the original group. It was later put on the approved list.

Western colleges of New England-New York origin that were still looking to the East for financial backing. Without the endorsement of this Society their chances of getting a hearing were slight. Its policy was to subject institutions to rigid scrutiny before approving their claims, with the result that a salutary check was imposed on the promoters of Western colleges so far as the New School Presbyterians and Congregationalists were concerned. Some sort of check was especially necessary at this time because of the frequency with which land speculation and the planting of paper colleges went hand in hand. In those days when land was cheap and colleges were thought to be an asset to a community, it seemed so simple for a new community or a group of promoters to set aside a section or two of land for a college with the assurance that the proposed school would attract more and better settlers, thus raising the value of all the land and making it possible ultimately to secure an endowment for the college. Or, as one critic put it, they had "embarked with all the credit of their sanctity upon the uncertain sea of traffic in wild lands & in building lots of cities yet to be."[66] There was nothing necessarily unreasonable or illegitimate in such a plan; unfortunately it fell into disrepute because so often the college never materialized, or died in the fledgling stage. Knox College, which had been founded in connection with land operations, was not placed on the accredited list by the Society for the Promotion of Collegiate and Theological Education until after an investigating committee reported that the college had not been founded for pecuniary gain. In the case of Iowa College a plan for creating an endowment through the sale of land was abandoned because of the opposition of this Society.

Iowa College was the child of the Iowa Band; before they left Andover the members of this Band planned to build a college in their field of labor. In 1844, the year following their arrival in the territory, a meeting of the men interested in the establishment of a college was held at Denmark, cradle of Iowa Congregationalism, and the Iowa College Association was formed.[67] It was decided to enter a tract of land

---

[66] L. Bacon, *Duties Connected with the Present Commercial Distress* (New Haven, 1837), 11.

[67] Two members of this Iowa College Association, Reuben Gaylord and J. A. Clark, had been members of an Iowa Educational Association at Yale, which had been formed for the purpose of founding a

from the Government, sell it out in parcels at an advanced price to settlers favorable to the project, and thus secure both an endowment for the college and a community in which it would prosper.[68] Asa Turner was sent East to obtain funds with which to buy the land, but the plan of combining land operations with a college did not meet with the approval of the newly formed College Society and was abandoned.[69] The men at the head of the College Society and others from whom the Iowa pioneers expected to receive financial help advised that a suitable site for the college be selected irrespective of any consideration connected with the sale of land, and promised that after the college was started they would support it in its efforts to secure money in the East. Davenport was accordingly chosen as the site for the college, which was opened in 1848. Iowa College, as it was then called, did not prosper at Davenport: in addition to the usual financial difficulties of most new colleges, there was trouble with the town authorities over streets; moreover, it was soon found that a Mississippi River town did not furnish a congenial atmosphere for a transplanted New England college. In 1859 the property was sold to the Episcopalians. Meanwhile another institution with similar aims had been founded at Grinnell, Iowa, by a colony from New England. There was no need for two New England colleges in Iowa, and so the two schools were merged, Iowa College being moved to Grinnell. By this change Iowa College secured a more central location in the state and property worth about forty thousand dollars, while it brought with it a small endowment, a library, the prestige of its name and its completed college classes, and the promise of assistance from

---

college in Iowa. The Yale Association came to nothing, but individual members went west as missionaries; "Early History of Iowa College," in *Minutes of the General Association of Congregational Churches and Ministers of the State of Iowa* (Hull, 1888), 106.

[68] E. Adams, *Iowa Band*, 105; "Early History of Iowa College," in *Minutes of the General Association of Congregational Churches...Iowa*, 107.

[69] Half a century after the event one of the founders of Iowa College, Julius A. Reed, was inclined to regret that they had not gone ahead with their land venture. "Thirty thousand dollars," he said, "invested there and then might have been worth more to Iowa College than all the gifts which have been bestowed upon it." Julius A. Reed, *Reminiscences of Early Congregationalism in Iowa*, 17.

friends at the East. Instruction began at Grinnell in September, 1859.[70]

A chain of colleges similar in origin and objects to those already described stretches across the continent clear to the Pacific Coast. In Wisconsin Beloit and Ripon stand as monuments to missionary zeal. The founders of Beloit College were Congregational and New School Presbyterian ministers who had been sent to Wisconsin by the American Home Missionary Society. As early as 1843 the possibility of founding a college was considered by these men at a meeting of the Presbyterian and Congregational Conference of that territory. The matter was brought up again the following year, and in 1845 they decided to locate the college, for which a charter was obtained in 1846, at Beloit. Western lands, which later brought the college more than fifty thousand dollars, were given to it by people in New England who were interested in Christian education in the West.[71] Ripon College, which seems to have started through the local pride and ambition of the citizens of the little town of that name, was offered to the Winnebago District Conference of Presbyterian and Congregational Churches in 1857. With the college went a debt which the churches were not able then to assume, but one of their members bought the property and held it for them. The first college instruction was given in 1863. Both Beloit and Ripon ultimately received the endorsement of the Society for the Promotion of Collegiate and Theological Education at the West.

Meanwhile other Presbyterian and Congregational missionaries were establishing Christian colleges on the Pacific Coast. When George H. Atkinson was making preparations to go to Oregon in 1847 as a representative of the American Home Missionary Society, Theron Baldwin, who had been a member of the Illinois Band, said to him: "You are going to Oregon. Build an academy that shall grow into a college, as we built Illinois College." Atkinson reached Oregon City in July, 1848, and within two months an association was

---

[70] G. F. Magoun, "Historical Sketch," in *Addresses and Discourse at the Inauguration of the Rev. George F. Magoun* (Chicago, 1865), 55-60; E. Adams, *Iowa Band*, 105-07; J. B. Grinnell, *Men and Events of Forty Years* (Boston, c. 1891), 328.

[71] *Exercises at the Quarter-Centennial Anniversary of Beloit College* (Beloit, 1872), 5-9, 57-58; H. M. Whitney, "Beloit College," in J. W. Stearns, ed., *Columbian History of Education in Wisconsin* (Milwaukee, 1893), 134-38.

formed and a board of trustees chosen for Tualatin Academy, which was incorporated in the following year. Cushing Eells, who had been associated with Dr. Marcus Whitman in the Indian mission, began instruction in the embryo college in 1849; the physical equipment consisted of a log house, twenty by thirty, with puncheon seats and desks.[72] In 1852 Atkinson made a journey to the East in behalf of the school. He collected over four thousand dollars in money, obtained books for the library, secured the endorsement of the College Society, and induced S. H. Marsh of New England to go to Oregon to take charge of the school. Out of this academy grew Pacific University. For many years it was dependent on the East for financial assistance. President Marsh made three trips East to solicit aid and obtained about seventy thousand dollars in money, besides valuable books for the library; the list of contributors contains the names of Samuel F. B. Morse, Henry Ward Beecher, Collis P. Huntington, Frederick Billings, and other nationally prominent men.[73]

Samuel H. Willey, one of the first representatives of the American Home Missionary Society in California, had not been long on the Pacific Coast before he began to make plans for a college. In 1849 he wrote to Dr. William M. Rogers, of Boston, one of the Overseers of Harvard College, asking advice on the subject. In 1853 Henry Durant, who had gone to California with the idea of starting a school, opened the Contra Costa Academy in Oakland with the support of the Presbytery of San Francisco and the Congregational Association of California. This academy had grown into the College of California by 1855, and Mr. Willey, who was then in the East, was asked to solicit funds for it. This he found a very difficult task. Why should people send money to California, where it was thought by Easterners that gold was almost as plentiful as water? He secured a few thousand dollars in small sums, however; Mr. Aspinwall of the Pacific Mail Steamship Company, C. R. Roberts, who later founded Roberts College, William E. Dodge, and Anson G. Phelps

---

[72] M. Eells, *Father Eells* (Boston, 1894), 163-65.

[73] G. H. Atkinson, "Memorial Sketch of Tualatin Academy and Pacific University," in N. S. Atkinson, *Biography of Rev. G. H. Atkinson* (Portland, 1893), 239-44; Pacific Coast Congregational Alliance, *Christian Education by Congregationalists in the Seven Pacific Coast States* (San Francisco, 1893), 31-33.

were among the contributors.[74] The Society for the Promotion of Collegiate and Theological Education at the West put the College of California on its list of institutions worthy of aid, but this of itself brought no money. In 1860 another appeal was made to the East for assistance, and at this time much was made of the fact that the College of California was not under the control of any one denomination; Presbyterians, both Old and New School, Congregationalists, Baptists, and Episcopalians in California had joined their forces to build a better college than any of them could have established alone. President Woolsey of Yale warmly commended this arrangement: "The plan of embracing within the Board of Directors of the Institution representatives of all evangelical denominations of Christians who will take part in the enterprise, and seek no exclusive college of their own, is," he said, "a happy one, and well calculated to meet the exigencies of a region where Christian cooperation is pre-eminently wanted. The great evil in regard to our country, and more particularly in regard to the western parts of it, is not that there is a want of colleges, but that there are too many of them; so many that they must be starvelings and competitors, and must appeal to sectarian love of power and influence."[75] In 1867 the legislature of California created a State University with which the College of California was merged; thus was formed the present University of California.[76]

After the Civil War the New School Presbyterians, now reunited with their Old School brethren, withdrew from participation in the activities of the College Society, leaving it entirely to the Congregationalists. Although controlled now by men who belonged to one denomination, it still emphasized nonsectarian Christian education. According to its rules as announced in 1873 no college which was not entirely free of state control on the one hand and of ecclesiastical domination on the other was placed on its list.[77]

[74] Commodore Vanderbilt was one of those who refused to contribute; in emphatic words he wished California no good. "Things had evidently been going wrong in his Nicaragua Steamship Line." S. H. Willey, *History of the College of California* (San Francisco, 1887), 14.

[75] T. D. Woolsey, in M. Kellogg, *Statement in Behalf of the College of California* (n.p., [1860]), 11.

[76] S. H. Willey, *History of the College of California*, 1-15; S.P.C.T. E.W., *Twenty-fifth Report* (1868), 86-87.

[77] *Home Missionary*, XLVI (1873), 194; S.P.C.T.E.W., *Thirtieth Report* (1873), 44.

The report of the Society for the year 1872 showed that Western Reserve, Oberlin, Marietta, Wabash, Illinois, Knox, and Beloit colleges had attained to a degree of strength which enabled them to stand without further assistance. Seven colleges were at that time receiving aid: Olivet, Ripon, Iowa, Pacific, Washburn, Carleton, and Berea. The origin of each of the first four in this list has already been noticed in this chapter. Berea, in Kentucky, was primarily for the mountain whites of "Appalachia." Washburn College in Topeka, Kansas, was a child of home missions and of New England antislavery enthusiasm. When Eli Thayer and Charles Robinson planted their colony at Lawrence, Kansas, they set aside a tract of land for a college. A short time later the Congregationalists of Kansas, under the leadership of S. Y. Lum of the American Home Missionary Society, tried to establish there Monumental College in honor of those who fought and died in the Free State War. The project failed, but in 1858 the Kansas Association of Congregational Churches voted to establish a college in Topeka. At first it was called Topeka Institute; when incorporated as a college in 1865 it was called Lincoln College. The name was later changed to Washburn College in honor of a benefactor, Ichabod Washburn, of Worcester, Massachusetts.[78]

In Minnesota missionaries sent out by the American Home Missionary Society began as early as 1856 to make plans for a college. "Father" Charles Seccombe, who, with Richard Hall, laid the foundations of Congregationalism in Minnesota, was especially active in this work. Intensely loyal to the Union cause during the Civil War, he asserted that "the Church and School house had been largely instrumental in bringing victory to the North."[79] About 1865 the Congregational churches in that state gave their support to Northfield College; its name was later changed to Carleton, in honor of William Carleton, of Charlestown, Massachusetts.[80]

In 1873 Doane College at Crete, Nebraska, received the coveted recognition of the College Society. The history of Congregational education in Nebraska began at the first

---

[78] *Home Missionary*, LXXII (1900), 226-28.

[79] W. Upham, ed., *Congregational Work of Minnesota, 1832-1920* (Minneapolis, 1921), 40.

[80] D. L. Leonard, *History of Carleton College* (Chicago, [1904]), 44-60.

meeting of the Territorial Association in October, 1857, when it was voted that it was expedient "to take measures to lay the foundations of a literary institution of a high order in Nebraska." A site was selected at Fontenelle where already an ambitious project for a "Nebraska University" under Baptist auspices had been launched and abandoned.[81] In 1858 the Congregationalists secured a charter from the legislature, and raised and borrowed enough money to erect a small college building. But unfortunately by that time the effects of the panic of 1857 were being felt in the West. The storm swept over Nebraska and "scattered the inhabitants of Fontenelle like chaff before the wind." Lands were left unimproved; buildings were unfinished; the college was suspended. In 1865 Reuben Gaylord, the father of the school, visited the East and raised enough money to enable it to open its doors with one teacher.[82] After a few more years of struggle the enterprise was abandoned;[83] then the Congregationalists of Nebraska threw their support to Doane College, which had been established in 1872 and named in honor of Thomas Doane, of Massachusetts, chief engineer of the Burlington and Missouri River Railway in Nebraska.[84] Doane College stood in the center of the Congregational scheme of education in Nebraska. As feeders to it, though with no organic connection, were four academies widely distributed over the state: Chadron in the northwest, Gates at Neligh in the northeast, Weeping Water in the southeast, and Franklin in the south central section.[85]

In 1875 Colorado College at Colorado Springs, a school opened under the auspices of Colorado Congregationalists in 1874, received recognition by the College Society. This institution, thanks to the vision and energy of its second president, E. P. Tenney, formerly a home missionary in Central City, Colorado, became one of the distinctive Con-

---

[81] "Minutes of Trustees of Nebraska University," MS. Show papers, State Hist. Soc., Lincoln, Neb.; [Mrs. R. Gaylord], *Life and Labors of Rev. Reuben Gaylord*, 420-31.

[82] L. H. Jones, in *Home Missionary*, XXXIX (1866), 32-33.

[83] The college at Fontenelle closed in 1872. V. C. Fuhlrodt, "The Pioneer History of Fontenelle, Nebraska," M.A. thesis, University of Nebraska, MS., State Hist. Soc., Lincoln, Neb.

[84] M. A. Bullock, *Congregational Nebraska* (Lincoln, 1905), 213.

[85] H. Bross, "Congregational Church," in J. S. Morton, *Illustrated History of Nebraska* (Lincoln, 1905-13), II, 500.

gregational colleges of the West. When Mr. Tenney took charge of the school in 1876 Congregationalism was still very weak in Colorado, and Colorado Springs was only a small straggling village. Colorado, admitted to the Union that year, had a population of approximately one hundred thousand persons. It was almost impossible to raise money in Colorado outside Colorado Springs for the new college, because the country was new, the future insecure, and much of the capital tied up in speculative ventures. Other towns and cities had troubles enough of their own without helping Colorado Springs "boom" its real estate by starting a college there. Congregationalists in the East had already listened to so many appeals for money for Western colleges that they were not likely to respond generously to a call for just another small college, and that one in a state so sparsely settled that it had little more than one inhabitant for each square mile. But President Tenney was an ecclesiastical statesman. He made an appeal for Colorado College on the basis of its relationship to a vast area to which he applied the name "New West." It was not to be a mere local college, useful as those were; it was to stand as the symbol of Protestant Christianity in the whole Rocky Mountain region and the Southwest. It was to stand like a lighthouse in a land which to his way of thinking was dark with the errors of Roman Catholicism and Mormonism. The material advantages and the spiritual desolations of the great Southwest were described by Mr. Tenney in a little book entitled *The New West as Related to the Christian College.* First issued from the press in December, 1877, it passed through at least five editions within two years. It called on Christian philanthropists to share in a great movement. It pointed out that the chief asset of the new college was a great opportunity. "The founding of Colorado College was, therefore," to quote Mr. Tenney in retrospect, "put at once upon broad national grounds, the beginning of an extended movement, which would affect the intellectual and moral condition of a third part of the United States, then opening to emigration under the well-known law of the westward movement of population in America.... At a providential hour, it fell to Colorado College to be the herald for presenting to the philanthropic East, the opening of another vast area of unknown America that had been relatively hidden from the eyes of men between the valley of the Mississippi and the Pacific

slope."[86] In certain editions of the New West pamphlet[87]
Mr. Tenney included an outline map of the United
States showing what the colleges of the older West had done
for home missions. It indicated by dots and circles nearly
two thousand localities where work under the auspices of
the American Home Missionary Society had been done by
the students of three theological seminaries (Lane, Oberlin,
and Chicago), and of ten colleges (Marietta, Oberlin, Western Reserve, Olivet, Wabash, Illinois, Knox, Beloit, Ripon,
and Iowa). The map was intended to show by contrast, and
did, the need for at least one home missionary training
school in the New West. This map, which was reproduced
in such periodicals as the *Home Missionary*, the *Congregationalist*, and the *Advance*, had an estimated circulation of
75,000 copies within two years. Colorado College, as was
hoped, did receive many substantial gifts from the East.[88]
As a missionary center in the West, it sponsored for a time
academies in Salt Lake City and Santa Fé. These were later
taken over by the New West Education Commission,[89] an
organization which was in a sense an outgrowth of the
interest in the Southwest aroused by the writings of President Tenney.

Drury College at Springfield, Missouri, named in honor
of Mr. S. F. Drury, of Olivet, Michigan, was endorsed by
the College Society in 1875. In 1883 the Society extended
its aid to Whitman College at Walla Walla, Washington.
Whitman College, which was chartered in 1859, was planned
as a memorial to Dr. Marcus Whitman by his friend and
former colleague, Cushing Eells, but it is likewise a monu-
ment to the sacrifices and heroic efforts of its founder. It is
said that there were times when Mr. Eells lived on dried
salmon and water at a cost of twenty-five cents a week in
order that every cent he could raise might go to keep alive
the college to which he had dedicated his life.[90]

In 1882 the College Society reported that since its forma-

[86] E. P. Tenney, *Looking Forward into the Past* (Nahant, Mass.,
1910), 80-83.

[87] E. P. Tenney, *New West as Related to the Christian College* (5th
ed., Colorado Springs, 1879), 37.

[88] American College and Education Society, *Third Report* (1877),
18.

[89] See below, page 403.

[90] S. B. L. Penrose, in *Home Missionary*, LXVIII (1895), 66.

tion about forty years earlier,[91] it had been the agency through which more than $1,300,000 had been transferred from the East to twenty-eight different Western colleges. To some the help given had been slight; to others it had meant life and the opportunity for continued service. The great majority of the colleges helped had been founded by Presbyterians and Congregationalists, although in the list appear Wittenberg College and Heidelberg College in Ohio and German Evangelical College in Missouri.[92]

PRESBYTERIAN COLLEGES

The original College Society having passed into the hands of Congregationalists, the Presbyterians founded one of their own. The movement was launched in 1877 when the General Assembly appointed a committee to consider enlarging the functions of the Board of Education so as to provide larger endowments for the Presbyterian colleges and theological seminaries. The committee reported that there was a need for more colleges in the West and an opportunity for the Presbyterians to foster higher education not only as a means of self-preservation but as a service they owed to the country. As a result of the adoption of this report the Assembly created in 1883 the Presbyterian Board of Aid for Colleges and Academies. Among the members of the first Board elected at this time were Benjamin Harrison, of Indianapolis, later president of the United States, and Cyrus H. McCormick, Jr., of Chicago.[93] The first annual report of the new Board indicated that it had divided about twenty-nine thousand dollars among nine institutions, the greater part of the amount having been given to four of them. These four were Salt Lake Collegiate Institute, which had been founded by the Presbyterian Church in the Mormon capital in 1875; the College of Emporia, which had been launched by the Synod of Kansas; the Presbyterian University of Southern Dakota, which had been founded at Pierre in 1883; and the College of Montana at Deer Lodge, which had been started originally as a nondenominational college but

---

[91] In 1874 the Society for the Promotion of Collegiate and Theological Education at the West was merged with the American Education Society.

[92] *Home Missionary*, LV (1882), 127-28.

[93] *Minutes of the General Assembly of the Presbyterian Church*, N.S. VII (1883), 581-89, 645-46.

had been turned over to the Presbytery of Montana. According to the second report of the Board, assistance ranging in amount from $107.80 to $2500 had been given to twenty-one different schools in the fiscal year 1884-85.[94]

In its fifth year the Board distributed about thirty-one thousand dollars among thirty-six colleges and academies. Obviously no large awards were made to any one institution, but the fact that it was on the approved list of the Assembly's Board made it easier for a college to secure special gifts. The Congregational College Society had restricted closely the number of schools to which it granted recognition; the Presbyterian Board distributed smaller sums among a larger number of institutions. Apparently one of the results of the formation of the Presbyterian Board of Aid for Colleges was the stimulation of the establishment of new colleges. In its report to the General Assembly in 1888 the Board stated that of the thirty-six institutions to which it was giving aid, only nine were organized and at work in 1883, the year in which the Board began its operations.[95] In the year 1890-91 fifteen colleges were receiving aid from the Presbyterian Board.[96] It appears that at least half of the schools to which financial assistance was given during this period have ceased to exist, and that only three of them, Park College in Missouri, Jamestown College in North

---

[94] Help was given to the following institutions: Albany Collegiate Institute (Oregon), Albion Academy (Franklinton, N. C.), Bellevue College (Nebraska), German Theological School (Dubuque, Iowa), Emporia College (Kansas), Galesville University (Wisconsin), Geneseo Collegiate Institute (Illinois), Hastings College (Nebraska), Lenox College (Hopkinton, Iowa), College of Montana at Deer Lodge, Oakdale Seminary (Nebraska), Park College (Parkville, Mo.), Parsons College (Fairfield, Iowa), Pierre University (Dakota), Presbyterian College of the Southwest (Del Norte, Colo.), Princeton Collegiate Institute (Kentucky), Salt Lake Collegiate Institute (Utah), Sedalia University (Missouri), Sumner Academy (Washington), Union College of Southern Illinois, Washington College (Tennessee). *Minutes of the General Assembly of the Presbyterian Church*, N.S. VIII (1885), 806.

[95] *Ibid.*, XI (1888), 265.

[96] The colleges receiving aid in 1890-91 were: Greenville and Tusculum (Tennessee), Washington (Tennessee), Galesville (Wisconsin), Emporia (Kansas), College of Montana, Pierre (South Dakota), Bellevue (Nebraska), Hastings (Nebraska), Presbyterian College of the Southwest (Colorado), Whitworth (Washington), Albert Lea (Minnesota), Coates (Indiana), Oswego (Kansas), Alma (Michigan). *Minutes of the General Assembly of the Presbyterian Church*, N.S. XIV (1891), 299. Daniel Baker College (Texas) and Occidental College (California) were added to the list in 1892.

Dakota, and Occidental College at Los Angeles, are now on the approved list of the Association of American Universities.[97] Whether it was a wise policy to encourage the establishment of so many small colleges with tiny libraries and meager laboratory equipment is questionable; but in judging the wisdom of the policy pursued it must be remembered that the purpose of the Board was to encourage Christian education under Presbyterian control, and that the teacher may be and often has been a more important educational agency than library or laboratory.

EPISCOPAL COLLEGES

The first great builder of Episcopal colleges in the West was Bishop Philander Chase. He saw the need for training clergy for the West in the West, and shortly after he was elected Bishop of Ohio began to plan for a college within his diocese. Just as the Congregationalists of the West had looked to New England for assistance in founding colleges, so Bishop Chase looked to old England for help. In 1823, in the face of strong opposition within his own denomination, he went to England and was able to interest many influential people in his plans. Altogether he secured about thirty thousand dollars for his proposed school, to which was given the name of Kenyon College in honor of Lord Kenyon, one of the chief benefactors; another donor, Lord Gambier, was remembered in the name given to the town in Ohio where the college was located.[98] The financial assistance received from England was not sufficient for the college, consequently Bishop Chase made an appeal also to his American brethren.[99] He secured some money but more prestige for the new school. Episcopalians from all parts of the country sent their sons there. Northern and Southern students were thrown together; there were two literary societies, one for each group, and it was taken as a matter of course that a student would affiliate with the society patronized by the men from his section.[100]

---

[97] Association of American Universities, *Journal of Proceedings ... Thirty-eighth Annual Conference ... 1936*, 30-35.

[98] P. Chase, *Reminiscences*, I, 209 ff.

[99] P. Chase, *Plea for the West*.

[100] B. C. Steiner, *Life of Henry Winter Davis*, 25; Salmon P. Chase, in "Recollections of School Days at Worthington" (in "Kenyon College Statements" in Harvard Library), tells how he was called up before his uncle, the bishop, for kicking one of his fellow students who had called him a Yankee.

Bishop Chase's success in establishing Kenyon College in good standing among the Episcopalians of the United States is all the more remarkable because of the opposition he encountered when he went to England to solicit gifts for the proposed school. Objection was made that it was beneath our national dignity to make such an appeal to a foreign nation, and Bishop John Henry Hobart even went so far as to go to England and oppose his colleague's plan by issuing printed circulars and by putting notices of warning in the newspapers.[101] On the other hand, there were some Americans who suspected the British of sinister motives in making gifts to an American college. Henry Caswall, an Englishman who was for a time a student at Kenyon College, relates one of his experiences which illustrates how such ideas might be held by ignorant and narrow-minded persons. Stopping one night at a house in Ohio, he was received with customary frontier generosity until he announced that he was from Kenyon College. His host at once became silent and reserved, but in the morning he told Caswall plainly that he regarded Kenyon College as imminently dangerous to the country. "I have fought the British," said he, "in the revolutionary war; I have again encountered them in the last war [1812] ; and I know something of their character. I know they would not contribute so many thousands to build a college in Ohio without a sinister object. I am, therefore, convinced that Bishop Chase is an agent employed by them to introduce British dominion here. The college is, in fact, a fortress,[102] all you students are British soldiers in disguise, and when you think you have the opportunity, you will throw off the mask and proclaim the King of England."[103]

After Bishop Chase's unhappy experience at Kenyon

---

[101] G. White, *Apostle of the Western Church*, 48.

[102] The style of architecture adopted at Kenyon led some of the rustics to imagine that the college building was a fort; see G. White, *Apostle of the Western Church*, 50-51.

[103] H. Caswall, *America and the American Church* (London, 1839), 45-46; it is of interest also to note that Bishop Chase, who was a great admirer of English forms and ceremonies, tried "to naturalize the students' Oxford caps and gowns at Kenyon, but the gown was not a convenient garment to chop wood in, the silk tassel of the cap would make love to the boughs of the forest, its hard flat top rocked to and fro like a drunken man in every gust, and the impatient sons of the West were undergoing perpetual metamorphosis from a gownsman into a Buckeye in shirt sleeves—till the effort was abandoned as against the nature of the Western man." B. C. Steiner, *Life of Henry Winter Davis*, 31.

College, as narrated briefly in a preceding chapter,[104] and his temporary residence in Michigan, he was elected Bishop of Illinois in 1835. Again he proposed to found a college, and again he turned to England for help, but with less success than when he made his earlier appeal. Some of the friends who helped him then had died; the Church of England was becoming more interested in her sons and daughters in Canada and Australia. Bishop Chase's plea for help was based principally on the number of English settlers in Illinois and the danger of their loss to the Episcopal Church, together with the activities of the Roman Catholic Church in that region.[105] In April, 1836, he returned to the United States with about ten thousand dollars, with which he founded Jubilee College.

A school for the training of preachers was an essential part of Dr. James Lloyd Breck's associate mission plan[106] which he tried on three successive frontiers, in Wisconsin, in Minnesota, and in California. At Nashotah, Wisconsin, Dr. Breck, who was a martinet in discipline, ruled his school for the prophets with an iron hand; he himself rang the bell at five o'clock in the morning to wake the students; five minutes later there was another tap which called them all to the door of a small central building where the roll was called. Then they returned to their rooms to finish dressing, to make their fires, and to study until six when the bell rang for chapel. And so it went through the day.[107] In Minnesota he established a cluster of schools at Faribault: one for Indians; St. Mary's for girls; Shattuck School for boys; and Seabury Divinity Hall. In 1867 Dr. Breck moved to California and founded there St. Augustin's Institute at Benicia. In all of these ventures Dr. Breck was dependent almost entirely on the voluntary gifts of friends in the East. Each time he began with almost nothing, but the necessary gifts came, as he believed, in response to prayer. While still at Nashotah he wrote to one of his friends in the East:

We came West without pecuniary means to accomplish a great work.... Five years have almost elapsed since entering upon this Mission, and without resources save the *alms* of the Church to rely

---

[104] See above, page 211.

[105] G. White, *Apostle of the Western Church*, 69-70; P. Chase, *Reminiscences*, II, 362-63, Note, for letter to Queen Adelaide.

[106] See above, page 265.

[107] T. I. Holcombe, *Apostle of the Wilderness* (New York, 1903), 22.

upon. We do now find ourselves free from all pecuniary liabilities. We have a valuable tract of land of 465 acres, and accommodations for five-and-twenty brethren.... I am certain that Nashotah would not have been in existence at the present time had we begun our work with thousands of dollars at our command; but, having had to struggle along, we have gained that experience which no amount of money could have brought, and which, now gained, no money could take away from us. If we were to start forth tomorrow on a new mission, it should be Nashotah all over again. We do not want immense sums of money; but *faith* is required, and this is the Gift of God.[108]

BAPTIST AND METHODIST COLLEGES

The work of the other major denominations in founding colleges in the West was perhaps no less important than that of those thus far considered, but less attention can be paid to it here because it was less a missionary enterprise and more a local undertaking. Baptist and Methodist colleges, for example, although founded with the same religious motives as those of Congregationalists and Presbyterians, have generally been more largely dependent on the people of their own local ecclesiastical units.[109] It is mainly with the exceptions to this generalization that we are here concerned.

John M. Peck, pioneer Baptist missionary in Missouri and Illinois, went out from New England with the idea of founding a college.[110] In 1818 he opened a school in St. Louis, under the name of the Western Mission Academy,[111] and when he moved to Illinois he established the Rock Spring Theological and High School. About 1831 this seminary was moved to Upper Alton, Illinois; in 1836 its name was changed to Shurtleff College in recognition of a gift of several thousand dollars from Dr. Benjamin Shurtleff, of Boston.[112] Kalamazoo College in Michigan was founded by another Baptist missionary, Thomas W. Merrill, who had gone to Michigan in 1829 following his graduation from

[108] C. Breck, *Life of James Lloyd Breck*, 55.

[109] Cf. A. Abernethy, *History of Iowa Baptist Schools* (Osage, Iowa, 1907), 49-174, for the story of the educational activities of Iowa Baptist conventions.

[110] J. M. Peck, Litchfield, Conn., May 23, 1817, to Isaac McCoy, McCoy MSS., I, No. 24, in Kansas State Historical Society.

[111] *American Baptist Magazine*, N.S. I (1818), 413.

[112] R. Babcock, *Memoir of John Mason Peck*, 225-33, 264-68; W. T. Stott, "American Baptist Education Work in Western States," in A. H. Newman, *Century of Baptist Achievements*, 341.

Colby College, Maine, and Newton Theological School. At first he taught a classical school in Ann Arbor, and then founded the Michigan and Huron Institute at Kalamazoo about 1833; later this was called Kalamazoo College.[113] In Oregon, Ezra Fisher, representative of the American Baptist Home Mission Society, took the lead in the establishment of a college for his denomination. The Oregon Baptist Education Society was formed, possible sites examined, and one chosen at Oregon City for which Fisher and other Baptist pioneers paid five thousand dollars. Of this amount Mr. Fisher gave $1250, nearly all of which he had obtained a short time before by labor in the gold fields of California.[114] In 1851 George C. Chandler and J. S. Read went out to Oregon under the auspices of the Baptist Home Mission Society to conduct the Oregon City College.[115]

The first Methodist College in America was Cokesbury College, which was located at Abingdon, Maryland, under a charter granted in 1794. Other colleges and academies were founded under Methodist auspices in this early period but none of them has survived. In 1820 the General Conference appointed a committee to investigate the educational system among the Methodists. The committee recommended that all the Annual Conferences establish as soon as practicable literary institutions under their own control and in such way as they thought proper. The General Conference of 1824 recommended again that each Annual Conference establish one or more institutions of learning. In accordance with this policy many Methodist colleges have been established all over the country, forty-two colleges and universities being listed in the *Manual of the Methodist Church* (North) in 1883. It too is a roll of honor; the oldest in the list is McKendree College, founded in Illinois in 1828; the names of many other well-known institutions appear, such as Albion in Michigan, Allegheny in Pennsylvania, Ohio Wesleyan, Indiana Asbury or De Pauw, Illinois Wesleyan, Northwestern, Lawrence in Wisconsin, Hamline in Minnesota, Iowa Wesleyan, University of Denver, Willamette in

---

113 W. T. Stott, *op. cit.*, 342-43.

114 *Correspondence of the Reverend Ezra Fisher*, 265-88.

115 C. A. Woody, "Baptists of the Pacific Slope," in A. H. Newman, *Century of Baptist Achievement*, 103; *American Baptist Register* (1852), 294.

Oregon, and the University of Southern California.[116] In addition the Methodist Church, South, had its roster of colleges which is quite as long as that of the Northern church.[117]

SCHOOLS AND ACADEMIES IN THE FAR WEST

In addition to colleges and universities scores of academies have been established throughout the West under religious influences and often as an expression of the missionary spirit. Of the Protestant denominations the Episcopalians were especially active in this respect in the nineteenth century, each bishop ordinarily having had one or more Church schools for boys and girls in his diocese. Bishop Randall of Colorado, for example, announced in 1867 his intention of establishing a boys' school in Golden (Jarvis Hall) and a high school for girls in Denver (Wolfe Hall), and made an appeal to the East for money.[118] In 1871 a single page of the *Spirit of Missions* carried information about a boarding school for girls and a collegiate institute for boys in Nebraska, St. Helen's Hall for girls and the Bishop Scott Grammar and Divinity School for boys in Oregon, St. Mark's School in Cheyenne, Wyoming, and St. Mark's School in Salt Lake City.[119] The latter school was regarded by Bishop Tuttle as an extremely important part of his missionary work,[120] and no doubt other missionary bishops felt the same way about the schools in their dioceses. In general the policy of Congregationalists, Presbyterians, Baptists, and Methodists has not been to found day or boarding schools for students of high school age or younger; they have preferred ordinarily to lend their support to the public schools of the community. In the Southwest after the Civil War, however, they all turned to such schools as the most effective means of getting a foothold among the Spanish-Americans,

---

[116] *Manual of the Methodist Church*, III (1883), 104; on the subject of Methodist education, see S. M. Duvall, *Methodist Episcopal Church and Education up to 1869* (New York, 1928).

[117] C. C. Jarrell, *Methodism on the March* (Nashville, 1924), 121-26, and Exhibit B; the list of schools connected with the Methodist Episcopal Church, South, comprises two universities, thirty-two Class A colleges for men or women or for both, five Class B colleges, twenty-eight junior colleges, twenty academies, and eleven mission schools.

[118] *Spirit of Missions*, XXXII (1867), 567, Appendix, 66.

[119] *Spirit of Missions*, XXXVI (1871), 357.

[120] D. S. Tuttle, *Reminiscences*, 360.

who had been trained in Roman Catholicism, and among the Mormons. Moreover, as a result of the backward character of the public-school system of the Southwestern territories, especially Utah and New Mexico, denominational schools supported from the East met a real need.

In 1875 the members of the local Presbyterian Church in Salt Lake City started a school which grew into the Salt Lake Collegiate Institute, "the best school in the Territory," said the Presbyterians with pardonable pride.[121] By 1889 the Presbyterians had thirty-one schools with fifty-four teachers and nineteen hundred pupils in Utah.

Both of the Baptist women's missionary societies took a lively interest in education in the Southwest. The Woman's American Baptist Home Mission Society, which had been formed in Boston in 1877, opened the first Baptist day school in Salt Lake City in 1883. After six years the school was discontinued for the reason that the opening of public schools in that city made the denominational school unnecessary. Similar schools were opened under the auspices of this Society in Ogden and Provo, Utah, about 1890. A second organization of Baptist women, the Women's Baptist Home Mission Society, also formed in 1877 but with headquarters in Chicago, began its educational work in Utah in 1882; practically all the young women it sent to work among the Mormons had received their preparation in the Baptist Missionary Training School in Chicago. There they had had actual training in social work in a great city and had learned, among other things, how to give instruction to girls in needlecraft and to boys in shop work. Inasmuch as the manual arts were not ordinarily included in the school program of that time, these young women were able to make their mission schools unusually attractive to the youngsters. But these women were missionaries first of all: they received a subsistence wage, and they made the establishment of Sunday schools and the building up of churches their chief aim. Day schools were a means to an end.[122]

In 1878 Congregationalists acting through Colorado College established academies in Salt Lake City and Santa Fé; in the following year one was started under the same

---

[121] *Minutes of the General Assembly of the Presbyterian Church,* N.S., XV (1892), 309.

[122] R. Maud Ditmars, "History of Baptist Missions in Utah, 1871-1931" (M.A. thesis, MS., University of Colorado Library), 26-32.

auspices in Albuquerque, New Mexico. Neither the College and Education Society nor the American Home Missionary Society because of charter limitations was willing to assume the responsibility for these schools.[123] Hence there was established in Chicago in 1879 a new society called the New West Education Commission. Colonel C. G. Hammond, formerly a resident of Salt Lake City and a superintendent of the Union Pacific Railroad, suggested the name and made the first gift.[124] The purpose of the organization was announced as "the promotion of Christian civilization in Utah, and adjacent States and Territories, by the education of the children and youth under Christian teachers, and also by the use of such kindred agencies as may be at any time deemed advisable."[125]

The Commission took over the Congregational academies at Salt Lake, Santa Fé, and Albuquerque, and soon started another at Las Vegas, New Mexico; elementary schools were set up at four places in Utah. The second report (1882) showed five academies, eleven free schools, twenty-nine teachers, and 1214 pupils.[126] The thirteenth report (1893) listed eight academies, forty-three schools, and 2481 students.[127] The teachers were sent out from the East and Middle West as missionaries. Their general instructions contained this statement:

> It must never be forgotten that New West Schools are sustained by Christian people who deem religious results of the very highest importance, and while the Directors do not desire to have the teacher discharge any religious duties in a narrow, sectarian spirit, they do expect that they will use all proper endeavor to instil into the minds of the pupils the great truths of the Bible.[128]

The Mormons were naturally opposed to this invasion of missionary teachers. Brigham Young, Jr., is reported to have warned his people from the Tabernacle against the schools, telling them that "he would rather throw a child

---

[123] In 1880 the constitution of the American Home Missionary Society was amended so as to permit the expenditure of money for schools. *Home Missionary*, LIII (1880), 50.

[124] E. L. Hood, *New West Education Commission* (Jacksonville, Fla., 1905), 9-10.

[125] New West Education Commission, *First Report* (1881), 5.

[126] New West Education Commission, *Second Report* (1882), 29.

[127] New West Education Commission, *Thirteenth Report* (1893), 47.

[128] New West Education Commission, *Tenth Report* (1890), 33.

of his into hell than send him to one of these gentile schools."[129] The teachers themselves met with varied receptions. One unburdened herself as follows:

> I am nearly frantic tonight. The people here seem determined to pull down and destroy this school. If they cannot by truthful words, they do not scruple to make use of lies. They accuse me of calling the children profane and detestable names, and they say things of me which I cannot write. I have tried in God's name to do right, but I feel that I cannot endure such slanders.[130]

From time to time the "New West" teachers in Utah met in conferences to console and encourage one another. At their second annual institute held in Salt Lake City in November, 1890, the program included talks and discussions on such topics as these: Industrial Training, Methods and Devices in Teaching, Physical Culture, Missionary Aspects of Our Work, and The Development of a Patriotic Spirit among Our Pupils.[131]

In one sense the "New West" and all other mission schools in Utah killed themselves off. One of the first and chief results of their establishment was an improvement in the public schools of the territory. The school term was lengthened, additional taxes were levied for educational purposes, the standard of teaching was raised, and the Mormons were stimulated to stress education, with the result that Utah presently came to be regarded as one of the most progressive states educationally.[132] As the public-school system of Utah improved the need for denominational private schools decreased, and ultimately most of them were closed.

The maintenance of schools in the Southwest is of significance also in connection with the growing interest of women in the home missionary movement. The various denominational women's home missionary societies quite generally took as one of their especial tasks the supervision of mission schools.

---

[129] New West Education Commission, *Third Report* (1883), 11.

[130] New West Education Commission, *Fifth Report* (1885), 11.

[131] *Christian Education and New West Gleaner*, VII (1890-91), 55-56.

[132] Cf. L. P. Ayres, *An Index Number for State School Systems* (New York, c. 1920), 45. According to the ranking system used in this book Utah rose from 28th place among the states in 1890 to 8th place in 1918.

To measure accurately the results of the home missionary movement is quite impossible, but any attempt at an evaluation of its importance must necessarily count its educational work as among the greatest of the services it has rendered. Said the Reverend Newell Dwight Hillis: "Grateful to our inventors, to our merchants and our railroad builders, we can never forget the debt we owe our educators. Among the most useful men in the republic are these home missionaries who have toiled tirelessly to found schools, build academies, erect libraries, endow colleges, and turn the children of the church toward the path that leads to the temple of wisdom and knowledge."[133]

[133] N. D. Hillis, "Home Missions and Education," in *Home Missionary*, LXXVIII (1904), 279.

CHAPTER XIII

SIGNIFICANCE OF THE HOME MISSIONARY MOVEMENT

They [the home missionaries] bore the burden and the heat of the day, they toiled obscurely and died unknown, that we might come to a glorious heritage.—*Theodore Roosevelt.*

SPIRITUAL forces cannot be measured with mathematical exactness. The significance of the home missionary movement cannot be stated with finality; its results cannot be weighed with precision. It might be possible to estimate the amount of money spent for home missions in the United States in the nineteenth century, to count the churches and colleges founded, and even to estimate the number of converts made, but these are superficial tests of achievement. The more important results were intangible, and a statement of their significance is necessarily an excursion into the realm of opinion.

Certain tangible facts, however, should be noted. Up to 1894 the five Protestant denominations to which most attention has been devoted in this book had contributed to organized home missions through their various agencies and societies at least seventy million dollars. Of this amount Old and New School Presbyterians had given more than nineteen millions. The receipts of the American Home Missionary Society, which had been supported by both Presbyterians and Congregationalists up to the Civil War, and by the Congregationalists alone after that date, amounted to about sixteen million dollars by 1894; those of the Methodist Episcopal Church, North, were put at thirteen and a quarter million dollars, while the estimated receipts of the Methodist Church, South, were more than five million dollars. The American Baptist Home Mission Society had had roughly eight million dollars to spend up to that date, while the Domestic Board of the Protestant Episcopal Church counted its receipts at seven and a quarter million

dollars. In proportion to the wealth of the country and the other expenditures of the people, the total sum was not large —but it had been given voluntarily.

Another statistical approach to the problem might be made by counting the number of churches planted and nourished in the West by home missionaries; but the number, whatever it might be, would be less significant than the proportion of the home missionary churches to the whole group. The Presbyterians in 1873 estimated that nine tenths of all their churches organized west of Pennsylvania and New York had been organized by home missionaries;[1] the Congregationalists credit four fifths of their Western churches to home missions; the estimates of the Baptists and Methodists range from four fifths to nine tenths.[2] In 1856 the American Home Missionary Society reported that it had helped six hundred churches in western New York, or four fifths of the Presbyterian and Congregational churches in that region; that it had given aid to practically every church of those two denominations on the Western Reserve; that it had planted four hundred churches within a radius of 150 miles from Chicago; and that in twenty-one years it had granted assistance to 170 churches in Wisconsin.[3]

But all such figures and statistics, useful though they may be, do not take us very far beneath the surface of the problem. What we really want to know about these home mission churches is how they affected thought, belief, and conduct. Who found through them a meaning in life and a hope in death? Who was inspired by them to higher ideals? To what extent did they raise the moral tone and improve the social life of their communities? These are hard questions to answer, and before an attempt is made certain other statistics should be examined.

At the opening of the nineteenth century pious Eastern Christians were fearful that the West would develop as the godless part of the country. It was to prevent this that missionaries were sent into the new states and territories. To what extent did they accomplish their purpose of saving the West from atheism and irreligion? According to the

---

[1] *Minutes of the General Assembly of the Presbyterian Church in U.S.A.*, N.S. II, 610.

[2] C. R. Reisner, "The West—Methodism's Promised Land," in W. Platt, ed., *Methodism and the Republic* (Philadelphia, [1910]), 55-56.

[3] A.H.M.S., *Thirtieth Report* (1856), 91-92.

statistics on church membership compiled by the Census
Bureau early in the twentieth century (1906)—there was
then a fairly close correlation between the number of inhabitants and the number of church members in all parts
of the United States. The five New England states with 7.1
per cent of the population had 8.6 per cent of the church
members—but this slight surplus on the side of formal
godliness is no more than might be expected in this old
center of Puritanism. New York with 9.8 per cent of the
inhabitants claimed 10.9 per cent of the communicants.
Illinois, which had once been missionary territory, had in
1906, 6.4 per cent of the population and 6.3 per cent of the
church adherents. In Ohio the number was 5.3 per cent
in both cases. In both Wisconsin and Minnesota the balance
tipped slightly on the side of church membership: Wisconsin
with 2.7 per cent of the inhabitants had 3 per cent of the
communicants, while in Minnesota the two figures were 2.4
per cent for population and 2.5 per cent for church members. Colorado and Washington each had 0.7 per cent of the
population and 0.6 per cent of the church members. In California the figures were respectively 2.0 per cent and 1.9
per cent; in Montana, 0.4 per cent and 0.3 per cent; in
Wyoming they were 0.1 per cent in each instance.[4]

Although most of the Western states and territories fell
somewhat short of their proportionate number of church
members, the discrepancy was not great; and we may conclude that in so far as church membership is any criterion
the West was not markedly less godless than the East. However, it must be recognized at once that these figures which
present the West in so favorable a light as compared with
the East are not necessarily an indication of the success of
Protestant home missionary work, because in some Western
states the close correlation between the percentages of total
population and church members is obtained by counting the
adherents of certain religious bodies against whom Protestant missionaries inveighed year after year. Obviously New
Mexico, with its large Roman Catholic population, and Utah,
stronghold of the Latter-day Saints, cannot be presented
as evidence of the success of Protestant home missions, even
though the former with 0.3 per cent of the population had
0.4 per cent of the church members, and the latter with 0.4

---

[4] U. S. Census Bureau, *Religious Bodies: 1906*, Part I, 42-43.

per cent of the inhabitants of the United States claimed 0.5 per cent of the church adherents.

A fairer test of the achievement of the home missionaries is to be found through an examination of the number of communicants in the various religious bodies per thousand of population. In 1906 in continental United States 241 persons out of every one thousand were enrolled as members in some Protestant church. Protestantism was relatively strongest in the South Atlantic states, where on an average 363 in every thousand were church members. In the North Atlantic division, which may be regarded as the base from which the bulk of the money, men, and enthusiasm for the home missionary movement was sent forth prior to the Civil War, 184 persons a thousand were enrolled in Protestant religious bodies. In the North Central division, the region which was the great missionary field in the first half of the nineteenth century, the number was 232 a thousand. This is a favorable showing as compared with the Eastern base, but it is impossible to determine precisely to what extent it is the result on the one hand of the efficiency of the home missionaries or on the other of the congestion of large numbers of foreign-born Roman Catholics in the Eastern cities. In the Western division of the United States the number of Protestants in a thousand dropped to 132, the lowest in any of the major sections of the country.[5] This figure, however, does not mean necessarily that home missions in the Rocky Mountain and Pacific states and territories should be set down as a failure; there is both the possibility and the probability that the figure would have been distinctly lower had it not been for the men and money sent into the region for the establishment of churches and schools by the great national home missionary organizations.

If we break up the figures indicating the number of Protestants for a thousand of population into those for the various denominations whose home missionary activities have been recounted in this study we find equally satisfactory—or unsatisfactory—evidences of the degree of success attained. For continental United States in 1906, 67 out of every one thousand persons were enrolled in the several Baptist bodies. Baptist numerical strength was most in evidence in the South: in the South Atlantic states 174 a

---

[5] U. S. Census Bureau, *Religious Bodies: 1906*, Part I, 62.

thousand were Baptists, while in the South Central district the number was 140 a thousand. In the North Atlantic, the North Central, and the Western divisions the figures were respectively 24, 27, and 15 a thousand. In so far as the North Atlantic states were a base for Baptist missionary operations in the West, the showing made in the West may be regarded as satisfactory. It should be noted in passing that the part of the country in which for many years there was on the whole the least interest in organized missions among Baptists was the section in which the various Baptist bodies won their greatest successes so far as numbers were concerned. Obviously family connections and other personal predilections may be more significant in determining religious affiliations than formal missionary work.

For the entire United States in 1906 the Congregationalists numbered 8 a thousand. In New England, the old seat of Congregationalism, the figures ranged from 20 a thousand in Rhode Island to 65 a thousand in Connecticut. In the North Atlantic division, which includes New York, New Jersey, and Pennsylvania—states in which Congregationalism was not strong—as well as New England, the number of Congregationalists dropped to 14 a thousand. In the North Central and Western states and territories, both of which were regions of extensive Congregational missionary activities, either alone or in conjunction with the Presbyterians, the figures were 10 and 11 respectively. The lower figure (10) in the North Central district and the still lower figure of seven in New York may be due in part to the way in which the Plan of Union worked to the disadvantage of Congregationalists so far as numbers were concerned. Of the denominations whose home missionary activities are here recounted, Congregationalism is the least national, since it has made so little headway in the South. In the South Atlantic and South Central states Congregationalists numbered only one in a thousand in 1906. But inasmuch as Congregational missionary efforts have not been directed especially at this part of the United States the few adherents there of the New England Way give little or no indication about the success of Congregational home missions.

The distribution of Methodists throughout the United States did not show so much variation by sections as was true of both the Baptists and the Congregationalists. In the country as a whole, Methodists numbered 68 in a thousand.

The figures for the various sectional divisions were: North Atlantic, 41; South Atlantic, 128; North Central, 59; South Central, 92; and Western, 37.

Presbyterian numerical strength, although nowhere so great, was more uniformly distributed over the country than that of the Methodists. It ranged from 18 in a thousand in the South Central states and 19 in the South Atlantic division, through 21 in the North Central and 22 in the Western, to 26 in the North Atlantic states. Superficially at least these figures would seem to indicate both the general appeal of the principles and polity of the Presbyterians and the effectiveness of their methods of church expansion.

In 1906, 11 out of every thousand persons in the United States were communicants of the Protestant Episcopal Church. This was much below the average for the North Atlantic states of 20 in a thousand. It is probably more than a coincidence that in the North Central states—part of which were being settled at a time when the missionary spirit was weak among the Episcopalians—the number of their members was put at only 6 in a thousand, while in the Western division, a region which on the whole was settled later and at a time when Episcopalian missionary work was being prosecuted more vigorously, the figure stood at 11 in a thousand, the same as the national average for this denomination.[6]

The problem of the success of home missions may be approached also by way of an examination of the statistics on the number of congregations and total church membership. Since the West was the principal field of expansion for all of the denominations, the shift in relative strength that occurred in the nineteenth century gives some indication of the type of religion that appealed most to the people in the new settlements. At the beginning of the Revolutionary War it has been estimated that in numerical strength the churches in America ranked as follows: Congregational, 700; Baptist, 380; Church of England, 300; Presbyterian, 300; Lutheran, 60; German Reformed, 60; Dutch Reformed, 60; Roman Catholic, 52; Methodist societies, 30.[7] By 1860

---

[6] U. S. Census Bureau, *Religious Bodies: 1906*, Part I, 62.

[7] D. Dorchester, *Christianity in the United States*, 256; R. Baird, *Religion in the United States of America* (Glasgow, Edinburgh, and London, 1844), 225, sets the number of Congregational churches in 1775 at 600; his figures for the other denominations are as given above.

the order, based on the number of churches, had changed materially, as is shown by the following figures: Methodist, 19,833; Baptist, 11,221; Presbyterian, 5,061; Roman Catholic, 2,550; Congregational, 2,234; Protestant Episcopal, 2,145; Lutheran, 2,128; Christians or Disciples of Christ, 2,068.[8] In these shifts in position the most striking changes were the growth of the Methodists from thirty small societies in 1776 to nearly twenty thousand congregations in 1860, the rise of the Catholics from eighth to fourth place, and the appearance of a new religious organization, the Disciples of Christ; in one generation the latter had attained a size comparable with that of two older groups, the Episcopalians and Congregationalists. In 1890 the order of rank on the basis of the number of local church organizations was as follows: Methodist, 40,878; Baptist, 36,693; Presbyterian, 11,894; Lutheran (of all synods), 11,880; Roman Catholic, 10,239; Disciples of Christ, 7,246; Protestant Episcopal, 5,018; Congregational, 4,868. If total membership or communicants be taken as the basis for ranking, the principal change in the order for 1890 would be that the Roman Catholics would stand first. In the light of these important changes in numerical strength in a little more than a century the question arises as to what were the characteristics of the various denominations which hindered or helped their growth in the West.

First place among Protestants was taken and held by the Methodists. Their system of itinerant preaching was admirably adapted to the conditions which prevailed on the frontier. All over the West the circuit riders were the pioneers among Protestants. They were individualistic and had initiative, but still were subject to skillful guidance by their presiding elders and bishops. But probably more important in winning the West than an efficient organization was the doctrine preached: free grace, free will, and individual responsibility. Here were teachings that appealed to the frontiersman's sense of justice and fair play.[9] In place of a closely reasoned Calvinistic system, they taught a simple scheme of religion. They were not afraid to sing and shout when the spirit moved them; they had appealed

---

[8] *Statistics of the United States, ... in 1860* (Washington, 1866), 497-501.

[9] W. W. Sweet, *Rise of Methodism in the West*, 14.

from "the theology of the intellect to the theology of feeling."[10]

Next came the Baptists, who in church organization and in the character of their preaching were closely in harmony with the temper of the West. Their church polity was congregational, and the individual church was governed democratically. There was no gulf fixed between the pulpit and the pew. Before the Civil War their ministers in the West were often men of very little formal education, who received small remuneration from their congregations and who worked with their hands during the week just as did the people to whom they ministered. They taught a simplified form of Calvinism and appealed directly to the exact words of the Bible, rejecting all human authority and tradition. In this they reflected one characteristic of the West, its self-confidence, its self-sufficiency, its indifference to the past, and its contempt for tradition. The Baptists insisted on personal religion and moral obligation; in their preaching they appealed to the emotions; they exalted the "gifts of the Spirit."

Although the Presbyterians had not made such remarkable gains as the Methodists and the Baptists they had held their place in numerical ranking among the Protestants. Their church organization was republican and sufficiently rigid to afford unity of action and to check the spread of heresy. They had insisted on an educated clergy even at the cost of alienating some of their most earnest members in the West. In ability to preach the Presbyterian ministry ranked high; it surpassed that of the Methodists and Baptists in education; it was equal to that of the Congregationalists and Episcopalians in training, and on the whole more effective in methods of delivery. Presbyterianism stood for orthodoxy and sound doctrine. Unwilling to tolerate even slight divergences of opinion or practice from the accepted standards, it was disturbed again and again by discord and divisions. But Presbyterian insistence on orthodoxy did not necessarily alienate the people of the West. They were just as orthodox in their own way; it was the popular desire for a simpler—but still orthodox—theology, and for a system which would allow for more play of the emotions that

---

[10] J. L. Diman, "Religion in America, 1776-1876," in *North American Review*, CXXII (1876), 26.

prevented the Presbyterians from reaching the masses as did the Methodists and Baptists.

The Lutherans, who were practically as numerous as the Presbyterians in the United States in 1890, owed their strength primarily to immigration into America after 1830, hence need not be considered in the present connection. Next in order come the Disciples of Christ. Theirs is the only important Christian denomination in the United States, unless Mormonism be accepted as Christian, which was developed in the West. They started in the West early in the nineteenth century, and their strength has remained mainly in the Middle West. Their teachings were simple and clear; there was little occasion for worry about the soul's welfare, because they outlined a definite scheme of salvation: belief, repentance, confession, and baptism. Like the Baptists they appealed to the Bible as the sole authority, and they rejected all human creeds and statements. They pleaded for a union of all Christians on the basis of the Bible; their motto was: "Where the Bible speaks, we speak; where the Bible is silent, we are silent." The difficulty they have experienced in their efforts to bring about Christian union on this apparently simple platform has been due to differences of opinion regarding interpretation and emphasis, and the unwillingness of any Protestant denomination to admit that its beliefs and practices were in any way unscriptural.

For the comparatively slow growth of the Protestant Episcopal Church in the West at least three reasons may be advanced. In the first place, the strength of this Church in the East lay in the wealthier and more aristocratic groups in society; it had not attracted to itself large numbers of the poorer people, those who were most likely to move to the frontiers in search of a new and better opportunity. Secondly, there were many in the Episcopal Church who admitted that its beautiful and elaborate ritual did not appeal to the average "rough and ready" frontiersman. Finally, this Church was late in beginning serious missionary work in the West. Almos tnothing was done before 1835; adequate machinery was not provided until after the Civil War. But once the means were available, the zeal of the missionary priests and bishops, combined with the advantages of a centralized organization, did much to increase the number of Episcopal adherents in the West.

Of the denominations considered in the present connec-

tion the Congregational has gone from first to last place in numbers in the course of the nineteenth century. Perhaps one reason is to be found in the fact so many adherents of the New England Way have not cared especially how large their denomination was. Until comparatively late they manifested little interest in building up Congregationalism as such; their sense of denominational loyalty was not strong. They had insisted that faith, good will, and right conduct were more important in religion than connection with any particular organization and hence viewed with complacency for a time the operation of the Plan of Union. Congregational church organization was democratic, and each congregation was practically an independent unit; hence it was found difficult to introduce Congregationalism into the West except in those places where there were enough people from earlier centers of New England influence to make a fairly strong church at the outset. The trouble was not in the polity; Baptist and Disciples churches were also congregational in church government, but ordinarily it took a much shorter time for one of their congregations to become strong enough to stand alone because of their greater popular appeal. And yet in proportion to their numbers the Congregationalists gave more money for organized home missions throughout the nineteenth century than any other one of the denominations we have considered in this study. The conclusion to be drawn is not that the home missionary movement was unprofitable to the Congregationalists as a denomination, but that to it they owe the fact that they have not remained a sect localized in New England, and one with a declining influence.

Among the Protestant denominations whose home missionary activities have been examined, the tendency throughout the nineteenth century has been towards greater similarity in doctrine and practice. Methodist meetings, once denounced as noisy, are now quiet and decorous; Baptist preachers, once despised as ignorant by their more learned colleagues, now include some of the foremost thinkers and scholars in the field of religion; in Congregational and Presbyterian pulpits little attention is paid now to the old Calvinistic doctrines. In so far as the home missionary movement has represented an attempt to maintain traditional barriers and distinctions among the denominations, it has been only partly successful.

Significant also is the bearing of the home missionary movement on the success of the voluntary system of church management and support. The United States generally abandoned the age-old system of state support for religion at the close of the eighteenth century. Conservatives were alarmed lest religion should be neglected. The last ties connecting church and state were being severed just at the time that the opening of the trans-Allegheny West threw a burden of unprecedented magnitude on American Christians. Long before the end of the nineteenth century it was evident that they had risen to the occasion and that the separation of church and state had not resulted in irreligion. It has been estimated that at the outbreak of the Revolution there were in this country about 1950 churches, or one church to 1700 people;[11] at the opening of the Civil War there were about 54,000 churches, or one to 574 people;[12] in 1890 there were more than 151,000 churches in the United States, or one for 414 inhabitants.[13] Leaving out of account the factor of seating capacity, on which we have no estimates for the earlier period, it appears that in proportion to population there were three times as many churches in this country in 1860 as in 1775, and more than four times as many in 1890. Essentially the same story is told by the increase in the ratio of church members or communicants to the whole population. In 1800 it has been estimated that there was one communicant in 14.50 inhabitants; in 1850, one in 6.57; in 1890, one in 4.53. This creditable showing is due in no small degree to the money and enthusiasm furnished by the home missionary movement.

While recognizing that the home missionary movement has revealed clearly one of the best features of the voluntary system of church support—the opportunity for individual initiative and personal religious enthusiasm and generosity to manifest themselves in grappling with a problem without direction or interference from the outside—it must not be forgotten that it also brought into sharp relief the wasteful character of the system. The rivalry between the churches in the West has generally been friendly, but it has been planless; they have often worked at cross-purposes; they

[11] D. Dorchester, *Christianity in the United States*, 256.

[12] *Statistics of the United States ... compiled from the Eighth Census*, 497-501.

[13] D. Dorchester, *Christianity in the United States*, 755.

have duplicated churches needlessly in some places and entirely neglected others. The Plan of Union of 1801 was an attempt on the part of the Presbyterians and Congregationalists to prevent such evils so far as they themselves were concerned. The attempt failed under the stress of the growing spirit of sectarianism that characterized the period preceding the Civil War. In 1874 the secretaries of the American Home Missionary Society and the Board of Missions of the Presbyterian Church, North, adopted a set of resolutions that were aimed to prevent duplication of churches of those two denominations in places where there was room for but one church. Their joint statement read in part as follows:

> We therefore most earnestly recommend to all Presbyterians and all Congregationalists, . . . to be careful so as to advise and act with respect to all unorganized communities that, if possible, there may be but one strong and harmonious Church organization at first, whether it be Congregational or Presbyterian; to avoid the wicked waste of funds in the support of two feeble Churches, both of which must be weak, and which might become involved in bitter, protracted and unholy strife. . . . With regard to places where both a Presbyterian and a Congregational church already exist, but where both are weak and but one is necessary, we would recommend that such churches meet together with prayer and conference, seek to become one on any basis that is equitable and that promises good results.[14]

About 1893, when the question of competition in the West was becoming acute, a conference of the representatives of all the evangelical missionary boards was called to consider the problem. Only the Presbyterian, the Reformed, and the Congregational boards were represented, but these three made a compact for the settlement of all questions that might arise among them as to right of occupancy of new territory. It was found that the written law of each of these boards was explicitly against the invasion of one another's territory and the overcrowding of home missionary churches. The declared principle of the Presbyterian Board was "to avoid interference improperly with existing organizations or multiplying churches from mere sectarian considerations"; the written rule of the Congregational Home Missionary Society was never to plant a new church on ground "which in the proper sense of the word is cared for by other evangelical denominations."[15]

---

[14] *Home Missionary*, XLVII (1874), 162.
[15] *Home Missionary*, LXXVII (1903), 54.

Whatever may have been accomplished by such an *entente cordiale* between the Presbyterians and the Congregationalists, it did not prevent competition between either one or both of them and other denominations. Attention was again drawn sharply to the problem in the closing years of the nineteenth century. In the period of financial depression that followed the panic of 1893 all the missionary societies and boards were forced to retrench or struggle with heavy deficits. When money had been fairly plentiful questions had been raised as to the advisability of four or five rival denominational missionary societies keeping alive the same number of competing churches in the same small town; but when they were all struggling to keep afloat it seemed worse than folly. A writer in the *Independent* in 1897 expressed the opinion that the reason the contributions to the various missionary societies had fallen off was that the people had lost faith in denominational missions with their emphasis on sectarian aggrandizement. His indictment of the system ran in part as follows:

> The cry of debt is heard at the treasury of every one of the denominations. Thoughtful men and women in all branches of the Church have come by common enlightenment of opinion to see that our present system is not only wasteful of men and money, but is proving to be positively destructive of the higher social interests of our new communities.

After discussing the evil of overlapping and the waste of money in unnecessary church buildings and the payment of salaries, he added, with reference to a typical Western village, this opinion:

> Back of this material loss in men and money lie the deeper spiritual injuries to this community. At the very heart of its communal life division and wicked competition are instituted. The religion of Christ comes as a minister of disintegration, debate and pettiness. Back of this lies a deeper curse. This little community, broken into helpless fragments must hang for years upon the charity of others. The people are pauperized at the very altars of their worship.[16]

The competitive system must also meet the charge that the money and effort spent in duplicate work might otherwise have been spent in places comparatively overlooked by all missionary agencies. Overlooking was sometimes

---

[16] J. H. Ecob, "Home Missions and Debt," in *Independent*, XLIX (1897), 1166-67.

a more obvious error than overlapping. From the results of an investigation made in Colorado in 1909 it appears that this was true in that state. According to this survey 11 per cent of home mission money spent in Colorado went to places in which there was but one church; 11.2 per cent to small towns where two or more mission boards were giving aid; 77 per cent went to the nine largest cities in the state— the so-called "strategic centers." The survey also revealed that there were 153 towns and villages in Colorado ranging in population from 150 to 1000 without any Protestant church; one hundred of these had no Roman Catholic church. In addition to these towns and villages there were 428 other communities of sufficient importance to have post offices that had no church of any sort.[17] These figures suggest that overlapping in small communities and unwise denominational subsidies to weak competing churches were not so common as was generally supposed, but they also show the unfinished nature of the home missionary task.

It must also be remembered in any discussion of duplication of missionary effort that it is in one sense a part of the price that we pay for our religious freedom. Multiplicity of sects is the logical outcome of the Protestant Reformation. Protestantism stands for the right of the individual to select his own form of religious thought and expression. When half a dozen church bells ring out at the same time in the same western village they do not necessarily sing a song of discord, strife, and jealousy. Perhaps the bells are saying, "Freedom of thought," "Toleration in religion," "Come here if you please," "Go there if you prefer." However desirable it may be to reduce the number of competing churches, it is not likely, so long as people have likes and dislikes in religion and so long as America retains its democratic principles, that any method of shuffling the worshipers about so as to form congregations of ideal size will work.

There remain for consideration certain intangible but very real results of the home missionary movement. Missionaries threw their influence on the side of spiritual as opposed to material values. Conditions of life in the new settlements were generally such as tended inevitably to drag the pioneers down in the social scale. If on the one hand

---

[17] E. B. Sanford, *Origin and History of the Federal Council of the Churches of Christ in America* (Hartford, 1916), 513-15.

such virtues as hospitality, courage, and resourcefulness were prized, on the other the amenities and niceties of life had to give way before the stark necessities of existence. In the very nature of things the frontier was materialistic. The missionaries did what they could to turn the thoughts of men from material to spiritual concerns; they did inspire the youth of countless Western communities with a desire for a better education; they did use their influence to curb the passions of lawless men. They were a wholesome leaven in Western society. An editorial in the *Outlook,* about the time that the frontier was disappearing from the American scene, put it this way:

> The home missionary, who to many people is hardly more than a man with a wife and several children somewhere out West, to whom a barrel full of odds and ends is sent, and from whom is received a letter full of gratitude and accounts of prayer-meetings, is in reality one of the most dominant agents in the making of history that the world has ever known. Compared with the settlement and civilization of Europe the spread of civilization over the territory which now comprises the United States has been startling in its swiftness. No armies ever achieved so thorough or so speedy a triumph as the American pioneers did. And among the pioneers none were more courageous, none were more steadfast, and none more in earnest, or, on the whole, more successful in attaining their purposes, than the men who went, not for the sake of extracting wealth from the soil, but for the sake of establishing righteousness in the new communities. In the midst of greed, or what may at best be called the spirit of acquisitiveness, they injected the spirit that seeks not to get but to give, the saving spirit of service, the leaven of the Nation.[18]

One specific illustration of the effect of the establishment of churches in frontier communities is to be found in the relatively unimportant matter of dress and deportment. A man who had watched the development of Illinois attributed the improvement in the dress and personal appearance of the young people of the state after 1830 in part to the habit of church attendance. The man who wrote the following knew human nature, even if he could not marshal documentary evidence to prove his contention that:

> [For this advancement in civilization,] the young people [of Illinois] were much indebted to their practice of attending church on Sundays. Here they were regularly brought together at stated times; and their meeting, if it effected no better end, at least accustomed them to admire and to wish to be admired. Each one wanted to make as

---

[18] *Outlook,* LXXIV (1903), 1050-51.

good a figure as he could; and to that end came to the meeting well-dressed and clean, riding on a fine horse elegantly caparisoned. This created in them a will to exert more than the old measure of industry; and taught them new notions of economy and ingenuity in business, to get the means of gratifying their pride in this particular. This again led to settled habits of enterprise, economy and tact in business, which once acquired and persevered in, were made the cause of a thriftiness unknown to their fathers and mothers.... I have observed very carefully ... that in those neighborhoods where the people habitually neglect to attend public worship on Sundays, such improvements rarely, if ever, take place. In such places the young people feel no pride, and do not desire improvement. They scarcely ever throw aside their everyday rough apparel to dress up neat and clean on Sunday. On that day the young men are seen with uncombed heads, unshorn beards, and unwashed linen, strolling in the woods hunting; or on the race-course, or at grocery contracting habits of intoxication, or lounging sullenly and lazily at home. The young women in appearance, dress, manners and intelligence, are fit companions for their brothers. Sunday brings to them no bright skies, no gladness, no lively cheerful thoughts, and no spirits renovated by mixing in the sober, decent, quiet, but gay assemblage of youth and beauty. Their week of labor is not cheered by anticipations of the gay and bright fête with which it is to close. Labor through the week to them is drudgery; and is performed with surliness and grudging; and their Sabbaths are spent in heedless sleepy stupidity....[19]

Of the definite results of the home missionary movement one of the most important—the founding of colleges and schools—has already been discussed.[20] But here again the intangible outweighs the tangible in importance. Granted that with the exception of the State universities the great majority of all the colleges more than sixty years old west of the Alleghenies have been the product of missionary zeal or religious enthusiasm,[21] the question of how they have molded the lives of their students and what influences they have exerted in their communities remains unanswered—but the answer to this question is far more significant than the number of their graduates, the value of their endowments, or the size of their libraries, however impressive those figures might be. Anyone who might attempt to answer this question—and who is wise enough?—should consider, for example, the effect of Kenyon College on Rutherford B. Hayes, of Illinois College on the youthful William Jennings Bryan,

---

[19] T. Ford, *History of Illinois*, 95.

[20] Chapter XII.

[21] Cf. P. G. Mode, *Frontier Spirit in American Christianity* (New York, 1923), 59-65.

or of Oberlin on the daring spirits of Lucy Stone and An-
toinette Blackwell. He should try to find out the effect of
Iowa College (Grinnell) on Jesse Macy, distinguished political economist, of Beloit on George Burton Adams, historian,
of Carleton on Marion L. Burton, university president, and
of Wabash on James Bassett, missionary to Persia, to mention only a few of the men and women trained in these mid-
western home missionary colleges.

Probably we shall never know exactly the answer to these
questions, but we may be sure that by and large these institutions with their poorly paid yet devoted teachers
influenced for good the lives of the eager and earnest young
men and women who came to them from the neighboring
farms and small towns, often as a result of great sacrifices
on the part of their parents. But if on the one hand these
schools built character and stressed the Christian virtues,
on the other, too often, they tended to stifle free inquiry
and to resist changes in thought. They naturally frowned
on deviations from the accepted theological beliefs of their
ecclesiastical sponsors, and some of them resisted the inroads of scientific ideas, such as the theory of evolution,
which seemed contrary to the Bible.

In general the home missionary movement was an expression of nationalism. It is true that at some times and
in some places the arrival of a home missionary intensified
sectional antipathies. Viewed from one angle the movement
seemed to grow out of a feeling of superiority on the part
of the people of the North and East over their less fortunate
fellows in the South and the West. But this aspect of the
movement was not so significant as the more encouraging
expressions of disinterested good will. Nationalism as applied to religion and morals, that is, a desire that the whole
country might be dedicated to sound principles and free,
democratic institutions, was a more important motive than
sectional pride. De Tocqueville, in commenting on the fact
that cultured and prosperous New Englanders left their
homes to lay the foundations of Christianity and freedom
on the banks of the Mississippi or the Missouri, said:

Thus religious zeal is continually warmed in the United States by
the fires of patriotism. These men do not act exclusively from a consideration of a future life; eternity is only one motive of their devotion to the cause. If you converse with these missionaries of Christian
civilization, you will be surprised to hear them speak so often of the

goods of this world, and to meet a politician where you expected to find a priest. They will tell you that "all the American republics are collectively involved with each other: if the republics of the West were to fall into anarchy, or to be mastered by a despot, the republican institutions which now flourish upon the shores of the Atlantic Ocean would be in great peril. It is, therefore, our interest that the new states should be religious in order that they may permit us to remain free."[22]

Just as patriotism was a more important motive than local or selfish interest in the home missionary movement, so in its results nationalism outweighed sectionalism. Moral and spiritual ties had been drawn between the East and the West that were stronger than the forces that tended to drive them apart. When the test of the Union came in 1861 the Northwest, in defiance of geography and old economic interests, took its stand with the Northeast. In explaining this momentous decision—a decision on which really depended the outcome of the struggle—several factors must be taken into account: the building of railroads had diverted to Atlantic ports commerce which had formerly gone down the Mississippi; economic and social differences had developed between the upper and lower parts of the Mississippi Valley; the Germans and other foreign-born who had settled in the Northwest were opposed to the South's "peculiar institution"; the Northwest had drawn its native American population mainly from the Middle and North Atlantic states, since people who moved West tended to follow their own line of latitude. All these are important, but to them should be added the intangible moral and spiritual ties that connected the Northeast and the Northwest. These ties were based on religious convictions; they had been stretched from New England towns to the prairies of Illinois and Iowa by missionary preachers and teachers. Again and again this point of view, often no doubt in uncritical and exaggerated language, was set forth by the men who in Civil War days were interested both in the preservation of the Union and the salvation of the West. Henry Ward Beecher, militant spokesman for the Northern point of view, said in 1863:

The enemies of liberty have attempted to draw us [in the East] from the West and the Northwest. Why have they not done it? It looked as if they might accomplish their foul purpose. The superficial

---

[22] A. de Tocqueville, *Democracy in America*, I, 392; cf. E. D. Adams, *Power of Ideals in American History*, 109.

aspect of the population of those regions would have led one to suppose that they were ready to go with the South. What saved them to the North? It has been the secret working of the truth of Christ's Gospel that has thus far held them back from going over to the side of those who are striving to put down freedom in this country.[23]

From the West came the answering statement of a Chicago minister:

Who does not know that the loyalty of the West, which along with the East has gone down against the South, as did the hordes of Northern Europe, has been produced to a large extent by the sturdy influence of pioneer missionaries? Everywhere patriotic, everywhere rallying the people, and using their pulpits for recruiting stations, they have but reaped the fruit of their former teachings in the enlistment-rolls that have often taken away their sons and the strength of their temporal support. By responses to a recent circular, we learn that the Congregational churches of Illinois have sent into the war one in *eight* of their male members; Wisconsin, one in *nine;* Minnesota, one in *seven;* Iowa, one in *five;* . . .[24]

The War between the States had shown, to quote the words of another observer, that "bonds stronger than those created by the flow of rivers or by the rising of mountain barriers—bonds athwart them, and defying all such obstructions—link the East and the West."[25] And these bonds, which were "moral and sacred, and therefore indissoluble," had been drawn by the humble home missionaries.

While the East was thus putting the stamp of its ideas and institutions on the West through the home missionary movement, the West was also reacting on the East in certain ways.[26] Attention has already been called to the growth of denominational consciousness among Congregationalists in the years preceding the Civil War and to the significance of the West in the development of this feeling of unity.[27] Similarly, the more radical antislavery Congregationalists and Presbyterians in the West appear to have stimulated the American Home Missionary Society to take a more pronounced stand on the slavery question.[28] Probably more im-

---

[23] *Home Missionary*, XXXVI (1863), 112.

[24] *Home Missionary*, XXXVI (1863), 91.

[25] S.P.C.T.E.W., *Nineteenth Report* (1862), 44-45.

[26] Cf. H. A. Stimson, "Some Contributions which the West may be Expected to make to the Congregationalism of the Future," in *The New Englander*, XXXIX (1880), 124-37.

[27] See above, page 253 f.

[28] See above, page 291.

portant than these influences, but even more intangible, is the psychological or spiritual reaction which must have come to those Easterners who participated in a movement intended to minister to the needs of other people in other parts of the country. Those who shared in the movement either by the contribution of money or the filling of a missionary box had widened their interests; those who read the reports of the missionaries in their religious periodicals had probably broadened their horizons. Thus in reaching out from themselves to others the friends of home missions shared in the humanitarian spirit of the age. The home missionary movement was produced, in part at least, by the same forces which brought about the establishment of antislavery, temperance, prison reform, and woman's rights societies.

But above all the home missionary movement was religious in its motives, methods, and objects. It was an attempt to bring men to God in accordance with the principles of Protestant Christianity. In general it may be said that the movement was conservative in its tendencies and results. The sponsors of the movement in the East and those who went out as missionaries were those who prized most highly their own religious institutions and who were most anxious to conserve and spread them. Through their efforts essentially the same type of religious life that prevailed among Eastern Protestants in the first half of the nineteenth century was transplanted in the West. It was practical rather than mystical; it put emphasis on individual righteousness and personal salvation after death rather than on social righteousness and community salvation now; it did not entirely escape the unchristian notion that men may attain goodness by the observance of rules rather than by a change of heart; it was strongly orthodox in its theology, which meant more specifically that it was Trinitarian, that it believed in the literal interpretation and the verbal inerrancy of the Bible, and that it visualized heaven as a city of gold and hell as a place of eternal torment. In short, the Puritanic theological concepts and practices were set up and cherished in the West through home missions.

The conservative effect of home missions extended to social as well as purely religious institutions. A Kansas missionary, aware of the significance of the work he and his fellows were trying to do in the West, wrote in 1880:

The *conservative influence* of the Presbyterian Church should not be overlooked in these farming communities, such as we have in this State. We have Free Lovism, Spiritualism, Materialism and such like cropping out here and there. A good solid Presbyterian Church stands as a stone wall against the fiery darts of such enemies. The home missionary is not only a pioneer doing duty as a picket in front of the main army, but he must stand guard over ground already won, sometimes defending and protecting institutions as old as the human race and as sacred as the Bible, as the institution of marriage and the holy Sabbath.[29]

It is not by chance that the South and Middle West have been the strongholds of fundamentalism and the chief centers of such traces of Puritanism as remain in this country.

The home missionary movement, as it has been presented here, represented an attempt on the part of pious Christians in the East, particularly those in New England and the Middle States, to control religion and education in the West. It was an effort, as its proponents often said, to prevent the people in the new settlements from lapsing into heathenism and to establish among them those forms of Protestantism that were dominant in the older states. It did its work mainly through devoted men who shared the hardships of the frontier, not primarily in order to enjoy its material blessings, but to make their contributions to the development there of the good life. They toiled obscurely and laid down their lives freely in order that others might live more abundantly. They were spiritual leaders who stood for idealism in the midst of materialism. They believed that righteousness exalteth a nation and that sin is a reproach to any people. They served their country, according to their light, quietly and faithfully, and well did they deserve the tribute paid them by President Theodore Roosevelt at the Presbyterian Centennial of Home Missions in 1902:

The century that has closed has seen the conquest of this continent by our people. To conquer a continent is rough work ... ; but it would be difficult to overestimate the value of the missionary work of those who go out to share the hardships, and while sharing it, not to talk about but to wage war against the myriad forms of brutality.... It is because of the spirit that underlies the missionary work, that the pioneers are prevented from sinking perilously near the level of the savagery against which they contend. Without it the conquest of this continent would have had little but an animal side. Without it the pioneers' fierce and rude virtues and somber faults would have been

---

[29] *Presbyterian Monthly Record*, XXXI (1880), 207-08.

left unlit by the flame of pure and loving aspiration. Without it the life of this country would have been a life of inconceivably hard and barren materialism.... Honor, thrice honor, to those who for three generations, during the period of the people's great expansion, have seen that the force of the living truth expanded as the nation expanded.

SELECTED BIBLIOGRAPHY

MANUSCRIPT SOURCES

American Home Missionary Society papers (including United Domestic Missionary Society papers, 1822-26), 1822-93 (name changed to Congregational Home Missionary Society in 1893) : reports from missionaries and miscellaneous correspondence (although the letters, which now fill 23 four-drawer filing cases, have not been counted, the number is estimated at about 200,000) ; Minutes of Executive Committee (25 vols., 1826-92) ; Letter Books (163 vols., 1826-1904). This material was in the possession of the Congregational Home Missionary Society, 287 Fourth Avenue, New York, when I first used it in 1917. The letter books (in which many of the copies are now illegible as a result of fading) and most of the missionary reports have since been transferred to the Hammond Library of the Chicago Theological Seminary. I have attempted to check there all of my references taken originally in New York; my references, unless otherwise indicated, are to the present location of the material in the Hammond Library (missionary reports, except for four bound volumes of letters, 1845-46, are filed in chronological order by the state or territory of origin). Abbreviation used in notes: A.H.M.S. papers, C.T.S. However, I have been unable to locate in Chicago all the documents I used in New York; in such cases I have given my original references to the Congregational Home Missionary Society archives, where the papers were numbered for each year of the Society's history and stored in wooden boxes. Abbreviation used: C.H.M.S. I have been informed by the officers of this Society that some years subsequent to my first use of this material, at a time when storage space in New York was both scarce and expensive, and before a depository was found in Chicago, an effort was made to clear out file accumulations which had become valueless, and that in this process some of the reports and other valuable documents in the collection may unfortunately have been destroyed. So far as my observations go, the gaps in the Chicago collection occur mainly in two periods: (1) 1822-26; (2) 1877-93. The American Home Missionary Society papers are not listed in W. H. Allison, *Inventory of Unpublished Material for American Religious History* (Washington, 1910).

Chicago Theological Seminary (Hammond Library). American Home Missionary Society papers (see above) ; MS. thesis: Evah I. Ostrander, "The American Home Missionary Society in Oregon, 1849-70," (M.A.).

Colorado, University of. MS. theses: R. Maud Ditmars, "A History of Baptist Missions in Utah, 1871-1931," (M.A.) ; Lynn I. Perrigo, "A Social History of Central City, Colorado, 1859-1900," (Ph.D.).

Congregational Home Missionary Society. See American Home Missionary Society.

Connecticut Home Missionary Society papers, Congregational House, Hartford. Reports of missionaries examined for the period 1798 to 1820. Allison, *Inventory*, 3-4.

Harvard University. Letter from Bishop John Ettwein to Benjamin Trumbull.

Kansas Historical Society, Topeka. Isaac McCoy papers.

Lambeth Palace, London. Papers relating to the American colonies and MS. Journals of the Society for the Propagation of the Gospel. C. M. Andrews and F. G. Davenport, *Guide to the Manuscript Materials for the History of the United States to 1783,...* (Washington, 1908).

Library of Congress, Washington. Transcripts: Great Britain (copies of S.P.G. correspondence).

Missouri Historical Society, St. Louis. Hempstead papers.

Nebraska Historical Society, Lincoln. Show papers; MS. thesis: V. C. Fuhlrodt, "The Pioneer History of Fontenelle, Nebraska," (M.A.).

United Domestic Missionary Society. See American Home Missionary Society.

Warner, Fanny. Diary and letters. In possession of Miss Martha Morrison, Denver.

Wisconsin Historical Society, Madison. Jackson Kemper papers.

Yale University. MSS. relating to the missionary work of the General Association of Connecticut and the Missionary Society of Connecticut.

PRINTED MATERIAL

This list of books, pamphlets, and magazine articles is not a compilation of all titles mentioned in the footnotes; those referred to incidentally and with no close relationship to the home missionary movement have been omitted. In the case of periodicals and reports of societies, the dates given are for the years consulted.

ABERNETHY, ALONZO. *A History of Iowa Baptist Schools.* Osage, Iowa, 1907.

ADAMS, EPHRAIM. *The Iowa Band.* Boston, 1870; rev. ed., 1902.

ADAMS, EPHRAIM DOUGLASS. *The Power of Ideals in American History.* New Haven, 1913.

ALEXANDER, ARCHIBALD. *Biographical Sketches of the Founder and Principal Alumni of the Log College.* Philadelphia, [1851].

ALEXANDER, GROSS. *History of the Methodist Episcopal Church, South (Amer. Ch. Hist. Ser., XI).* New York, 1894.

ALLEN, IRA W. "Early Presbyterianism in East Central Illinois," *Transactions of the Illinois State Historical Society for the year 1916* (Pub. No. 22 of the Ill. State Hist. Lib.), 71-78. Springfield, 1917.

ALLEN, W. O. B., and McCLURE, EDMUND. *Two Hundred Years: the History of the Society for Promoting Christian Knowledge, 1698-1898.* London, 1898.

AMERICAN BAPTIST HOME MISSION SOCIETY. [Annual] Reports. New York, 1833-1909.

———. Baptist Home Missions in North America. New York, 1883.

———. Proceedings of the Convention Held in the City of New-York, ...for the Formation of the American Baptist Home Mission Society.... New York, 1832.

American Baptist Magazine and Missionary Intelligencer (title varies). Boston, 1817-30.

American Baptist Register, for 1852. Ed. by J. Lansing Burrows. Philadelphia, 1853.

American Church History Series. Edited by Philip Schaff, H. C. Potter, Samuel M. Jackson. 13 vols. New York, 1893-97.

AMERICAN COLLEGE AND EDUCATION SOCIETY. See American Education Society.

AMERICAN EDUCATION SOCIETY. Address to the Directors of the American Education Society. Boston, 1817. Pamphlet.

———. [Annual] Reports. Andover, 1816-17; Boston, 1818-74.

———. Quarterly Register and Journal (title varies). Andover, 1829-30; Boston, 1831-43.

AMERICAN HOME MISSIONARY SOCIETY. [Annual] Reports. New York, 1827-93.

———. Our Country; Its Capabilities, Its Perils, and its Hope.... New York, 1842.

———. A Plea for Home Missions. New York, 1858.

———. Reply of the Executive Committee of the American Home Missionary Society to a Communication in Behalf of a Commission of the General Assembly of the Presbyterian Church. N.p., 1860. Pamphlet.

AMERICAN SOCIETY FOR EDUCATING PIOUS YOUTH FOR THE GOSPEL MINISTRY. See American Education Society.

ANDERSON, JAMES S. M. The History of the Church of England, in the Colonies and Foreign Dependencies of the British Empire. 3 vols. London, 1845-56.

Annales de l'Association de la Propagation de la Foi. Paris and Lyons, 1827-51.

APTHORP, EAST. Consideration on the Institution and Conduct of the Society for the Propagation of the Gospel in Foreign Parts. Boston, 1763.

———. A Review of Dr. Mayhew's Remarks on the Answer to his Observations on the Charter and Conduct of the Society for the Propagation of the Gospel in Foreign Parts. London, 1765.

ARMITAGE, THOMAS. A History of the Baptists; ...New York, 1887.

ARTHUR, DORA FOWLER. "Jottings from the Old Journal of Littleton Fowler," in Texas Historical Association Quarterly, II, No. 1 (July, 1898), 73-84.

ASBURY, FRANCIS. The Journal of the Rev. Francis Asbury, ...3 vols. New York, 1821.

ASPLUND, JOHN. The Annual Register of the Baptist Denomination in North-America; ...N.p.,n.d. [1791].

ATKINSON, JOHN. *Centennial History of American Methodism.* New York, 1884.

———. *History of the Origin of the Wesleyan Movement in America.* ...Jersey City, 1896.

ATKINSON, NANCY BATES [compiler]. *Biography of Rev. G. H. Atkinson, D.D....* Portland, 1893.

AVERY, JOSEPH. "Visit of Rev. Joseph Avery," (ed. by Frank H. Severance) in *Publications of Buffalo Hist. Soc.*, VI (1903), 223-30.

BABCOCK, RUFUS. *Forty Years of Pioneer Life: Memoir of John Mason Peck.* Philadelphia, [1864].

BACKUS, ISAAC. *An Abridgment of the Church History of New England, from 1602 to 1804....* Boston, 1804.

———. *A History of New England, with Particular Reference to the Denomination of Christians called Baptists.* 2 vols. 2nd ed., Newton, Mass., 1871.

BACON, LEONARD. *The Duties Connected with the Present Commercial Distress....* New Haven, 1837. Pamphlet.

———. *The Old Way: Commemorative Discourse for the 50th Anniversary of the American Home Missionary Society.* [New York, 1876]. Pamphlet.

BACON, LEONARD WOOLSEY. *A History of American Christianity (Amer. Ch. Hist. Ser., XIII)*, New York, 1897.

BADGER, JOSEPH. *A Memoir of Rev. Joseph Badger;* ... Hudson, Ohio, 1851.

BAILEY, J. W. *Knox College, by Whom Founded and Endowed;* ... Chicago, 1860.

BAIRD, ROBERT. *The Progress and Prospects of Christianity in the United States of America;* ... London, [1851].

———. *Religion in the United States of America.* Glasgow, Edinburgh, and London, 1844.

———. *State and Prospects of Religion in America;* ... London, 1855.

BAIRD, SAMUEL J. *A History of the New School, and of the Questions Involved in the Disruption of the Presbyterian Church in 1838.* Philadelphia, 1868.

BALDWIN, ELIHU W. *Address Delivered in Crawfordsville, Indiana, July 13, 1836.* Cincinnati, 1836. Pamphlet.

BANGS, NATHAN. *A History of the Methodist Episcopal Church.* 4 vols. New York, 1857.

BAPTIST HOME MISSION SOCIETY. See American Baptist Home Mission Society.

Baptist Home Mission Monthly. New York, 1878-88.

Baptist Missionary Magazine. See *American Baptist Magazine.*

BARNES, ALBERT. *Home Missions, A Sermon in Behalf of the American Home Missionary Society....* New York, 1849. Pamphlet.

———. *Plea in Behalf of Western Colleges....* Philadelphia, 1846. Pamphlet.

BARNES, LEMUEL C. See de Blois, Austen Kennedy.

BATCHELDER, JAMES L. *The United States, the West, and the State of Ohio as Missionary Fields.* Cincinnati, 1848.

BEACH, JOHN. *A Calm and Dispassionate Vindication of the Professors of the Church of England, against the Abusive Misrepresentations and Falacious Argumentations of Mr. Noah Hobart,* . . . Boston, 1749.

BEARDSLEY, E. EDWARDS. *The History of the Episcopal Church in Connecticut,* . . . 2 vols. 2nd. ed., New York, 1869.

————. *Life and Correspondence of the Right Reverend Samuel Seabury,* . . . Boston, 1881.

————. *Life and Correspondence of Samuel Johnson, D.D., Missionary of the Church of England.* . . . New York, 1874.

BEATTY, CHARLES. *The Journal of a Two Months Tour; with a View of Promoting Religion among the Frontier Inhabitants of Pennsylvania,* . . . London, 1768.

BEECHER, CATHERINE E. *Educational Reminiscences and Suggestions.* New York, 1874.

————. *To the Board of National Popular Education.* N.p.,n.d. (Printed, not published). Pamphlet.

————. *The True Remedy for the Wrongs of Woman;* . . . Boston, 1851.

BEECHER, EDWARD. *The Papal Conspiracy Exposed, and Protestantism Defended, in the Light of Reason, Science, and Scripture.* Boston, 1855.

BEECHER, LYMAN. *Autobiography, Correspondence, etc., of Lyman Beecher, D.D.* Ed. by Charles Beecher. 2 vols. New York, 1864.

————. *A Plea for the West.* Cincinnati, 1835.

BELOIT COLLEGE. *Exercises at the Quarter-Centennial Anniversary of Beloit College. July 9, 1872.* Beloit, 1872.

BENEDICT, DAVID. *A General History of the Baptist Denomination in America,* . . . 2 vols. Boston, 1813.

BERNHEIM, G. D. *History of the German Settlements and of the Lutheran Church in North and South Carolina,* . . . Philadelphia, 1872.

BILLINGTON, RAY. "Anti-Catholic Propaganda and the Home Missionary Movement, 1800-1860," in *Miss. Val. Hist. Rev.,* XXII (Dec., 1935), 361-84.

————. *The Protestant Crusade 1800-1860.* New York, 1938.

BLAKE, S. LEROY. *The Separates or Strict Congregationalists of New England.* Boston, [1902].

BOARD OF NATIONAL POPULAR EDUCATION. *[Annual] Reports.* Cincinnati, 1848-58.

BOEHM, JOHN PHILIP. "The Writings of the Rev. John Philip Boehm, Founder of the Reformed Church in Pennsylvania," trans. and ed. by William J. Hinke, in *Jour. Pres. Hist. Soc.,* VI, 295-324; VII, 24-60, 113-41, 274-303, 305-33, 353-84; VIII, 70-89, 97-113, 162-83, 210-25, 258-81 (1912-16).

BOUTON, NATHANIEL. "History of the Origin and Organization of the American Home Missionary Society," in *Home Missionary,* XXXIII (Nov., 1860), 157-66.

BOWDEN, JAMES. *The History of the Society of Friends in America.* 2 vols. London, 1850-54.

BOWEN, L. P. "Makemie and Rehoboth," in *Jour. Pres. Hist. Soc.*, VI (1911-12), 153-67.

BRECK, CHARLES. *The Life of the Reverend James Lloyd Breck,...* New York, 1883.

BREWER, CLIFTON HARTWELL. *A History of Religious Education in the Episcopal Church to 1835.* New Haven, 1924.

BRIGGS, CHARLES AUGUSTUS. *American Presbyterianism: Its Origin and Early History.* New York, 1885.

BROOKS, CHARLES WESLEY. *A Century of Missions in the Empire State. ...Work and Growth of the Baptist Missionary Convention,...* Philadelphia, 1909.

BROSS, HARMON. "Congregational Church," in J. Sterling Morton, *Illustrated History of Nebraska*, II, 481-507. Lincoln, 1905-13.

BRUNSON, ALFRED. "A Methodist Circuit Rider's Horseback Tour from Pennsylvania to Wisconsin in 1835," in *Wisconsin Historical Collections*, XV, 264-91. Madison, 1900.

BUCKLEY, J. M. *A History of Methodism in the United States. (Amer. Ch. Hist. Ser., V).* New York, 1896.

BULLOCK, MOTIER A. *Congregational Nebraska.* Lincoln, 1905.

BURLESON, HUGH LATIMER. *The Conquest of the Continent.* New York, [1911].

BURRAGE, HENRY S. *History of the Baptists in Maine.* Portland, 1904.
———. *A History of the Baptists in New England.* Philadelphia, 1894.

CANNON, JAMES, III. *History of Southern Methodist Missions.* Nashville, 1926.

CARRIEL, MARY TURNER. *The Life of Jonathan Baldwin Turner.* N.p., 1911.

CARROLL, HENRY KING. *The Religious Forces of the United States....* *(Amer. Ch. Hist. Ser., I).* New York, 1893.
———. *Missionary Growth of the Methodist Episcopal Church.* Cincinnati, 1907.

CARROLL, J. M. *A History of Texas Baptists....* Dallas, 1923.

CARTWRIGHT, PETER. *Autobiography of Peter Cartwright, the Backwoods Preacher.* Ed. by W. P. Strickland. Cincinnati and New York, [1856].

CASWALL, HENRY. *America, and the American Church.* London, 1839.

CATHCART, WILLIAM. *The Baptist Encyclopedia.* 2 vols. Philadelphia, 1881.

CHANDLER, THOMAS BRADBURY. *The Life of Samuel Johnson, D.D. The First President of King's College, in New-York....* New York, 1805.

CHASE, PHILANDER. *Address delivered before the Convention of the Protestant Episcopal Church, Springfield, Illinois, June 16th, 1845.* St. Louis, 1845. Pamphlet.
———. *Appeal by Bishop Chase, in behalf of a Protestant Episcopal Theological Seminary for the Diocese of Illinois.* London, n.d. Pamphlet.

————. *Bishop Chase's Reminiscences: an Autobiography.* 2 vols. 2nd ed., Boston, 1848.

————. *A Plea for the West.* Philadelphia, 1826. Pamphlet.

CHASE, SAMUEL. *Malignity Exposed; or a Vindication of Bishop Chase.* ... Peoria, 1847. Pamphlet.

————. *Review of Jubilee College.* [Peoria, 1843]. Pamphlet.

CHAUNCY, CHARLES. *A Letter to the Reverend Mr. George Whitefield, Publickly calling upon him to Vindicate his Conduct or Confess his Faults.* Boston, 1744. Pamphlet.

————. *A Letter from a Gentleman in Boston to Mr. George Wishart, ... Concerning the State of Religion in New-England.* Edinburgh, 1742.

————. *Seasonable Thoughts on the State of Religion in New England.* Boston, 1743.

Christian Education and New West Gleaner. See New West Gleaner.

CLARK, JOSEPH B. *Leavening the Nation.* New York, [1903].

CLARK, JOSEPH S. *Historical Sketch of Congregational Churches in Massachusetts. 1620-1858.* Boston, 1858.

CLARK, RUFUS W. *Popery and the United States....* Boston, 1847. Pamphlet.

CLARY, DEXTER. *History of the Churches and Ministers Connected with the Presbyterian and Congregational Convention of Wisconsin,* ... Beloit, 1861.

CLEVELAND, CATHERINE C. *The Great Revival in the West, 1797-1805.* Chicago, [1916].

CLEWELL, JOHN HENRY. *History of Wachovia in North Carolina: The Unitas Fratrum or Moravian Church in North Carolina....* New York, 1902.

COBB, SANFORD H. *The Rise of Religious Liberty in America.* New York, 1902.

CONKLIN, GABRIEL. *Examination of a Pamphlet titled "Truth as it is,"* ... Alexandria, D. C., 1839. Pamphlet.

CONGREGATIONAL CHURCHES, CONNECTICUT. *Contributions to the Ecclesiastical History of Connecticut;* ... New Haven, 1861.

CONGREGATIONAL EDUCATION SOCIETY. See American Education Society.

CONGREGATIONAL HOME MISSIONARY SOCIETY. See American Home Missionary Society.

————. *Reports.* New York, 1894-1901.

CONNECTICUT. *The Public Records of the Colony of Connecticut.* 15 vols. 1850-90.

Connecticut Evangelical Magazine. Hartford, 1800-07.

Connecticut Evangelical Magazine and Religious Intelligencer. Hartford, 1808-15.

CONNECTICUT, GENERAL ASSOCIATION. *An Address, of the General Association of Connecticut, to the District Associations on the Subject of a Missionary Society;* ... Norwich, 1797. Pamphlet.

————. *An Address to the Emigrants from Connecticut, and from New England generally, in the New Settlements in the United States.* Hartford, 1817. Pamphlet.

————. *A Narrative of the Missions to the New Settlements according to the Appointment of the General Association of the State of Connecticut:* ... New Haven, 1794. Pamphlet.

————. *A Continuation of the Narrative of the Missions to the New Settlements,* ... New Haven, 1797. Pamphlet.

CONNECTICUT MISSIONARY SOCIETY. *The Constitution of the Missionary Society of Connecticut: With an Address from the Board of Trustees, to the People of the State,* ... Hartford, 1800. Pamphlet.

————. *An Act to Incorporate the Trustees of the Missionary Society of Connecticut:* ... Hartford, 1803. Pamphlet.

————. [ANNUAL] *Narrative on the Subject of Missions* (title varies). Hartford, 1802, 1805, 1806-10, 1812-23.

————. *A Second Address from the Trustees of the Missionary Society of Connecticut, to the People of the State,* ... Hartford, 1801. Pamphlet.

CORDLEY, RICHARD. *Pioneer Days in Kansas.* Boston [1903].

CORWIN, EDWARD TANJORE. *A Manual of the Reformed Church in America* ... *1628-1878.* 3rd ed., New York, 1879.

COSSIT, F. R. *The Life and Times of Rev. Finis Ewing.* ... Louisville, [1853].

COWLES, HENRY. *A Defence of Ohio Congregationalism and of Oberlin College, in reply to Kennedy's Plan of Union.* [Oberlin, 1856?]. Pamphlet.

CRAM, JACOB. *A Journal of a Missionary Tour in 1808 Through the New Settlements of Northern New Hampshire and Vermont.* (*Rochester Reprints,* XI). Rochester, 1909.

CROSS, ARTHUR LYON. *The Anglican Episcopate and the American Colonies (Harvard Historical Studies,* IX). New York, 1902.

[DAGGETT, MRS. L. H., ed.]. *Historical Sketches of Woman's Missionary Societies in America and England.* Boston, [1883].

DAVENPORT, FREDERICK MORGAN. *Primitive Traits in Religious Revivals.* New York, 1905.

DAVIDSON, ROBERT. *History of the Presbyterian Church in the State of Kentucky;* ... New York, 1847.

DAVIES, SAMUEL. *The State of Religion among the Protestant Dissenters in Virginia;* ... Boston, 1751.

DE BLOIS, AUSTEN KENNEDY, and BARNES, LEMUEL CALL. *John Mason Peck and One Hundred Years of Baptist Home Missions, 1817-1917.* New York, 1917.

[DEXTER, FRANK, ed.]. *A Hundred Years of Congregational History in Wisconsin.* Wisconsin Congregational Conference, 1933.

DIMAN, J. L. "Religion in America, 1776-1876," in *North American Review,* CXXII (Jan., 1876), 1-47.

DIXON, JAMES. *Personal Narrative of a Tour through a Part of the United States and Canada: with Notices of the History and Institutions of Methodism in America.* ... 3rd ed., New York, 1850.

DODDRIDGE, JOSEPH. *Notes on the Settlement and Indian Wars, of the Western Parts of Virginia & Pennsylvania,* ... Wellsburg, Va., 1824; new ed., Albany, 1876.

DORCHESTER, DANIEL. *Christianity in the United States,* ... New York, 1888.

DOUGLASS, HARLAN PAUL. *The New Home Missions.* ... New York, 1914.

DOUGLASS, TRUMAN O. *The Pilgrims of Iowa.* Boston and Chicago, [1911].

DOW, LORENZO. *Perambulations of Cosmopolite; or Travels and Labors of Lorenzo Dow, in Europe and America.* ... Rochester, 1842.

DOYLE, SHERMAN HOADLEY. *Presbyterian Home Missions:* ... Philadelphia, 1902.

DRURY, CLIFFORD MERRILL. *Henry Harmon Spalding.* Caldwell, Idaho, 1936.

——. *Marcus Whitman, M.D., Pioneer and Martyr.* Caldwell, Idaho, 1937.

DUBBS, JOSEPH HENRY. "The Founding of the German Churches of Pennsylvania," in *Pennsylvania Mag. of Hist. and Biog.,* XVII (1893), 241-62.

——. *The Reformed Church in Pennsylvania.* Lancaster, 1902.

DUNNING, ALBERT E. *Congregationalists in America.* ... Boston and Chicago, n.d.

[DUTTON, S. W. S.]. "Popular Education in the West by Female Teachers from the East," in *The New Englander,* VII (Nov., 1849), 593-610.

DUVALL, SYLVANUS MILNE. *The Methodist Episcopal Church and Education up to 1869* (Teachers College, Columbia University *Contributions to Education,* No. 284). New York, 1928.

DWIGHT, TIMOTHY. *Travels; in New-England and New-York.* 4 vols. New Haven, 1821-22.

DYER, JOHN L. *The Snow-Shoe Itinerant.* ... Cincinnati, 1890.

EATON, W. H. *Historical Sketch of the Massachusetts Baptist Missionary Society and Convention, 1802-1902.* Boston, [1903].

ECKENRODE, H. J. *Separation of Church and State in Virginia.* Richmond, 1910.

EDWARDS, JONATHAN. *A Faithful Narrative of the Surprising Work of God in the Conversion of Many Hundred Souls,* ... 3rd ed., Boston, 1738.

——. *Some Thoughts Concerning the present Revival of Religion in New England.* ... Boston, 1742.

EDWARDS, MARTHA L. "Religion in the United States, 1815-30," in *Miss. Val. Hist. Rev.,* V (March, 1919), 434-49.

EELLS, MYRON. *Father Eells;* ... Boston, 1894.

EGGLESTON, N. H. "Chicago Theological Seminary," in *The New Englander,* XVII (May, 1859), 335-56.

ELSBREE, OLIVER WENDELL. *The Rise of the Missionary Spirit in America 1780-1815.* Williamsport, Pa., 1928.

EMERY, JULIA C. *A Century of Endeavor 1821-1921: A Record of the First Hundred Years of the Domestic and Foreign Missionary Society of the Protestant Episcopal Church....* New York, 1921.

ENGLAND, JOHN. *The Works of the Right Rev. John England, First Bishop of Charleston,...* 5 vols. Baltimore, 1849.

EVANS, W. M. See Hinkhouse, J. F.

FAIRCHILD, JAMES HARRIS. *Oberlin: the Colony and the College, 1833-1883.* Oberlin, 1883.

————. *Oberlin. Its Origin, Progress and Results....* Oberlin, 1871.

FINLEY, JAMES B. *Autobiography of Rev. James B. Finley;...* Ed. by W. P. Strickland. Cincinnati, 1854.

————. *Sketches of Western Methodism:...* Ed. by W. P. Strickland. Cincinnati, 1857.

[FISHER, EZRA]. *Correspondence of the Reverend Ezra Fisher....* Ed. by S. F. Henderson, N. E. Latourette, K. S. Latourette. Privately printed, 1919.

FLINT, TIMOTHY. *Recollections of the Last Ten Years....* Boston, 1826.

FOOTE, WILLIAM HENRY. *Sketches of Virginia Historical and Biographical.* Philadelphia, 1850.

FORD, R. CLYDE. See Hoyt, Charles O.

FOSTER, FRANK HUGH. *A Genetic History of the New England Theology.* Chicago, 1907.

[FRERI, JOSEPH]. *The Society for the Propagation of the Faith and Catholic Missions, 1822-1900.* Baltimore, 1902.

FRIES, ADELAIDE L., ed. *Records of the Moravians in North Carolina* (Publications of the North Carolina Historical Commission). 4 vols. Raleigh, 1922-30.

GADDIS, MAXWELL PIERSON. *Foot-Prints of an Itinerant.* Cincinnati, 1857.

GALLAGHER, DANIEL W. See Mahan, Asa.

GATES, ERRETT. *The Early Relation and Separation of the Baptists and Disciples.* Chicago, 1904.

GAVITT, ELNATHAN CORRINGTON. *Crumbs from my Saddle Bags....* Toledo, 1884.

[GAYLORD, MRS. REUBEN]. *Life and Labors of Rev. Reuben Gaylord ... by his Wife.* Omaha, 1889.

GERMAN REFORMED CHURCH. See Reformed Church.

GEWEHR, W. W. "Some Factors in the Expansion of Frontier Methodism, 1800-1811," in *Journal of Religion*, VIII (Jan., 1928), 98-120.

GILLETT, E. H. *History of the Presbyterian Church in the United States.* 2 vols. Philadelphia, 1864.

GOOD, JAMES I. *History of the Reformed Church in the United States, 1725-1792.* Reading, Pa., 1899.

————. *History of the Reformed Church in the U. S. in the Nineteenth Century.* New York, 1911.

[GOODWIN, DANIEL, ed.]. *A Letter Book and Abstract of Out Services Written during years 1743-1751 by the Revd. James MacSparran.* Boston, 1899.

GOODYKOONTZ, COLIN B. "Protestant Home Missions and Education in the Trans-Mississippi West, 1835-1860," in J. F. Willard and C. B. Goodykoontz, eds., *The Trans-Mississippi West* (Boulder, 1930), 65-86.

GORDON, GEORGE A. *Humanism in New England Theology.* Boston and New York, 1920.

GORRIE, P. DOUGLASS. *The Churches and Sects of the United States:* ... New York, 1850.

GRACEY, J. T. See Reid. J. M.

GRAVES, ANSON ROGERS. *The Missionary Work of the Church in the West* (Hale Memorial Sermon No. 3), Chicago, 1908. Pamphlet.

GREEN, ASHBEL. *A Historical Sketch or Compendious View of Domestic and Foreign Missions in the Presbyterian Church.* ... Philadelphia, 1838.

GREEN, F. M. *Christian Missions and Historical Sketches of Missionary Societies among the Disciples of Christ,* ... St. Louis, 1884.

GREEN, WILLIAM MERCER. *Memoir of Rt. Rev. James Hervey Otey,* ... New York, 1885.

GRINNELL, JOSIAH BUSNELL. *Men and Events of Forty Years:* ... Boston, c. 1891.

GROSE, HOWARD B. *Baptist Missions on the Frontier.* New York, n.d. Pamphlet.

GUILDAY, PETER. *The Life and Times of John England First Bishop of Charleston (1786-1842).* 2 vols. New York, 1927.

GUMMERE, AMELIA M. See Jones, Rufus M.

HADDEN, ARCHIBALD. *Congregationalism in Minnesota, 1851-1891.* Minneapolis, 1891.

HAMILTON, J. TAYLOR. *A History of the Church known as the Moravian Church, or the Unitas Fratrum,* ... (Moravian Historical Society, *Transactions*, VI). Bethlehem, Pa., 1900.

———. *A History of the Missions of the Moravian Church,* ... Bethlehem, 1901.

HARBAUGH, H. *The Life of Rev. Michael Schlatter;* ... Philadelphia, 1857.

HARWOOD, THOMAS. *History of New Mexico Spanish and English Missions of the Methodist Episcopal Church from 1850 to 1910.* 2 vols. Albuquerque, 1908-10.

HAWKINS, ERNEST. *Historical Notices of the Missions of the Church of England in the North American Colonies,* ... London, 1845.

HAWKS, FRANCIS L., and PERRY, WILLIAM STEVENS. *Documentary History of the Protestant Episcopal Church.* ... Nos. 1-9. New York, 1862-63.

HENDERSON, SARAH FISHER, et al., eds. See Fisher, Ezra.

HICKEY, EDWARD JOHN. *The Society for the Propagation of the Faith.* ... (*Catholic University of America Studies in American Church History*, III), N.p., 1922.

HICKOK, LAURENS P. *A Nation Saved from its Prosperity only by the Gospel.* ... New York, 1853. Pamphlet.

HILL, TIMOTHY. *Historical Outlines of the Presbyterian Church in Missouri.* Kansas City, 1871. Pamphlet.

HINES, GUSTAVUS. *A Voyage Round the World: with a History of the Oregon Mission:* ... Buffalo, 1850.

HINKE, WILLIAM J. *Life and Letters of the Rev. John Philip Boehm,* ... Philadelphia, 1916.

————. "Diary of the Rev. Michael Schlatter," in *Jour. Pres. Hist. Soc.,* III (1905), 105-21, 158-76.

HINKE, WILLIAM J., and KEMPER, CHARLES E., eds. "Moravian Diaries of Travels through Virginia," in *Virginia Magazine of History and Biography,* XI, 113-31, 225-42, 370-93; XII, 55-82, 134-53, 271-81 (1903-05).

HINKHOUSE, J. F., and EVANS, W. M., eds. *One Hundred Years of the Iowa Presbyterian Church.* Cedar Rapids, 1932.

HOBART, NOAH. *A Serious Address To the Members of the Episcopal Separation in New-England.* ... Boston, 1748.

————. *A Second Address to the Members of the Episcopal Separation in New England.* ... Boston, 1751.

HODGE, CHARLES. *The Constitutional History of the Presbyterian Church.* ... 2 vols. in one. Philadelphia, [1851].

HOLCOMBE, THEODORE I. *An Apostle of the Wilderness James Lloyd Breck,* ... New York, 1903.

Home Missionary. New York, 1828-1906.

HOOD, E. LYMAN. *The New West Education Commission 1880-1893.* Jacksonville, Fla., 1905.

HOPKINS, MARK. *An Address delivered in Boston, May 26, 1852, before the Society for the Promotion of Collegiate and Theological Education at the West.* Boston, 1852. Pamphlet.

HOTCHKIN, JAMES H. *A History of the Purchase and Settlement of Western New York, and of the Rise, Progress and Present Status of the Presbyterian Church in that Section.* New York, 1848.

HOYT, CHARLES O., and FORD, R. CLYDE. *John D. Pierce Founder of the Michigan School System.* Ypsilanti, 1905.

HUBBARD, JOSEPH W., chairman. *The Presbyterian Church in Iowa 1837-1900.* ... Cedar Rapids, 1907.

HUBBARD, WILLIAM. *A General History of New England.* ... Cambridge, 1815.

HULBERT, ARCHER B. "Undeveloped Factors in the Life of Marcus Whitman," in J. F. Willard and C. B. Goodykoontz, eds. *The Trans-Mississippi West* (Boulder, 1930), 87-102.

HULBERT, ARCHER BUTLER, and DOROTHY PRINTUP, eds. *Overland to the Pacific.* 8 vols. [Colorado Springs] and Denver, 1932 ————.

HUMPHREY, EDWARD FRANK. *Nationalism and Religion in America, 1774-1789.* Boston, 1924.

HUMPHREYS, DAVID. *An Historical Account of the Incorporated Society for the Propagation of the Gospel in Foreign Parts,* ... London, 1730.

HUNT, J. R. E. *Lutheran Home Missions.* Rock Island, Ill., 1913.

IOWA COLLEGE. *Addresses and Discourse at the Inauguration of the Rev. George F. Magoun, A.M., as President of Iowa College, July 19, 1865.* Chicago, 1865. Pamphlet.

IOWA CONGREGATIONAL CHURCHES AND MINISTERS. *Minutes of the General Association of Congregational Churches and Ministers of the State of Iowa. From 1840 to 1855....* Hull, Iowa, 1888.

JACKSON, SHELDON. "Iowa Movement for Home Missions," in J. F. Hinkhouse and W. M. Evans, eds., *One Hundred Years of the Iowa Presbyterian Church,* 359-69.

JAMES, CHARLES. *Documentary History of the Struggle for Religious Liberty in Virginia.* Lynchburg, Va., 1900.

JAMESON, J. FRANKLIN. "The American Acta Sanctorum," in *American Historical Review,* XIII (Jan., 1908), 286-302.

JARRATT, DEVEREUX. *The Life of the Reverend Devereux Jarratt ... Written by himself in a Series of Letters....* Baltimore, 1806.

JARRELL, CHARLES C. *Methodism on the March.* Nashville, etc., 1924.

JARVIS, SAMUEL FARMAR. *A Sermon, preached before the Auxiliary Education Society of the Young Men of Boston,...* Boston, 1822. Pamphlet.

JENNINGS, WALTER WILSON. *Origin and Early History of the Disciples of Christ....* Cincinnati, [1919].

[JOHNSON, S.]. *A Candid Examination of Dr. Mayhew's Observations on the Charter and Conduct of the Society for the Propagation of the Gospel....* Boston, 1763.

JOHNSTON, JAMES H. *A Ministry of Forty Years in Indiana....* Indianapolis, 1865. Pamphlet.

JONES, JOHN G. *A Concise History of the Introduction of Protestantism into Mississippi and the Southwest.* St. Louis, 1866.

JONES, RUFUS M., assisted by ISAAC SHARPLESS and AMELIA M. GUMMERE. *The Quakers in the American Colonies.* London, 1911.

JORDAN, PHILIP D., ed. "William Salter's 'My Ministry in Iowa, 1843-1846,'" in *Annals of Iowa,* 3d Ser., XIX (Jan., Apr., 1935), 539-53, 592-613; XX (July, 1935), 26-49.

JUDD, BERTHA GRIMMELL. *Fifty Golden Years:... Woman's American Baptist Home Mission Society, 1877-1927.* New York, c. 1927.

[JUDSON, E.] "The Evangelization of the West. How Shall it be Effected? and by Whom?" in *The New Englander,* IV (Jan., 1846), 29-39.

KEELER, ELLEN COUGHLIN. *The Balance Wheel: A Condensed History of the Woman's Home Missionary Society of the Methodist Episcopal Church, 1880-1920.* New York, [1920].

KEITH, GEORGE. *A Journal of Travels from New-Hampshire to Caratuck,...* London, 1706.

[KELLOGG, MARTIN]. *A Statement in behalf of the College of California, 1860.* Signed Martin Kellogg, Vernon, Conn., July, 1860. Pamphlet.

KEMPER, CHARLES E. See Hinke, William J.

KENNEDY, WILLIAM S. *The Plan of Union: Or a History of the Presbyterian and Congregational Churches of the Western Reserve;* ... Hudson, Ohio, 1856.

KINCAID, WILLIAM. "Home Missionary Work of Congregationalism," in Ohio Church History Society, *Papers,* VII (1896), 76-97.

KINGSLEY, H. C. "Roman Catholic Contributions and Missions," in *The New Englander,* XVII (Feb., 1859), 93-110.

KIP, WILLIAM INGRAHAM. *The Early Days of My Episcopate.* New York, 1892.

KIRK, EDWARD NORRIS. *The Church Essential to the Republic. A Sermon.* ... New York, 1848. Pamphlet.

KIRKPATRICK, JOHN ERVIN. *Timothy Flint: Pioneer, Missionary, Author, Editor 1780-1840* ... Cleveland, 1911.

[KITCHEL, H. D.]. "The Congregational Convention," in *The New Englander,* XI (Feb., 1853), 72-92.

KOFOID, CARRIE PRUDENCE. "Puritan Influences in the Formative Years of Illinois History," in *Transactions of the Illinois State Historical Society,* 1905 (Pub. No. 10 of Ill. State Hist. Lib.), 261-338. Springfield, 1906.

LADIES' SOCIETY FOR THE PROMOTION OF EDUCATION AT THE WEST. *Annual Reports.* Boston, 1847-51.

———. *History of the Formation of the Ladies' Society.* ... Boston, 1846. Pamphlet.

LATHROP, DANIEL. See Mahan, Asa.

Latter Day Luminary. Philadelphia, 1818-25.

LAUER, PAUL E. *Church and State in New England.* (Johns Hopkins Univ. Studies in Hist. and Pol. Sci., 10th Ser., Nos. II-III). Baltimore, 1892.

LEE, JESSE. *A Short History of the Methodists, in the United States of America.* Baltimore, 1810.

LEONARD, DELAVAN L. *A Century of Congregationalism in Ohio.* Oberlin, 1896.

———. *The History of Carleton College.* ... Chicago and New York, [1904].

LORE, D. D. "Missions in America," in *Methodist Quarterly Review,* XL (April, Oct., 1858), 241-56, 589-605; XLI (April, 1859), 265-87.

McCLURE, EDMUND. See Allen, W. O. B.

McCONNELL, S. D. *History of the American Episcopal Church.* 3rd ed., New York, 1891.

McDONNOLD, B. W. *History of the Cumberland Presbyterian Church.* Nashville, 1888.

McILWAINE, HENRY R. *The Struggle of Protestant Dissenters for Religious Toleration in Virginia.* (Johns Hopkins Univ. Studies in Hist. and Pol. Sci., 12th Ser., IV), Baltimore, 1894.

[McNARAMA, JOHN]. *Three Years on the Kansas Border.* New York and Auburn, 1856.

M'NEMAR, RICHARD. *The Kentucky Revival;* ... New York, 1846.

MAGOUN, GEORGE FREDERICK. *Asa Turner;* ... Boston and Chicago, [1889].

[MAHAN, ASA, LATHROP, DANIEL W., GALLAGHER, JAMES (committee)]. *A Report of the Minority in the Convention on Domestic Missions, Held in Cincinnati, November, 1831.* Cincinnati, 1831. Pamphlet.

MASSACHUSETTS. *Journals of the House of Representatives of Massachusetts 1715-1717.* Mass. Hist. Soc., 1919.

——. *Records of the Governor and Company of the Massachusetts Bay in New England.* 1628-86. 5 vols. Boston, 1853-54.

Massachusetts Baptist Missionary Magazine. Vols. I-IV. Boston, 1803-16.

Massachusetts Missionary Magazine (merged with *Panoplist,* 1808). Salem, 1803; Boston, 1804-07.

MASSACHUSETTS MISSIONARY SOCIETY. *A Brief Abstract of the Proceedings and Fund of the Massachusetts Missionary Society.* ... [Boston, 1800]. Pamphlet.

——. *An Historical Sketch of the Missions of the Massachusetts Missionary Society. From May, 1800 to May, 1801.* [Boston, 1801?]. Pamphlet.

——. *To All, who are desirous of the Spread of the Gospel.* ... Boston, 1799. Pamphlet.

MASTERS, VICTOR I. *Baptist Missions in the South:* ... [Atlanta], 1915.

MATHEWS, LOIS KIMBALL. *The Expansion of New England:* ... Boston and New York, 1909.

——. "Some Activities of the Congregational Church West of the Mississippi," in *Essays in American History Dedicated to Frederick Jackson Turner,* 3-34. New York, 1910.

MATTESON, JAMES. See Reed, Andrew.

MAXSON, CHARLES HARTSHORN. *The Great Awakening in the Middle Colonies.* Chicago, 1920.

MAYHEW, JONATHAN. *A Defence of the Observations on the Charter and Conduct of the Society for the Propagation of the Gospel.* ... Boston, 1763.

——. *Observations on the Charter and Conduct of the Society for the Propagation of the Gospel.* ... Boston, 1763.

MEADE, [WILLIAM]. *Old Churches, Ministers and Families of Virginia.* 2 vols. Philadelphia, 1857.

MEANS, JAMES H. "The First Home Missionaries of New England," in *The Congregational Quarterly,* X (April, 1868), 167-71.

MERENESS, NEWTON D. *Travels in the American Colonies.* New York, 1916.

METHODIST EPISCOPAL CHURCH. *Journals of the General Conference.* Vols. I-III. New York, 1855-56.

——. *Minutes of the Annual Conferences.* Vols. I-VIII. New York, 1840-61.

——. *Minutes of the Methodist Conferences, Annually held in America, From 1773 to 1794, inclusive.* Philadelphia, 1795.

METHODIST EPISCOPAL CHURCH, BOARD OF CHURCH EXTENSION. *Church Extension Annual,* ... Philadelphia, 1877.

METHODIST EPISCOPAL CHURCH, MISSIONARY SOCIETY. [*Annual*] *Reports.* New York, 1820-98.

Methodist Review (title varies). New York, 1818-96.

MILBURN, WILLIAM HENRY. *The Pioneers, Preachers, and People of the Mississippi Valley.* New York, 1860.

———. *Ten Years of Preacher-Life:* ... New York, 1859.

MILLER, ADAM. *Origin and Progress of the German Missions in the Methodist Episcopal Church,* ... Cincinnati, 1843.

MILLER, SAMUEL. "Historical Review of the Church (Old School Branch) since 1837," in *Presbyterian Reunion: A Memorial Volume, 1837-1871,* 1-49. New York, 1870.

MILLER, W. G. *Thirty Years in the Itinerancy.* Milwaukee, 1875.

MILLET, JOSHUA. *A History of the Baptists in Maine;* ... Portland, 1845.

MILLS, SAMUEL J., and SMITH, DANIEL. *Report of a Missionary Tour.* ... Andover, 1815.

MILLS, SAMUEL J. See also Schermerhorn, John F.

MISSIONARY SOCIETY OF CONNECTICUT. See Connecticut Missionary Society.

MISSOURI BAPTIST GENERAL ASSOCIATION. *Missouri Baptist Centennial 1906.* ... Columbia, 1907.

MODE, PETER G. *The Frontier Spirit in American Christianity.* New York, 1923.

———. *Source Book and Bibliographical Guide for American Church History.* 1921.

MONETTE, JOHN W. *History of the Discovery and Settlement of the Valley of the Mississippi.* ... 2 vols. New York, 1846.

MOORES, CHARLES W. *Caleb Mills and the Indiana School System* (Indiana Hist. Soc. Pub., III, No. 6), Indianapolis, 1905.

MOREHOUSE, HENRY L. "Historical Sketch of the American Baptist Home Mission Society for Fifty Years," in *Baptist Home Missions in North America,* 291-540. New York, 1883.

MORSE, SAMUEL F. B. *Foreign Conspiracy against the Liberties of the United States: the Numbers of Brutus,* ... New York, 1835.

———. *Imminent Dangers to the Free Institutions of the United States through Foreign Immigration,* ... New York, 1854. Pamphlet.

———. *Samuel F. B. Morse His Letters and Journals.* Ed. by Edward Lind Morse. 2 vols. Boston and New York, 1914.

NEWMAN, A. H. *A Century of Baptist Achievement.* Philadelphia, 1901.

———. *A History of the Baptist Churches in the United States* (*Amer. Ch. Hist. Ser.,* II), New York, 1894.

NEW WEST EDUCATION COMMISSION. *Annual Reports.* Chicago, 1881-93.

New West Gleaner (title varies). Boston, 1884-93.

NICHOLS, ROBERT HASTINGS. "The Plan of Union in New York," in *Church History*, V (March, 1936), 29-51.

NORTHRUP, CYRUS. "The Influence of New England Ideas on the History of the Country," in *Centennial Papers published by ... Congregational Churches in Connecticut*, 202-06. Hartford, 1877.

O'GORMAN, THOMAS. *A History of the Roman Catholic Church in the United States (Amer. Ch. Hist. Ser., IX)*, New York, 1895.

OHIO CHURCH HISTORY SOCIETY. *Papers.* Vols. I-XII. Oberlin, 1890-1901.

PACIFIC COAST CONGREGATIONAL ALLIANCE FOR THE PROMOTION OF EDUCATION. *Christian Education by Congregationalists in the Seven Pacific Coast States.* San Francisco, 1893.

PADELFORD, FRANK W. *The Commonwealths and the Kingdom....* Philadelphia, 1913.

Panoplist (title varies). Boston, 1805-20.

PARKER, EDWIN POND. *Historical Discourse in Commemoration of the One Hundredth Anniversary of the Missionary Society of Connecticut.* Hartford, 1898. Pamphlet.

PASCOE, C. F. *Two Hundred Years of the S. P. G.:...* London, 1901.

PAYNE, RAYMOND. "Annals of the Leopoldine Association," in *Catholic Historical Review*, I, 51-63, 175-91.

PEET, STEPHEN D. *History of Early Missions in Wisconsin,...* Madison, 1886. Pamphlet.

———. *History of the Presbyterian and Congregational Churches and Ministers in Wisconsin....* Milwaukee, 1851.

PERRY, WILLIAM STEVENS. *The Alleged "Toryism" of the Clergy of the United States at the Breaking out of the War of the Revolution.* ... N.p.,n.d. Pamphlet.

———. *The History of the American Episcopal Church 1587-1883.* 2 vols. Boston, 1885.

———. *Historical Collections Relating to the American Colonial Church.* 5 vols. Hartford, 1870-78.

———. *Missions and Missionary Bishoprics in the American Church.* Privately printed, 1877. Pamphlet.

PERRY, WILLIAM S. See also Hawks, Francis L.

PETERS, ABSALOM. *A Brief Answer to an Official Reply of the Board of Missions of the General Assembly to Six Letters of the Rev. Absalom Peters....* New York, 1831. Pamphlet.

PHELAN, MACUM. *A History of Early Methodism in Texas 1817-1866.* Nashville, [1924].

PHILADELPHIA BAPTIST ASSOCIATION. *Minutes of the Philadelphia Baptist Association from A. D. 1707 to A. D. 1807.* Ed. by A. D. Gillette. Philadelphia, 1851.

PHILLIPS, SADLER. *The Early English Colonies....* London, 1908.

PIERCE, GEORGE F. *Incidents of Western Travel:...* Nashville, 1857.

PIERSON, HAMILTON W. *In the Brush; Or, Old Time Social, Political and Religious Life in the Southwest.* New York, 1881.

PLATT, WARD. *The Frontier.* New York, 1908.

POLK, WILLIAM M. *Leonidas Polk Bishop and General.* New ed., 2 vols. New York and London, 1915.

PORTUS, GARNET V. *Caritas Anglicana....* London, [1912].

POSEY, WALTER BROWNLOW. *The Development of Methodism in the Old Southwest 1783-1824.* Tuscaloosa, Ala., 1933.

PRESBYTERIAN CHURCH IN THE UNITED STATES OF AMERICA. *Acts and Proceedings of the Presbyterian Church in the United States of America.* Philadelphia, 1789-1802.

————. *Addresses delivered at the Centennial Celebration of the General Assembly....* Philadelphia, [1888].

————. *A Digest Compiled from the Records of the General Assembly.* ... Philadelphia, 1820.

————. *1802 Centennial 1902 of Home Missions in Connection with the one hundred and fourteenth General Assembly....* Philadelphia, 1902.

————. *Extracts from the Minutes of the General Assembly ... 1789-1820.* 4 vols. Philadelphia, 1802-20.

————. *A Historical Sketch of the Board of Home Missions of the Presbyterian Church....* 1802-88. [New York, 1888].

————. *Minutes of the General Assembly.* New Series, Philadelphia, 1872-1900.

————. *Records of the Presbyterian Church....* Prepared by W. M. Engles. Philadelphia, [1841?].

————. *Relations of the Presbyterian Church to the work of Home Missions....* New York, 1860. Pamphlet.

PRESBYTERIAN CHURCH, BOARD OF DOMESTIC MISSIONS OF THE GENERAL ASSEMBLY. *Annual Reports.* Philadelphia, 1833-59.

PRESBYTERIAN CHURCH, STANDING COMMITTEE OF MISSIONS. *Missionary Intelligence;* ... Philadelphia, 1811. Pamphlet.

PRESBYTERIAN CHURCH, EDUCATION SOCIETY. *An Address from the Managers of the Education Society,* ... Philadelphia, [1818?]. Pamphlet.

————. *First Annual Report....* Philadelphia, 1819.

Presbyterian Monthly Record. Philadelphia, 1870-86.

PRINCE, THOMAS JR. *The Christian History, Containing Accounts of the Revival and Propagation of Religion in Great Britain & America. For the year 1743.* Boston, 1744.

PROTESTANT EPISCOPAL CHURCH. *Proceedings of the Board of Directors of the Domestic and Foreign Missionary Society of the Protestant Episcopal Church....* Philadelphia, 1831.

PROTESTANT EPISCOPAL CHURCH, BOARD OF MISSIONS. See *Spirit of Missions.*

PUDDEFOOT, W. G. *The Minute Man on the Frontier.* New York, [1895].

RAMMELKAMP, CHARLES H. "Illinois College and the Anti-Slavery Movement," in *Transactions of the Illinois State Historical Society for the year 1908* (Pub. No. 13 of the Ill. State. Hist. Lib.), 192-203. Springfield, 1909.

RANDALL, MABLE. "Bishop Chase in Gilead, 1832-1836," in *Michigan Pioneer Collections*, VII (1884), 358-65.

REED, ANDREW, and MATTESON, JAMES. *Narrative of the Visit to the American Churches by the Deputation from the Congregational Union of England and Wales.* 2 vols. New York, 1835.

REED, JULIUS A. *Reminiscences of Early Congregationalism in Iowa.* Grinnell, 1885. Pamphlet.

REFORMED CHURCH IN THE UNITED STATES. *Minutes and Letters of the Coetus of the German Reformed Congregations in Pennsylvania 1747-1792....* Philadelphia, 1903.

REICHEL, LEVIN T. *The Moravians in North Carolina....* Salem, N. C., and Philadelphia, 1857.

REID, J. M., and GRACEY, J. T. *Missions and Missionary Society of the Methodist Episcopal Church.* 3 vols. New York and Cincinnati, 1879.

RICE, CYRUS. "Experiences of a Pioneer Missionary," in Kansas Historical Society, *Collections*, XIII (1913-14), 298-318.

ROBINSON, WILLIAM A. *Jeffersonian Democracy in New England.* New Haven, 1916.

Rocky Mountain Presbyterian. Denver, 1872-86.

ROEMER, THEODORE. *Ludwig-Missionsverein and the Church in the United States (1838-1918). Franciscan Studies*, No. 12. New York, 1933.

ROGERS, JAMES R. *The Cane Ridge Meeting-House. To which is Appended the Autobiography of B. W. Stone....* Cincinnati, [1910].

ROWE, HENRY KALLOCK. *The History of Religion in the United States.* New York, 1924.

ROY, J. E. "Salmon Giddings," in *The New Englander*, XXXIII (July, 1874), 513-32.

———. "Fifty Years of Home Missions in Illinois," in *The New Englander*, XXXV (July, 1876), 561-80.

RUPP, I. DANIEL, ed. *An Original History of the Religious Denominations at Present Existing in the United States....* Philadelphia, 1844.

SALTER, WILLIAM. See Jordan, P. D.

SCHERMERHORN, JOHN F., and MILLS, SAMUEL J. *A Correct View of that Part of the United States which lies West of the Allegany Mountains with regard to Religion and Morals.* Hartford, 1814.

SCHMAUK, THEODORE EMANUEL. *A History of the Lutheran Church in Pennsylvania (1638-1820)....* Philadelphia, 1903.

SCHOULLER, JAMES B. *History of the United Presbyterian Church of North America (Amer. Ch. Hist. Ser.,* XI, 145-255), New York, 1894.

SCHWARZE, WILLIAM NATHANIEL. "Early Moravian Settlements in America," in *Papers of the American Society of Church History,* 2nd Ser., VII, 71-88.

SCOTT, JAMES L. *A Journal of a Missionary Tour through Pennsylvania, Ohio, Indiana, Illinois, Iowa, Wiskonsin, and Michigan....* Providence, 1843.

[SECKER, ARCHBISHOP]. *An Answer to Dr. Mayhew's Observations on the Charter and Conduct of the Society for the Propagation of the Gospel in Foreign Parts.* London, 1764.

SEEBACH, MARGARET R. *Missionary Milestones:...* New York, [1917].

SEMPLE, ROBERT B. *A History of the Rise and Progress of the Baptists in Virginia.* Richmond, 1810.

SHARPLESS, ISAAC. See Jones, Rufus M.

SMITH, DANIEL. See Mills, S. J.

SMITH, JOSEPH. *Old Redstone; Or, Historical Sketches of Western Presbyterianism....* Philadelphia, 1854.

SMITH, JUSTIN A. *History of the Baptists in the Western States East of the Mississippi.* Philadelphia, 1896.

SMITH, LAURA CHASE. *The Life of Philander Chase....* New York, 1903.

[SMITH, WILLIAM]. *A Brief State of the Province of Pennsylvania,* ... London, 1755. Pamphlet.

SOCIETY FOR THE PROMOTION OF COLLEGIATE AND THEOLOGICAL EDUCATION AT THE WEST. *Annual Reports.* New York, 1844-74.

———. *Facts in Reference to the Society....* New York, 1858. Pamphlet.

———. *Final Effort of the Society....* New York, 1856. Pamphlet.

———. *Proceedings at the Quarter-Century Anniversary of the Society....* Marietta, Ohio, November 7-10, 1868. New York, 1868.

———. *Results and Wants of the Society....* New York, 1859. Pamphlet.

SOCIETY FOR THE PROPAGATION OF THE GOSPEL. *An Account of the Society for Propagating the Gospel....* London, 1706.

———. *Classified Digest of the Records of the Society for the Propagation of the Gospel in Foreign Parts 1701-1892.* London, 1893.

Spirit of Missions. Burlington, N. J., 1836-98.

SPRING, GARDINER. *A Brief View of the Facts which gave rise to the New-York Evangelical Missionary Society of Young Men....* New York, 1817. Pamphlet.

———. *Memoirs of the Rev. Samuel J. Mills,...* New York, 1820.

STAUFFER, VERNON. *New England and the Bavarian Illuminati.* New York, 1918.

STEARNS, JONATHAN F. "Historical Review of the Church (New School Branch) since 1837," in *Presbyterian Reunion: A Memorial Volume, 1837-1871,* 50-102. New York, 1870.

STEINER, BERNARD C. *Life of Henry Winter Davis.* Baltimore, 1916.

———. "Rev. Thomas Bray and his American Libraries," in *American Historical Review,* II (Oct., 1896), 59-75.

STEVENS, ABEL. *History of the Methodist Episcopal Church.* 4 vols. New York, 1864-67.

STEWART, ROBERT LAIRD. "The Mission of Sheldon Jackson in the Winning of the West," in *Jour. Pres. Hist. Soc.,* VI (1911), 49-68.

———. *Sheldon Jackson: Pathfinder and Prospector of the Missionary Vanguard in the Rocky Mountains and Alaska.* New York, [1908].

STILLMAN, SAMUEL. *A Discourse Preached in Boston before the Massachusetts Baptist Missionary Society, May 25, 1803....* Boston, 1803. Pamphlet.

STIMSON, H. A. "Some Contributions which the West may be Expected to make to the Congregationalism of the Future," in *The New Englander*, XXXIX (Jan., 1880), 124-37.

STOCKER, HARRY EMILIUS. *A Home Mission History of the Moravian Church in the United States and Canada.* N.p., 1924.

STONE, BARTON W. See Rogers, James R.

STRICKLAND, W. P. *History of the Missions of the Methodist Episcopal Church,...* Cincinnati, 1850.

STRONG, CYPRIAN. *A Sermon, Preached...before the Board of Trustees of the Missionary Society in Connecticut....* Hartford, 1800. Pamphlet.

STURTEVANT, JULIAN M. *American Emigration; a Discourse in behalf of the American Home Missionary Society,...* New York, 1857. Pamphlet.

———. *An Autobiography.* Ed. by J. M. Sturtevant, Jr. New York and Chicago, [1896].

———. *Historical Discourse.* [At Quarter-Century Celebration at Illinois College]. New York, [1855]. Pamphlet.

———. "Collegiate Education in the Western States," in *The New Englander*, IV (April, 1846), 274-88.

SWEET, WILLIAM WARREN. *Circuit-Rider Days in Indiana.* Indianapolis, 1916.

———. "The Coming of the Circuit Rider Across the Mountains," in *Miss. Val. Hist. Asso. Proceedings* (1916-17), 271-82.

———. *Religion on the American Frontier: The Baptists 1783-1830.* ... New York, 1931.

———. *Religion on the American Frontier Vol. II: The Presbyterians 1783-1840....* New York and London, 1936.

———. *The Rise of Methodism in the West....* Nashville, etc., c. 1920.

TALBOT, ETHELBERT. *My People of the Plains.* New York, 1906.

TAPPAN, LEWIS. *History of the American Missionary Association....* New York, 1855.

TAYLOR, JAMES B. *Memoir of Rev. Luther Rice,...* Baltimore, 1840.

TAYLOR, JOHN. "Journal of Rev. John Taylor's Missionary Tour through the Mohawk & Black River Countries, in 1802," in O'Callaghan, *Documentary History of the State of New York*, III, 1105-50. Albany, 1850.

TAYLOR, WILLIAM. *Seven Years' Street Preaching in San Francisco.* New York, 1856.

TENNEY, E. P. *Looking Forward into the Past.* Nahant, Mass., 1910.

———. *The New West as Related to the Christian College and the Home Missionary.* 2nd ed., Cambridge, 1878; 5th ed., Colorado Springs, 1879.

TEWKSBURY, DONALD D. *The Founding of American Colleges and Universities Before the Civil War....* Teachers College, Columbia University *Contributions to Education*, No. 543. New York, 1932.

THOMPSON, CHARLES LEMUEL. *The Soul of America: the Contribution of Presbyterian Home Missions.* New York, etc., [1919].

THOMPSON, ROBERT ELLIS. *A History of the Presbyterian Churches in the United States (Amer. Ch. Hist. Ser., VI).* New York, 1895.

THOMPSON, THOMAS. *An Account of Two Missionary Voyages By the Appointment of the Society for the Propagation of the Gospel....* London, 1758.

TIFFANY, CHARLES C. *A History of the Protestant Episcopal Church in the United States of America (Amer. Ch. Hist. Ser., VII).* New York, 1895.

TRACY, JOSEPH. *The Great Awakening....* Boston, 1842.

TROWBRIDGE, M. E. D. *History of the Baptists in Michigan.* N.p., 1909.

TURNER, ORSAMUS. *History of the Pioneer Settlement of Phelps and Gorham's Purchase,...* Rochester, 1851.

TUTTLE, D. S. *Reminiscences of a Missionary Bishop.* New York, [1906].

TUTTLE, JOSEPH F. *An Address in behalf of the Society for the Promotion of Collegiate and Theological Education at the West....* New York, 1854. Pamphlet.

———. *Baccalaureate Sermon: The Christian College in its Relations to the Institutions of a New Country.* New York, 1865.

———. "Caleb Mills and the Indiana Common Schools," in Moores, *Caleb Mills and the Indiana School System, q.v.,* 380-96.

———. *The Origin and Growth of Wabash College....* Logansport, Ind., 1876. Pamphlet.

———. "The West and Western Eloquence," in *Biblical Repository and Classical Review,* 3rd Ser., IV (Oct., 1845), 638-69.

TYERMAN, L. *The Life and Times of the Rev. John Wesley....* 3 vols. London, 1875.

TYLER, BENJAMIN BUSHROD. *History of the Disciples of Christ* (in *Amer. Ch. Hist. Ser.,* XII). New York, 1894.

UNITED DOMESTIC MISSIONARY SOCIETY. *First Report of the United Domestic Missionary Society,...* New York, 1823. Pamphlet.

UPDIKE, WILKINS. *History of the Episcopal Church in Narragansett, Rhode-Island;... With an Appendix,... "America Dissected,"* by the Rev. J. Macsparran. New York, 1847. 2nd. ed., revised and enlarged by Daniel Goodwin, 3 vols. Boston, 1907.

UPHAM, WARREN. *Congregational Work of Minnesota 1832-1920....* Minneapolis, 1921.

VAIL, ALBERT L. *The Morning Hour of American Baptist Missions.* Philadelphia, [1907].

VEDDER, HENRY C. *A Short History of the Baptists.* New ed. Philadelphia, [1907].

VENABLE, WILLIAM HENRY. *Beginnings of Literary Culture in the Ohio Valley,...* Cincinnati, 1891.

WALKER, GEORGE LEON. *Some Aspects of the Religious Life of New England....* Boston, 1897.

WALKER, WILLISTON. *The Creeds and Platforms of Congregationalism.* New York, 1893.

————. *A History of the Congregational Churches in the United States (Amer. Ch. Hist. Ser., III)*, New York, 1894.

WATSON, JOHN F. *Annals of Philadelphia and Pennsylvania....* 2 vols. Philadelphia, 1844.

WAYLEN, EDWARD. *Ecclesiastical Reminiscences of the United States.* New York, 1846.

WEBER, HERMAN C. *Presbyterian Statistics Through One Hundred Years 1826-1926....* N.p., 1927.

WEBER, SAMUEL EDWIN. *The Charity School Movement in Colonial Pennsylvania.* Philadelphia, [1905].

WELSH, WILLIAM. *Letters on the Home Missionary Work of the Protestant Episcopal Church,...* Philadelphia, 1863. Pamphlet.

WENTZ, ABDEL ROSS. *The Lutheran Church in American History.* Philadelphia, [1923].

WESTERN EDUCATION SOCIETY. *Report of the Directors....* Utica, 1819. Pamphlet.

WHIPPLE, HENRY BENJAMIN. *Lights and Shadows of a Long Episcopate.* New York and London, 1899.

WHITE, GREENOUGH. *An Apostle of the Western Church: Memoir of the Right Reverend Jackson Kemper....* New York, 1900.

WHITE, WILLIAM. *Memoirs of the Protestant Episcopal Church in the United States of America....* Philadelphia, 1820. 2nd ed., New York, 1836.

WHITEFIELD, GEORGE. *A Continuation of the Reverend Mr. Whitefield's Journal. From his Embarking ... to his Arrival at Savannah in Georgia.* London, 1740.

————. *A Continuation of the Reverend Mr. Whitefield's Journal. After his Arrival at Georgia,...* London, 1741.

————. *A Continuation of the Reverend Mr. Whitefield's Journal, From a few Days after his Return to Georgia....* London, 1741.

————. *A Letter to the Reverend Dr. Chauncy....* Philadelphia, 1745.

WHITTLES, THOMAS D. *The Parish of the Pines: The Story of Frank Higgins....* New York, etc., [1912].

WILLEY, SAMUEL H. *Decade Sermons.* San Francisco, 1859.

————. *A History of the College of California.* San Francisco, 1887.

WILLISTON, SETH. "The Diaries of the Rev. Seth Williston, D.D. 1796-1800," ed. by John Quincy Adams, in *Jour. Pres. Hist. Soc.*, VII, 175-208, 234-54.

WITTEN, ROBERT R. *Pioneer Methodism; or Itinerant Life in Missouri.* ... Hannibal, Mo., [1881?]. Pamphlet.

WOODS, H. *The History of the Presbyterian Controversy, with Early Sketches of Presbyterianism.* Louisville, 1843.

WOODS, JAMES. *Recollections of Pioneer Work in California.* San Francisco, 1878.

WOODWARD, JOSIAH. *An Account of the Rise and Progress of the Religious Societies, in the City of London....* 3rd ed., London 1701.

WOOLMAN, JOHN. *The Journal and Essays of John Woolman.* Ed. by Amelia Mott Gummere. New York, 1922.

WRIGHT, MARY EMILY. *The Missionary Work of the Southern Baptist Convention.* Philadelphia, [1902].

WRIGHT, STEPHEN. *History of the Shaftsbury Baptist Association. From 1781 to 1853.* Troy, N. Y., 1858.

INDEX

Adams, Ephraim, 250 n., 252
Adams, George B., 422
Adams, G. H.: quoted, 326
Adams, Harvey, 250 n.
Adams, William, 267
Alabama, missions to, 198, 264
Albany Collegiate Institute, 395 n.
Albany Conference, 151, 301
Albert Lea College, 395 n.
Albion Academy, 395 n.
Albion College, 400
Alden, Ebenezer, 250 n.
Alden, Lucius, 177
Allegheny College, 400
Allen, William, 54
Allison, John, 76
Alma College, 395 n.
American Baptist Home Mission Society:
organization, 204; methods, 205 f.; in
Middle West, 258; in Texas, 258 f.; on
Pacific Coast, 283-85; after Civil War,
358 f.; receipts up to 1894, 406; mentioned,
156, 202, 301
American Bible Society, 172, 178, 206
American Board of Commissioners for
Foreign Missions, 139, 273, 292
American Education Society, 172, 241, 366,
394 n.
American Home Missionary Society: origin,
173-79; early operation, 179-88;
distribution of missionaries, 180; policies,
181 f.; pay for missionaries, 182
f.; relations with ecclesiastical bodies,
184 f.; relations with missionaries, 185-
87; publicity, 187 f.; experiences of
missionaries, 188-95; and Illinois Band,
195-97; relations with Presbyterians,
198-200, 238-43, 417; and Roman Catholics,
234; repudiated by Old School Presbyterians,
241; co-operation of New
School Presbyterians and Congregationalists,
243; and panic of 1837, 244 f.;
missionary boxes, 245-48; missionaries
to Iowa, 248-54; to Wisconsin, 254-56;
to Minnesota, 256 f.; to Oregon, 272-78;
to California, 278-82; and slavery, 289-
94; missionaries to Kansas and Nebraska,
294-99; withdrawal of New School
Presbyterians, 299-301, 341 f.; and Civil
War, 302-05; missionaries to Colorado,
315 f.; to Utah, 316-18; to Black Hills,
318; name changed, 342; missionaries to
Northern prairies, 343-47; to logging
frontier, 347 f.; new fields on Pacific
Coast, 348 f.; Oklahoma, 349-51; denominational
comity, 351-54, 417-19;
and education, 368 f.; and colleges, 381-
94, *passim;* receipts up to 1894, 406;
achievements in West, 407; mentioned,
74, 148, 164, 214, 366, 403. *See also*
Congregational Home Missionary Society
American Missionary Association, 292
American Peace Society, 173
American Society for Educating Pious
Youth for the Gospel Ministry. *See*
American Education Society
American Society for Promoting Temperance,
173
American Tract Society, 172, 219

Amistad Committee, 292
Anderson, James, 74
Andover Theological Seminary, 139 176,
195, 249, 274, 297, 385
Anglican Church, in colonies: 41-49, 65;
in Revolutionary period, 88-90; relation
to state, 94 f.; number of congregations,
411. *See also* Episcopalians; Society
for the Propagation of the Gospel
Apthorp, East, 48
Arizona, missions to, 320, 323, 326, 359
Arkansas, missions to, 264
Arminianism, 67, 85, 202
Asbury, Francis: experiences on frontiers,
100 f.; during Revolutionary War, 104
f.; bishop, 106; missionary journeys,
106 f.; celibacy among itinerants, 158;
collections for missions, 162; mentioned,
86, 160
Aspinwall, William H., 388
Associate mission plan, 265 f.
Associate Reformed Church, 149, 174, 178,
179 n.
Association of the Holy Childhood, 120
Atkinson, George A., 273 f., 276, 387
Atkinson, John: quoted, 157 f.
Augustana Synod (Lutheran), 339 f.
Austin, Moses, 146 n.
Avery, Joseph, 137

Backus, Isaac, 84, 108
Bacon, Leonard: quoted, 364
Badger, Joseph, 125 f., 131-33
Badger, Milton, 290
Baird, L. O., 349 n.
Baldwin, Theron: quoted, 194, 387; and
Illinois Band, 196 f.; and The College
Society, 384
Bangs, Nathan, 206
Baptist associations: Bowdoinham, 153;
Chemung, 258; Crooked Creek, 205;
Miami, 257; Philadelphia, 83, 108, 153;
Redstone, 212; Shaftsbury, 152; Warren,
84, 108
Baptist Education Society of New York,
366
Baptist Missionary Training School, 402
Baptists: aid from England, 62; and
Great Awakening, 73, 83-85; missions in
eighteenth century, 83-85; after the
Revolutionary War, 107-09; characteristics,
108 f.; missions in early nineteenth
century, 152-56; General Missionary
Convention, 154-56, 200; home
missions, 1820-35, 200-06; opposition to
missions, 201 f., 204 f., 257 f.; American
Baptist Home Mission Society, 204,
257 f., 283-85, 301 f., 358 f., 406; and
the Campbells, 212 f.; Pacific Coast missions,
283-85; division over slavery, 301;
missions after the Civil War, 358 f.;
colleges, 399 f.; schools in Utah, 402;
proportion of home missionary churches,
407; ratio to population, 409 f.; number
of churches, 411 f.; success in West,
413; mentioned, 29, 31, 33 f., 87, 93, f.,
126, 138, 140 f., 157, 173, 161, 378, 391
Barnes, Romulus, 197
Barrows, W. M.: quoted, 328
Barton, Thomas: quoted, 89

Date Due

MAY 3 '65			
NOV 18 '65			
DEC 6 '65			
DEC 28 '65			
JAN 11 '66			
APR 12 '66			
APR 18 '66			
MAY 4 '67			

D1545648